Come Unto Me

By

E. E. CLEVELAND

Associate Secretary

Ministerial Association, General Conference of Seventh-day Adventists

Author of Mine Eyes Have Seen

This book is published in collaboration with the Missionary Volunteer Department as an enrichment of the Morning Watch devotional plan.

REVIEW AND HERALD
WASHINGTON, D.C.

Dedication

To my faithful wife and little son,
whose understanding has made possible my
ministry to millions.

TO BE OR NOT TO BE

Then Agrippa said unto Paul, Almost thou persuadest me to be a Christian. Acts 26:28.

On this first day of the new year, 1969, let us place first things first. "To be or not to be," that is the question. To be a Christian is to be. Agrippa said unto Paul, "Almost thou persuadest me." "Almost sweet is unsavory; almost hot is lukewarm; almost a Christian is like Micah, who thought himself religious enough because he had gotten a priest into his house; almost a Christian is like Ananias, who brought a part but left a part behind; almost a Christian is like Eli's sons, who took more than their share of the sacrifices, like the fig tree which deceived Christ with leaves, like the virgins with lamps without oil."

A pious old man was one day walking to the sanctuary with a New Testament in his hand when a friend greeted him, "Good morning!"

"Ah, good morning," replied he. "I am reading my Father's will as I walk along."

"Well, what has He left you?" asked his friend.

"Why, He has bequeathed me a hundredfold more in this life, and in the world to come life everlasting."

When Dr. Judson went on his missionary journeys through the villages and jungles of the poor benighted Karens, he was called by the natives, "Jesus Christ's man." What a distinction for us to covet on this first day of this new year.

"And the Spirit and the bride say, Come. And let him that heareth say, Come. And let him that is athirst come. And whosoever will, let him take the water of life freely" (Rev. 22:17). This gracious invitation comes from One who demonstrated in a manner that cannot be contradicted that He loves us with an everlasting love. His life of constant torture at the hands of His enemies, His death at Calvary for our sins, His invitation sealed in His own blood, "Come unto me," should find a response in every heart.

On this day let there be a renewal of Christian vows by those who have already accepted Christ as Saviour, and a return to the foot of the cross by all those who have denied the faith.

3

WHEN GOD TOOK A CHANCE

Choose you this day whom ye will serve. Joshua 24:15.

Faced with the problem of making man, God had two alternatives. He could make man in such a way that he would *have* to serve Him; that is, without the power of choice. Or He could make him a free moral agent with a sovereign will. But what if man should use his will against his Creator? Why not play safe, make a puppet and be sure? But a wise and loving God wants no extracted affection. Man's praise must be freely offered; love without coercion.

That man is free to decide his destiny few will deny. "To whom ye yield yourselves servants to obey, his servants ye are to whom ye obey" (Rom. 6:16). Notice, "ye yield yourselves." Concerning the sin of Adam and Eve in Eden, Adam said: "*I* did eat" (Gen. 3:12). Eve said: "And *I* did eat" (verse 13). Each was personally responsible for his action, for each made a decision. And this is true of each of us. "Keep thy heart with all diligence; for out of it are the issues of life" (Prov. 4:23). The power to decide is God-given. To surrender the will to Him and exercise it to His glory is the prime virtue.

Pressures affecting the will are many and continuous. Our own human nature is not the least of these strong influences. Add to this the additional pressure of a sin-charged environment. And, of course, there is always a personal devil to tempt and deceive. These are the negative forces that war against the spirit. Only through watchfulness and prayer may they be overcome. Daily submission to the will of Christ, a Heaven-directed will, is the secret of successful living.

When General Lee was coming up Chambersburg Road to Gettysburg, a young Pennsylvanian lass grabbed a poker and started down the road to meet the enemy. Lee came right on, and at that place a decisive battle was fought.

Later at a quilting party, Mrs. Bamberger said to Hannah, "What did you expect to do with that poker against the Southern army?"

Replied Hannah, "Nothing, except to let them know what side I was on."

Which side are you on? The right or the wrong? There is no middle ground, no in between. The power to decide is yours.

4

LET US MAKE MAN

Thus saith the Lord, Let not the wise man glory in his wisdom, neither let the mighty man glory in his might, let not the rich man glory in his riches. Jer. 9:23.

The world has three standards by which it evaluates men; namely, wisdom, power, and wealth. But one may have cunning without character, power without self-restraint, and wealth without compassion. Yet such men receive the plaudits of their fellows and are the subjects of unrestrained adulation. In this we worship strange gods. For wisdom, riches, power, blessings within themselves, have ceased to be means and are now ends. For this they were never intended.

What then is the fairest of life's ambitions? To what can a young man aspire that is more worthy than wisdom, riches, and power? "But let him that glorieth glory in this, that he understandeth and knoweth me, that I am the Lord" (Jer. 9:24). Now, this puts first things first.

A young man in travel-stained clothes was observed sitting on the steps of a great city church day after day.

"What do you want?" the minister asked him. "Can I help you financially?"

"No," replied the boy.

"Is it instruction that you seek?"

"No."

"Do you want to be a bishop?" the minister asked.

"No!" shouted the boy. "I don't want your money, wisdom, or position. I seek your Master!"

Whom seek ye? Do you give yourselves to Him each day through prayer and the study of the Word? Remember, God alone makes men. But what kind of man do you want to be? Rich, wise, powerful? Then be a good man first. Seek first the kingdom, and all or some of these will be added. It is the hard way but also the infinitely better one.

The kingdom of God first is the secret to better living. "Christ in you, the hope of glory." This living experience is possible to all of us by faith in Him. Reformation based on human resolution is temporary at best, but transformation based on surrender to the Lord Jesus Christ is thorough and lasting.

5

HOW SHORT MY TIME

Remember how short my time is. **Ps. 89:47.**

This strange prayer of the psalmist expressed his utter desperation. The enemies of Israel were pressing from advantage to advantage. In this dark hour David pictures the Lord as hiding from Israel, but not without cause. Israel had forsaken God and this David knew. But he was wide awake to passing *time* and *opportunity.* He expected action from God *in his day,* and longed to advance the cause through personal effort. "Remember how short my time is," was his plea to God. He did not want to be left out. He wanted to see Israel safe from her enemies *in his time.*

My friend, have you considered the shortness of your time? "Oh, I have plenty of time," is an expression often heard. But have you? The international situation indicates the contrary. And further, your personal life span is an uncertainty. And how far are we from the "standing up of Michael" and the close of probation? Perhaps a more serious question would be, how near are you to the close of your personal probation? These questions are enough to make that "plenty of time" quip freeze on one's lips. *Now* is the time to surrender that sinful thought, act, or manner of speech. *Today* is the day to give the message in tract, sermon, or Bible study. Now is the hour to right some wrong, and to pray with David: "Remember how short my time is."

> "The clock of life is wound but once,
> And no man has the power
> To tell just when the hands will stop
> . . . at late or early hour.
> Now is the only time you own;
> So live, love, toil with a will;
> Place not faith in tomorrow,
> For the clock may then be still."

On his way to the scaffold, Lord William Russell handed his watch to the physician with these last words: "Will you kindly take my timepiece and keep it? I have no use for it. I am now dealing with eternity." Soon shall we all. This day is yours; make the most of it.

LORD, I BELIEVE

And he said, Lord, I believe. John 9:38.

This confession of faith followed a miracle. A blind man had received his sight. Grateful lips intoned the words: "Lord, I believe." But the enemies of faith are many—some within ourselves, some without. From within, human nature is at war with living faith. A man realizes this when he transgresses, often against his own desire. Repeated transgression is discouraging. Faith must be sought from above through prayer. This alone can conquer the inner tendency to transgress.

Second, there is the pressure of environmental evil. This also tends to inhibit faith. Evolutionary teaching, the moral decay of our society, and the disheartening quest of science for more lethal weapons have in themselves little to encourage one's faith.

The text relates an experience in personal faith. The blind man's own religious leaders sought to shake his faith. Of Jesus they said, "We know that this man is a sinner" (John 9:24). Around him the controversy raged. So intense was the conflict that he was ultimately cast out of the synagogue. Through it all his faith remained unshaken. "One thing I know, that, whereas I was blind, now I see" (verse 25).

You, too, can have this experience with Christ, an excursion with Him through life by faith. But how does one build faith in a faithless age? "So then faith cometh by hearing, and hearing by the word of God" (Rom. 10:17). The Bible is a faith-building book. There is a mysterious life-giving element in its words. To one who prayerfully reads its pages, faith comes. This also explains the necessity of church attendance. The church is the place where prayer is made and the Word of God is read. These activities feed our faith.

Also, faith, like muscles, must be exercised to grow. This involves obedience to the law as an act of faith. How true are the words of the familiar song:

"Yield not to temptation, For yielding is sin,
Each victory will help you Some other to win."

Faith grows fastest in the atmosphere of obedience. What think ye of Christ? Have you such faith as to trust Him with your life?

CALM SEAS OR TROUBLED WATERS?

Then said they unto him, What shall we do unto thee, that the sea may be calm unto us? Jonah 1:11.

Jonah had fled from the presence of the Lord and lay asleep in the bottom of the ship. The waters were troubled and the ship appeared ready to sink. When it was finally discovered that the man of God asleep in the hold was the cause of their peril, the sailors were reluctant to deal harshly with him, realizing that how they treated him would affect their own peace.

"What shall we do unto thee, that the sea may be calm unto us?" How few of us realize that our own "seas" are not calm because we have not dealt fairly with our fellows. And indeed, how little peace of mind is possible to one who mistreats another, for whatever reason. Poverty, personality differences, physical deformity, lack of mental aptitude, racial origins, are all of little consequence in man's attitude toward his brother, for the human family is interrelated by creation. "If a man say, I love God, and hateth his brother, he is a liar: for he that loveth not his brother whom he hath seen, how can he love God whom he hath not seen?" (1 John 4:20).

One day Sir Walter Scott threw a rock at a stray dog, intending to drive it away. Unintentionally, he broke the dog's leg. Instead of running away, the dog came limping up to Sir Walter and licked the hand that threw the rock. Said Scott: "That dog preached the Sermon on the Mount as few people ever practice it."

The sharp words, hasty judgments, snide criticisms, all spring from a spirit that is foreign to Christ. The prayer of the psalmist may well be our own: "Create in me a clean heart, O God; and renew a *right spirit* within me" (Ps. 51:10). And as a companion prayer, we should pray for the infilling of the love of God by the Holy Spirit. Then shall we know how to deal with others and enjoy calm seas on our own shores.

What we do affects others. Had Jonah remained aboard the ship, he might have carried all on board to destruction with him. It is impossible to live for Christ without leading some soul to Him. Perhaps that is why there will be no starless crowns in heaven.

8

THE PRAYER HABIT

Pray without ceasing. 1 Thess. 5:17.

Psychologist William James has graphically described the power of habit thus: "The drunken Rip Van Winkle in Jefferson's play, excuses himself for every fresh dereliction by saying, 'I won't count this time.' Well, he may not count it, but . . . deep down among the nerve cells and fibers, the molecules are 'counting it.' Thus habit, whether good or bad, becomes engraved."

May this be true of the prayer habit. The text does not imply that one must be continually upon his knees. Nor that prayer is to be indulged in at the expense of the business of making a living. It does suggest an attitude or state of mind; prayer-conditioned molecules, fibers, and nerve cells. "Prayer is the breath of the soul." We breathe with no conscious effort on our part. But are our souls dying for want of spiritual breath?

Unceasing prayer is a trait we do not usually look for in a military man, but General Stonewall Jackson was a man of deep faith in persistent prayer. "I have so fixed the habit of prayer in my mind," he said, "that I never raise a glass of water to my lips without asking God's blessing, never seal a letter without putting a word of prayer under the seal, never take a letter from the post without a brief sending of my thoughts heavenward, never change my classes in the lecture-room without a minute's petition for the cadets who go out and for those who come in."

An ill-clad old man stood weeping at the White House gate, forbidden to enter. Young Tad Lincoln, playing on the lawn, asked what was the matter.

"My son is to be shot at dawn and only Mr. Lincoln can help. But these soldiers won't let me see him."

"I'll take you to him," shouted Tad. "He's my father. He'll see me at any time!"

And God is our Father. He'll hear us any time. Angels marvel that grace so freely offered is so seldom sought. Have you prayed today? How often? Without prayer, we are not safe for a single hour, for except the spirit of man is fed it will wither and die.

REPENT

I tell you, Nay: but, except ye repent, ye shall all likewise perish. Luke 13:3.

The word "repent" is one with which everyone should become familiar. John the Baptist disturbed the stillness of the wilderness with it. "Repent," shouted Peter to the multitudes assembled at the Beautiful Gate of the Temple. Our text contains the Master's solemn warning that those who refuse to repent will perish. Just what does the word mean? Perhaps the most accurate definition is "a change of attitude." Another has defined it as being sorry enough for sin to quit. All are agreed that repentance involves a *break* with sin. It is the *point of turning.*

But how does one repent? Can a man repent at will? The answer to the first question provides a clue to the second. Repentance is initiated by the reproof of the Holy Spirit. "He will reprove the world of sin" (John 16:8). It is under the convicting power of the Holy Spirit that a man submits to change. When a man repents, he places his will against the sin that destroys him.

There are three conditions under which a man repents:

1. "The goodness of God leadeth thee to repentance" (Rom. 2:4). The cross of Christ is the clearest expression of His goodness. Read the story of Calvary prayerfully, and it will break your heart.

2. "Godly sorrow worketh repentance to salvation" (2 Cor. 7:10). Personal remorse for having displeased Christ has led many to change.

3. The heavy hand of judgment, as in the case of Jonah. In the stomach of the leviathan he repented, and given another chance, made good. But that is doing it the hard way.

Dwight L. Moody tells of his experience at a railroad station. He inquired whether the train standing there was going to Boston. He was told that it was. After boarding it, he asked the conductor, who said, "No, this train goes to Albany." Now, Moody could sit there, knowing he was on the wrong train, and land in the wrong place; or he could *change trains.* Since he did the latter, he repented, figuratively speaking. Isn't it about time for us to "change trains"? Christ is waiting for the fruits of repentance in our lives today.

BE CONVERTED

Repent ye therefore, and be converted, that your sins may be blotted out, when the times of refreshing shall come from the presence of the Lord. Acts 3:19.

Conversion is that act whereby God takes control of the surrendered life. The stubborn will, yielded to God, acknowledges: "I am crucified with Christ: nevertheless I live; yet not I, but Christ liveth in me" (Gal. 2:20). Conversion does not destroy human nature; under this experience, Christ controls it. "I keep under my body, and bring it into subjection" (1 Cor. 9:27). But the body will not be kept under without a fight. "So fight I, not as one that beateth the air" (verse 26). Nor is the Christian promised a continual string of victories. But if he falls and is sincerely repentant, divine provision has been made. "And if any man sin, we have an advocate with the Father, Jesus Christ the righteous" (1 John 2:1).

Man's tendency to sin is no reflection on Christ's ability to keep him from sinning, but rather on man's inclination toward carelessness in matters spiritual. That Christ can keep the life pure is fully attested to in Jude 24: "Now unto him that is able to keep you from falling." It is man's watchfulness and prayer life that must be perfected through progressive sanctification. So take heart and press on! Only the faithless are lost. It is the persevering, though erring, Christian that Satan fears.

The test of conversion? It is nothing more or less than obedience to God. A candidate for admission to a certain church related before the membership a dream to substantiate his conversion.

The pastor said: "We do not wish to despise a good man's dream. But we will tell you what we think of the dream after we see how you live when you are awake."

To be converted is to be acted upon by the Spirit of God. True, we cannot change ourselves but we can be changed by yielding to the Spirit's power. This is the good news of the gospel. It is not mere reformation based on human desire and effort, but transformation through the power of God to recreate that which He originally created in His own image.

11

A SURE THING

Being confident of this very thing, that he which hath begun a good work in you will perform it until the day of Jesus Christ. Phil. 1:6.

Hesitancy to accept Christ most often springs from fear of the future rather than from lack of present conviction. What assurance have we that it is possible to maintain a high level of spirituality for hours, days, weeks, months, and even years? Can I be sure now that, having honored my Lord, I will not disgrace Him later? This, for many, is the "missing link" inhibiting their acceptance of the new-birth experience.

Our text assures us that our spiritual development does not rest alone with us. Christ began in us this work of grace. He promises that He will perform it in us until the end of time.

1. Divine energy will be available for our strength and deliverance until the day of Christ.

2. If our hearts are kept in tune with Christ through prayer and Bible study, His promise is to keep us in the days ahead.

3. We must therefore live a day at a time, trust Him a day at a time, and we will find Him adequate hour by hour.

"Now unto him that is able to keep you from falling" (Jude 24) certifies forever Christ's ability to save. We must discipline ourselves to watchfulness and prayer. This is the area of progressive sanctification. Through experience we learn the folly of self-assurance and the wisdom of absolute dependency on God. This is the work of a lifetime, for each new day renews the conflict.

A little girl fell into a cistern and called loudly for help. Her mother hastened to her rescue. Telling how she was saved, the little girl said, "I reached up as far as I could, and mother did the rest." So Christ saves the sinner. Have you reached up as far as you can?

The problem for most of us is looking at the future as if it were one united whole. To envision year after year of unlimited time during which we are obligated to live for Christ overwhelms our faith. But life is so uncertain that we might not be alive tomorrow. Constant dependency upon Christ is the only safe course to follow.

12

TOO YOUNG FOR BAPTISM?

And now why tarriest thou? arise, and be baptized, and wash away thy sins, calling on the name of the Lord. Acts 22:16.

At what age is it best to join the church? Isn't it best to wait until one realizes the full significance of this important act, and doesn't that demand maturity?

"And so," concluded one youth, "I think I'll wait until I am sure." Should he? He will probably wait a long time, for *waiting* and *being sure* are not consistent with each other in spiritual matters. The longer one waits, the less certain he is. Faith is strengthened by action.

"And now why tarriest thou?" What are you waiting for? Feeling, is that it? You may ask, "Must I feel different as others say I should or as they say they do? Must I be moved to tears? Can a man be converted without weeping?"

No, faith is not feeling. It is trust, simple trust. One may trust with or without tears. Jesus Christ has declared His love for you. Believe Him. He declares all your sins forgiven according to your faith. Believe Him! He affirms His ability to heal human weakness. Try Him! And if, in sincere effort, we sometimes fail, He promises to forgive and restore. Place your trembling hand in His today.

Arise! Conditions will never be more favorable than they are today. The outlook grows dimmer by the hour. Within are filthy rags. Only the uplook counts. Arise and be baptized. Baptism will burn the bridges behind you. It is an act of separation.

"Be baptized, and wash away thy sins." Sin must be expunged from the record in heaven as well as from our hearts. As in baptism the water covers our bodies, so the blood of Christ covers our sins on earth and in heaven. Glorious privilege! Matchless love!

Out on the cattle ranches of the West the unbranded calves that roam at large are known as mavericks. They are claimed by the first man who catches them and brands them. A Western girl came to Christ and was baptized. She testified: "I was a little maverick out on the prairie when the evangelist found me, branded me for Jesus by baptism, and now the world knows that I am His child."

13

ANOTHER MAN

And the Spirit of the Lord will come upon thee, and thou shalt prophesy with them, and shalt be turned into another man. 1 Sam. 10:6.

Saul was chosen to be Israel's first king. Coming from the "least of all the families of the tribe of Benjamin," he shrank from the responsibilities of leading so great a people. "Wherefore then speakest thou so to me?" he inquired of the prophet. "Thou shalt be turned into another man," came the answer. *Another man.* Challenging thought! Have you ever wished you were someone else? With the same family and name, of course, but better equipped to meet life's challenges. Or have you envied the spiritual strength of others and longed to be like them? Have you looked within and hated what you saw—a craven weakness, hated, but yielded to—and longed to be *another man?* The Bible says you can.

For Saul it involved a delicate operation. "God gave him another heart" (1 Sam. 10:9). For us the requirement is no less. Without the new heart, the new man is impossible. Transformation must precede reformation, and this Christ has promised to all who believe. There is no spiritual excellence to which we cannot attain through repentant faith. My friend, seek Him with the passion of a thirsty man in a waterless desert. And if you lack this thirst, pray for it. Wrestle like Jacob until you prevail with God. Hold on until you begin to think, feel, and act like *another man.*

In a certain village there was a very mean man who sold wood to his neighbors. He always took advantage of them by cutting the logs shorter than the customary four feet. One day the report was circulated that the man had been converted. No one believed it.

"How do you know?" people asked.

"I went out and measured the wood that he cut," said a customer. "It's a good four feet long."

He was indeed *another man.* In Christ you may be also. The experience must radiate from the inner man. May our works be simply our characters shining through, and in the time of testing there will be no erosion of our faith or faithfulness.

14

THE COUNSEL OF THE UNGODLY

Blessed is the man that walketh not in the counsel of the ungodly. Ps. 1:1.

The counsel of the ungodly has a special appeal to our human nature. That is why we are prone to listen and act upon the suggestions of the enemy of our souls. But the man who seeks counsel of the saints puts himself in the way of God's blessing. Good advice can only come from the good. One who has Christian parents is especially fortunate. Advice from such parents may sometimes sound like preachments of a bygone age, but principles never change. Character is built the same today as yesterday, and forever.

It is not old-fashioned for youth to come home at a decent hour at night; it is right. Nor is it out of fashion for a young woman to consult her mother about her dates, or a young man his father. The young man who refuses to drink or smoke, and chooses the path of moral living is labeled a "square." Better to be square than squalid. And when in doubt, seek counsel of that Christian parent, teacher, or friend. The counsel of the ungodly can only lead to more ungodliness, and those who follow it eventually stand "in the way of sinners." Such advice can only serve to pollute the thought stream, making good behavior doubly difficult. Evil counsel ridicules that which is best in life.

And because the world current runs the downward course, it takes little more than the power of suggestion to draw one to its polluted stream. The counsel of the ungodly has permeated every facet of our communication system. On television and radio, and in magazine and newspaper, the downward pull is felt. Resistance will demand that the best within us be committed to that which is above us. Only in Christ may we hope to overcome.

"If you would go to Wartburg, they will show you a dark spot on the wall made by the ink bottle which Martin Luther threw at the devil. I know that some deny that it was the devil. But this much is sure: Luther thought it was and he let fly the ink!"

Would to God that there were more men who in their hatred of evil would "let fly" at the very thought of sin.

15

THE SEAT OF THE SCORNFUL

The scorners delight in their scorning, and fools hate knowledge. **Prov.** 1:22.

Cynicism has become the god of this age. Yes, men literally worship their doubts. It has indeed become fashionable today to question truth and integrity. That there is something wrong with everything and everybody is an unspoken but universal belief. If this be true, then there is nothing reliable, and ideas of the absolute are obsolete. Doubt reflects no particular credit on its possessor, nor is it evidence of exceptional mental capacity. The smart set specialize in questioning established values and thereby give evidence of their immaturity. When older and wiser, the folly of it all will overwhelm as relentlessly as does the incoming tide.

To some there is something wrong with everything but wrong. To them Sabbath school is too early and church service too late; youth activities are not adult enough and prayer meetings are too adult. But a midtown movie or dance, a dusk-to-dawn party, or a wild ride with the hot-rodders is the life. Such is the appetite perverted by sin. It is a craving never satisfied, an unquenchable fire that will burn to the lowest hell.

"Come unto me, all ye that labour and are heavy laden, and I will give you rest," said Jesus. The heart where Jesus dwells is at rest with God, man, and itself. Such a person moves to correct that which can be helped and in prayerful patience bears that which cannot. He discerns beauty in the simple and finds joy in Christian fellowship. To him the brassy tinsel of worldly pleasure is a transparent sham. He has decided for Christ and is at rest. It is said that deep within the ocean there is an area of calm that can never be disturbed. High winds may turn the ocean surface into choppy seas or mountainous waves, but the area of perpetual calm flows smoothly on. May you find that place of perpetual calm.

The misery of cynicism is a thing seldom discussed. The negative frame of mind feeds its poison to the system of its possessor. The Bible says, "Blessed is the man that . . . sitteth [not] in the seat of the scornful" (Ps. 1:1).

16

BLESSED IS THE MAN

Blessed is the man that doeth this, and the son of man that layeth hold on it; that keepeth the sabbath from polluting it, and keepeth his hand from doing any evil. Isa. 56:2.

The Sabbath day is a day of gladness and rejoicing. It should be called "a delight" (Isa. 58:13). Of all the days of the week, this one should be the most desired. It is a day dedicated to the worship of Jehovah. On it there is a cessation of physical labor. Business and secular pleasure are put aside. The Christian today attends two schools: (1) The church, where he studies the Word of God, and (2) the outdoors, where God is studied through nature.

Some hate to see the Sabbath come because it will interfere with a football or basketball game, or the telecast of a baseball game. Others are reluctant to leave the radio or television set quiet for twenty-four hours. Still others find it hard to resist the temptation of the usual long gossip sessions on the telephone during Sabbath hours. To all such people the Sabbath is a burden. Their love for the Lord of the Sabbath has been short-circuited, for those who love the Lord cannot hate His day.

Years ago I visited a church in the State of Ohio. Times had been hard with me, and I knew few people in that city. During the preaching service I noticed an elderly man studying me closely. At the conclusion of the meeting he approached me and asked, "Are you Bill Cleveland's son?" I answered in the affirmative.

"I know your father," he said, "and any son of my friend Bill is a son of mine. Welcome to my home."

He was happy to see me because he loved my father. Likewise, the man who loves the Lord will find the Sabbath a delight, for it is His. He will rejoice at its coming and mourn its passing.

Youth is naturally restless, but in many a young person there is an unnatural restlessness. It is natural that youth should be impatient to get on with living. Youth seeks definition through experimentation but it is tragic when these years of wide-eyed exploration are dissipated on the shoals of reckless living. Happy is the youth who finds in the Sabbath twenty-four hours for sober reflection.

GOD'S WAY REJECTED

They say unto God, Depart from us; for we desire not the knowledge of thy ways. Job 21:14.

We live in an age that is restive under moral restraint. In international diplomacy, sacred treaties are no more permanent than the paper on which they are written. The marriage vow is losing its hold on those who take it. Chastity is elective. Business agreements are evaded for profit. And from many pulpits of the land, prelates thunder their defiance of the law of God. Organized crime is recognized as another world, the underworld, that is. Our world works twenty-four hours a day at casting away the Lord's cords.

Such is the deceptiveness of sin that it blinds the eye of man to the fact that the prohibitions of Jehovah are for man's good. "No good thing will he withhold from them that walk uprightly" (Ps. 84:11). This applies to whatever man craves for recreation, diet, companionship, or habit. Whether or not we see the danger, if God forbids it, death lurks concealed within the thing we seek. The laws of God are protective restraints and privileges, and only our fallen natures would "cast away their cords."

Discipline is heaven's tool for the development of character. Hence, the grace of God operates continually to bring man's thoughts, words, and acts into harmony with divine law. Submission to the will of God is man's first spiritual privilege. Resistance to internal and external temptation must hinge on our acceptance of God's will for our lives. He who surrenders his will to Christ finds the law his delight. Disregard of the law of God is an invitation to danger. The laws of God are given as an expression of His love for us. Submission to those laws reveals our love for Him.

An Indian convert was asked to go to America to lecture the church on its obligation to send more missionaries.

"Has not Christ told them to do it?" he asked.

"Yes," came the reply, "but we must remind them of their duty."

"But," he said, "if they will not mind Christ, they'll not obey me."

And it is so. Obedience is rooted in spiritual growth, and only as we love Christ will our behavior be perfected.

A LIFTER UP

But thou, O Lord, art a shield for me; my glory, and the lifter up of mine head. Ps. 3:3.

All of us have at one time or another done, thought, and said things of which we were ashamed. "For all have sinned, and come short of the glory of God" (Rom. 3:23). However, we are called to victory in Christ and not defeat. At Calvary the death of the only-begotten Son of God provided enabling atonement and strength to meet this standard. In the heart of the Christian there is constant consciousness of the gap between the ideal and his own unworthiness, and this serves to discourage many. This need not be, for David said, "Thou, O Lord, art . . . the lifter up of mine head."

This gap between profession and performance is not a permanent one for the persevering Christian. This is an essential difference between the Christian and the hypocrite. The hypocrite makes no effort to close the gap between the standard and his own behavior. Indeed, he may let it widen without concern. The Christian, however, is locked daily in a life-and-death struggle to close the gap. Sometimes he succeeds, sometimes he fails. In moments of disappointment he asks Christ to be "the lifter up" of his head, and as his faith seizes God's power he revives. He does not regard the "door of mercy" as an excuse to transgress, but as a restoration of privilege to the repentant. To him the outstretched hands at Calvary are an invitation to the fallen to rise again and again to the challenge of Christian living.

The gap is a challenge and not a "great gulf fixed," for there is always help at hand. The believer is encouraged that Christ has offered Himself as a substitute for sin and stands as man's covering in heaven, while in faith he determinedly fights the good fight on earth.

Only a failure in faith can remove this covering. Repeated deliberate transgression is destructive to faith. It is this that leads to the deadening of the conscience and eventually to the unpardonable sin. The ear of Christ is ever tuned to the prayer of the penitent. To seek Him early and often is our highest privilege.

I COME

And, behold, I come quickly; and my reward is with me, to give every man according as his work shall be. Rev. 22:12.

These words were uttered more than nineteen hundred years ago. With the passage of time a persistent skepticism has grown over the question of the soon coming of our Lord. How quick is *quickly?* Indeed, some have despaired that Christ will come at all, and have begun to smite their fellows. Just what may we expect? Has the Lord delayed His coming?

Let us first consider the international situation. Because of the efficiency of death-dealing weapons, men of no religious persuasion agree that we have little time on this earth. We have truly reached a time of perplexity, with no way out. If there existed no additional evidence, man's bloody history in human relations forecasts an early end of life on this earth as we know it. Add to this the fact that the signs of the end clearly outlined in Matthew 24 and Luke 21 are ominously multiplying in frequency and intensity, and with certainty we conclude that this generation shall not pass before it witnesses the coming of our Lord. How else can it be? While it would be a mistake to tie this event to a day-hour prediction, it will be fatal to ignore passing events that foretell His coming. How sad it is to contemplate that whenever the Lord returns, it will be too soon for some.

However, our faithfulness must not depend on whether His second coming is soon or delayed. Whether or not the coming of Christ is when we think, we must be faithful. We should serve Him because we love Him. Then are we ready if death should claim us prior to the hour of His appearing.

"What would you do, son, if you received word that the king would visit your home tonight?" asked the teacher.

"I'd get ready," came the reply.

"What would you do if you learned he would come next week?"

"I'd be ready," the little one answered.

"And what if you knew he would come but did not know when?"

"I'd stay ready," the little boy answered triumphantly. May it be so with us.

SOURCES OF CONFIDENCE

For thus saith . . . the Holy One of Israel; . . . in quietness and in confidence shall be your strength. Isa. 30:15.

No more pitiable person exists than one who has lost his confidence. So important is faith to human existence that God has dispensed a measure to all men (Rom. 12:3). To be sure, much of this God-given faith has been misplaced, but those who are without it are the living dead. To whom, then, may we look, and in whom may we safely put our trust?

First, the God of heaven deserves our deepest trust. By creation and redemption He has justified our confidence. Absolute confidence in Him is the key to life here and hereafter. We must believe that He is and that He loves us. We must take His Word, the Bible, the book of God, from cover to cover. Believe His miracles from the manifestations before Pharaoh to the raising of Lazarus. Believe His power to save. In this we must have confidence. Believe that all men have a heaven to gain and a hell to shun. Have faith in God!

Second, believe the church, for it is the depository of the word of life and the testimony of Jesus Christ. Defective though it may be in practice, it is pure in principle. And it is to the purest principle that we are called. There may be those in the church who are not what they profess. This must not damage our confidence nor dim our witness.

Third, let us believe in one another. This is possible despite betrayal. Indeed, one man's treason does not warrant loss of confidence in all. And even during the period of His betrayal, Christ could call Judas friend. To be sure, there are some things that one would not trust in the hands of a sworn enemy. But many of us have found that for every person who disappoints us, there is another who will lend a helping hand. It is important to our peace of mind that we believe in someone. The perpetually suspicious are the eternally miserable. Judges are they, assigning motives to meaningless actions and reading sinister meanings into harmless statements.

If confidence in God, the church, and our fellow men is to survive, it must be fed with prayer, Bible study, and fellowship. Thus through trustful contact we grow in favor with God and man.

21

WHY LIVE?

I am come that they might have life, and that they might have it more abundantly. John 10:10.

Since the splitting of the atom, every baby that is born is conceived in the "valley of the shadow of death." Since that dread day, bombs, awesome in their destructive potential, and rockets capable of carrying them, have narrowed the already shrinking lane in which statesmen maneuver for peace. Many youth, shocked by the immediacy of impending disaster, are living the sin-life to the hilt. "Eat, drink, and be merry, for tomorrow we die" (if not today) has become their philosophy of defeat. Appeals for disciplined living are met with a cynical rebuff. Why prepare for life in the face of death?

But is not death itself a good reason for acceptance of the more abundant life? All of us are born with one life, a physical one. Christ offers a second life to all who will accept it—the spiritual life. It is this additional life that is more abundant. To be sure, the physical life is foredoomed by both time and circumstance. But the surrendered life that is hid with Christ in God, produces a hope that will survive the grave. I, therefore, conclude that the uncertainty of this present physical existence should generate genuine interest in eternal verities.

And, further, indulging in soul-destroying, body-damaging, mind-defiling habits is not *really* living. They get most out of life here who explore by faith the privileges of divine grace while accepting its discipline. They live abundantly who have found in Christ the answer to life's questions and the solution to its problems. Their faces reflect a beauty that need not be painted on, and a joy that springs from the soul. "Joy is the flag that is flown from the castle of the heart when the King is in residence there."

It is paradoxical that in our times death has been substituted for life and life for death. The hippie revolt has tried to establish a reversal of values. The way of death is glorified as the way of life and its extreme advocates in the name of love refuse to bathe, work, or persevere in purposeful enterprises. But the Bible is still true, its standards are binding, and the way of abundant life is still found therein.

DO IT

Whatsoever thy hand findeth to do, do it with thy might; for there is no work, nor device, nor knowledge, nor wisdom, in the grave, whither thou goest. Eccl. 9:10.

Our world suffers today from tasks half done and shoddy performances. "Anything worth doing at all is worth doing well."

Total application to any worthy assignment is implied in the text. The apostle Paul was able to say, "This one thing I do." To prepare for his lifework, he was educated in the school of the rabbis. When he stood at last on the threshold of service his credentials were unquestioned. Many are the temptations to turn aside before one's education is complete for more practical pursuits. But the text reminds us that "there is no knowledge nor wisdom in the grave." Therefore, what one gets must be crowded into life's rapidly passing years.

The admonition also applies to the spiritual man. Spiritual preparation must be pursued diligently and wholeheartedly if excellence is to be achieved. Christ must be desired, sought, pursued with the passion of the hart for the water brook. Christianity requires that the whole man be employed in the search for Christ. "Do it with thy might." This task requires the sum total of man's consummate energies.

In answering any call to service, "do it with thy might." However menial the task, do it faithfully, for even the proper use of a broom is essential to character development. He who has visions of scaling mountain peaks, dreams in vain except he traverses well the valley.

> "The way to be master is to be servant;
> The way to get up is to get down!
> The way to receive is to give;
> The way to be rich is to be poor;
> The way to be wise is to be a fool;
> The way to be exalted is to abase yourself;
> The way to live is to die."

The doctrine that after death man will get another chance is a dangerous one. Our text with great emphasis focuses on the now, with death as the ultimate limit of human probation. It accents urgency. It is an invitation to excellence, with promise of enduring reward.

23

IN THE VALLEY

Multitudes, multitudes in the valley of decision: for the day of the Lord is near in the valley of decision. Joel 3:14.

The valley of Jehoshaphat is known to Bible students as the valley of decision. Here the armies of Pharaoh Necho defeated the armies of Josiah. It was here that Sennacherib's hopes of an easy conquest of Israel were dashed. Historically, this narrow valley was a place where accounts were settled and issues were decided in the crucible of war.

This picture is used to illustrate mankind's position in the last days. Humanity has reached its valley of decision internationally. Rapidly developing circumstances give our diplomats little room to maneuver. They have reached the point of no return. And now, each day of man's existence is a day of fateful decision. The judgment sits in heaven as tension mounts on the earth. Hence, each day of man on earth, destiny is being decided in heaven. For us each day is indeed a day of spiritual decision. From this dread hour of commitment there is no turning aside. The human family, like Balaam's ass, is in a strait place, and there is naught to do but face what is before.

The issue is clear. Will you have this world or the next? We cannot have them both. Heaven and earth have little in common; so little in fact that to love one is to hate the other. God requires the whole man —body, mind, and spirit. In none of these areas can one serve two masters. All three parts of man may be schooled in the divine art of subservience to Christ. In this, however, His grace alone is sufficient. Through prayer and the daily study of God's Word we may ensure our emergence from the valley of decision into the sunlight of God's love.

Griffith Thomas once told the story of a man who was a helpless slave to drink. He tried again and again to free himself, but to no avail. One day he declared his resolve to quit, and kneeling, committed himself to Christ.

Someone said, "So at last you have got the mastery of the devil."

"No," he replied, "but I've got the Master of the devil."

We, too, may have victory through Christ by faith in Him.

OIL THROUGH THE PIPES

And I answered again, and said unto him, What be these two olive branches which through the two golden pipes empty the golden oil out of themselves? Zech. 4:12.

The two olive branches pictured by the prophet Zechariah are interpreted to be the Old and the New Testament. The golden oil represents spiritual nourishment that flows into the soul from the Word. Of the Scriptures Christ said, "They are they which testify of me" (John 5:39). Is not then the knowledge of Jesus and His Word the golden oil that feeds the soul? Be it also noted that the oil is conducted to the soul by pipes of gold. Is not this the agency of the Holy Spirit, to give men access to Christ?

What priceless treasure lies hidden in the Word! The Bible has been accurately depicted as the world's most neglected best-seller. Do you read it daily? Do you daily expose your soul to the life-giving flow of the golden oil? The treasures of the Book are legion: Divine direction, encouragement, doctrine, rebuke, prophecy, and Heaven's approbation are all there. For what on earth can we exchange for the priceless oil from golden pipes? This hour of deepening crisis demands deeper consecration. A faltering world needs your firm commitment. God alone has the answers for this hour. Man may find them through companionship with Him.

This is the hour to seek the divine gift of the Holy Spirit. It is He who guides men to Christ. "I will send him unto you," said Jesus (John 16:7). He is available now on a scale heretofore unknown.

A man under conviction of sin accepted Christ.

"But it won't last," taunted a companion. They were working near a water mill.

"What makes that wheel turn today?" the new convert asked.

"The stream," was the answer.

"What will turn it tomorrow?"

"The stream, of course."

"And the days after?" asked the man.

"The stream. It never fails," was the knowing reply.

Likewise, God's spirit is available for every hour.

25

PEOPLE THAT DO KNOW

But the people that do know their God shall be strong, and do exploits. Dan. 11:32.

Interpreted within the framework of its immediate prophetic context, our scripture refers to the glorious accomplishments of the apostolic church and onward. However, the expression itself is marvelous as a concise summary of the divine operation. Acquaintance with Christ as a personal Saviour is the first essential. As individuals we must seek Him as our Lord and Friend. We must yield to Him our unreserved trust, and give verbal expression of this act in daily prayer. Thus our faith in Him will grow and our relationship ripen into inseparable companionship. Through daily commitment of the will to Christ strength is received to meet life's emergencies.

To be sure, we have not been promised immunity to temptation. But Christ does offer strength to resist. "I will strengthen thee; yea, I will help thee; yea, I will uphold thee" (Isa. 41:10) are His quiet assurances. "God is faithful, who will not suffer you to be tempted above that ye are able" (1 Cor. 10:13). These promises are genuine, certified by the "shedding of blood." Their realization is dependent on our faith.

Strength of character, the power to say No, strength of will and purpose are the prized possessions of men who know the Lord. It is our relationship with God that makes us what we are. If we know Him, we shall be strong. And with His strength, we shall do exploits. Strength is consequent to personal knowledge, and performance follows the impartation of power. A knowledge of this sequence is important. To know the Lord, to reflect His character-image, and to witness faithfully to others is the cycle of salvation. A weakness on any point undermines the others. Faithfulness in all three is essential to the development of the whole man. How is your relationship with Christ today? Have you surrendered your will to Him? How is your witness? Have you spoken for Him to others? God help us to make all else on earth secondary to our knowing God. Men who do exploits for God cannot live insignificant lives. Whatever they put their hands to do must prosper. But complete consecration is necessary.

BEATING THE AIR

I therefore so run, not as uncertainly; so fight I, not as one that beateth the air. 1 Cor. 9:26.

"Find your life's purpose and press toward the mark with certainty," is the message of today's text. Uncertain runners and beaters of the air have claimed more than their share of the human family. Wasted years and pitiable frustration are the lot of the aimless. Decide now on a life profession and begin an early march toward its fulfillment.

In choosing one's lifework, God's direction and guidance should be sought before all else. "Lord, what wilt thou have me to do?" is a prayer childlike in simplicity but powerful in portent. It is not enough to be efficient and successful. We must be what God wants us to be or we shall be plagued by a vague but persistent uneasiness throughout our days. To use a timeworn phrase, we want to be in the "center of God's will," otherwise it is better not to exist.

Also, the matter of motive is important. In the choice of life's occupation, service to others must be the supreme motivation. It can never be said of a man who serves well the cause of God and others, he "beateth the air." Whatever the profession, may it be a tributary to human need. Furthermore, resolve to be the very best in your chosen field. This involves present sacrifice for future excellence, but in the end a grateful world will call you blessed.

One time two cowpunchers went into the mountains to bring in a wild steer. To do the job, they took along a little gray donkey. Arriving in the mountains, they tied the donkey to the steer with a thick rope and left them alone. The steer threw the donkey all over the place. He banged him against trees and rocks and dragged him into bushes. After a week, the donkey appeared at the ranch headquarters and with him was the steer, now tame. How had the donkey done it? Simple. Every time the steer threw him down, he got up and took a step toward the corral. The donkey had a purpose.

With every failure, then, arise and take another step toward the kingdom, and one day you will appear at heaven's sparkling gates, battle scarred perhaps, but serene in the security of the Master's presence.

LOVE THYSELF

Thou shalt love thy neighbour as thyself. Matt. 19:19.

The emphasis in this text to love our neighbors can easily obscure the fact that we have directives from heaven to seek the best for ourselves. Self-appreciation is a Christian duty when we think of what price God paid for our redemption. To properly evaluate our worth we must (1) recognize our status as a child of God, made in His image (Gen. 1:27); (2) believe in what we may become through Christ; and (3) cheerfully accept the disciplines of the gospel for our everyday conduct.

Seeking fulfillment through any one of these three practices will result in improved behavior. To appropriate all three is to develop into a full man in Christ, and into greater favor among men, for the psalmist says, "men will praise thee, when thou doest well to thyself" (Ps. 49:18). Self-respect is one of the most dynamic motivations for a Christian to live up to his potential as a steward of God's love.

Twentieth-century youth find proposition three especially difficult. So attractive is the world's tinsel, and so magnetic its pull, that any restraint is regarded as a relic of "old-fashioned" ideals. Indeed, to be a "square" is well-nigh unpardonable. But let's face the truth. Although there are some things that God refuses to tolerate in His children, He will take nothing beneficial from them. "For . . . no good thing will he withhold from them that walk uprightly" (Ps. 84:11). The child of God recognizes in His prohibitions a guide to life. If a thing is good, it is permitted; if harmful, it is forbidden. The Christian's highest privilege is the grace of humble submission that God's greatest favor may be upon him.

It is ironic that God should love us more than we love ourselves, and that self-destroying habits are naturally appealing to us. We should indeed love ourselves too much to stoop to popular evil customs and practices. The key to unsullied self-love, of course, is love for God. When our relationship with Him is normal our view of ourselves and of our fellow man assumes the proper perspective. Then are we prepared to say, "All that the Lord hath said will we do."

THAT THOU MAYEST DO

But the word is very nigh unto thee, in thy mouth, and in thy heart, that thou mayest do it. Deut. 30:14.

This text of Scripture is a capsule expression of God's requirement with a built-in formula to meet it. The demand? "That thou mayest do it." The supply? "The word is very nigh." The writer of this interesting passage removes forever any excuse for lack of performance. "It is not hidden from thee" (verse 11). "It is not in heaven, that thou shouldest say, Who shall go up for us to heaven, and bring it unto us" (verse 12). "Neither is it beyond the sea, that thou shouldest say, Who shall go over the sea for us, and bring it unto us?" (verse 13). But God has made the Scriptures available to all of us and has agreed to write them in our hearts that we may obey them. And the curt warning of verses 17 and 18 deserves our attention, "But if thine heart turn away, so that thou wilt not hear, . . . ye shall surely perish."

Does the Word of God claim first place in your home? Or is it a poor second to television, novel reading, or other amusements? Do you find reading the Bible dull and uninteresting? This is a sure sign that other channels of communication are receiving more than their share of attention, and thereby destroying the spiritual appetite.

A man came to R. A. Torrey and said to him, "The Bible is as dry as dust to me. I must find a way to love the Bible as others do or cease to be a Christian. You tell me how."

"Take a book of the Bible and read it every day for a month."

This he did, and his appetite for spiritual things became insatiable.

A skeptical world beholds the lives of Christians. They eagerly seize upon any small flaw in the Christian experience as an excuse for their own wrongdoing. If the Christian would not negate his own Christian witness, he must provide a demonstration of the character of Christ for those with whom he lives, and this is possible only by the power of the indwelling Christ. A high-powered automobile was seen sputtering as it noisily climbed a small hill.

"Hey," shouted a bystander, "why run a fine car on cheap fuel?"

Like the laboring car, many lives are run on the inferior fuel of human effort rather than on the adequate power of divine grace.

THY BREAD

Cast thy bread upon the waters: for thou shalt find it after many days. Eccl. 11:1.

A service of love is never without its compensations. And yet it requires none. To help another with the thought of personal return stamps the act as legitimate employment or selfishness. Love asks only that others be helped; it serves for the sake of service. Love finds satisfaction in the relief of the oppressed. A grateful smile from a sickbed is reward enough for an all-night vigil.

But our text for today contains the assurance that unselfish deeds performed on earth, are recorded in heaven and will be rewarded. God's response may not come soon nor even in this life, but it will come. Children have often benefited from the kindness of their parents to others. "Your father did me a good turn at a time I was in need. Welcome to my home." How often some such greeting has been made between strangers around the circle of the earth.

But some acts of kindness will be repaid in the kingdom, literally "after many days." It is not unusual to meet Christians whose sole joy is helping others. Their life's deepest motivation tritely expressed is, "What can I do for you?"

A victor at the Olympic games was asked, "Spartan, what will you get by this victory?"

He answered, "I shall have the honor to fight foremost in the ranks of my prince."

The reward of one good deed may be the privilege of doing another. For the heart of love this is enough. In the Tate Gallery in London you will see one of the last and most notable of the paintings of George Frederick Watts. On the wall in the background of the painting are these words, "What I spent, I had. What I saved, I lost. What I gave, I have." How true!

But in this matter motive is all important. We do not cast our bread upon the water that we may find it after many days. We do not give to become recipients, nor do we serve to be served. Those truly motivated by love give without regard to return or compensations. They serve merely for the joy of serving.

A COMPANION OF FOOLS

He that walketh with wise men shall be wise: but a companion of fools shall be destroyed. **Prov. 13:20.**

The human heart is lonely and we crowd together for warmth, but this natural tendency to associate has its problems. Great care should be exercised in the selection of friends. Yes, friends should be selected. We are to love all men, saints and sinners, but our associates should be carefully chosen, and character should be the basis of that choice. All other considerations are secondary to this. That one should find his associates among the God-fearing is true for the following reasons:

1. Association provides exposure to the weaknesses of one's friends as well as to their virtues. This subjects one to unnecessary negative pressures in addition to his own personal shortcomings.

2. Selection of friends of low repute has a damaging effect on one's reputation. One should guard well his influence, for it is this that speaks louder than words.

3. One should always consider ultimate consequences. "A companion of fools shall be destroyed." One rotten apple can infect a bushel, necessitating the destruction of all. The counsel of today's text is preventive in nature. Christ would have us choose Christlike companions, and thus enhance our own spiritual nature.

This principle also holds true for those contemplating marriage. To be unequally yoked is an invitation to tribulation. Let not an appeal to emotion becloud your reason. The Creator knows the creature. Take His word. "We ought always to make choice of persons of such worth and honor for friends, that if ever they ceased to be so, they will never abuse our confidence, nor give us cause to fear them as enemies."—ADDISON.

In the Garden of Eden the bond of friendship between the Creator and His creature was a thing of beauty until severed by sin. But even then God hastened to re-establish the relationship, this time on an even firmer basis, not by natural creation, but by the sacrifice of Himself, the miracle of re-creation. And he who is a companion of Christ will never be a companion of fools.

31

THERE IS A WAY

There is a way which seemeth right unto a man, but the end thereof are the ways of death. Prov. 14:12.

This present era may properly be labeled "the age of the counterfeit." Right and wrong have been rationalized to the point of mergence, making distinction difficult if not impossible. The evil one has driven his stake as close to the line of right as possible; so close indeed that many find it difficult to differentiate between the true and the false. To those with faulty spiritual eyesight, the gray twilight area expands, and the path of death seems right.

How the evil one confuses good with evil is clearly illustrated in the story of Eve's temptation and fall. It should be noted that at the outset Eve knew right from wrong. The lines were clearly drawn. Her initial statement to the devil indicates this. But the devil begins to question God's motive. "For God doth know that in the day ye eat thereof, then your eyes shall be opened, and ye shall be as gods, knowing good and evil" (Gen. 3:5). This explanation made the way of death seem attractive. Suddenly the clear line between good and evil became blurred. Continued meditation erased it completely, and the woman fell. And just what was it that made wrong seem right? Well, if not "right" then not "so bad"? What would lead this woman to doubt her God for just one moment? She was told that by transgression she would be like Him. Confusion compounded! And as an added bonus, she was told, "Ye shall be as gods." All of this the devil confirmed with the oath, "God knows." "So God is withholding that which is good to prevent my knowing what He knows," mused Eve as the line between good and evil disappeared in a haze of spiritual confusion. And she ate.

Trust in the word of God and a prayer of faith would have prevented this tragedy of the ages. The antidote is still available.

The secular view sees glory in the way of sin. It appears as a mirage in the desert. It is never real, only apparent. It "seemeth right unto a man." Death dressed in attractive garb masquerades as life. Only those who through prayer and the study of God's Word sharpen their perceptive senses have the discerning eye.

THE FRUIT AS THE TREE

But of the fruit of the tree which is in the midst of the garden, God hath said, Ye shall not eat of it, neither shall ye touch it, lest ye die. Gen. 3:3.

Only God can know good and evil without temptation. God as God cannot be tempted, for He is absolute in wisdom and power. Being neither all-wise nor all-powerful, created beings are without this immunity. Our only hope of life eternal rests in our faith in the wisdom and power of the Creator. This was true of men and angels in their unfallen state. It is equally true today.

Unlimited knowledge without absolute power is a fatal equation. And the mere knowledge of evil is corruptive. Knowing this, God withheld from men and angels this knowledge.

The tree of knowledge of good and evil still stands in the midst of earth's tarnished garden. It is still unsafe to expose ourselves to its forbidden fruit. That it still appeals to the senses is not surprising. For the original fruit was "good for food," "pleasant to the eyes," and productive of a dubious brand of wisdom. And how did partaking affect our first parents? It weakened their bodies, debased their natures, and stripped them of God's righteous character, which was their covering. Experimenting with evil can have only one sure result—spiritual and physical death. Then let us guard more closely the avenues of the soul. Let us resolve henceforth to abstain from reading books, viewing programs, and attending gatherings that provide an education in evil or that have no character-building value. Let us strive through prayer and Bible study to be like God in character, which is indeed our only security against sin. May we spend our short lives, not in the profiteers' search for new forms of evil, nor for an experimental knowledge of the old, but in the ceaseless search for excellence in Christ. Then shall we know "the joy of the Lord" in this life and assurance of life in the world to come.

But there is no power in man to resist the fruit of the forbidden tree. Only the power of God can render him immune to the tug of external temptation or the internal tendency toward waywardness. It is this power that we must seek with all our heart.

GIVE HIM NO REST

And give him no rest, till he establish, and till he make Jerusalem a praise in the earth. Isa. 62:7.

An officer complained to General Stonewall Jackson that some soldiers were making a noise in their tent. "What are they doing?" asked the general. "They are praying," was the reply. "Is that a crime?" the general demanded. "The articles of war order punishment for any unusual noise," was the reply. "God forbid that praying should be an unusual noise in this camp," replied the general.

Prayer is defined by one author as "the soul of religion" and "the breath of the soul." We breathe with unconscious effort. Is this the meaning of 1 Thessalonians 5:17, "Pray without ceasing"? My father counseled me as a little boy, "Son, in life you will develop many habits. You can do nothing more profitable than learn to pray."

There are those who fear that a spiritual program of this nature will reduce prayer to a mere ritual, a form without meaning. I answer, better this, than that prayer be relegated to the hallowed sanctuary of some seldom-visited trophy room. These are twin evils, to be sure, but few Christians are guilty of the former.

That prayer changes things is undoubtedly true. But I strongly suspect that prayer more often changes people so that they can change the things that can be changed and endure the things that cannot. "Give him no rest," the Bible says, until His promise is fulfilled. Nothing else can satiate the hunger pangs of the soul. That restless, uneasy feeling is the heart's call to prayer. It will accept no substitutes. You may give it instead a new round of parties, jazz, intoxicants, or opiates. These will but intensify the craving. The soul can find its rest only in God. Some learn this early, others late. The sooner the better. You can pray without prayer book, prayer wheel, or beads. Prayer is communicating with God. There can be no relationship without it. Have you talked to God today?

God does not weary of our repeated approaches to the throne of grace. Unchanging prayer based on the unchanged need is music to His ear. He regards neither rhetoric nor oratory. The essential ingredient is an expectant faith based on a repentant heart.

GOD REMEMBERS

Can a woman forget her sucking child, that she should not have compassion on the son of her womb? yea, they may forget, yet will I not forget thee. Isa. 49:15.

It is said that there is a tribe of people in a far-off land that knows nothing of arithmetic. They never count. A man asked one of them how many sheep he had. "Don't know," came the reply. "Then how do you know if one is missing?" he asked. "Because of the face that I would miss."

Yes, God remembers us individually. Three and a half billion people populate this globe. But to Him, we are more than a digit on a heartless computer. He knows us both by name and by need. "I have graven thee upon the palms of my hands." Midst severest trial, when deserted by friend and foe alike, Jesus says, "I will never leave thee, nor forsake thee." During the Flood, amid the world's worst natural upheaval, the Scriptures say that "God remembered Noah."

Just prior to the destruction of Sodom and Gomorrah, God paused in His march to administer judgment to give Abraham a chance to pray for his nephew. And later, while effecting the rescue of Lot, the angel revealed Heaven's concern for the individual with this question, "Hast thou here any besides? son in law, and thy sons, and thy daughters, and whatsoever thou hast in the city, bring them out of this place." And later to Lot himself, "Haste thee, escape thither; for I cannot do any thing till thou be come thither."

Life has a way of overwhelming the strongest of God's children, demanding resources beyond our supply. It is comforting to know that in every emergency Jesus is always near. Indeed, he is always just a prayer away. With Him, there are no problems—only solutions. Even the fowl of the air receive His personal attention. "Are ye not much better than they?"

Then let us take courage, finding refuge in the promise, "I will never leave thee nor forsake thee," and these tension-producing times will have little affect on our inner peace. We are graven upon the palms of His hands. We may, therefore, face the day with hopeful hearts.

THE LANGUAGE OF OUR LIVES

Let your light so shine before men, that they may see your good works, and glorify your Father which is in heaven. Matt. 5:16.

"Are you a Christian?" asked Gypsy Smith, the evangelist.

"Yes," was the reply.

"How long have you been one?" he asked.

"Twenty-eight years off and on," the man answered.

Answered Gypsy, "More off than on, I presume, and it will be that way until you become 'out and out.'"

It is a fact that the language of our lives outweighs the words of our mouths. Yes, men are more impressed with what we do than with what we say. The Christian ideal is that we match our high profession with performance. We then become shining examples to others.

A great preacher closed his sermon with an earnest gospel appeal. A woman of wealth and social distinction came forward. She asked to speak a few words to the audience. "I want you to know just why I came forward tonight. It was not because of any words spoken by the preacher. I stand here because of a little woman who sits before me. Her fingers are rough with toil. She has served my home for years. I have never known her to be impatient, speak an unkind word, or do a dishonorable deed. I know of countless little acts of unselfish love that adorn her life. In the past, I have sneered at her faith. Yet when my little girl was taken away, it was this woman who caused me to look beyond the grave and shed my first tears of hope. The sweet magnetism of her life has led me to Christ. I covet the thing that has made her so beautiful."

I was sitting across the table from the president of a sovereign country. Beside me was a missionary who for eighteen years had served the church in that far-off land. The chief executive of this state said, "I like you Adventists. You have helped me build my country. Pastor Henry here came to my country when it was struggling educationally and brought that school of yours to a fine standard where it is making a contribution to the life of the nation. You Adventists are always welcome here."

36

WHOM SHALL I FEAR?

The Lord is my light and my salvation; whom shall I fear? the Lord is the strength of my life; of whom shall I be afraid? Ps. 27:1.

"You will work today," barked the sergeant to the new recruit, and ordered him out of the barracks on the double. It was Sabbath morning, a crisp November day in 1917. My father was marched to a pile of rock. A shovel was put in his hand and he was ordered to work. Looking up he spied six rifles all aimed at him. The voice of the sergeant split the silence into a thousand atoms. "Work or die," he said. With a prayer on his lips my father allowed the shovel to fall to the ground. The air was filled with invectives, to my father's relief. He had expected bullets. "You have one more chance," said the soldier, leaning the shovel against him. Once again the rifles were raised. The shovel hit the ground—there was a pause. "Go to your barracks," came the order. This, our soldier was glad to do. The date of the court-martial was set. With a prayer on his lips, my father entered a room filled with high Army officials.

For the next two hours he was interrogated mercilessly. Each officer, according to his own personality, alternated between verbal abuse and calm cunning. Finally someone asked, "Soldier, what would you do if a robber entered your home, threatened your wife and child—and you had a rifle near?"

Prayerfully father replied, "If the Lord lets me get into this kind of situation, He will help me out of it."

The commanding officer dismissed the court, came down and took a chair opposite my dad and said smilingly, "I know you Adventists. I know your health habits and all about your Sabbath. You may keep Sabbath for the rest of the time you are in the Army. I left my family in the care of an Adventist housekeeper."

The power of example is far reaching. The fidelity of that housekeeper blessed the life of an unknown soldier in trouble.

And as for my father, the strength of his life was also his strength in death. Like David, he could walk through the valley of the shadow of death without fear of evil, for God was with him. He looked for a city that has foundations, whose builder and maker is God.

REMEMBER

Remember the sabbath day, to keep it holy. Ex. 20:8.

A new recruit in the United States Army stood with one foot up-raised, polishing his boots. "You're in the Army now," rang through the corridors as lusty young voices sang the refrain. But the young soldier was worried. He had requested Sabbath privileges and been denied. "We have no Sabbath in the Army," were the words that kept ringing in his ears. But he just had to go to church. All good Adventists do— when the Sabbath comes.

"There must be a way," he mused as he continued to prepare for the Sabbath. Finally his uniform was pressed and everything was in order. The crimson rays of the setting sun slanted skyward in a final salute to the oncoming day of rest. Jehovah's day of rest was here. The young Army private prayed earnestly before retiring that God would make it possible for him to attend church next morning.

His deep sleep was broken by the piercing sound of a trumpet. It was an unexpected call to inspection. Soldiers tumbled from their bunks into uniforms in varying stages of disorder. Why hadn't someone warned them? They would have been ready. "Fall out," barked the sergeant. "Attention," he shouted. Hundreds of men lined the parade ground as the commanding officer, riding a snow-white steed, rode up and down the line berating his troops for their disheveled appearances. Suddenly he stopped. Standing before him was one man with boots shined and uniform pressed. "Step forward, soldier," he snapped. "What is your name?"

"William Cleveland, sir," came the answer.

"Follow me," he ordered. They marched to a platform. "Soldiers," he shouted, "look at this man. His uniform is pressed and his boots clean and shined. He is the only man in this company ready for inspection. Soldier, you have the day off to do as you please."

A happy young man made his way to church that day secure in the knowledge that it pays to be ready for the Sabbath. How proud I am that this man was my father.

THEM THAT CURSE

But I say unto you, Love your enemies, bless them that curse you, do good to them that hate you, and pray for them which despitefully use you, and persecute you. Matt. 5:44.

The troopship was about to embark. The year was 1917. The soldiers had been issued their thick winter coats before sailing. My father had received a coat with a thick fur collar. The Army issue was not so uniform in those days as now. He prized this coat, for it was both attractive and warm.

The day before the ship sailed, the coat was stolen. Where could it be? Who had it? Sadly my father applied for and received another coat. Bemoaning his misfortune, he contented himself with a coat of lesser quality.

One day aboard ship, far out over the Atlantic, he spotted his coat. Rushing up to the man wearing it, he claimed it as his own. But the new owner refused to give it up, and became abusive. The other soldiers roared with laughter as my father recoiled under the hail of abuse. To say that he was not tempted to reply in kind would be to claim more for him than the facts would justify. However, he resisted the impulse to retaliate and slowly walked away.

Months later on the battlefields of France the soldier who had stolen my father's coat lay gasping for breath, a victim of poison. The Germans had poisoned the pool from which he had drunk. "Help," he moaned. The only medic near with the help he needed was my father, the man from whom he had stolen the coat. He gasped his apology from a grateful heart as the man that he had previously humiliated knelt to give him aid.

Is it not best to bless our enemies and treat with kindness those who slander us? Only those who through faith have claimed the divine nature of our Lord, are capable of this.

Human nature tends to just the opposite, for by nature we bless those who bless us and curse those who curse us. We pick our friends among those who have a flattering opinion of us and tend to shun those whom we consider to be our critics.

Christianity alone can produce in one a compassion for his enemies.

YOUR WORK

For God is not unrighteous to forget your work and labour of love, which ye have shewed toward his name, in that ye have ministered to the saints, and do minister. Heb. 6:10.

It is human to want to be appreciated and remembered. My own heart aches as I remember that tired, careworn mother who worked so hard to put her son through school and decided to surprise him on graduation day. A proud day it was when the seniors, resplendent in cap and gown, chatted informally prior to the processional. This mother, in neat but frayed garments, approached her son and put her hand on his arm. Wheeling around, he saw her stooped form and worn clothes, and his countenance froze. He spoke to her curtly as if she were a stranger. And in the processional, he proudly turned his back and walked away. Forgotten were the days of toil and sacrifice. He was ashamed of his mother.

But our text assures us that "God is not unrighteous to forget our work." What comforting words. Many of the most vital deeds performed go unnoticed by other men. Lack of appreciation is a sign of our times. And it sometimes happens that another gets credit for what you do. At such times many find it necessary to set the record straight.

Perhaps most grievous to bear is having one's best severely criticized. To be sure, our best may be inadequate, but any deed has merit if it constitutes one's own best effort.

God remembers—blessed thought—the word of cheer, the care of the sick, the Bible study held, and the visit to the prison to bring cheer to the captives. All are written in the book of God's memory.

A man was pinned beneath his car on a U.S. highway as flames licked at the framework of the automobile. Bystanders stood help-lessly listening to the groans of the victim when suddenly there appeared a giant of a man. With almost superhuman strength, he lifted the car off the wounded driver and then quietly slipped away.

When word of this heroic deed was spread around the town, search was made, and the modest giant was found quietly working at a service station. A hero's reward was given him, and a grateful city remembered. Men often forget, but God remembers.

THY THOUGHTS

*How precious also are thy thoughts unto me, O God! how
great is the sum of them!* Ps. 139:17.

It is a sad fact that many of God's children know little of what He
thinks. Our ignorance of God's will is a prime cause of our sin. That
this ignorance is inexcusable constitutes our shame. The opinions of
the Almighty should be our first concern. "In all thy ways acknowledge
him." There is nothing that concerns us that does not involve Him.
His interests and ours are identical. "In him we live, and move, and
have our being." The well-ordered, happy, significant life is, then, of
necessity a Christ-centered one.

God has not spared Himself to make known His thoughts to us.
Originally man could commune with God face to face. With the advent of sin, He chose more indirect methods of communication.
Prophets, preachers, and special messengers are all used to reveal God's
will. Their essential purpose was to make known God's thoughts to
man.

Then came the masterpiece of revelation in the person of Jesus
Christ. He it was who most perfectly demonstrated the mind of God
in human flesh, for "in him dwelleth all the fulness of the Godhead
bodily." His coming into the world pierced the curtain of satanic
censorship—that the will of God might flood the earth.

Do you study the Word of God each day? Has it produced in you
such change of heart that you treasure His thoughts? How else will
we ever know the reality of the experience mirrored in Philippians
2:5: "Let this mind be in you, which was also in Christ Jesus"?

I am comforted to know that God's thoughts are of man and his
welfare. Why else would He spend thirty-three years on this earth
giving His full attention to the needs of the human family? And what
of His death at Calvary for our sins? May we not faithfully conclude
that we are in the very center of the thoughts of God? How great
indeed is the sum of them—His attention to little Zacchaeus up in
the tree, to the woman with an issue of blood for twelve years, to the
crippled man by the pool, to the demon possessed. God is likewise
thinking of us today. Are we thinking of Him?

41

PRECIOUS SEED

He that goeth forth and weepeth, bearing precious seed, shall doubtless come again with rejoicing, bringing his sheaves with him. Ps. 126:6.

Jesus saves! This is the precious seed contained in the gospel. It must be borne to every living person. Its very nature demands it. The needs of man require it. For the gospel seed is life itself—life here and life hereafter.

The Christian religion deals with the whole man—body, mind, and spiritual attitude. There are very specific messages in the Scriptures dealing with all three. Obedience to these laws is essential to physical, spiritual, and mental health. The gospel seed is indeed precious. But its influence is limited when it is not shared.

The rewards of sharing one's faith are many and satisfying, not the least of which is "rejoicing" when we see souls added to the kingdom.

I had just finished a sermon when a man staggered up the aisle and clasped my hand. "I am lost," he said, "I need help." I knelt in prayer with this drunken man in tattered garments. He had no job, and his family had left him. How was I to know that God would hear and heal that very night? Today he is a baptized member of the church. He has a good job and his home is intact. Now, with clear eye and steady step, he makes his way resolutely toward the kingdom of God.

In Port of Spain, Trinidad, a seventeen-year-old girl reacted quickly to the good news of the gospel sown like seed in her own heart. She, in turn, planted it in her mother's heart and in that of her grandmother, her three sisters, and her brother. It was my privilege to baptize the entire family.

This young woman was tested in the matter of Sabbath observance. She was fired from her job for keeping the Sabbath. But the seed had been faithfully sown, and she was content to suffer for Christ's sake. But she was called back, and the father of the manager of the store insisted that she not only be rehired, but be given her regular salary and extra work be found for her to do.

You may be sure that I came again with rejoicing over the fruit of seed sown in that wonderful city, and so may we all rejoice in God.

WILD GRAPES

What could have been done more to my vineyard, that I have not done in it? wherefore, when I looked that it should bring forth grapes, brought it forth wild grapes? Isa. 5:4.

Seriously, what more can Jesus do to save our souls? Witness His thirty-three-year struggle on earth to ensure man's salvation. The humble circumstances of His birth were an insult to His status. Pursued by a bloodthirsty king at the age of two years, repudiated by many of His own followers—He literally trod the winepress alone.

Clothed in human form, Christ will carry the scars of His sacrifice through eternity. What love—what matchless love—that Divinity would so limit Himself! What more can Jesus do?

Why, then, this negative response, these "wild grapes"? If we will but yield our hearts to Christ, His love will produce in us fruit for the kingdom. Having fulfilled the requirements of divine love, Christ can do no more than offer us the benefits of His atoning act. The rest is up to us. He does not compel the conscience.

For the "wild grapes" in their lives, some blame heredity. They would thrust upon their parents responsibility for their deeds. Let none deny the power of heredity. To a great extent, the lives of children are shaped by parents. But there is a higher power than heredity. "I will strengthen thee; yea, I will help thee; yea, I will uphold thee with the right hand of my righteousness" (Isa. 41:10). This promise can break the power of heredity. It is also effective against social and other environmental pressures. How else can you explain the conversion of Peter, the transformation of the apostle Paul, or the changed life of Mary Magdalene? The power of Christ literally changes lives!

Jacob is a prime example of a man who by faith and struggle broke the power of heredity. He was by nature a deceiver, and was encouraged in this nefarious work by his mother. He continued in this life of deception, deceiving and being deceived, until he approached the armies of Esau, his brother. It was then that he had that famous all-night struggle with his Master. "I will not let thee go, except thou bless me," he agonized. It was then that the hand that touched his hip touched his heart, and Jacob was a new man in Christ Jesus.

LIVING FOR HIM

Who redeemeth thy life from destruction; who crowneth thee with lovingkindness and tender mercies. Ps. 103:4.

"Is it a sin to take my own life?" This question spoken in a desperate voice revealed a desperate need. A few tactful questions brought out the fact that the man on the phone had indeed decided to end his own life. "What is there to live for?" he challenged. Such questions as the Sabbath, tithing, abstemiousness in dress and diet, suddenly took their proper place in the Christian order of things. These things are indeed outgrowths of a more vital experience involving life itself. These themes, vital in their place, could not help now. Life in its initial sense was at stake here. The question: "What is there to live for?" intrigued me. The answers came thick and fast.

"Live to serve God," was my first reply.

"But He can do without me," the man answered.

"But you cannot do without Him," I shot back, "and that is why you are considering taking your life. You are separated from Him." Then the texts began to come to mind. "I am come that they might have life, and that they might have it more abundantly" (John 10:10). "I am crucified with Christ: nevertheless I live; yet not I, but Christ liveth in me" (Gal. 2:20). "Accept Christ as Lord of your life and He will become at once the source and reason for living."

Second I said to him, "You must live to save your fellow man. Your death leaves God one pair of hands less with which to roll back the darkness. Your fellow man has deep spiritual, physical, and mental needs. You have no right to retire from life until you have done your part to meet those needs."

"How can I meet those needs," he asked, "when I have them myself?"

I answered, "Our inter-dependence is a redemptive fellowship. It is like the man who with his friend was traversing the cold wasteland of Antarctica. One collapsed in the snow and begged his companion to go on. Knowing that the man would freeze to death, his friend knelt and lifted him to his shoulder and struggled on. They both arrived at a place of safety. As a result of the struggle to save his friend, both were saved from death that day. So it is with us all."

HUMBLE YOURSELVES

Humble yourselves in the sight of the Lord, and he shall lift you up. James 4:10.

A little girl in the Orient was being examined for baptism: "Do you know what it means to be baptized?" the kindly pastor asked.

"Yes, sir, I know," was her firm reply.

"Have you been truly converted?" was the next question.

"Oh, yes." Again the reply was firmly stated.

"But how do you know you have been converted?"

"Because I used to be hardheaded and now I am not," she said.

This is indeed the universal test of true conversion—submission to God. Sin produced in man a fatal willfulness. This, the God of heaven cannot allow. A runaway planet in our skies can be catastrophic. A runaway man even more so. Submission involves humility. "Humble yourselves therefore under the mighty hand of God, that he may exalt you in due time" (1 Peter 5:6). Genuine humility demands self-denial—confession to God without reservation. Indeed, if He demanded all, on what moral ground can we stake our claim or base our objections?

"The earth is the Lord's and the fulness thereof." We are the creatures of His hands but He allows man nine tenths of his income and six sevenths of his time, requiring only obedience to His will. "Submit yourselves therefore to God. Resist the devil, and he will flee from you" (James 4:7).

One of the world's leading psychologists asserts that the only thing that keeps any of us out of the insane asylum is just five cents' worth of iodine in the thyroid gland. This picture of our fragile selves should teach us dependence upon the great Creator.

Adam and Eve were physically, mentally, and emotionally, as well as spiritually, dependent upon God. When sin separated them from their Creator, death began to set in. They were assailed with intellectual doubts, physical weakness, emotional instability, and spiritual declension.

So is it with us all. Our only hope is in absolute and total dependence upon that strong arm that never fails.

BEHOLD THE MAN

Then came Jesus forth, wearing the crown of thorns, and the purple robe. And Pilate saith unto them, Behold the man! John 19:5.

In this our day man is strangely preoccupied with himself. This accounts in part for his obvious boredom. To be sure he does experience temporary periods of artificial excitement stimulated by scientific advance or the madness called the sports craze. Failing this, he resorts to entertainment or stronger opiates to satiate his taste. He neglects the only source of peace, found in the invitation of Jesus, "Come unto me, all ye that labour and are heavy laden, and I will give you rest" (Matt. 11:28). Christ should be our first and constant concern. Pilate's advice is inspired counsel: "Behold the man!"

1. Behold His creative power. "It is he that hath made us, and not we ourselves" (Ps. 100:3). "The heavens declare the glory of God; and the firmament sheweth his handywork" (Ps. 19:1). What a sense of capability pervades when Christ is near.

2. Behold His redemptive power. "I have blotted out, as a thick cloud, thy transgressions, and, as a cloud, thy sins: return unto me; for I have redeemed thee" (Isa. 44:22). What power to save!

3. Behold His character. Of His mercy it is written: "For the Lord your God is gracious and merciful, and will not turn away his face from you, if ye return unto him" (2 Chron. 30:9). And of His justice it is written: "Be not deceived; God is not mocked: for whatsoever a man soweth, that shall he also reap" (Gal. 6:7). By beholding we become changed. Our character is the measure of that which claims our first and most constant attention.

There is something fascinating about Christ. Secular historians have dated history by His life. The claims He made, the miracles He performed, and the profound teachings contained in His sermons have been a basis not only for changed lives but for philosophical speculation for more than nineteen hundred years. No, He cannot be ignored, and the day will come when, willingly or unwillingly, men must stand before the judgment bar of God. And at the judgment of the great white throne, they will behold Him in all His glory.

TO BREAK A HABIT

For sin shall not have dominion over you: for ye are not under the law, but under grace. Rom. 6:14.

The first portion of our text makes it clear that the reign of sin can be broken, and that disobedience is not a necessity. "Sin shall not have dominion." But what can be done to break the power and dominion of sin in the life?

1. It takes faith, for unless a man believes that a habit can be broken he is hardly likely to exert the effort required to break it.

2. Prayer is a necessity. There are some habits that cannot be broken without divine power, and there are no habits that are beyond the power of divine grace.

3. There must be a supreme exercise of the will. God has given to each man a will, and with this will he can control the mind and the activities of the body. It is like a steering wheel in an automobile. It is the point of ultimate control. Some habits will never be broken until the full force of the human will is turned against them.

In the army of Alexander the Great, a soldier who had been caught leaving the post without permission was brought before him. Alexander the Great addressed him: "I understand that your name is also Alexander. Is that correct?"

The man said, "It is, sir."

"Then I will ask you, are you guilty of all the crimes of which you are accused?"

"I am guilty, sir."

"Then you will have to change your name or change your ways," said Alexander.

Is this not true to a greater degree in our relationship to Christ? How often do we commit sins that misrepresent His name and character. My father often said, "Before you do what you do, remember who you are."

The sin pattern can be broken, the nature of the habit notwithstanding. Our problem is a problem of faith, and if faith is in need of foundation, there is ample evidence in Scripture, and in what Christ has done for others, of the power of Christ to deal with any habit.

SPIRITUAL REST

Come unto me, all ye that labour and are heavy laden, and I will give you rest. Matt. 11:28.

Many have read this text and looked upon it as being the working man's scripture. They reason: "I labor and am heavy laden. The Bible promises me rest ultimately from my labors." But the scriptural context indicates that this is not its intent at all. The very next verse says: "My yoke is easy, and my burden is light." The yoke refers to the law of God, the great moral law of the Ten Commandments. Obedience to it is made easy by first coming to Christ. There are too many people who are laboring without divine assurance.

"Come unto Me," said He, "all who are having a difficult time following, and I will make it for you a restful experience."

My little boy was trying to climb a tree, but without success. Up he would climb and down he would slide, up and down, fruitlessly seeking to reach the lower limb. Suddenly he got a bright idea. His little feet pounded the grass toward the kitchen where I was watching.

"Daddy, Daddy, come here please." And I followed him to the foot of the tree. "Daddy, if you will just give me a lift I think I can make it to the lower limb." With that I boosted his little body into the air close enough for him to pull himself up. He labored in vain on his own to achieve his objective, but when he came to me the same burden that was frustrating to him was made light, and the yoke was made easy.

It is to this Jesus refers when He gives the invitation to all weary and heavy-laden laborers to come unto Him and He will give them just the boost they need to see them through today.

I have lived in an area where hurricanes frequently make their way during the season. There is something peculiar about these monstrous storms. It is said that in the very eye of the hurricane all is calm. But the mighty winds that churn around this eye of calm are justifiably feared for their destructive nature.

A true Christian experience is an eye of calm. There is, indeed, a place of quiet rest near to the heart of God.

THE NECESSITY OF FAITH

Jesus saith unto him, Thomas, because thou hast seen me, thou hast believed: blessed are they who have not seen, and yet have believed. John 20:29.

A little boy was flying a kite high in the sky. So far out was it that it was difficult to discern. A man came by and wanted to know: "Little boy, what are you doing?"

The boy pulled away at the string and replied, "I am flying a kite, mister."

The man scanned the sky and said, "I don't see any kite."

"Oh, but it is out there, sir," said the boy.

Searching the sky again in vain the man said to the lad, "But son, I still don't see it. How do you know that it is out there?"

The boy replied, "Sir, I know it is out there, for you see I hold the string and I feel the pull."

We must know in our hearts that there is a God and that those who seek Him do not seek in vain. We must be sure that He is indeed a rewarder of them that seek Him diligently. There are many things promised to those who seek Him by faith. Just to mention a few: There are pardon, peace, power, cleansing, and the great promise of life—the more abundant life here and the glorious life of the hereafter. All of this is possible to us through faith in Christ. We may not see Him but the evidence is there that He is alive and interestedly active in the affairs of our lives.

An infidel was put in a room with a Christian. Toward early morning the infidel was seen rushing from the room in obvious anxiety. "What is wrong?" inquired the innkeeper.

"Find me another room," shouted the infidel. "Just five more minutes in the room with that man and I would become a Christian."

"But how could that be?" cried the innkeeper. "Aren't you an infidel?"

He said, "I cannot stand that man's prayers. He prays as if he really believes there is a God listening to him. Find me another room."

One man's stout faith can dispel the doubt of ten faithless men.

49

EVERY WORD

Man shall not live by bread alone, but by every word that proceedeth out of the mouth of God. Matt. 4:4.

An old violinist was poor but he owned a violin that never failed to charm others with its beautiful tone. Someone asked the violinist about his instrument. He held it tenderly in his hand and said, "A great deal of sunshine must have gone into this wood, and what has gone in comes out."

According to our text the Word of God is to us more vital than bread. In fact, a day should not pass without the individual partaking thereof. That which goes in comes out. Feed the mind with that which is constructive and cultural and spiritual and we will reap a harvest of disciplined behavior that will be a credit to our families, to our church, and to our God.

In John 6:63 Jesus said, "The words that I speak unto you, they are spirit, and they are life." It is literally true that the Bible is more than an instrument for the cultivation of the intellect. It literally breathes spiritual life into the heart of the believer.

The foreman on a ship deck once said to Clyde the carpenter: "Are you one of those who say they know they are saved?"

"Yes, thank God," said Clyde, "I am sure I am saved from sin."

"Well now," replied the foreman, "that is something I don't understand. How can you know that you are saved as long as you are in this world?"

"Well," replied Clyde, "I do not think it presumption to say I am saved from sin, for it is real and I know it. Let me ask you, what is the breadth of this planking?"

The foreman, astonished, said, "Why, fourteen inches all around."

"But," asked Clyde, "what makes you sure it is fourteen inches?"

"Why," answered the foreman, "here it is in the book I got from headquarters, and I am going by the book."

"That is exactly how I know that I am saved from sin," said Clyde, "I am going by the Book. I have met its requirements, and the Book comes from headquarters and it says that I am saved by grace through faith in the Lord Jesus, and I believe it."

A QUESTION OF AUTHORITY

The most High ruleth in the kingdom of men, and giveth it to whomsoever he will, and setteth up over it the basest of men. **Dan.** 4:17.

There are three levels of authority that exercise themselves in our world. They are—human authority, angelic authority, and divine authority. When God created man it was His purpose to control man Himself. This is understandable, for man was made in the image of God and only God could give him adequate guidance and supervision. But sin altered all this, and the theocracy that God intended was supplanted by an era of faulty human rule. For six thousand years now this world has been under the control of one nation after another, each clearly demonstrating its incapacity to govern the rest of the world. This is the sad story of the rise and fall of nations, and it is a sad commentary that our heroes are bloody men. Great war lords of the ages have dominated the pages of human history.

But human beings are also confronted with angel power. There are literally in this earth thousands of fallen angels, according to Revelation 12:7-9. These angels, under the direction of Lucifer, go forth to deceive the whole world, and it is their studied purpose to interpose their will and their authority between man and God. God gave man dominion at Creation. But he lost it through sin. Both human and fallen angelic authority are presumptive.

Divine authority is the only justifiable power in the world today. We must remember that it is God who created us and it is God who has redeemed us. It is Creation and redemption that form the basis of the only authentic authority in this world. And when there is a conflict between angelic and human authority on the one hand and divine will of God on the other, we ought to obey God rather than man.

This was so in the case of Daniel. The law was passed in the kingdom requiring that only the king should receive worship for thirty days. To Daniel his course was clear. He had to recognize the only legitimate authority in the earth, and that is the voice of God. He must be obeyed first. Daniel cast himself upon the mercy of God, and his victory was a glorious one.

GO YE

And he said unto them, Go ye into all the world, and preach the gospel to every creature. Mark 16:15.

Someone said to John W. Foster in China: "What right have you Christians to come over here and bother these poor people with your religion?"

Dr. Foster replied, "It is our right to give to others something that is too good to keep."

At a meeting some young people were discussing the text: "Ye are the salt of the earth." One suggestion after another was made as to the meaning of the salt in the verse. Said one, "Salt imparts a desirable flavor." Another suggested, "Salt preserves from decay." But I like best the words of a little Chinese Christian girl who said, "Salt creates thirst." We are indeed the salt of the earth, but have souls been made thirsty for the Lord Jesus Christ because of our attitude and example? Do men want to know Christ because they know us?

A man who was visiting a railroad yard saw a big engine sidetracked. He said, "The engine looks as if it could go. Why is it switched off here?"

"Oh, it can pull itself all right," said the workman, "but there is something wrong with it. It can't pull anything else."

The Christian who merely keeps himself going is not much of a Christian. It is the business of a Christian to draw others to Christ. Have you shared your faith with someone today?

Standing in line at a cafeteria at a camp meeting recently, I noticed a small boy eying me intently. I asked him what he wanted to be in life. Hearing his reply, I talked with him briefly about becoming a soul saver. His eyes lighted up as if by magic.

"Do you think I could do it?" he asked.

My answer was, "Of course." And I talked further with him about the nature of this spiritual work. Today I received a letter from that little boy, and apparently the fires of the love of God are burning even more brightly than ever in that young heart. He seems almost impatient to get out and teach others of the message. And he is only thirteen years of age. Are you making soul-saving contacts for Christ?

SELF-DENIAL

Then said Jesus unto his disciples, If any man will come after me, let him deny himself, and take up his cross, and follow me. Matt. 16:24.

On one occasion Rubinstein was playing for a company of musicians. When they began to applaud he requested: "Friends, please do not applaud; your applause directs my thoughts from the music to myself and I cannot play."

The unhappy people in our world are those who spend their time thinking of themselves. Man is usually guilty of self-congratulation or self-pity. And the root of most human misery may be traced to these. Pride is folly and self-pity ego, and both are rooted in selfishness. Self-denial is a Godlike trait and is denied us only if we persist in our estrangement from Christ. To fellowship with Christ is to partake of His righteous character, and the more we walk with Him, the more like Him we become. This is the key to Enoch's translation. He walked with God through prayer, through the study of His will, and through meditation on His promises, and became so like his Creator that God could not bear another moment of separation from this godly saint and took him to Himself.

Upon being asked, "What is the first thing in religion?" Saint Augustine replied, "Humility."

And when asked for the second and third requirement, "Humility," he again replied.

Said Jesus: "I am meek and lowly in heart." To be meek is to be Godlike. To be proud and self-assertive is to imitate Lucifer, the original transgressor. There is a remedy for pride and self-pity. We may truly overcome through prayer, the study of God's Word, and service to others. It is thus that we grow out of ourselves into the divine likeness.

But there is more involved in our textual injunction than self-denial. We are admonished to take up His cross. His was a cross of obedience, a cross of service, and a cross of witnessing. This brought Him into conflict and eventually led to His crucifixion. It may also lead to ours. However, we cannot back away from either the cross or the cup. It is our privilege to enter into the fellowship of His sufferings.

HERE AND HEREAFTER

There is no man that hath left house, or parents, or brethren, or wife, or children, for the kingdom of God's sake, who shall not receive manifold more in this present time, and in the world to come life everlasting. Luke 18:29, 30.

The rewards of Christian living are often believed to be limited strictly to the hereafter while the pleasures of the present are generally conceded to be the privilege of sinners. In our text we are assured that becoming a Christian has its advantages "in this present time." Christianity adds to the happiness and zest of everyday living. It is indeed the more abundant life. God has denied man nothing that is for his best good in this life or in the life to come. Indeed, the only genuine happiness in our world today is that which is based upon man's perfect relationship with his Maker. To begin and end each day with a period of communion with God makes that day an experience of high adventure.

The Christian faith has its compensations here in life and when one faces the silent halls of death, but its rewards do not end there. The Christian may die knowing that there is a resurrection of the dead and that the eternal joys of another world await him.

For the first time a young boy was taking his minister to see his mother, eagerly leading him up the rickety stairs of a tenement building. After interminable flights, they knocked at a door and a cheery voice said, "Come in." They were greeted by a beautiful but invalid Christian woman, her face radiating sunshine. The room was clean, though sparsely furnished, contrasting with the squalor just passed through.

Noticing the shock on the minister's face, the mother said, "Pastor, it's not what it ought to be down here but, thank God, things are better higher up."

If, indeed, there were no rewards in this life for serving the Lord, eternity would be worth it all.

> "A tent or a cottage, O why should I care?
> They're building a palace for me over there!
> Though exiled from home, yet still I may sing:
> 'All glory to God, I'm a child of the King.'"

THE CALL OF DUTY

So likewise ye, when ye shall have done all those things which are commanded you, say, We are unprofitable servants: we have done that which was our duty to do. Luke 17:10.

For a job well done we may receive either praise or criticism or both. However, the accomplishment of one's task requires neither. Our text suggests that we are to do our duty whether or not we are praised and indeed in spite of criticism. We need not be reminded that there are those in our world who must be praised for what they do or duty remains unperformed. There is a milder form of this malady that expresses itself in this way. In the absence of praise the job is often done grudgingly, and obviously without relish or efficiency.

There are yet others who, though not needing praise, cannot stand criticism. They have a thin skin. Our text suggests that we obey and that we perform our duties with faith and efficiency, in the absence of praise and in the face of criticism. Such an attitude is contrary to human nature and is only possible to a truly converted man. "Marvel not that I said unto thee, Ye must be born again" (John 3:7). It is only when the life is daily submitted to the will of God that one does not need artificial stimulation from external sources, whether it be the whiplash of criticism or the heady elixir of praise.

I visited Okinawa and saw the rugged escarpment from which Desmond Doss lowered seventy-five wounded men to safety, in full view of enemy gunners. This was a heroic feat and deserving of the highest honors that a nation could give one of its soldiers. Over the many years since this I have had occasion to study the remarks of this young man so highly honored for doing such deeds of obvious bravery. Not once has he acknowledged the praise showered upon him or assumed credit for having done anything unusual. His remarks appropriately polarize around two things: (1) gratefulness to God for his safety and the safety of his men, (2) a job had to be done and he was proud to have the privilege of doing it. Such humility is rare.

It can be cultivated, you know. Perhaps the best way to do it is to continually give God and our fellows credit for any success that may come our way, and pray that the spirit of Christ may be our own.

DO YOU KNOW HIM?

And hereby we do know that we know him, if we keep his commandments. 1 John 2:3.

Mark Twain was traveling in Europe with his little daughter and being feted in many cities by celebrities in varying spheres of life. One day the little girl asked him, "Papa, you know everyone but God, don't you?" The penetrating honesty of this little girl is a sad but true commentary on the spiritual condition of many in our world. They have managed to acquaint themselves with everyone but the One who really matters—God. Mysterious as this practice is, it is understandable, for man is by nature a sinner, and sin's chief tactic is diversion.

While traveling in Liberia I came to a sign in the middle of the road. It said, "Diversion." As I sat puzzling over the word I noticed that road repairs were being made and that there was a side road to be taken. It was then that I smiled, understanding that the Liberian use of the word *diversion* was equivalent to the American use of *detour*. Anything that will make a man deviate from the main road is the design of the archdeceiver and, oh, how well he accomplishes his purpose. It requires more than human strength to concentrate on first things. "But seek ye first the kingdom of God, and his righteousness; and all these things shall be added unto you" (Matt. 6:33). It is ironic that that which should be first is last and that which is last is first in human thinking. But the happiest people I know on earth are those who put Christ first in all the affairs of their lives and who consult Him about the minutest details. These are God-conscious people. He will never forsake those who make Him first.

Those who claim to be Christians, but willingly transgress God's law certainly do not "know" Him. If they did, they would know better than to pursue this course. If they knew Him, they would know that He hates sin, and that He will punish the sinner. If they knew Him, they would know that His grace and love cannot cover up unconfessed sin. If they knew Him, they would know that God searches the intents and purposes of the heart, and therefore no hypocrisy could possibly succeed. Those who know God know that He requires obedience, and surrendered to Him, they do His will by His grace.

THE TRUTH

And ye shall know the truth, and the truth shall make you free. John 8:32.

Some years ago a passenger train was speeding into New York as another train was emerging. There was a head-on collision. Fifty lives were snuffed out. An engineer was pinned under his engine. Tears were running down his cheeks. In his dying agonies he held a piece of yellow paper crushed in his hands and said, "Take this, it will show you that someone gave me the wrong orders."

For years the world has been traveling on the wrong orders, until today it knows not its Creator and Redeemer. Today there is little excuse for this, for Bibles are available at the cheapest prices. This marvelous Book, which is in fact sixty-six books, offers 31,173 verses of inspired counsel. Written over a period of 1,500 years, the Bible revelation of God is amazingly harmonious, in spite of the fact that many of the writers lived in different countries and at different periods of earth's history and wrote often without a knowledge of what the others had written. It is in this divine Word that God has chosen to reveal His truth to the human family. The Bible constitutes the holy counsels of Heaven, and we find our greatest security living in harmony with them.

It has been said that although the Bible is the best-seller it is the least-read book of all. How can this be among those who claim to love the Lord? One of the surest signs of love is the desire to communicate. We communicate with God through prayer and God communicates with us through His Holy Word. No marriage relationship can flourish without communication, nor can man's relationship with God be strengthened without confidence that His Word is true.

A skeptic in London said recently in speaking of the Bible: "It is quite impossible to believe in any book whose author is unknown." A Christian asked him if he knew the compiler of the multiplication tables. "No," answered the skeptic.

"Then, of course," said the Christian, "you do not believe in them."

"Oh, yes," said the skeptic, "I believe in them because they work."

"So does the Bible," answered the Christian.

57

A MAN'S LIFE

And he said unto them, Take heed, and beware of covetousness: for a man's life consisteth not in the abundance of the things which he possesseth. Luke 12:15.

Dr. D. S. Stuart tells a story of a man who stayed ashore during the days of Sir Francis Drake and who grew sleek and prosperous. As a consequence he pitied one of his townsmen who sailed with Drake but who had little of material value to show for his adventures. Said the landlubber, "You have not made much out of these years."

"No," said the other, "I have not made much. I have been cold, hungry, shipwrecked, desperately frightened, but I have been with the greatest captain who ever sailed the seas."

It is not often that a Christian can count his wealth in terms of material goods, though occasionally men with great riches prize the pearl of great price above all else. Riches and spirituality are not mutually exclusive, as the lives of Joseph of Arimathea and Nicodemus would testify. However, it is common knowledge that most of the Master's followers came from the poorer people. Say the Scriptures, "The common people heard him gladly."

The Christian is often derided because of apparent lack in material goods. There are those who conclude that the Christian life is not worth living. They point to the requirements of the Scriptures that restrict behavior and call for self-denial. But we know what true riches are, and that they cannot be measured with dollar values. Because a choice must be made I will take an empty purse and a full heart rather than to throw my lot in with the lovers of mammon.

In a Midwestern city a few years ago a ragged peddler, who was thought to be totally impoverished, died in the hovel in which he had spent his last years. The new tenants who cleaned up his place before they moved in found a fortune of $61,000 in bonds and currency stored in various places around the premises. In tobacco cans, in an old trunk, in a dresser drawer, and in out-of-the-way places he had secreted his wealth. The certificate of death was stark in its tragic brevity, bearing the single word, "Malnutrition."

Covetousness always leads to impoverishment of mind and heart.

LIVE PERSEVERINGLY

Seek the Lord and his strength, seek his face continually.
1 Chron. 16:11.

A young girl said to her mother just after a white-haired visitor had left their home: "If I could be such an old lady as that—so beautiful, serene, sweet, and lovable—I should not mind growing old."

To which the mother replied: "Well, if you want to be that kind of old lady, you had better begin making plans today. She does not impress me as a piece of work that was done in a hurry. It has taken a long time to make her what she is. If you are going to paint that sort of portrait of yourself to leave the world, you had better start mixing your colors right now."

The counsel is especially applicable to the formation of Christian character. Character is not suddenly made. What we are to be we are even now becoming. Character is not immediately developed nor spontaneously bestowed. It is the product of a day-to-day, personal relationship with Christ, and we must start mixing our colors now so that in the day of testing we shall be ready.

It is a common failing of humanity to look forward to the day when we can do some great thing or make some great change. This is at the seat of all procrastination. We mean well, but often it takes some rude experience to arouse us to the necessity of perseverance. Spasmodic service to God is destructive to a sturdy faith. Daily dedication of our powers and consistent witness for Him mold us in the image of God.

I think of the apostle Peter. For three years he followed our Lord's ministry, observing Him personally and assisting in the public services. But he neglected the deeper work of grace that should be going on in each individual heart day by day. Then came the great test. Before the crowing cock had sounded his second alarm, Peter had denied his Lord thrice, with cursing and swearing. This led him to Gethsemane, where on bended knee he surrendered at last his hard heart to Christ and was a broken man. But the Spirit of the Lord possessed him, and the new creature that emerged from the Garden was the man of power at Pentecost.

SUBMIT AND RESIST

Submit yourselves therefore to God. Resist the devil, and he will flee from you. James 4:7.

A young man from the Belgian Congo stood one evening at a mission station watching young girls sewing. He noticed how the cotton thread always followed the needle. That evening when he knelt to pray, he prayed, "O Lord, Thou art the needle and I am the cotton." I have never heard it more accurately expressed. O to be led by Christ as the thread is led by a needle! There is no resistance, only perfect submission, and this is the key to change in our lives—submission to the will of God. At times this seems to be most difficult, for we have our own wills, you know, and add to this the unrelenting pressure of demon forces, and we understand man's interference with the divine operation on his own heart. Submission involves true surrender. There can be no cherished idol in the heart if Christ is to occupy the heart's throne. "I the Lord thy God am a jealous God" we read (Ex. 20:5). Christ wants all or none, and He will not be satisfied with less. Coupled with our submission to God must be an active resistance to that which is evil.

A little boy was observed standing before a fruit stand staring at some beautiful apples. The boy's hand would go up and forward to an apple and he would bring it back. Again and again he repeated this until the fruit vendor approached him. "What are you trying to do, my boy?"

"Oh," said the little boy in embarrassment, "I am trying not to steal one of your apples." The spirit of resistance to evil must be deeper than this. It must be so deep that we will avoid personal contact with that which would tend to weaken our defenses wherever possible. It may mean the formation of new acquaintances and getting rid of life-time friends, but whatever it takes we will count all loss but for the excellency of Jesus Christ, and we will resist unto blood any assault of the enemy that would tend to estrange us from our God. In submission to Him lies our power to resist all evil.

God grant us this strength today, and every day, for resistance to sin is a daily experience.

BROTHERLY LOVE

By this shall all men know that ye are my disciples, if ye have love one to another. John 13:35.

Soon after a man bought a farm he met his nearest neighbor. "Have you bought this place?" asked the neighbor.

"Yes," was the reply.

"Well, sir, I claim your fence down there is ten feet on my side of the line, and I am going to take the matter to court and prove my claim to it."

The newcomer said: "Oh, no, don't do that. If the fence is on your side of the line we will just take it up and move it."

"Then," said the neighbor, "that fence stays just where it is. A man with an attitude like yours doesn't need to be sued."

Christian, brotherly love had made a friend. Hate often does more harm to the hater than the hated. Adrenalin is pumped into the blood, stimulated by the excitement of hatred, thus the body is kept tense and prepared for emergencies that often never come. This has a debilitating effect upon the body and upon the nerves and indeed upon the mind. The hater is literally killing himself. His attitude produces dangerous hypertension. "There are no happy haters."

A story is told of three Arabs who were discussing the philosophy of night and day. "How do you know," asked one, "when night is past and day is come, and darkness will never more return?"

Answered one: "When I need not the light of the candle to show me my direction, then I know that night is past and day has come."

"And you?" he asked the second one.

"Oh," came the answer, "when I am able to thread a needle without the use of artificial light, then I know that night is past and day is come."

"Both of you are wrong," said the third Arab. "There is but one proof that night is past and day is come. It is when you look into the face of your brother and recognize in him the image of God, regardless of the color of his skin or the texture of his hair or the language that he speaks. Then you may be sure that night is past and day is come, and darkness will nevermore return."

THY SPEECH

And after a while came unto him they that stood by, and said to Peter, Surely thou also art one of them; for thy speech bewrayeth thee. Matt. 26:73.

Archbishop James Ussher and Dr. Preston, well known alike for their piety and their learning, often met to converse on science and knowledge generally. On these occasions it was customary for the good archbishop to conclude: "Come, Doctor, let us say something about Christ before we part." Of all the subjects upon which men converse there is none more appropriate than the subject of salvation through Jesus Christ. It is ironic that men concern themselves with trivialities when there is available such a wealth of strengthening material on which to concentrate the mind and on which the tongue may dwell. Make no mistake, men judge us by our conversation.

In the case of Peter they were sure that he was "one of them," for his speech betrayed him. David prayed: "Let the words of my mouth, and the meditation of my heart, be acceptable in thy sight, O Lord, my strength, and my redeemer" (Ps. 19:14). He recognized that the words of his mouth were a consequence of the meditations of his heart and only as the heart was cleansed could the words be pure.

The Christian simply is not interested in low-level thinking or speech. If the conversation of the gutter appeals to you, this is the surest sign of a backslidden state. Words are powerful. They may kill and they may make alive. If we realized how powerful for good or evil our words are, with what great care would we choose and use them. "The tongue is a little member, and boasteth great things. Behold, how great a matter a little fire kindleth! And the tongue is a fire, a world of iniquity: so is the tongue among our members, that it defileth the whole body, and setteth on fire the course of nature; and it is set on fire of hell" (James 3:5, 6).

One philosopher has said, "Think twice before you speak, and then shut up."

Only Christ can bridle the heart and thus control the tongue. May we submit our hearts to Him today.

THAT WHICH IS LEAST

He that is faithful in that which is least is faithful also in much: and he that is unjust in the least is unjust also in much. Luke 16:10.

A psychologist once hired a man to work on his woodpile but instructed him not to chop the wood. Instead he was simply to strike the log with the back of the ax. He would be paid the regular wage that he got for wood chopping. In no time at all the man came in to report that he was quitting. He said he could not stand that sort of job any longer. He had to see the chips fly. Instinctively we know what he meant. Few of us can keep our morale for very long when we are working at a job that has no meaning for us or in which we can find no sense of accomplishment or progress.

Are you the typist in an office? Do you toil unnoticed day after day in an obscure corner of the building while others get the glory for the work that you do? Are you an engineer down in the hold of a ship while others promenade on deck enjoying the fruits of your labors? How many of us can labor in anonymity, contributing to the whole but never knowing the extent of the contribution?

W. T. Ellis reminds us that Jeremiah was imprisoned in an old cistern and in danger of dying from thirst and hunger. It was lowly Ebed-melech who dared to go in to the king and plead for the prophet's life. This obscure, unknown man saved the first prophet in the land.

Thousands of people labor in obscurity making the records for which others get credit. Their names may never be known, but it is sure that the wheels could not turn without them.

Various versions have been told of the following story: An organist was giving a concert on an old-fashioned pump organ powered by a little boy in the back who manned the bellows. The artist always received thunderous applause but never gave any credit to his unseen helper who pumped the necessary air to the instrument.

One day the boy decided not to pump. Imagine the embarrassment of the artist. When reproached for not having done his duty, the lad said, "Sir, I decided that it's about time you shared the credit. Either I am necessary or I am not."

63

THE LAW OF CHRIST

Bear ye one another's burdens, and so fulfil the law of Christ.
Gal. 6:2.

The motto of an old African chief is this: "When you pass through the jungle be careful to break a twig so that the next man can find his way." Christianity is more than abstaining from negative vices. There is a positive program of Christian service that possesses therapeutic value. While it is true that we are not saved from sin by what we do, it is equally true that by obedience to the positive requirements of the law of Christ, we are thereby strengthened to perform more perfectly the will of God. The physical body has to be exercised in order to develop strong body tone. It is equally true that unless the Christian graces are exercised they will cease to exist in the human heart. There is strength in helping others.

The Egyptian hieroglyphic representing charity is a naked child with a heart in his hand giving money to a bee without wings. The child represents the humility of charity, the heart in his hand the cheerfulness of charity. Giving money to the bee without wings represents the worthiness and helplessness of the object of charity.

There is a song that says, "No man is an island, no man walks alone." We cannot sit in splendid isolation while our burden-bearing brethren struggle on to meet life's minimal requirements. To all has been committed something to be shared by someone else.

Recently on the battlefield in Vietnam a group of American soldiers were standing in conversation when suddenly a hand grenade landed in their midst. Shouting a warning, a soldier immediately threw his body on the death-dealing missile just in time for an explosion that literally tore him apart. But in doing this he had saved his buddies. And to a man they expressed their gratitude when later in Washington a distinguished service medal was presented as an award for his heroism. He literally gave his life to save others.

Herein lies life's highest happiness that we would share with others that which God has so generously given us, whether it be money, talent, or the advantages of our education. We are bound by the law of Christ to bear one another's burdens.

MEASURE OF MY DAYS

Lord, make me to know mine end, and the measure of my days, what it is; that I may know how frail I am. Ps. 39:4.

In the industrial nations of the world the clock plays an important part in everyday life. Time is indeed of the essence. Men awaken by the clock and go to bed by the clock, and between awaking and sleeping they live by the clock. Life is never long enough. Death is seldom welcome.

Alfred North Whitehead recognizes two kinds of time: (*a*) Time as a transition between duties and occasions that we can measure by the clock and calendar; (*b*) time as unattached to beginnings and endings, its relation to the concept of past, present, and future without defining historical periods. The first is not hard to understand, for that is transitional time by which the life span is measured. We are familiar with the Biblical allotted threescore years and ten as the norm for human existence. In this compass is found probationary time. What man plans to accomplish must be achieved between the cradle and the grave.

But time as a relative thing, though hard to understand in the sense in which Whitehead uses it, may be illustrated concerning spiritual relationships. In conversion, for instance, time is irrelevant, for it is not a calendar concept, but a continuing experience. We are not always conscious of its beginning and certainly we have only a vague idea of its relation to eternity. Indeed, in terms of everlasting life, conversion is a timeless thing. Our darkness changes to eternal day even here, and we better understand the promise, "At evening time it shall be light." That marvelous change of the character of the earthly to the character of the heavenly should be sought in transitional time, for that is all we have. We know not what hour the Grim Reaper will pay his visit to our doors.

I had twenty minutes to live. Had not the doctor operated within that twenty-minute period, it is his judgment that I would have been a dead man. I did not at that time know how short my time was, but when apprised of the situation, the fact that I had lived a rather busy life in service to my fellow man was a comforting thought.

3

BIBLE MORALITY

Let not sin therefore reign in your mortal body, that ye should obey it in the lusts thereof. Rom. 6:12.

Mass media such as television, the press, and magazines have produced in our world a sex consciousness that amounts to sickness. Man's preoccupation with physical pleasure amounts to a new form of idolatry. The twofold effect of this planned assault on the morals of the world is as follows:

1. A vague consensus that everyone is breaking the seventh commandment.

2. It is the thing to do.

This twofold effect has produced a bandwagon complex and a sense of inevitability on youth until he cries, "If I haven't I will, so why not now?"

Only the power of the gospel can counteract this flood tide of evil, and we have the blessed assurance of Scripture that sin can be resisted successfully. "Being confident of this very thing, that he which hath begun a good work in you will perform it until the day of Jesus Christ" (Phil. 1:6). He "is able to keep you from falling." However, there must be active resistance on the part of the individual if he is to escape. We must resist our own polluted imagination, we must shun evil companions, we must cease to read literature that would inflame the imagination, and resist the temptation of looking at movies on TV that do the same.

Now, power to do these things rests with Christ, and through prayer and the study of the Word of God we may gain this power. Those who indulge in modern forms of evil, experience a sevenfold loss: (1) loss of innocence, (2) loss of self-respect, (3) loss of influence, (4) loss of spirituality, (5) loss of self-control, (6) loss of social ideals, (7) economic loss.

To all who feel helpless before the internal and external drives of human nature come these words: "Fear thou not; for I am with thee: be not dismayed; for I am thy God: I will strengthen thee; yea, I will help thee; yea, I will uphold thee with the right hand of my righteousness" (Isa. 41:10).

ONE OF YOU

And as they did eat, he said, Verily I say unto you, that one of you shall betray me. Matt. 26:21.

Paul Louis Lehmann has said: "Out of all the history of the night veiled in its mysterious darkness and crisscrossed with its threads of passion and pride, laughter and lamenting, slumber and sickness, gaiety and grieving, dreams and death, there has never been a night like that one described by the apostle Paul as 'the same night in which he was betrayed.' It was stabbed wide open with the white blade of the moon that exposed the heart of Christ bleeding in Gethsemane and laid bare to the view of history the black desperation of hell that haggled Jesus like the merchandise of crime on the counters of the priest's court and through the halls of Pilate. The sacred agonies of His prayer must have wrung the heart of His Father and the dew that fell on the forms of the sleeping disciples was distilled with the tears of angels."

"One of you," said Jesus, "shall betray me." And one of them did! But the black night of betrayal did not end there. Throughout succeeding centuries men and women have continued to betray the only-begotten Son of God. And His heart hurts no less now than it did then. He has every right to expect so much of us, considering all the honor He has conferred upon us. He is the one common source of all our hopes.

Said Charles H. Spurgeon: "There was a time when I lived in the strong old castle of my sins and rested on my work. There came a trumpeter to the door and bade me open it. I, with anger, chided him from the porch and said he ne'er should enter, then there came a goodly personage with loving countenance. His hands were marked with scars where nails were driven and His feet had nailprints too. He lifted up His cross, using it as a hammer. At the first blow the gate of my prejudice shook; at the second it trembled more; at the third down it fell and in He came, and He said: 'Arise, stand upon thy feet, for I have loved thee with an everlasting love.'"

May we all have experiences with Christ that are just as personal as was this, that the testimony of our lives and of our lips may move others to accept the Christ that we love.

67

GOOD FRUIT

Either make the tree good, and his fruit good; or else make the tree corrupt, and his fruit corrupt: for the tree is known by his fruit. Matt. 12:33.

"How wise I am!" cried the finger post to the willow stump by his side.

"Are you?" asked the willow.

Indignantly retorted the post, "Do you see my arms? Are not the name of the great town and the distance from it plainly written there?"

"Oh yes," said the willow.

"Then you must acknowledge how superior I am to you. I am a public teacher," answered the finger post.

"True, indeed," answered the willow, "and learned you are, but I see little difference between you and me. You know the way to the city, I believe, and are the means of enabling many to find it, but here you have stood these past twenty years and I don't see that you have gotten a step farther on the road than I have, who don't profess to understand anything about it."

How tragically true of so many of us who point others to the cross, but by example are no nearer than are they who know not what we know.

Dr. Albert Camus said: "Here is what frightens me, to see the sense of this life dissipated; to see our reason for existence disappear; that is what is intolerable. Man cannot live without meaning." No man need live without meaning. To glorify God and to serve our fellow man is the true reason for our existence. And the significance of this purpose deepens with the collapse of prevailing values and with man's disillusionment with himself.

"Belief is not faith without evidence, but commitment without reservation." Yes, to the twofold purposes of our being we must commit ourselves without reservation and we will be more than mere signposts on the byway pointing the traveler to his destination. But we will become guides to that traveler and accompany him to that destination. The world is in need of more guides, living guides, rather than dead signposts.

THOU ANSWEREDST ME

In the day when I cried thou answeredst me, and strengthenedst me with strength in my soul. Ps. 138:3.

Dr. John Timothy Stone tells of a visit he paid to the old church of Robert Murray M'Cheyne. The aged sexton showed him around. Taking Dr. Stone into the study he pointed to a chair and said, "Sit there, that is where the master used to sit." Then he said, "Now, put your elbows on the table." This was done. "Now, bow your head upon your hands." Dr. Stone did so. "Now let the tears flow, that is the way the master used to do."

The visitor was then taken into the pulpit and the old sexton said, "Stand there behind the pulpit." Dr. Stone obeyed. "Now," said the sexton, "lean your elbows on the pulpit and put your face in your hands." This having been done he said, "Now let the tears flow, that is the way the master used to do." Then the old man added a testimony that gripped the heart of the hearer. With tearful eyes and trembling voice he said, "He [meaning Dr. M'Cheyne] called down the power of God upon Scotland and it is with us still." Such is the power of a man who achieves strength of soul. Long after his death his influence for good remains. So may it be with us all. But the bestowal of power is not limited to any age or race. Nor is it necessary that we live with our weaknesses. Indeed there can be no peaceful coexistence with the same. Our sins must be dealt with. They will not of themselves go away.

"Except ye repent," said Jesus, "ye shall all likewise perish" (Luke 13:3). Yes, our attitudes, which are favorable toward sin by nature, must be changed, and this is possible only as, like Dr. M'Cheyne, we literally pray down the power of God upon our lives. This must be done daily and within the twenty-four-hour day, prayer must become habitual, as habitual as breathing, for prayer is the breath of the soul. It is through the power lines of prayer that God reaches the soul.

Samson is a classic example of this. The Philistines thought they had him trapped in a city with a heavy gate. But Samson prayed to the Lord and was strengthened, and lifted the giant gate off its hinges and carried it away. The power of God is real, and the strength of God is effective, and it is as available today as ever.

I WILL SPARE THEM

And they shall be mine, saith the Lord of hosts, in that day when I make up my jewels; and I will spare them, as a man spareth his own son that serveth him. Mal. 3:17.

On one of the bridges of Ghent in Flanders are two bronze statues. They represent a father and a son and are memorials of their mutual affection. On account of some grave political offense both were condemned to die by the headsman's ax. Such was the popular esteem in which they were held that an executioner could not be found. A strange proposition was made them, that one should save his life by becoming the executioner of the other. The proposal was hailed with melancholy pleasure by both because each saw how one life at least could be saved. Each urged the other to accept the terms.

By earnest entreaties the father prevailed, and the son consented. The day of execution came. A vast multitude assembled to watch the strange sight. There was the horrid block and broad ax. Father and son were there, the one to be beheaded by the other. The father kneels and places his neck on the wood and awaits the final stroke that will sever the gray head from the body. The son, with a pale face and wild look, seizes the ax and lifts it with trembling hand. Will he strike? No! He flings the deadly weapon from his hand and falls on the bared neck of his father, bathing it with his tears and exclaiming: "No, no, my father, we die together!"

The vast crowd, whose feelings were strung to the highest pitch, gave vent to their admiration in the wildest applause and demanded pardon for the men, which was granted, and the memorial statues were erected in honor of their mutual affection.

The sin of Adam caused great perplexity in the courts of glory. A problem existed that must be solved. The law required that man should die for his own sins. The Creator of man stood with the ax of divine judgment poised in His hand. Would He strike? No, the great heart of love would not permit this. He decided that He would become as a man, not that they should die together, but offering Himself to die in man's stead. Thus He was wounded for our transgressions and bruised for our iniquities.

LASTING FAME

Behold, at that time I will undo all that afflict thee: and I will save her that halteth, and gather her that was driven out; and I will get them praise and fame in every land where they have been put to shame. Zeph. 3:19.

A biologist tells how he watched an ant carrying a piece of straw that seemed a big burden for it. The ant came to a crack in the earth that was too wide to cross. It stood for a time as though pondering the situation, then put the straw across the crack and walked over it. What a lesson for us! How comforting that in time God will undo all that afflicts us so that our burdens may become steppingstones to higher achievement. The promise is further made: "I will get them praise and fame in every land."

Alexander Pope said, "Unblemished let me live or die unknown; Oh, grant an honest fame or grant me none!" The fame promised in this text is the only lasting one. It is fame based on trust in God and obedience to His revealed will.

A friend of mine in India used to work on the docks during the war as a stevedore. He heard the message preached and accepted the Sabbath truth. After much difficulty he was able to get Sabbath privileges, after which he was baptized. Of course, he had to take a cut in pay, but the financial loss meant little to him compared with the salvation of his soul. One Sabbath while he was in church there was a terrific explosion on the dock—an ammunition ship had blown up in the harbor. Rushing to the scene after the service he saw many of his old friends dead and terribly mutilated. Had he been there that day he might have been killed.

It was my privilege to baptize a woman who was in deadly fear of her husband's learning that she was becoming a Seventh-day Adventist. Upon discovery of her purpose he persecuted her terribly. One night she awakened, and he was standing with a gun in his hands staring intently at her. He not only threatened her life, but threatened my life as well. Unfortunately for him, retribution was swift in coming. He was overtaken by a mysterious illness, and the good wife whom he had persecuted had to care for him until the day of his death.

THE POWER OF INFLUENCE

By faith Abel offered unto God a more excellent sacrifice than Cain, by which he obtained witness that he was righteous, God testifying of his gifts: and by it he being dead yet speaketh. Heb. 11:4.

The two sons of Adam were called to sacrifice before God. They were given specific instructions as to the procedures to be taken. Abel took God at His word and obeyed Him, bringing a lamb to the altar for sacrifice. Cain used his own reasoning powers, surmising that the fruit of the ground would be as adequate as the lamb of the flock and indeed more convenient since he was a farmer. The two presented themselves before the Lord, and the Lord honored Abel's sacrifice by fire. This enraged the jealous Cain and he slew his brother in a fit of temper. But our text avers that Abel being dead yet speaketh, and so he does, and what he says is important to each of us today. The lesson is that God requires absolute obedience, and this He honors with divine favor.

What stories will your influence tell after you are dead? We are determining this even as we live from day to day. Our influence will speak through our families, and what our closest friends say of us. What we do has a positive or negative effect on all whom we contact. "For none of us liveth to himself, and no man dieth to himself" (Rom. 14:7).

A drunkard father heard in vain the tearful pleas of his wife to quit drinking if only for the sake of their little son. Then one day, having staggered through the snow to the tavern, he was lifting the dread cup to his lips when he heard a sound. Looking down, there he saw his little boy. He had been followed that day but he wondered how. As he stepped outside the tavern, it was for the last time, because he could see that in the snow he had left plain footprints, and his little boy had walked therein.

We all leave behind us footprints. Whither do they lead others? We may be sure we are the only sermon that some soul will ever hear and the only Bible he will ever read, and after we are dead we shall not be able to change one whit of the story. The time to change is now.

THE DAYSPRING FROM ON HIGH

Through the tender mercy of our God; whereby the dayspring from on high hath visited us. Luke 1:78.

The meaning of the word "dayspring" translated from the original languages means the dawn, or a rising of light. The coming of Christ into the earth nineteen hundred years ago was literally to us as a sun rising and a diffusing of light throughout the world, for to the individual Christian He does more than light the pathway externally. According to John 1:9: "That was the true Light, which lighteth every man that cometh into the world." Christ provides an inner spark of inspiration to every life. He imparts to the tiniest baby the vigor to live. This indwelling power moves men under most adverse circumstances to forge ahead and to triumph over handicaps.

How easy it is for the everyday affairs of life to become dull and monotonous, for after all, for most of us tomorrow will be like today in terms of our duties. There is a sameness in life. Every day has its familiar pattern. The problem is how to preserve the joy and the adventure of day-to-day living. How to greet each new day as a new opportunity to push back frontiers and to do some fresh thing, to move mountains of difficulty. Life and enthusiasm should characterize our every activity.

It is said that Mithridates, king of Pontus, became interested in an old musician who had performed at a feast for him. One morning on his awakening, the old man saw the tables in his house covered with vessels of silver and gold, a number of servants around him who offered him rich garments, and a horse standing at the door as was usual among the king's friends. The old man was astonished and would have fled the house but the servants detained him and told him that the inheritance of a rich man had been conferred upon him by the king and that these were but the first fruits of this fortune. At last believing the reports, he put on the royal robe, mounted the horse, and riding through the city, he cried out: "All these are mine! All these are mine!"

Jesus Christ, the Dayspring, has arisen in our hearts, and this has conferred upon us a royalty that naught in this world can match.

NO CLOAK

If I had not come and spoken unto them, they had not had sin: but now they have no cloke for their sin. John 15:22.

The guilt complex is a by-product of transgression, and because the sinful deed cannot bear the light of exposure there is a tendency to cover up. This was true of our first parents when they sinned against God. They hid from His presence and made cloaks of fig leaves with which to cover themselves. The old "cover up" began then and has continued ever since.

Jesus said, "Men loved darkness rather than light, because their deeds were evil." But in Psalm 139, beginning with verse 11, we read: "If I say, Surely the darkness shall cover me; even the night shall be light about me. Yea, the darkness hideth not from thee; but the night shineth as the day: the darkness and the light are both alike to thee."

A rich landlord once cruelly oppressed a poor widow. Her son, a little boy of eight years, saw it. He afterward became a painter and painted a likeness of the dark scene. Years later he placed it where the landlord saw it. The man turned pale, trembled in every joint, offered any sum to purchase it that he might put it out of sight. But there is an invisible Painter drawing on the canvas of the soul a likeness reflecting correctly all the passions and actions of our spiritual history on earth. Eternity will reveal them to every man. We must meet our earth life again. And more than likely we will meet it in this life as we face those who know us best.

It is said that after Julius Caesar was murdered Marcus Antonius brought forth his coat all bloody and cut and laid it before the people saying, "Look, here you have the emperor's coat thus bloody and torn," whereupon the people were presently in an uproar and cried out, "Slay the murderers," and they took their tables and stools that were in the place and set them afire and ran to the houses of them that had slain Caesar and burnt them. The sight of the bloody coat changed their attitude toward their once distinguished leader.

And so it is with us as we look to Calvary by faith and witness the shed blood of the Lord Jesus Christ. How it should change our attitude toward the sins that put Him there and lead us to the foot of the cross.

EVERY SPIRIT

Beloved, believe not every spirit, but try the spirits whether they are of God: because many false prophets are gone out into the world. 1 John 4:1.

In our text for today a merciful God exercises His protective powers in behalf of His children. He is anxious that they be not deceived, for there are many false spirits that pass as angels of light. The Bible sets the bounds of safety with reference to the faith of the believer. It is clear as to what we can and cannot believe with safety. Many are the spirits that compete for the attention of man. There are the millions of evil angels that have been in the earth since the fall of Lucifer. "And the great dragon was cast out, that old serpent, called the Devil, and Satan, which deceiveth the whole world: he was cast out into the earth, and his angels were cast out with him" (Rev. 12:9).

Demons are not creatures of myth; they are very real and very powerful. This explains in part the strength of overmastering temptation, and why some of us are afflicted with habits that appear unshakable. These habits are fastened on us by demon power and can be broken only by divine power. These evil spirits do more than tempt us to sin. They spend much of their time insinuating doubt as to the truthfulness of the Word of God, knowing full well that the person who does not read and believe the Word of God is hopelessly lost.

Of these fallen angels the apostle Paul has appropriately written: "For such are false apostles, deceitful workers, transforming themselves into the apostles of Christ. And no marvel; for Satan himself is transformed into an angel of light. Therefore it is no great thing if his ministers also be transformed as the ministers of righteousness; whose end shall be according to their works" (2 Cor. 11:13-15).

Today, spiritualistic manifestations have assumed pseudoscientific forms and in some instances spiritualism is masquerading as a religion. Whatever face suits its deceitful purposes best, that these evil spirits will assume. They would go so far as to convince some people that they do not exist. It is understandable then that we are admonished not to believe every spirit that has gone out into the world. Our only safety is in the Word of God.

THE ROOT

For the love of money is the root of all evil: which while some coveted after, they have erred from the faith, and pierced themselves through with many sorrows. 1 Tim. 6:10.

Poverty is no evidence of piety, nor are riches a sign of divine favor. Money is a trust and its possessor is a steward. We are indebted both to God and to man for the wise and benevolent use of our resources. Referring to a man who having adequate resources continued to add land to land, Jesus said, "Thou fool." The attitude of this cynical and materialistic age is "You get yours as I got mine." But the spirit of Christ requires more of His disciples. "If a brother or sister be naked, and destitute of daily food, and one of you say unto them, Depart in peace, be ye warmed and filled; notwithstanding ye give them not those things which are needful to the body; what doth it profit?" (James 2:15, 16).

A man was one day relating to a Quaker a tale of distress and concluded by saying, "I could not but feel for him." Replied the Quaker, "Verily, friend, thee did right in that thee did feel for thy neighbor, but did thee feel in the right place? Did thee feel in thy pocket?"

John Wesley says: "Get all you can without hurting your soul, your body, or your neighbor. Save all you can, cutting off every needless expense. Give all you can. Be glad to give and ready to distribute, laying up in store for yourselves a foundation against the time to come that you may attain eternal life."

One observer has said: "By the legitimate use of money the individual faculties are developed and at the same time mutual dependence is promoted. It feeds the hungry, clothes the naked, shelters the homeless, builds hospitals for the sick, wipes the tears of widows, hushes the cries of the fatherless, diffuses education and knowledge, circulates the Bible, builds places of religious worship, sends the missionary to the heathen and supports the ministries at home."

When Alexander the Great was asked why he did not gather money and lay it up in a public treasury, he replied, "For fear lest being the keeper thereof, I should be infected and corrupted."

76

THE LOWLY

Though the Lord be high, yet hath he respect unto the lowly: but the proud he knoweth afar off. Ps. 138:6.

In our class-conscious world respect for the lowly is a scarce commodity. The apostle James directly stated the prevailing attitude in James 2, beginning with verse 2: "For if there come unto your assembly a man with a gold ring, in goodly apparel, and there come in also a poor man in vile raiment; and ye have respect to him that weareth the gay clothing, and say unto him, Sit thou here in a good place; and say to the poor, Stand thou there, or sit here under my footstool: are ye not then partial in yourselves, and are become judges of evil thoughts?"

Jesus illustrated again and again His respect for the lowly. He and His disciples were standing at the Temple one day observing the many contributions that were being placed at the disposal of the church. There were the rich men in their fine garments putting in their lavish gifts with prideful flourishes, when finally and almost furtively there appeared a poor woman who placed her mite into the treasury and silently slipped away. Taking note of her Jesus said: "Verily I say unto you, That this poor widow hath cast more in, than all they which have cast into the treasury: . . . even all her living" (Mark 12:43, 44).

The text does not imply that God does not love the rich nor that He has lack of respect for them. There were indeed many rich followers of Christ, men in the category of Joseph of Arimathea and the great Gamaliel. Rather our text suggests that there is adequate respect accorded to the rich while the poor, because of their poverty, are despised or ignored. Neither the spirit nor the teachings of the Christian faith will allow this. The gospel of Christ has a special appeal to the poor for this very reason. The church is the one place on earth where rich and poor mingle with absolute equality and freedom.

Said one, "The ground is level at the foot of the cross." Said Jesus in Luke 22:25, 26: "The kings of the Gentiles exercise lordship over them; and they that exercise authority upon them are called benefactors. But ye shall not be so: but he that is greatest among you, let him be as the younger; and he that is chief, as he that doth serve."

YE SHALL BE WITNESSES

But ye shall receive power, after that the Holy Ghost is come upon you: and ye shall be witnesses unto me both in Jerusalem, and in all Judaea, and in Samaria, and unto the uttermost part of the earth. Acts 1:8.

J. Hudson Taylor once told of a Chinese pastor who, upon meeting a young convert, asked him if it were true that he had only known the Lord for three months. "Yes, it is blessedly true," he replied.

The pastor continued, "How many have you won to Jesus?"

"Oh," said the convert, "I am only a learner and I have never possessed the complete New Testament until yesterday."

"Do you expect a candle to begin to shine when it is burned halfway down?"

"No," came the reply, "but as soon as it is lighted."

And so it is with us. The best time to begin witnessing is when one has received the light. There is no credence in the theory that one has to become a Christian and practice it for a while before witnessing to others. What happens is that one grows cold with inactivity, and it is far more difficult to start later than it is at the outset of one's Christian experience. There is such a thing as initial love growing cold, and it is against this that one must guard. Spreading the message of salvation to others preserves the warmth of one's soul.

Hobart D. McKeen said: "The gospel must be shared, the story must be told, the secret must be passed on and out to every soul frigid with faithlessness and fear. And this we do best by two simple means—conversation and contagion, and the conversation need seldom be that of one who argues a cause, but it must always be that of one who witnesses to a fact.

"Our chief business, whether in the pulpit or in the pew, is to bear simple, straightforward testimony as to what Christ is and does and means. And the contagion—well, that will always follow, and flow out and beyond the conversation. True religion, like good health, good music, and true beauty, is contagious; it is catching, it spreads like some holy flame from candle tip to candle tip, from life to life."

CHRISTIAN PERFECTION

Be ye therefore perfect, even as your Father which is in heaven is perfect. Matt. 5:48.

Pliny informs us that Zeuxis once painted such a realistic picture of a boy holding a dishful of grapes that the birds were deceived and flew to the grapes to peck at them. Zeuxis, notwithstanding, was dissatisfied with the picture, "For," he explained, "had I painted the boy as well as he ought to have been painted, the birds would have been afraid to touch them." And so it is with our lives. Our very best always seems to leave something to be desired. In short, our best is not enough. Perfection always eludes us. How then can the spirit of our text ever be realized. The answer is in Colossians 1:27, 28: "To whom God would make known what is the riches of the glory of this mystery among the Gentiles; which is Christ in you, the hope of glory: whom we preach, warning every man, and teaching every man in all wisdom; that we may present every man perfect in Christ Jesus."

In this life absolute perfection lies only in Christ, and as we receive Him by faith as our Saviour, He substitutes His perfection for our imperfection and declares us righteous before God. Now, this is based, not on any good deed that we may do, but on the absolute righteousness of His own character and on His merits alone. Having declared us perfectly united with Him as sons and daughters in the family of God, He then begins the progressive work of changing our characters into the likeness of His own. This requires time, patience, and effort, not only on the part of God, but on our own part as well. We must be willing to diligently cooperate with God in counteracting the evil influences of our nature. We must through prayer and the study of the Word of God surrender our stubborn wills to Him, and though the growth process may not be discernible, the end result certainly will. We will find ourselves being shaped in the divine likeness of the Son of God.

This daily and progressively becomes the Christian's experience. What he first accepts by faith becomes living reality in fact and the change may be unmistakable and permanent, for the cure is real.

VICTORY

But thanks be to God, which giveth us the victory through our Lord Jesus Christ. 1 Cor. 15:57.

The word for victory in our text is *nikos,* meaning "a conquest," or "a triumph." Our text contains the assurance that we may become true overcomers. This includes internal weakness, external and environmental pressures, as well as demoniac intrusions. Through Christ the victory may be had and sin need not be our master.

One's concept is likely to shape the nature of his struggle. It is important that we aspire to total and absolute victory. Those who will settle for peaceful coexistence with sin are not likely to struggle too diligently against it. But the knowledge that the prize may be had is sufficient to elicit from each of us a peak performance.

A vicar of the Church of England was troubled with a violent and apparently ungovernable temper. Many times he had prayed about it with tears and had struggled much to conquer it, but he had been beaten and was almost in despair. One day after he had prayed and confessed his sin and believed that he had obtained help to keep down the violent temper, he left his study to go about his duties. But alas, it was not long before he re-entered his study beaten and almost brokenhearted. In his sorrow he fell asleep and dreamed that he saw a figure coming toward him. He seemed conscious that his guest was the Lord Jesus Christ. He swept and dusted the room but the more he worked the more untidy it became. Finally the Stranger knocked. "Oh, what shall I do?" he said to himself. "I cannot let Him into a room in such disorder as this," and he kept on sweeping and dusting until the stranger knocked again and again. "Oh," he said, "I cannot open while the room is so unfit to receive Him." But all his efforts were in vain, and when the Stranger knocked again, overpowered with shame and confusion, he opened the door, saying, "Master, I can do no more, come in if Thou wilt into such a room."

The Master came in and to the astonishment of the vicar the dust was laid, the disorder disappeared, and all was bright and clean and joyful. The Master's presence alone had done all that his utmost effort had failed to accomplish.

THE VISION

*And I heard a man's voice between the banks of Ulai, which
called, and said, Gabriel, make this man to understand the vision.*
Dan. 8:16.

The vision referred to here has as its contextual background
verse 13, relating to the 2300-day-year prophecy and the cleansing
of the sanctuary. We know that at the time of the utterance of this
prophecy the sanctuary on earth had long passed away, but while it
lasted it was "the pattern of things in the heavens." It is then clear
that the sanctuary to be cleansed was the heavenly sanctuary of
which Paul writes in Hebrews 8:2: "A minister of the sanctuary, and
of the true tabernacle, which the Lord pitched, and not man." The
2300-day prophetic period stretching from 457 B.C. to A.D. 1844
marked the time of the beginning of the judging of the people.
When in A.D. 31 Christ ascended on high He went into the holy
place of His great temple in the sky, there to begin a work of intercession, substitution, and mediation for those who would be heirs of
salvation.

For 1,813 years He continued this phase of His ministry. In 1844,
the end of the 2300 days, a new and solemn significance was added
to His ministry, for in the Most Holy Place of the sanctuary He began
the work of the investigative judgment, or the cleansing of the sanctuary. Since that date we have been in the last serious period of
probation for this sinful world. The anger of the nations on earth,
the total collapse of long-cherished spiritual values, the militant
atheism that is invading religion, juvenile and parental delinquency,
utter disregard for the law of God—all of these things indicate that
impressive scenes are now taking place in heaven and that Christ, the
righteous Judge, is in the very final stages of the solemn work of
judgment. It is appropriate then that the mightiest angel in heaven
be sent to Daniel with a commission to "make this man to understand," and it is from his pen our eyes have been opened to one of
the most sacred truths contained in the Scriptures.

The pre-Advent judgment, called investigative, is soon to close.
Are you using your probation wisely? Is your heart right with God?

ABUNDANT HONOR

And those members of the body, which we think to be less honourable, upon these we bestow more abundant honour. **1 Cor. 12:23.**

It is a common experience that we feel at times insignificant and unnecessary and one may wonder just why he was born. We look at others and the duties they perform and covet their capacity and the acclaim they receive. This text indicates that those portions of the body that are feeble are as necessary to the function of the body as are those more prominent parts.

An automobile manufacturer may get all the credit for his product and have his name spread to the ends of the earth by the news media but what would he be without thousands of production workers who assemble his automobile and the engineers who in research contrive newer and better parts for the improvement of the product?

We go to church, we see the minister finely dressed and hear his inspiring sermon and compliment ourselves on having such a wonderful pastor, but what of his good wife who faithfully toils to provide moral support and spiritual encouragement for the divine operation? And what of his little children who back him up? Yes, behind every prominent man there is someone standing in the shadows performing a function necessary to his success.

The apostle Paul is anxious that each member of the church recognize his importance to the church whether he occupies a position of prominence or is simply a lay member in the church without organizational responsibility.

In a lawsuit involving a great train wreck some years ago the signalman on the scene of the accident was charged with criminal negligence. On the witness stand he was asked, "Were you on duty the night of the wreck?" "Did you wave your lantern?" "Did you wave it on time?"

To each query he answered, "Yes."

The jury deliberated and found him not guilty. As he went out of the courtroom he whispered to a friend, "They did not ask me the main question. They should have asked me, 'Was the lantern lighted?'"

THESE SIGNS

And these signs shall follow them that believe; In my name shall they cast out devils; they shall speak with new tongues. Mark 16:17.

The skeptical world in which we live is looking for men and women who give evidence of having been with Jesus and learned of Him. Christ has given us many evidences that are demonstrable and unmistakable evidence of our fellowship with Him. "In my name shall they cast out devils," Christ says. This is done every time a sinner is converted to Christ. This phrase also meets its fulfillment when men have become mediums, literally possessed of evil spirits, and are confronted with the power of God and delivered. "They shall speak with new tongues." This was fulfilled at Pentecost and is being fulfilled today as men proclaim the gospel in foreign countries, using languages unfamiliar to their natural homelands. As we near the end of time who can say that God will not do it again to glorify His name?

"They shall take up serpents." A man was telling another about people handling snakes. He said: "Doesn't the Bible say that we can pick up vipers? Didn't Paul pick one up?"

"Yes," came the answer, "but Paul was not hunting snakes but sticks to make a fire. God had need of Paul and He saved him."

If in the exercise of a divine command we find ourselves attacked by serpents, we have the assurance that through prayer and confidence in God we may be saved. But this text is no command to look for serpents. Rather we should look for souls.

"If they drink any deadly thing, it shall not hurt them." This is literally being fulfilled daily in the lives of our missionaries and in lands where they eat things to which they are unaccustomed, and apparently suffer no ill effect.

"They shall lay hands on the sick, and they shall recover." This is happening now in the great and extensive work being done in our hospitals across the land; and further, there are miraculous faith healings taking place among us daily. I could spend hours relating personal experiences in this regard. But fidelity to the Word is our great assurance of acceptance with God, not the performing of miracles.

THE CHRIST OF GOD

He said unto them, But whom say ye that I am? Peter answering said, The Christ of God. Luke 9:20.

Many are the evidences of the divinity of the Lord Jesus Christ, not the least of which are His miraculous birth, His absolutely perfect life, His death at Calvary for the sins of men. We also think of His miracles, many that have been imitated but few duplicated, and greatest among these, the raising of men from the dead and the conversion of sinners from sin to salvation. But through it all there runs a golden thread which proves above all else the divine nature of the Son of God and that is His utter unselfishness. He was born into the world for us and unto us (Isa. 9:6). His thirty-three and a half years on this earth were spent unselfishly for others, specifically for us (Rom. 5:10). And when on Calvary He suffered, bled, and died, that too was for us.

Sacred history records that He rose from the dead. This, according to the apostle Paul, was "for our justification." He ascended on high according to Hebrews 9:24 "to appear in the presence of God for us," and He will come again. And for what purpose? From His own lips come the words: "I will come again, and receive you unto myself; that where I am, there ye may be also." What love! What matchless love! And from our lips should spring the cry of Peter in grateful, humble acknowledgment of His divine lordship—"Thou art the Christ, the Son of the living God."

From the pen of an imaginative writer, we read, "As the planets get further from the sun, their light and heat diminish, their flowers and fruits lose sweetness. Their summers shorten. What must it be in the most remote Neptune three hundred times as far away as our earth. Oh, star of perpetual ice and winter, without bird or flower or leaf! So is it in that life where Christ's divine nature is denied and that heart is crowded back far away from the center of divine warmth and light, leaving it without a flower or a leaf or a trace of summertime."

"The Lord God is a sun and shield." Is He the central figure in your life? God grant that henceforth it shall be so.

The apostle Peter's acknowledgment that Jesus is "the Christ of God" must become our own.

THE CERTAINTY OF THOSE THINGS

It seemed good to me also, having had perfect understanding of all things from the very first, to write unto thee in order, most excellent Theophilus, that thou mightest know the certainty of those things, wherein thou hast been instructed. Luke 1:3, 4.

We live in an age of disturbing transition and rampant uncertainty. Values long held in sacred esteem are now marked as badges of obsolescence. Agreements—personal, national, and international—are cheaper today than the paper on which they are written. Vows are no sooner taken than broken, and a legitimate question forces itself to the forefront of many hearts: "Is there anything on earth I can trust?" The answer is good: There is.

We can trust the Bible. It is a Book tested by time, its enemies, and its friends, and it has survived all three. It offers the only plausible explanation of life, its origin and its destiny, and of death, its cause and its remedy. It offers man the way of life at its best, and the happiest, most productive people that I know on earth are those who follow its teachings.

Basically the problem of certainty resolves itself in this: God is the foundational certainty in all the universe. The Bible is His message to the human family. It follows then that men lack confidence and certainty because they neglect the message of God to their own hearts. The inclusion of Christ in the everyday affairs of life produces in the Christian confidence and faith. The emotional insecurities that characterize our age are largely absent from the lives of the true followers of Christ. They are surrounded by a pool of serenity, and when things go wrong with them they are somehow mysteriously confident that ultimately all things will right themselves and that every occurrence has its positive result, however negative in nature.

An old lady was observed in the midst of an earthquake, serenely rocking in a rocking chair and singing a hymn. When it was all over she was asked: "Grandmother, how could you remain so calm in the midst of this terrible earthquake? Were you not afraid?"

To which she smiled and replied: "No, I was not afraid. I simply rejoiced that the God I serve has the power to shake the world!"

THE NEW BIRTH

That which is born of the flesh is flesh; and that which is born of the Spirit is spirit. John 3:6.

The necessity of the new birth is the burden of our text today. We are informed that to be born of the flesh is only to be half born and that natural birth does not provide the basis for entry into the family of God. "Marvel not that I said unto thee, Ye must be born again," said Jesus. Natural birth is physical birth. Spiritual birth is of heaven and it is quite another thing. And because physical birth cannot provide it, a new birth is a necessity. And though there exists no relationship between the two, in many instances they are similar.

1. In physical birth the child does not initiate his own beginnings. In spiritual birth this is also true, for the source of the first impulse that one feels in his heart to follow Christ is divine.

2. There is no physical birth without pain and the shedding of blood. Similarly there could be no spiritual birth had not the only begotten Son of God initiated it by the suffering He endured on Calvary for our sins. "Without shedding of blood is no remission."

3. We refer to the newly born child as a baby. Similarly the Scriptures refer to a man born into the kingdom of God as a newborn babe, desiring the sincere milk of the Word that he may grow thereby. And the analogy continues. As the newborn babe grows into spiritual adolescence and manhood, he is referred to later on in these words: "When I became a man, I put away childish things." One has indeed not fully lived until he has experienced the new birth. The testimony of a few who refused this blessed privilege serves as warnings to all.

Mirabel the atheist said, "Give me laudanum that I may not think of eternity." Voltaire said, "I am abandoned by God and man, I shall go to hell. Oh, Christ, oh, Jesus Christ." Charles IX, king of France, said, "What blood, what murders, what evil counsels I have followed. I am lost, I see it well." And Thomas Paine said, "I would give worlds if I had them, if the *Age of Reason* had never been published. Oh, Lord help me, Christ help me, stay with me, it is hell to be left alone."

In contrast to these is the exultant cry of many a Christian at the portal of death.

WORSHIP

O worship the Lord in the beauty of holiness: fear before him, all the earth. Ps. 96:9.

Thousands occupy church pews weekly, observing the form of worship without receiving the intended blessing. Motives for attending church are many and varied; not all of them holy. In a negative vein, men attend (*a*) to preserve an image, (*b*) for the children's sake, (*c*) for professional reasons, (*d*) to meet friends, (*e*) for fear of hell, (*f*) because of a desire for heaven. However, worship is rewarding only if entered into with proper motivation. This does not include going to church to hear "a good sermon," "good music," or to exhibit one's talent in the exercise of church office responsibilities.

The true worshiper loves his Lord so much that he eagerly awaits the call to worship, for he is there to meet his Lord. He has little time for small talk or observing the passing fashion parade. Awaiting the beginning of the service, he is deep in meditation. His faith reaches up and out for the hand of God. He joins heartily in the singing, enters into the spirit of the morning prayer. During the sermon he is less interested in the minister's style or delivery than in the message from the Book. He can expect to get something out of worship, for he puts something in!

It is said that one pound of honey represents the concentrated sweetness of 62,000 clover blooms. To collect that amount the bees make 2,700,000 trips to and from the flowers and travel about 5 million miles in gathering honey. It is literally true that we get out of a thing what we put in. This is especially true of worship.

There is also the question of the life that one lives during the week. Worship comes natural to one who lives daily in close fellowship with his Maker. We do not imply that only the righteous should worship. Rather that righteousness lends itself more naturally to worship. But in every congregation there are wounded consciences and frayed characters. These have greater need to worship than all others. And let all such remember that "the oyster mends its shell with a pearl," and "men may rise on stepping stones of their dead selves to higher things."

DOERS OF THE LAW

For not the hearers of the law are just before God, but the doers of the law shall be justified. Rom. 2:13.

Napoleon was reviewing his troops on horseback when he accidentally dropped the reins of his steed, which leaped forward and was soon galloping wildly away. An alert unranked soldier risked his life to grab the reins, bringing the horse to a standstill. "Thank you, captain," shouted Napoleon gratefully. "Of which regiment, sir?" asked the soldier, sensing his sudden promotion. "Of my guards," came the reply. The soldier immediately dropped his sword and marched stiffly up to and began to mingle with the elite guard. "And have you mistaken your place, soldier?" inquired a guard. "No, I am your captain," replied the soldier. "By what authority?" he was asked. "Napoleon himself," came the answer. This soldier believed his emperor's word and acted upon it. This is the nature of faith as taught in the Bible.

We are justified by faith in Christ as our Saviour. But this is not passive faith. There are those in our world who have a detached belief that maintains interest but avoids involvement. Saving faith acts! Disobedient faith is dead. The doers of the law are the firm believers. The Christian's obedience is the outgrowth of his faith. As a healthy tree yields its luscious fruit to bless mankind, so the tree of faith yields as its precious natural fruit the works of the law.

Faith inspires obedience based on love. It is, therefore, joyful obedience, not that of a "quarry-slave at night, scourged to his dungeon, but, sustained and soothed by an unfaltering trust," the Christian approaches each new duty trusting that God knows what is best. Faith in God is never blind. Whoever follows God walks in the light.

The other evening I was driving in the city of Columbus, Ohio. I had pulled out of a bright service station and assumed that all was well when a man rolled up beside me in his automobile and said, "Say, mister, turn on your lights."

My intentions were good. I had a sense of security. I felt that my lights were on, but had that been an officer I would have been fined for violating the law. Good intentions notwithstanding, there is no substitute for compliance to Heaven's requirements.

HEAVEN IS ASSURED IN HIM

If in this life only we have hope in Christ, we are of all men most miserable. 1 Cor. 15:19.

A skeptic said to a Christian, "Suppose you miss the worldly pleasure that you Christians avoid and at the end find that there is no heaven?" "Well," replied the Christian, "I am having such a happy time on my journey that I would say it was all worth while. But tell me, suppose you take in all of the Bible-forbidden pleasures and at the end find that there is a hell. What then?" That ended the debate.

The Christian life is doubly rewarding. It provides grace for the joys and sorrows of everyday living and eternity in the world beyond. The hope of life in the hereafter has inspired followers of God in all ages. Abraham "looked for a city that hath foundations, whose builder and maker is God." And all of his spiritual successors have regarded themselves pilgrims and strangers here. To them the promised joys of the hereafter make the death-dealing pleasures of this present world pale by comparison.

But is there a city out there in space? The Bible states plainly that there is! "He hath prepared for them a city" (Heb. 11:16). "I John saw the holy city" (Rev. 21:2). "He . . . shewed me that great city" (verse 10).

The Christian knows that heaven is out there. From the Bible he receives messages from out there every day. Through prayer he sends back his own. The Christian knows that Christ is there. This increases his desire to go there. It is with great difficulty that one is even temporarily separated from his loved ones. Love requires ultimate reunion. The high privilege of face-to-face communion with Christ is reward enough of itself. For it was He who was wounded for our transgressions, bruised for our iniquities. He died our death that we might live His life. Heaven will be worth it all just to behold His face.

One of our astronauts on completion of his several orbitings of the earth declared, "It's dark out there." Only planets and worlds can reflect light; in space itself there is no response to its rays. So only in Christ has the true light shone, and all men are lost in darkness except His life be seen in us.

PREFERRING ONE ANOTHER

Be kindly affectioned one to another with brotherly love; in honour preferring one another. Rom. 12:10.

Selfishness is the mother of all other sins. When its own interests are involved, it is often blind to the needs of others. A popular secular philosopher says, "Self-preservation is the first law of nature." The Christian religion asserts that interest in others and care for their needs are basic to self-preservation. There is an old proverb that says, "Every man for himself and God for us all." But God's favor does not rest upon anyone who is all for himself to the neglect of others.

In one of our local conferences some years ago, the conference committee judged it necessary to replace a worker who seemed untrained for his official responsibilities. They talked to him kindly, setting forth the reluctance with which they sought his successor. The incumbent worker was agreeable and even suggested a man who he thought would fill the need. Like Daniel, he showed such "an excellent spirit" that the committee found other work into which he fitted with distinction. Oh, how the church needs more of this "preferring one another."

A certain king had a minstrel whom he commanded to play before him. It was a day of high feasting, and many guests were assembled. The minstrel laid his fingers upon the strings of his harp and woke them to the sweetest melody, but the hymn was to the glory of himself. In high-sounding strains he sang of himself and all of his glories. When the feast was over, he went to the monarch and said, "O king, have I not performed well? I await my pay." Then the king replied, "Thou hast sung unto thyself. Pay thyself. Thine own praises were thy theme. Be thyself the paymaster." But the harper cried, "Did I not sing sweetly, O king? Give me thy gold." The king answered, "So much the worse for thy pride that thou should'st lavish such sweetness upon thyself. Get thee gone. Thou shalt not serve in my court." The sweetness of many a life, like the sweetness of the harper's song, is lost when it is centered in one's own self, but that perfume is most admired that has the widest exposure, and the perfume of our lives gladdens the world most when widely spread.

TO EVEN THE SCORE

Dearly beloved, avenge not yourselves, but rather give place unto wrath: for it is written, Vengeance is mine; I will repay, saith the Lord. Rom. 12:19.

The tendency to get even is present with all of us. It is natural not to want to be taken advantage of by anyone, and this is a common trait of human nature. You will, therefore, not consider yourself a person apart if from time to time you are tempted to repay in kind some evil deed committed against your person or interest, nor is it a sin to be so tempted. However, divine love requires that we resist the temptation. The law of love will not allow that we repay in kind any grievance committed against us. We are bound first by the example of our Lord, who submitted to every indignity that could be heaped upon a person without vengeful response. Second, we are bound by the laws of persuasion.

Is it possible for us to render evil for evil, an eye for an eye, and a tooth for a tooth and win a soul to Christ? If such a one practices the religion we practice, what kind of Christian will he be?

Third, we are bound by the laws of spiritual preservation. To render evil for evil destroys as nothing else can one's own spiritual nature and befouls the atmosphere of purity that should fill and surround the Christian. Diogenes, being asked by what means a man might revenge himself upon his enemies, replied, "By becoming himself a good and honest man."

A high official in England once went to Sir John Eardley-Wilmot in great wrath and narrated a story of great insult he had received. He closed by asking him if he did not think it would be manly to resent it. "Yes," said his friend, "it would be manly to resent it, but it would be Godlike to forgive it."

An English criminal, notorious for his crimes, was sentenced to execution. While in prison he became thoroughly convicted of the enormity of his sins and was truly repentant. He found pardon and his heart was so filled with the love of God that he cried out continually, "He is a great Forgiver, He is a great Forgiver." When the love of God fills our hearts, we too become great forgivers.

NOT MEAT

For the kingdom of God is not meat and drink; but righteousness, and peace, and joy in the Holy Ghost. Rom. 14:17.

The religion of the Pharisee concerns itself with external forms without eternal, internal realities. The thirty-three years of Christ's ministry on this earth were an effort to reverse this spiritual tragedy. Christ taught the primary necessity of the transforming power of God changing the heart. He sought to establish a oneness with the individual, an inseparable relationship that would enable him to endure all trials and overcome all temptation. He saw that transformation of the heart was necessary before the life could be reformed or any change seen in the habits of man. The changed habit pattern was indeed to become the manifestation of the inner relationship that had been formed between Christ and His disciple. As we judge a tree by the fruit, so may the life be judged by the deeds. While the kingdom of heaven is not the external behavior itself but rather the transformation of the inward man, the kingdom of God is made manifest through the righteous deeds of the newly converted Christian. It is in this sense that our lights "so shine before men, that they may see your good works, and glorify your Father which is in heaven."

The custom prevails in Paris of giving old buildings a new appearance by recutting the stones of the walls. By this means the church of Ste. Genevieve (now the Panthéon) has been modernized and beautified, but it is so identified with the bloody massacre of St. Bartholomew's that no renovation can obliterate its foul blot. Its stains will not out nor its vile memories die. Old sinners seek to quiet their consciences in the same way. They recast and polish the outside with remarkable success, but the deep stains of sin will not depart except by the application of the blood of Christ. Let us beware of confounding the reformation with conversion. Bloody memories cluster about the church of Ste. Genevieve and bleaching bones fill its vaults in spite of its external renovation, and so it is with us. We must be transformed by the renewing of our minds if genuine reform is to be our experience. And it is the will of God that everyone who bears the Christian name give daily evidence of that inward renewal.

92

BE YE SAVED

Look unto me, and be ye saved, all the ends of the earth: for I am God, and there is none else. Isa. 45:22.

Our text reveals the source of all true salvation. "Look unto me," Jesus says, "and be ye saved." The text also makes it clear that man cannot save himself. "Be ye saved," or "be acted upon." Salvation is an externally executed act that reaches deep into the very heart of man's being. Many personal testimonies concerning salvation tend to confuse rather than clarify the process. This in turn causes many thinking people to turn away from the church and from religion on the grounds that if what they hear is true, they want none of it. By the descriptions used, salvation is often pictured as an emotional experience. The truth of the matter is, religion is not emotion. It is the implantation of the character of Christ into the soul of man. We cannot explain this process in its detail but of this we are sure, it is a fact, a beautiful fact. However, it may or may not be accompanied by emotional reaction. Many factors will determine this. If one finds his desires changed and his will to live a new life present, he must not underestimate the depth of his experience because of the absence of the emotional factor.

An ungodly man said to a minister, "Sir, I hope to be saved at last." Came the reply, "It would be better, friend, to be saved at first. Let us go down on our knees and seek the blessing now." And it is true that to be saved at last we must be saved at first. "For by grace are ye saved through faith; and that not of yourselves: it is the gift of God" (Eph. 2:8).

We can claim no credit for our own salvation any more than a swimmer who is hopelessly lost and drowning. The rescuer may have to knock the faltering swimmer out cold with a sharp blow in order to reduce him to helplessness and be able to drag him to shore. It is a fact that such a man cannot save himself, and no effort on his part can get him to safety. Similarly it is the divine love of God operating through the offering of the Lord Jesus Christ that initiates the salvation of every sinner saved by grace. It is when divine love is accepted in the heart and the Saviour is embraced as friend and Lord that the fact of salvation is accomplished in the life.

I AM READY

And he said unto him, Lord, I am ready to go with thee, both into prison, and to death. Luke 22:33.

The words of this text are the words of a consciously committed man. He is sincere as far as he can see. He commits himself to the twin extremes of the shame of prison and the tragedy of death. He can think of no other circumstance in between that might separate him from the love of Christ. He could not foresee that a few hours hence he would deny his Lord, making mockery of his pronouncement, "I am ready."

We must all face the fact that all spiritual readiness is the exclusive property of God, and there is no merit in man that Heaven recognizes. We conclude, then, that all human readiness is Heaven imparted and implanted. We can appreciate more the statement of our Lord, "Marvel not that I say unto thee, Ye must be born again." There are two methods by which the genuineness of one's conversion may be tested: (1) Obedience, (2) adversity. It seems that without the furnace fires of affliction man is ill-prepared to face such extremes as imprisonment and death. Christ knew this and gently rebuked His ardent disciple. Later on Peter was thoroughly converted and suffered the martyrdom of death steadfastly. He was indeed at that moment ready.

Through prayer and the study of the Word of God, man may condition his soul for the reception of divine power that will produce in him a readiness to meet whatever comes. An example of this is Restituta, an African virgin in the time of Valerian. She was arrested as a Christian at Carthage and condemned by a judge named Proculus to be placed in an old boat filled with pitch and other combustibles and set adrift. She was bound fast in the boat, the pitch was lighted, and the wind blew offshore, and the martyr sped swiftly in her fiery bark, Elijahlike, toward the sea. But this girl was ready.

We are told that Latimer at the stake shows us how the boweddown frame can be strengthened for its terrible conflict. His mortal frame became invigorated at the prospect of the near approach of his journey's end. He no longer appeared a withered, crooked old man, his body bending under the weight of years, but he stood upright, as comely a father as one would desire to behold.

HE THAT BELIEVETH

Jesus cried and said, He that believeth on me, believeth not on me, but on him that sent me. John 12:44.

Christ here proclaims the essential unity of the Godhead. He was one with His Father from the beginning. In Him was life unborrowed, underived. He was and is the express image of the Father's person. In our text He expresses the impossibility of rejecting Him and believing on the Father. The Pharisees, because they "loved the praise of men more than the praise of God," rejected Him and did not confess Him lest they be put out of the synagogue. They reasoned without foundation that being in the synagogue could be significant without Christ, and in this they have much company in the twentieth century, for there are multiplied thousands who observe the ritual of going to church and putting in their offerings but who have never experienced in their hearts the saving grace of the Lord Jesus.

When will men understand that without the love of God all that we may do is without significance? Only Christ can make our service and ritual meaningful. Look at a railway train. All the coaches are crowded with passengers. They speed over high bridges, through dark tunnels, and the least mistake or fault of the engineer would produce a terrible accident. Do they see the man to whose care they have entrusted their lives? No. How then are they so calm and secure? Because they trust him. So may it be with each of us. We see not the Pilot of our lives but He is there. Having accepted this fact by faith we follow Him through dangers seen and unseen but without fear, because we trust Him. "This is the victory that overcometh the world, even our faith."

This text precludes our seeking to bypass Christ and enter the kingdom. "No man cometh unto the Father, but by me," He says. Therefore, the whole world will have to deal with Him. The Bible speaks of Him as the "stone" that the builders rejected. May I add, woe to the builders, for there is no other name under heaven whereby we must be saved but the name of Jesus.

How strange that man would make his peace with substitute gods, or seek other than sincere heart repentance to make his peace with Him.

SELF-CONTROL

But I keep under my body, and bring it into subjection: lest that by any means, when I have preached to others, I myself should be a castaway. 1 Cor. 9:27.

We live in an age when lack of self-control is lauded as a virtue and the preachment of old-fashioned self-discipline is ridiculed as a doctrine of a bygone age. In rather select circles these days strange voices are heard encouraging young people to indulge in previously forbidden licentious practices. It is being urged that standards of morality must be updated so as to remain relevant to those to whom they are addressed. The question here is: Should principles be adjusted to meet delinquent human behavior or should humanity be adjusted to meet divine requirements? Essentially it is a question of what needs adjusting, man or moral principle. To decide that moral principle must be adjusted is to proclaim a lack of faith in the sufficiency of divine grace. It is in effect a concession that it is impossible to reform man and therefore law must be made to conform. The Bible supports none of this. It counsels man with the assurance that there is a sufficiency of divine grace and that one may "keep under his body, and bring it into subjection," even in this dark and evil world.

Discipline of the mind is also possible. There are those who complain that they have no control over their thoughts and are guilty of having wandering minds, permitting them to stray into forbidden paths. They thus develop morbid imaginations that wreak havoc with the morals. The Bible encourages us to believe that even the mind may be brought under control. Indeed, Philippians 2:5 suggests, "Let this mind be in you, which was also in Christ Jesus." This is in fact the function of the will. As a driver may control the course of an automobile with the steering wheel, so a man may with his will control both thought and body behavior. But that the will might lead the mind and the body into pure paths, it is necessary that man voluntarily yield it to the will of God, earnestly pleading, "Not my will, but thine, be done." This must be done daily, and indeed several times a day; thus the surrendered will in the guidance of an all-wise God directs the mind and the body into "green pastures . . . beside the still waters."

DON'T TEMPT CHRIST

Neither let us tempt Christ, as some of them also tempted, and were destroyed of serpents. 1 Cor. 10:9.

That Israel tempted Christ during her exodus from Egypt is common knowledge. That she doubted God from the Red Sea to the banks of the Jordan is a matter of record. And, furthermore, she was loud in her murmurings against God and against His leaders. The Scriptures equate one with the other. Moses was bitterly complaining of the attitude of the children of Israel to God, and God commanded that he stand up, for they murmured not against Moses but against God Himself.

Is there not contained in this story a serious warning to modern Israel? They tempted Him by unbelief. They tempted Him by disobedience. They tempted Him with ingratitude while pining for the so-called luxuries of Egypt. They tempted Him by indulging in the "pleasures" of the heathen that surrounded them. They tempted Him by losing sight of their ultimate objective and that was to be a people separate and distinct in terms of their faith and practice, and yet a people very much involved with the society about them in terms of holy service.

To live in splendid isolation, oblivious to the spiritual, physical, and mental needs of those around us is a misrepresentation of Christianity and presumption on His mercy. We thereby "tempt Christ."

"Let believers beware of the folly of trying the Saviour's patience by insisting on retaining their old appetites, customs, and desires, instead of gladly abandoning everything that pertains to the old unregenerate life in favor of the provisions the Lord in love makes for them."—*The SDA Bible Commentary,* on 1 Cor. 10:9.

To do as little as we can for God on a sort of get-by program is another way of grieving the heart of Christ. The heart of devotion seeks to do its utmost to show its love. Out of the fullness of its joy it cries "How much more, Lord, can I do for Thee?" In this it seeks not merit, but a happy relationship.

We tempt Christ when we presume upon His love and power. "Only he who has true faith is secure against presumption. For presumption is Satan's counterfeit of faith."—*The Desire of Ages,* p. 126.

THE RESURRECTION

For I delivered unto you first of all that which I also received, how that Christ died for our sins according to the scriptures; and that he was buried, and that he rose again the third day according to the scriptures. 1 Cor. 15: 3, 4.

It is difficult, if not impossible, to transmit that which one has not himself received. The apostle Paul was careful not to transmit another's experience; rather he says, "I also received." And what was it he transmitted? (1) Christ died for our sins according to the Scriptures, and (2) that He was buried, and (3) He rose again the third day. It is to the resurrection that we now address our attention.

It is the resurrection of Christ that validates our faith. "And if Christ be not risen, then is our preaching vain, and your faith is also vain" (verse 14). If Christ be not raised, then all who die are perished. "And if Christ be not raised, your faith is vain; ye are yet in your sins. Then they also which are fallen asleep in Christ are perished" (verses 17, 18).

The resurrection of Jesus Christ tells us many things; chiefly, that if we live for Christ in this life and die, we may die with the hope of living again. The resurrection of Christ also tells us something about the body we will have in the resurrection morning. John 20:27, 28 indicates that Christ's body was recognizable. There were features about it that identified Him as being who He was. "Beloved, now are we the sons of God, and it doth not yet appear what we shall be: but we know that, when he shall appear, we shall be like him; for we shall see him as he is" (1 John 3:2). Christ was Himself when He returned from the grave. We will be ourselves but glorified. Christians should give more attention to the subject of the resurrection, for it is a symbol of the new life that we live in Christ, having died to sin. Baptism is spoken of as spiritual death. We arise to walk in newness of life. Those who know us have a right to expect us to live a different life from that we lived before we died to sin.

Through prayer and the study of the Word of God, we are led into a closer relationship with Christ, and die to sin. Having risen with Christ, let us walk with Him in newness of life.

HE IS NOT HERE

And he saith unto them, Be not affrighted: Ye seek Jesus of Nazareth, which was crucified: he is risen; he is not here: behold the place where they laid him. Mark 16:6.

That Christ is indeed risen is the cornerstone of the Christian faith. Let no man minimize the significance of His death, for without the shedding of blood there is no remission for sin. But what would have been the significance of His death had He not risen?

The triumphant words, "He is not here," assume deeper significance than what would first appear. That He is risen and is alive forevermore has a very personal bearing on each individual soul. (1) His resurrection ensures that death will eventually be conquered. Death is an enemy and spreads its gloom from family to family throughout the earth. What a joy to know that Someone has conquered death and that one day, because He arose, death will cease to be. (2) The resurrection of Christ means to us that we will one day be reunited with loved ones from whom we have been separated in death. Said the apostle Paul, "And if Christ be not raised, your faith is vain. . . . Then they also which are fallen asleep in Christ are perished" (1 Cor. 15:17, 18). (3) If Christ had not risen, then every sermon that a minister has preached is but hollow mockery and empty promises. "If Christ be not risen, then is our preaching vain, and your faith is also vain" (verse 14). (4) The resurrection of Christ ensures the immortalization of our bodies. "Behold, I shew you a mystery; We shall not all sleep, but we shall all be changed, in a moment, in the twinkling of an eye, at the last trump: for the trumpet shall sound, and the dead shall be raised incorruptible, and we shall be changed." In the book, *Bible Treasury,* the story is told of a party of sailors who went ashore on some island of the sea and ate freely of some plant that put them into a deep sleep. As they did not return, others came in search for their companions and found them lying apparently dead. Anxiously they set to work to arouse the drugged sleepers, and the recovery of the first was a glad omen that the rest erelong would be revived. So the resurrection of Christ is divine assurance to all His followers that as He is now alive from the dead, they too shall rise.

99

IN GOD WE TRUST

But we had the sentence of death in ourselves, that we should not trust in ourselves, but in God which raiseth the dead. 2 Cor. 1:9.

Human nature is not trustworthy in matters spiritual. Indeed, temporal matters are more efficiently dealt with when man depends spiritually upon a power superior to himself. This is the foundation of our faith in Christ; namely, a realization of our own inadequacy and of our dependence upon our Creator. "In him we live, and move, and have our being." The philosophy of self-reliance has its positive and negative aspects. If when we use the term we mean not depending upon other human beings for those things that are our personal responsibilities, then the term is meaningful to the Christian. If, on the other hand, it is misinterpreted to refer to the ability of man to go it alone, having no need of God, then it is a philosophy of folly.

There are those blind religious leaders who contend that God is dead. In this they are asserting the adequacy of the human machine to meet its own needs. They have substituted human mentality as the court of final appeal, displacing the living God as the all-wise Judge of mankind and the Director of human destinies.

The preachments of Charles Darwin, Sigmund Freud, and Karl Marx have done much to perpetuate this myth of human sufficiency. And the education systems of the world have caught up this theme and are propagating it with the authority of fact. The bankruptcy of this theory may be readily seen in the fact that with all of his vaunted intellect, man has solved none of his major problems, such as disease, crime, and the problems of war and its aftermath. Do not six thousand years of failure constitute sufficient documentary evidence of the insufficiency of the human unaided by the divine? What is our own practice? Do we go about our daily tasks without reading the Word of God for light and guidance, and neglect the high privilege of conversation with God through prayer? Is our spiritual experience anemic because of our laxity in these two character-building exercises? They are indispensable as a means of grace. Can it be that Christians are abetting the humanists by their spiritual slackness? God forbid!

OUR SUFFICIENCY

Not that we are sufficient of ourselves to think any thing as of ourselves; but our sufficiency is of God. 2 Cor. 3:5.

The sin of Adam alienated the human family from a loving Father and Creator, but the love of God would not permit this schism to long continue. The record is that God came walking in the cool of the day, seeking the sinner. His purpose is to restore in man the image of his Maker and to reconcile him with his Creator, but the price was too high for man to pay. Nothing less than absolute perfection would atone for man's imperfection, and this no man had or has of himself. The Creator moved to become man's deliverer. Christ offered Himself in atonement for all men's sins. This alone would be acceptable to God, and so He offers us His life for ours and His death for our second death. Further, He offers us eternal life, for which we have nothing to exchange.

"But our sufficiency is of God." We may now say with John Flavel, "Lord, the condemnation was thine that the justification might be mine; the agony thine that the victory might be mine; the pain was thine and the ease was mine; the strife thine and the healing balm issuing from them mine; the vinegar and gall were thine that the honey and the sweet might be mine; the curse was thine that the blessing might be mine; the crown of thorns was thine that the crown of glory might be mine; thou paidest the price that I might enjoy the inheritance."

It was a custom in ancient Israel on the Day of Atonement for a lamb without spot to be offered for the sins of the people. Their sins were confessed upon the head of this innocent animal and atonement was made with its blood for the sins of the people. So it is with Christ. His merits and His alone will suffice to appease the claims of divine justice. The sinner's penitent cry reaches up to God, "Nothing in my hand I bring, Simply to Thy cross I cling."

Our trust in Him is our only resource in coping with the ordinary affairs of life. Our day-to-day problems require a strength other than our own. Let us then lift up our eyes, not to the hills, but to the skies, where dwelleth the High and Holy One who inhabiteth eternity.

THERE IS LIBERTY

Now the Lord is that Spirit: and where the Spirit of the Lord is, there is liberty. 2 **Cor.** 3:17.

The desire for liberty is basic in human nature. The master may take his freedom lightly, but his slaves dream of living without shackles. Great revolutions of history all testify to the power of malcontent and the strength of the basic urge to be free residing in every man's bosom. There are, however, two major spiritual concepts of what freedom really is:

1. There are those who believe spiritual freedom to be freedom from obligation to observe God's moral law, the Ten Commandments. For many years, the popular pulpit, implemented by radio and television broadcasts, has boldly propounded the theory that man can somehow be saved from his sins while being at liberty to transgress the law. This accounts in no small measure for the great breakdown in twentieth-century morals and the lack of concern for spiritual things in the young people of this age.

2. There are those who take liberty to mean freedom from the law's condemnation but not from its binding obligations; freedom from transgression that means freedom from guilt. It is this that gives man a free conscience, a mind void of condemnation.

True liberty confines its expressions within the framework of the law of moral behavior. To violate this law is to subject oneself to the lowest form of slavery. True liberty is not freedom to do what one wants but to do what one ought.

It is said that a captive eagle was tethered to a stick by a chain ten feet long. It kept marching around in a circle till a deep track was worn, and months of practice confirmed the habit. At length its owner took off the chain and set it free. Still the bird pursued its usual circle, not claiming freedom until someone pushed it from the beaten track. As if astonished, it looked around, flapped its wings, and then fixing its eye on the sun soared upward and away.

So may it be with us. Christ's death at Calvary for our sins rescues us from the rut of the sinful habit pattern, and we enjoy the freedom He purchased for us.

JESUS CAME

This is a faithful saying, and worthy of all acceptation, that Christ Jesus came into the world to save sinners; of whom I am chief. 1 Tim. 1:15.

Four thousand years had passed since the sin of Adam. The hopes of man for ultimate redemption had been kept alive by a variety of means. From time to time Spirit-filled, God-called men were sent to encourage the hearts of the faithful and to rebuke the waywardness of sinners. Also through signs and wonders and supernatural manifestations, God spoke to the hearts of His people. But perhaps the most meaningful revelation of the plan of salvation lay in the system of animal sacrifices which were prophetic in nature of the ministry of Christ as the Saviour of the world. This was mankind's only hope, and is today. Hence the significance of the announcement of our text, "Jesus came into the world to save sinners." This simple announcement should dispel all self-consciousness from the hearts of those who are timid to follow Him on the grounds that they are unworthy. The Scriptures clearly indicate that you are the object of His search. To save sinners He came into the world. No matter how men hide behind pretense and earthly display, God's Spirit seeks them out.

It was said of Him that "foxes have holes, and the birds of the air have nests; but the Son of man hath not where to lay his head." But the scholarly need not contemn Him because of His lack of estate or His lowly birth, for at the age of twelve His wisdom exceeded that of the most scholarly teachers of His day. So profound were His observations on themes beyond the comprehension of His chronological age that they wondered at what school He had studied. Nor may the rich scorn Him because of poverty, for it was He who rescued a rich man from embarrassment by converting the water into wine at the marriage feast, revealing Himself as the key to endless resources. Nor may those who are considered socially unacceptable for race, education, or wealth reasons be shy of Him, for Christ in the flesh was without all of these from an earthly point of view. It is then clear that all men may respond to the gospel commission with no justifiable reservations.

Surrender your life to Him? You'll be glad you did.

THE GIFT

Neglect not the gift that is in thee, which was given thee by prophecy, with the laying on of the hands of the presbytery. 1 Tim. 4:14.

Traveling by automobile down one of our prominent highways, I was struck by the sight on the side of a hill of hundreds of shells of wrecked automobiles. These cars had once been active and serviceable, like the one I was driving, but now they were tossed aside and rusting idly in the weather beside the highway they had so often traveled.

On the Bowery in New York City, a similar, though different, situation exists. One may see once-useful lives now dissipated by drink, sitting idly beside the highway of life no longer useful but literally rusting in the weather of an aimless existence. "Neglect not the gift that is in thee." Our talents may be cultivated and become a blessing to the world that we touch and serve. The neglect of their development is evidenced by the thousands of aimless wanderers in this life who have become displaced persons. Our talents and gifts may be cultivated by academic training. There is indeed no substitute for the refinement that accompanies a good education, and those young people who forsake pursuit of their education in favor of some apparent temporary advantage, whether it be monetary or otherwise, are merely penalizing themselves in the long run.

Character development is essential to the cultivation of our gifts. Like a jewel in the snout of a pig is a gift in the possession of a dissolute, lawless person. To neglect the salvation of our souls is to tarnish the gift that is within us. Daily conversion based on prayer and Bible study is essential to the enrichment of our talents and gifts. It is not enough to be a good singer or doctor or minister or teacher or laborer, rather it is more important that we be a good person. "A good character is a coat of triple steel, giving security to the wearer, protection to the oppressed, and inspiring the oppressor with awe."

Only the Christ-consecrated gift can truly benefit the world. The great artists of all time often acknowledged divine inspiration. Their masterpieces speak of a source other than human. Man in the hand of the Almighty is at his best. Let us heed Paul's counsel to Timothy.

THEY THAT TRUST

They that trust in the Lord shall be as mount Zion, which cannot be removed, but abideth for ever. **Ps. 125:1.**

We live in an unstable, unsettled world. An explosion of treatment centers for the emotions has kept pace with the population explosion. There is a basic insecurity lurking beneath the surface of the man who struts. For all his apparent affluence, the average human being is worried and feels terribly insecure about his position in life. To the Christian, things are different. There is a deep abiding faith that brings him peace of mind and rest of soul. This is one of the immediate by-products of salvation. It is not merely "pie in the sky." It is most rewarding here and now. There is a sound experience based on depth of conviction that renders one secure in Christ. This is the experience of all who "trust in the Lord."

Jack Appleton was a newspaperman and a saint. For seventeen years he wrestled with an incurable disease and for seven years of that time lay helpless in bed. His room became a place of encouragement and inspiration to many, and his poems with their note of quiet courage have traveled far. "Jack, what do you do when you can't touch the bottom?" I asked him one day. "I swim," he answered. "And when you can't swim?" I asked. "Then I float," he answered, "and underneath are the everlasting arms." So it is with all who trust the Lord. They become as unmovable as Mount Zion.

It is sad enough to see sinners driven by the wind and tossed about. Their frustration is enough to bring tears from the eyes of the Saviour. But it is worse to know Christians who have no peace of mind and rest of soul. As one man put it, "They have too much religion to go to the dance hall and too little to go to prayer meeting." In short they are miserable. It is my firm belief that the Christian's life is the happiest one, and that only hypocrisy and sin breed misery. Said Jesus, "In the world ye shall have tribulation: but be of good cheer; I have overcome the world."

The second fruit of the Spirit of God in the life is joy. An unhappy man is an unstable man, but they that trust in the Lord shall "be as mount Zion, which cannot be removed."

THE JOYFUL SOUND

Blessed is the people that know the joyful sound: they shall walk, O Lord, in the light of thy countenance. Ps. 89:15.

The joyful sound in our text can refer to none else than the good news of the gospel of Christ. The song writer has said, "We have heard a joyful sound, Jesus saves." To the ears of a lost man there is no sound sweeter than that of a familiar voice.

On a newscast a story was told of the massacre of an entire village of innocent women and children by the Viet Cong. An eyewitness to the slaughter had himself been attacked and left for dead. He mentioned how he had remained immobile until he heard the motors of helicopters overhead, and he knew that he would be rescued. This thought so thrilled his heart that, forgetting his wounds, he was seen by those manning the whirlybirds to be jumping up and down and waving his arms and shouting with joy that salvation had come at last. In a very real sense this is true of those dead in trespasses and sin. No sweeter sound can grace the ear than the grand old story of salvation—Christ came into the world to save sinners and none are excluded from the glorious provisions of the gospel. The further assurance that the only requirement that God makes of the candidate is that he believe implicitly in His promises and accept by faith the gospel requirements is good news indeed. Thus are the lost found and the sick made whole by the precious blood of Jesus.

The glorious terms of the gospel awaken in man the heart's noblest impulses. There is indeed a song in every heart in tune with Christ.

Those imprisoned in old Bilibid prison in the Philippine Islands tell of the day when the American paratroopers staged a daring raid on the area to liberate the compound. Those incarcerated had every reason to believe they would have been lined up and shot had there been some forewarning of the imminent liberation. I have talked to some of the prisoners who survived this ordeal. One person told me that he has never heard a more welcome sound than the firing of American troops and the cheerful drawl of an American GI. It is even so with the gospel of the Lord Jesus Christ. It means liberty to the captives. It lets the oppressed go free. It is the most joyful of all joyful sounds.

IF WE SUFFER

If we suffer, we shall also reign with him. 2 Tim. 2:12.

We have all known the thrill of seeing soldiers on parade, and our hearts have felt the surge that accompanies martial music. Resplendent in his colorful uniform, his bayonet glistening in the sun, a soldier on parade makes a proud figure, but the test of a good soldier is not how he performs on parade but what he does on the battlefield. There amid the grime and the filth and discomfort of his miserable foxhole, the stench of death, the screams of the wounded, and the groans of the dying fill the air. He knows that each moment may be his last. A good soldier endures this hardness, and it is hardness that tests his worthiness as a soldier.

The philosopher Philemon has said, "In this thing one man is superior to another that he is better able to bear prosperity or adversity." And another has observed, "Most of our comforts grow up between our crosses."

Said the apostle, "Beloved, think it not strange concerning the fiery trial which is to try you, as though some strange thing happened unto you: but rejoice, inasmuch as ye are partakers of Christ's sufferings" (1 Peter 4:12, 13).

Difficult problems do indeed serve a useful purpose. It is hardness that strengthens one for the next trial and difficult decision. One day there will be a grand parade when Christian soldiers move toward the sky in celestial step with the music of angels, but this will be the reward and not the test. We will mount up with wings as eagles but only after on earth we have endured hardness as good soldiers.

One of our young Adventists who joined the Marines expressed his conviction with reference to bearing arms and Sabbath observance. He was brutally beaten in an effort to break his spirit. Insults to his courage were his daily fare. Frequent trips to the stockades, solitary confinement, all of these were weapons in the hands of his immediate superiors to change his mind. But young Barnett was a good Christian soldier and he later won the grudging admiration of his associates and superiors. Looking at him now, in the cheerful countenance and the buoyant spirit one reads: "It pays to stand like a good soldier."

HIGHER THAN I

From the end of the earth will I cry unto thee, when my heart is overwhelmed: lead me to the rock that is higher than I. Ps. 61:2.

Man is dependent by nature—physically, mentally, and spiritually. Hence, he is limited in his capacity. It is understandable, then, that there are times when life gets too big, and in the language of the text, the "heart is overwhelmed." In emergencies for which there seems to be no solution, it is a simple thing for a man to pray a prayer and to seek assistance from a power outside of and above himself. Someone has said, "Except that which is above us shall come unto us, that which is about us and within us will destroy us."

Our text recognizes that there is a Supreme Being and that we may repair to Him in moments of stress, confident that He will hear and answer prayer. Verse 3 gives reason for confidence: "For thou hast been a shelter for me, and a strong tower from the enemy."

In each man's life there are bitter things and sweet, and many of the problems we face are overwhelming—bereavement, economic privation, marital distress, to mention only a few that beset the human family. The waywardness of children has broken many a mother's heart, and what wife could be unaffected by a drunkard husband.

What a comfort to know that there is "the rock that is higher than I" unto whom we can repair in hours of stress! How much better it is to form the habit of communing with Him while the sun shines and in moments of prosperity. One enjoying such an experience finds little difficulty or embarrassment in turning to Christ in the time of storm.

Having tasted of His mercy and experienced His love, one can say with the psalmist, "So will I sing praise unto thy name for ever, that I may daily perform my vows" (verse 8).

During a hurricane that crashed into New Orleans, Louisiana, the waters of the Gulf and Lake Pontchartrain rapidly overspread the city. The cry went up from the terror-stricken inhabitants: "Higher ground." Automobiles clogged the city streets. Poisonous water reptiles added their stinging fury to the plague. "Higher ground" was a cry of desperation. And it should and must be the prayer of needy souls: "Lead me to the rock that is higher than I."

BORN AGAIN

Nicodemus saith unto him, How can a man be born when he is old? can he enter the second time into his mother's womb, and be born? John 3:4.

Nicodemus was puzzled at the pronouncement of the Saviour, "Except a man be born again, he cannot see the kingdom of God." Nicodemus was thinking of natural birth, whereas Christ was speaking of spiritual birth. Of course, the figure of being born into the kingdom is a good one, for there are similarities between natural and spiritual birth. There is a "quickening" in both instances. In natural birth the moment of conception is a "quickening." In spiritual birth the quickening of conscience, a new sensitivity to right and wrong, a movement toward a new life, is a part of the miracle of conversion.

The unregenerate human heart has been described in Ephesians 2:1 as "dead in trespasses and sins." A resurrection from this inert spiritual state is suggestive of the term "the new birth." It is new in the sense that it is distinct from the first, or natural, physical birth. The conversion, or new birth, experience is portrayed in the baptismal rite when the candidate rises to "walk in newness of life" (Rom. 6:4) with his Lord. He is "a new creature" (2 Cor. 5:17).

When Adam and Eve sinned in the Garden of Eden, it was with the knowledge of the divine fiat, "Ye shall not eat of it, neither shall ye touch it, lest ye die" (Gen. 3:3). In eating the forbidden fruit they did die, for in spiritual things disobedience always separates the offender from the Source of life. Cut off from communication with Heaven, Adam and Eve felt their nakedness and sewed together makeshift garments, substitutes for the glorious garment of light given them at Creation.

Since that tragic hour every individual born of woman has been in spiritual darkness until he finds reconciliation with God through Christ who died that men might live. That discovery of his Lord on the part of the sinner through recognition of His sacrifice for man comes slowly in the experience of some, in a flash of inspiration to others. The attending change in the life from darkness to light, from sinning to obedience, from despair to hope and joy, is the new birth experience.

SEEK MY FACE

I will go and return to my place, till they acknowledge their offence, and seek my face: in their affliction they will seek me early. Hosea 5:15.

The myth has somehow persisted that God is ever in pursuit of man and that man may presume upon His love without penalty to himself. Our text for today makes it clear that this is not the case. "I will go and return to my place, till they acknowledge their offence, and seek my face." That "God so loved the world, that he gave his only begotten Son" is an indisputable fact. The concern of this lesson is that we not take that love for granted and presume upon it until we are at last bereft of His presence without a spark of conscience left with which to build again our spiritual experiences.

In Genesis 6:3 we read, "And the Lord said, My spirit shall not always strive with man, for that he also is flesh." He demonstrated this impatience with presumptuous transgression by visiting the human family with punishment by water in the form of a cataclysmic flood; thus, the world had an example of what it means to presume on God's grace and to trample upon His mercy. Will you and I heed this warning?

In the common everyday affairs of life, do we consult God as to the best course to take? Are our prayer lives such that He can fulfill the promise made hundreds of years ago, "In all thy ways acknowledge him, and he shall direct thy paths" (Prov. 3:6)? There is a severe penalty for repeated willful transgression of the will of God. That penalty is threefold in nature: (1) In the mind of the presumptuous transgressor there is a searing of the conscience. (2) Confidence in the will of God and the way of life is destroyed. (3) The example set makes others to stumble, for no man liveth to himself.

The apostle Paul was on the road to Damascus. His mission was one of destruction, but suddenly he was stricken with a bright light from heaven and the voice of God inquiring as to why he was living as he lived. In his affliction Paul expressed his willingness to do the will of God. But why must it be this way? May we not volunteer our lives and our all to Christ without the heavy hand of justice being laid upon us? Is it not easier that we voluntarily submit our wills to Him?

NOAH FOUND GRACE

But Noah found grace in the eyes of the Lord. Gen. 6:8.

Grace is the unmerited favor of God. It is the love of God bestowed upon unworthy human beings. This grace provides pardon for past transgressions. The Bible speaks of this as justification. It provides strength for present and future emergencies. This is called sanctification, and it promises the believer eventual deliverance from the very presence of sin. This is called glorification.

These threefold privileges of grace constitute the Christian hope, and they form the seat of all spiritual rebirth. To be pardoned and cleansed under the terms of justification is an experience that covers the past, the present, and the future. To be the recipient of imparted strength from Jehovah on a day-to-day basis is, of course, one's present and future privilege, and the great promise of physical deliverance from this old world of sin and sorrow is a future experience, providing a goal toward which our weary footsteps tread.

There is a mistaken notion among thousands that grace was extended man only at the incarnation of Christ. The fact is, according to Titus 2:11 and 12, "the grace of God that bringeth salvation hath appeared to all men, teaching us that, denying ungodliness and worldly lusts, we should live soberly, righteously, and godly, in this present world." Our text makes it clear that God has not favored one generation above another in the dispensation of divine grace; for indeed, there has been no period in the history of man during which this beneficent expression of divine love has been absent from the earth.

It is, therefore, now each man's happy privilege to "come boldly to the throne of grace, that he may obtain mercy, and find grace to help in time of need."

A minister, after preaching a very interesting sermon, launched into a fervent appeal. The only one responding to this appeal was a little boy. After the service the minister asked the little fellow, "What about the sermon most impressed you?" To which the little one replied, "Sir, at the end of your appeal you said, 'Whosoever will, let him come.' 'Whosoever' is my name, and so I came."

That blessed "whosoever" beckons to you and me.

111

A SIGN

Moreover also I gave them my sabbaths, to be a sign between me and them, that they might know that I am the Lord that sanctify them. Eze. 20:12.

The Sabbath is not a hollow symbol without spiritual significance to the believer. It is a vital spiritual exercise, bringing many benefits of divine grace in its train. That the seventh day is the Sabbath is evident from the blessings that accompany the observance of the specific day God appointed. Not all days were blessed; only the Sabbath. "Blessed is the man that doeth this, and the son of man that layeth hold on it; that keepeth the sabbath from polluting it, and keepeth his hand from doing any evil" (Isa. 56:2).

Orlando Florian worked at the Voice of Prophecy Bible Correspondence School in Miraflores, Peru. He was attending night school in the city and had had no problem skipping his Friday night classes. But now he was confronted with a Sabbath examination. His professor was adamant and refused when he asked for exemption. He prayed for guidance, and his pastor suggested he see Dr. Lopez, the school director. Dr. Lopez was alone in his office when Orlando went to see him. When he introduced himself and said he worked at the radio Bible school, the director beamed. "You do?" he exclaimed. Then he pulled from his desk a diploma he had just received for work he himself had done at the school. Learning of Orlando's dilemma about the Sabbath examination, he told him not to worry. "I will arrange with your professor for some other day for the test." Orlando pedaled home with his heart singing praises to his heavenly Father. God always has the way prepared for those who are determined to serve Him at whatever cost.

Yes, the Sabbath is one of the signs of the sanctifying power of God, and when one keeps it, often at the loss of his job or friends and perhaps even his family, he reveals to the world that he loves God supremely and that the sanctifying power of the Spirit is a reality in his life. And aside from his positive witness to the world, the true Sabbath-keeper finds God's Spirit witnessing to his own heart that precious comfort that he is a child of God.

PEACE

There is no peace, saith my God, to the wicked. Isa. 57:21.

From the cradle to the grave man is engaged in an endless pursuit of peace of mind and rest of soul. Worry is one of the most common illnesses of our times, and it produces tensions, weakens the heart, disturbs the blood pressure, and unbalances the personality. But in this world of confusion there is an island of calm to the confident in heart. "There is a place of quiet rest." Our text, however, makes it clear that there is no peace for the wicked. "Come unto me, all ye that labour and are heavy laden, and I will give you rest," said Jesus. Peace of mind and rest of soul are natural products of a right relationship with Christ. This involves confidence in His Word and obedience to His requirements.

"O that thou hadst hearkened unto my commandments! then had thy peace been as a river, and thy righteousness as the waves of the sea" (Isa. 48:18).

In a class that I was teaching recently, one of my students objected rather sharply to a position I had taken. I proceeded to defend my point, but he felt that I had defended it with undue vigor. I was unaware of this; however, I did notice that during the next two class periods this young man did not enter heartily into the discussions as was his usual custom. Inquiring concerning this of a friend of his, I was informed that his feelings had been hurt in what I had considered to be a healthy exchange of opinions. Upon receipt of this information, I was miserable. I slept over it that night and went another day, pondering the course that I should pursue. I knew that I had no alternative than to approach my brother and to apologize for having offended him. Until I did this I had no peace of mind. Conversely, following our warm exchange of Christian understanding, the peace of God flooded my soul, and the bond between us was stronger than when the infraction was committed. This is the key to personal peace, keeping the soul channel clear between oneself and the Saviour. This involves a renunciation of pride and a show of humility. Are you prepared to pay the price? Here is the formula: "Great peace have they which love thy law: and nothing shall offend them" (Ps. 119:165).

UNCEASING LABOR

And daily in the temple, and in every house, they ceased not to teach and preach Jesus Christ. Acts 5:42.

The zeal with which the disciples pursued their work is a rebuke to the slothful believer today. Whatever we do should be done with enthusiasm and dispatch. Procrastination is hazardous. Opportunity often vanishes with delay.

Henry Ford's fireplace motto reads as follows: "Enthusiasm is the yeast that makes your hope rise to the stars; enthusiasm is the sparkle in your eye, it is the swing in your gait, the grip of your hand, the irresistible urge of your will and your energy to execute your ideas. Enthusiasts are fighters. They have fortitude, they have staying qualities. Enthusiasm is at the bottom of all progress. With it there is accomplishment; without it there are only alibis."

Enthusiasm was a secret of the apostle Peter's success. His sermons are not dead prose but living rhetoric, vibrant with the spirit of the speaker and the intensity of his convictions. The importance of enthusiasm is illustrated in the experience of Joash, king of Israel.

The prophet Elisha said to him, "Smite upon the ground. And he smote thrice, and stayed." The man of God was wroth with him and said, "Thou shouldest have smitten five or six times; then hadst thou smitten Syria until thou hadst consumed it: whereas now thou shalt smite Syria but thrice" (2 Kings 13:19).

Edward C. Butler has said, "Every man is enthusiastic at times. One man has enthusiasm for thirty minutes, another has it for thirty days, but it is the man who has it for thirty years who makes a success in life." Enthusiasm is contagious. One cannot have it without transmitting it to others, but the basis of enthusiasm is optimism. Some men literally get out of bed on the top side of the day. Such a man was Joseph. If any man had the slightest excuse to give up on life, it was this man. Abandoned in a pit, sold into slavery, thrown into prison on a false charge; at every stage of his life we see him fighting upward, until at last he is the second man in the Egyptian kingdom.

Through prayer and the study of the Word, we find God's promise in every challenge, and attack with vigor the duties of each day.

THY LIGHT IS COME

Arise, shine; for thy light is come, and the glory of the Lord is risen upon thee. Isa. 60:1.

In his original sinless state, man enjoyed the privilege of face-to-face communion with his Maker. Consequent to this relationship, the light of God like a luminous garment shrouded Adam and Eve. With the entrance of sin this high privilege of person-to-person communication was taken away and man was stripped of the glory of God. Through six thousand years of transgression the darkness has deepened, and the prophet, inspired by God, was constrained to say, "Darkness shall cover the earth, and gross darkness the people." But in every generation the light has shone, and men have had an opportunity to make their peace with God in the full glare of the good news of salvation.

From Adam to Christ there was an unbroken line of living witnesses. To name a few, there were Enoch, Methuselah, Abraham, Jacob, Isaiah, Jeremiah, and more. Since New Testament times men of God have arisen whose names are household words. After the first century there was a conspired effort by political, religious, and scientific forces to extinguish the pure primitive light of the gospel as taught by the apostles and prophets, which truth literally went into a tunnel and was for 1,260 years partially obscured. Then came the great Renaissance and the Reformation, and from 1844 on there has been a continuing revelation of original Christianity. As remarkable as the inventive genius of man in the scientific world, precious light from the Scriptures now floods the earth as the waters cover the sea. The language of our text is being fulfilled before our very eyes, "Thy light is come, and the glory of the Lord is risen upon thee." There remains now the exhibition of that glory before men so that the church may fulfill God's plan for restoration of the world to its original purpose, hence, the significance of the injunction, "Rise, shine."

Each convert must become a convert maker. The spreading of the gospel of the kingdom is the method by which the church may shine. The church is in its purest radiance when it reflects the character of the Master amid the rapidly deepening darkness that envelops the earth.

MY WORD

So shall my word be that goeth forth out of my mouth: it shall not return unto me void, but it shall accomplish that which I please, and it shall prosper in the thing whereto I sent it. Isa. 55:11.

This prophecy has been fulfilled in ten thousand ways. What is the secret of its power? "Because the Bible is the voice of a universal Father talking to His universal family. In it He tells of man as he was, as he is, and as he shall be. It can never be destroyed. Jesus said: Heaven and earth shall pass away, but My words shall not pass away. It is like the bush that burned with fire and yet remained unconsumed. God was in the bush, and God is in the Bible. Infidels have tried to destroy it. Instead they died and were soon forgotten, but the Old Book, though often banned and burned and ridiculed and neglected, continues to live through the centuries. It has come down to us floating upon a sea of blood—every page stained with the lifeblood of martyrs." —J. D. SNIDER, *I Love Books,* p. 216.

Charles Spurgeon tells of a young woman who in the freshness of the Saviour's pardoning love came to him one day bringing her little Bible. The Bible had been given her in early childhood by her dying mother, who had written these words on the flyleaf: "In this book a treasure lies. If you dig deep, you'll find the prize." The young woman said, "Oh, how often I've wondered what that meant; how often I've turned over these pages looking for the treasure, and now I have found it." Commenting further, Spurgeon said, "The Book—the one Book— the Book that is older than our fathers, that is truer than tradition, that is more learned than the universities, that is more authoritative than councils, that is more infallible than popes, that is more orthodox than creeds, that is more powerful than ceremonies, 'the sword of the spirit, the omnipotent Word of God, the wonder of the world, and the boon of heaven.'"

When Scott lay dying at Abbottsford, he turned to his beloved Lockhart and said, "Lockhart, reach me the Book." "What book?" his friend asked. "Ah," said the dying bard, "there is but one theme and one Book for a dying man and that is Christianity and the Bible."

116

MY FLOCK

And ye my flock, the flock of my pasture, are men, and I am your God, saith the Lord God. Eze. 34:31.

The marvel of the love of God is that He would condescend to identify Himself with human beings. This is the most inspiring aspect of the gospel. "The Word was made flesh, and dwelt among us" (John 1:14).

Spurgeon tells of a mother and father and infant child crossing the mountains of Vermont when a fearful storm came upon them. The wind roared and howled. The snow drifted in great heaps. The cold became intense. To add to their danger, they lost the road and at last, surrounded by drifting snow on every side, they could advance no farther. Then the husband and father left the wife and child to go in quest of assistance from some farmhouse. He found help, but in the darkness of night and the fury of the storm he was unable to retrace his steps so that the help he had obtained was unavailing. At length the morning dawned and the storm subsided. Then the neighbors and the anxious husband renewed the search. Toward noon the body of a woman was found, cold in death, partly enshrouded in the white mantle that had fallen from the clouds during the dreadful night, but wonderful to tell, the child was alive. "She stripped her mantle from her breast and bared her bosom to the storm, then sank upon the snow to rest and smiled to think her babe was warm."

How descriptive of the love of God, for Christ came into a world that rejected Him for thirty-three years, then covered it in mercy with His blood that was shed at Calvary. Is not this enough to give us hope?

It is clear that Christ has no illusions as to what constitutes His flock. "The flock of my pasture, are men." He therefore knows just what He can expect of each of us in terms of capacity, and He is also aware when we are giving Him less than our very best. He knows that our best will be something less than that of angels and yet He has every right to expect our behavior to measure in every aspect above that of brute creation. Yet how sad to contemplate that some of what God sees in men is no more than what He sees in the brute world.

117

THE SECRET OF HIS TABERNACLE

For in the time of trouble he shall hide me in his pavilion: in the secret of his tabernacle shall he hide me; he shall set me up upon a rock. Ps. 27:5.

That there is a temple or tabernacle in heaven is clearly taught in the Scriptures. Hebrews 8:1, 2 makes this clear. "Now of the things which we have spoken this is the sum: We have such an high priest . . . ; a minister of the sanctuary, and of the true tabernacle, which the Lord pitched, and not man." Verse one indicates that this tabernacle is in the heavens. In Revelation 15:5 John says, "And after that I looked, and, behold, the temple of the tabernacle of the testimony in heaven was opened."

The Seventh-day Adventist Church stands alone in proclaiming the twofold nature of the ministry of Christ in the heavenly sanctuary. Upon His ascension He entered the holy place of the sanctuary in heaven, and since 1844 He has been in the Most Holy Place performing a work of judgment in addition to His other ministry of grace. We have literally come to the time when we need to be hidden "in his pavilion: in the secret of his tabernacle," and we need to be set "up upon a rock." It is in the tabernacle that sins are now being fully and finally dealt with. The Lord is literally in His holy temple. Let all the earth keep silent before Him. Sins confessed now are covered in the tabernacle by the blood of Jesus Christ. In this sense we are hidden and, when justified, set upon a rock. Is not this the equivalent of the man referred to by Jesus, building his house upon a rock so that when the winds blow and the storm breaks in its fury, that house shall stand? Cleansing, pardon, and the impartation of divine power are the secrets of His tabernacle.

In our text the psalmist, David, apparently has in mind deliverance from his earthly enemies. However, the implications of the language of the text are far broader than this. The very existence of the work of atonement now going on in the heavenly sanctuary is to the world largely still a secret. Blessed is the man who through prayer and Bible study has received assurance in his heart of sins forgiven and that the blood of Jesus Christ has taken away all sin.

118

WHO NEEDS GOD?

For in him we live, and move, and have our being; as certain also of your own poets have said, For we are also his offspring. Acts 17:28.

"Who needs God?" It was a Sabbath afternoon, and a seventeen-year-old young person was sitting facing his pastor. "Look what science and technology have accomplished without Him and, mind you, many of these men are atheists or agnostics." The pastor sighed deeply and uttered a silent prayer, for he wanted so badly to convince this young man of the existence of God, and of His necessity in human need.

"Young man," the pastor began to talk slowly, "by whose laws are the scientists operating in the accomplishment of their designs? There is, as you know, a law of gravitation. Indeed, all nature is governed by natural law. Now, the scientist did not make these laws. He simply discovered them. In all of human history man has never created anything. He has only been able to produce new forms from existent matter. At best he is only a craftsman, using the laws of physics for his so-called creations. But science can account neither for origin nor destiny. It requires more faith to believe in the theories of evolution than it does to believe the scriptural account of Creation, and the theory of a utopian world built by scientists and philosophers has never gone beyond the dream. In fact, most of the voices from the scientific world are proclaiming the dangers of total annihilation. And, further," the minister continued, "what is the source of your strength?"

"Food grown by the farmers," the young man replied.

"And where did the seed originate?"

"Why, from the full-grown ear of corn or from the ripened tomato."

"Good," replied the pastor. "Now, where did the ripened tomato or the full-grown ear of corn originate? In short, which was first, the seed or the fruit; the chicken or the egg?"

To this the young man had no reply. The Bible declares that in the beginning God created the heavens and the earth. This is plausible, it is understandable, it is believable, it accounts for existing matter by paying tribute to a divine all-intelligent Power.

119

DIVINE STANDARD

For whosoever shall keep the whole law, and yet offend in one point, he is guilty of all. James 2:10.

There is a measuring stick by which all human behavior is judged. That standard is unchangeable. Right and wrong are not relative. They do not shift from one era to another. Nor are they determined by each individual. Right and wrong are not arrived at by trial and error, nor are they established by consensus thinking. Right and wrong are determined by divine fiat. The law of God—the Ten Commandments—is the standard. The moral law was not originated by man but was handed down to him. Thus judgment of right and wrong lies not in the hand of man but in the hand of the Lawgiver. The power to obey is a fruit of grace. It is the life of Christ imputed and imparted to the life of the Christian. There is in our time much talk about the "new morality." The new morality is nothing more than the old immorality. There is a growing tendency to flout the old moral standards and label virtue as Victorian and crass transgression as relevancy. To deny the existence of an arbitrary standard by which right and wrong are measured is in effect to make every man his own judge of human behavior. This, of course, is the grossest anarchy, for every man would decide for himself what is right or wrong. There would be no basic honesty.

A friend called on Rowland Hill to bring him to account for his too-severe, too-legal gospel. "Do you, sir," asked Mr. Hill, "hold the Ten Commandments to be a rule of life for the Christian?"

"Certainly not," replied the visitor. Mr. Hill rang the bell, and upon the servant's making his appearance, quietly added, "John, show that man the door and keep your eye upon him until he is beyond reach of every article of wearing apparel or piece of property in the hall."

And so it is. One's attitude toward the Ten Commandments is the test of his attitude toward God and his fellow man. God is able to read the heart but we human beings can only measure attitudes by deeds. The fruits of obedience to the law reveal the relationship between the believer and his God. We cannot dissociate what we do from what we think, for as a man "thinketh in his heart, so is he" (Prov. 23:7).

A RUMOR FROM THE LORD

The vision of Obadiah. Thus saith the Lord God concerning Edom; We have heard a rumour from the Lord, and an ambassador is sent among the heathen, Arise ye, and let us rise up against her in battle. Obadiah 1:1.

The book of Obadiah contains two key thoughts referred to as rumors from the Lord. The first is in the fifteenth verse of the chapter, "For the day of the Lord is near upon all the heathen." And the second is in verse 21, ". . . and the kingdom shall be the Lord's."

This twofold message of Obadiah has constituted the burden of God's counsel through His messengers in all ages. To wit: That the enemies of the Lord will be put to flight and that eventually truth must conquer wrong. Oppression is now and has been the partial lot of all of those who worship the true and the living God. The enemy of our souls would through persecution force us to relax the grip of faith on eternal verities, but the blessed hope of the ultimate triumph of right strengthens one to endure present trial.

The end of human rule will not mean the end of all things, rather the glorious beginning of the reign of Christ, for the kingdom shall be the Lord's. "And in the days of these kings shall the God of heaven set up a kingdom, which shall never be destroyed: and the kingdom shall not be left to other people, but it shall break in pieces and consume all these kingdoms, and it shall stand for ever" (Dan. 2:44).

We may, then, with justification look for a city that hath foundations whose builder and maker is God, and may we never lose our awareness of the nearness of the coming of the Lord. In the language of Obadiah, "the day of the Lord is near."

A little boy, the son of a war veteran, was observed feverishly going about his chores, helping mother with the house cleaning. A neighbor remarked, "Sonny, why all this unusual activity?"

"Why, haven't you heard?" replied the boy. "Dad is coming home."

"When do you expect him?" asked the lady. "Today?"

"I don't know," said the little boy. "That's why I'm in a hurry!"

Let us cultivate an expectancy that will please God.

121

BE THOU FAITHFUL

Fear none of those things which thou shalt suffer: behold, the devil shall cast some of you into prison, that ye may be tried; and ye shall have tribulation ten days: be thou faithful unto death, and I will give thee a crown of life. Rev. 2:10.

"Martyrdom" is a word generally associated with the witness of saints of the early centuries. We seldom think of any necessity for martyrdom in modern times. Yet the stout spirit of many believers exhibited in accepting the truths of the third angel's message partakes of the courage and fortitude of thousands who have suffered the rack and the flame in witness to the deathless quality of their faith. To take a stand for an unpopular truth requires moral heroism that arises out of a clear spiritual perspective, and God honors those who honor Him.

In a recent evangelistic campaign it was my privilege to baptize a woman who had the following experience: Three weeks after her baptism there was a knock on the door. It was the assistant pastor of the church of her former connection. "Greetings," he said to her. "I've come by to see just why we've missed you from church lately."

"Come in," replied our sister.

"Oh, I don't have time," said the man. "All I want to know is, Are you still with us?"

"Come in," again the woman said.

"Well, I can only stay for a while," the visitor said. She pointed him to a seat and soon returned with her baptismal certificate.

"Read this," she said. He sat for a few minutes scanning the beautiful certificate and its vital contents. Finally he looked up and said, "Have you joined this church too?"

"Yes, I have," she answered.

To her surprise the man replied, "The man that baptized you baptized my wife and three children. Be faithful, I'm coming too."

Sometimes withdrawal from another communion or from one's family in matters of faith does not turn out as happily as this. Yet though there be heartache and suffering in breaking earthly ties, God comes close to the faithful heart, making all the promises of His Word available for the faltering soul.

THIS MIND

Let this mind be in you, which was also in Christ Jesus.
Phil. 2:5.

The mind is the seat of all human behavior. It is the source of all thought, word, and deed. If the life is to be lived for Christ, the mind must be surrendered to His purposes. Hence, the injunction of the text, "Let this mind be in you, which was also in Christ Jesus." This admonition implies two things: (1) agreement, (2) active cooperation. Let us consider them separately.

The Bible is the will of God verbally expressed. It gives us some glimpse of the Master's mind. By the daily study of the Word and prayer for understanding and strength, we become partakers of the divine nature and our thinking becomes like Christ's.

Second, it is a spiritual law that the more we order our lives in harmony with the divine pattern, the more fully we identify with the Master's way of life. This conformity involves every aspect of our lives, but specifically must we guard the entrance of the mind against negative influences that would distort the image of Christ in the soul. We live in an age of mass communications, and these without doubt have contributed to the well-being of the human family in many areas, but they have not been an unmixed blessing. While we glory in the positive aspects of scientific achievement, attention must be called to some of its dangers. Great care must be given to the "brainwashing" aspects of mass media communications, and Christian discrimination must be exercised in their use. The mind that feeds in the gutter partakes of its nature. What goes into our minds is accurately reflected by what appears in our behavior. Says Paul, "But the fruit of the Spirit is love, joy, peace, longsuffering, gentleness, goodness, faith, meekness, temperance: against such there is no law" (Gal. 5:22, 23).

May the prayer of our hearts be "Give me a heart like Thine."

To pray for the meekness of Christ is to invite the persecution visited upon Him, for such is conducive to humility. The heavy blows of persecution rained upon the head of the innocent child of God are a test of his lowliness. The mind of Christ forbade retaliation on His oppressors. It will forbid it in us.

123

GOD HAS SPOKEN

The mighty God, even the Lord, hath spoken, and called the earth from the rising of the sun unto the going down thereof. **Ps. 50:1.**

Fortunately for sinful man, God has not broken off contact with him. The text says, "God . . . hath spoken." Often in this life when there is disagreement among people, they cease communicating with one another. This renders reconciliation difficult if not impossible, and so we read in the Scriptures that following the sin of Adam "they heard the voice of the Lord God walking in the garden in the cool of the day" (Gen. 3:8). God made provision for maintaining contact with us so that reconciliation might be effected.

Yes, God has spoken to man and continues to speak in a variety of ways. He has spoken to us in nature. "The heavens declare the glory of God; and the firmament sheweth his handywork" (Ps. 19:1). The beauty of sunset and sunrise, the multicolored flowers, waving grass, and rustling leaves caressed by the gentle breeze, all speak in language clear of the love of God for man.

> "In the beauty of the lilies Christ was born across the sea,
> With a glory in His bosom that transfigures you and me;
> As He died to make men holy, let us die to make men free,
> While God is marching on."

God has also spoken to man through the Scriptures, His Holy Word. To the ends of the earth has He thus spoken, for thanks to the miracle of printing, the Bible is now available to men and women around the globe, and in so many translated languages that few men can disclaim accountability for the light contained therein.

God has also spoken to man through special messengers—ministers of His in all generations. Mysteriously men have been called from the ordinary pursuits of life and given a heavy burden for the salvation of their fellow men, often against their own wills and under circumstances not of their own choosing.

Perhaps the voice most clearly heard is the voice of Calvary, for God hath in these last days spoken unto us by His Son in a revelation of love unparalleled in the annals of communication.

124

THE WORSHIPFUL ATTITUDE

Keep thy foot when thou goest to the house of God, and be more ready to hear, than to give the sacrifice of fools: for they consider not that they do evil. Eccl. 5:1.

God is "the high and lofty One that inhabiteth eternity." A vision of His awesome majesty would certainly impel one to tread softly in His presence. There has occurred, however, through the years a pagan form of worship that emphasizes exhibitionism in the form of body contortions, shrill utterances, and in some instances general rowdiness. This worship attitude is clearly rebuked in verse 2 of our chapter. "Be not rash with thy mouth, and let not thine heart be hasty to utter any thing before God: for God is in heaven, and thou upon earth: therefore let thy words be few."

It is a mark of pagan religions to rant and dance and shout and even to abuse the flesh in the act of worship. The worship of God in the temple has ever been associated with solemnity, sobriety, and awe. This is certainly no invitation to Laodicean coldness. Services can become so formal and stilted that a fervent Amen would elicit a turning of heads and a craning of necks. Indeed, in some congregations to shed a tear is to exhibit unwarranted emotionalism. To be pitied are those cold souls to whom the singing of ordinary hymns is a distressful exercise. The fervent hymnody of the Advent Movement will ever live in the hearts of those who love the Lord's appearing.

While prudence is to be exercised and exhibitionism discouraged, be it known that God is to be worshiped "in spirit and in truth." Dr. John Robertson tells of a Scottish village where years ago all the hearth fires had gone out. It was before the days of matches. The only way to rekindle the fires was to find some hearth where the fire was yet aglow. The search was fruitless until at last a flaming hearth was found away on a hill. One by one the villagers came to this hearth and lighted their peat, put it carefully in a pan, shielding it from the wind, and soon fires were burning brightly throughout the community.

It is a revival of fervency in worship we all need and want. God has plenty of fire on the hill. Let us in worship climb up into His presence through the path of surrender.

125

CONTENTMENT

Better is an handful with quietness, than both the hands full with travail and vexation of spirit. Eccl. 4:6.

Semiramis built a monument for herself with this inscription, "Whatever king wants treasure, if he opens this tomb, he may be satisfied." Darius, therefore, opening it found no treasure; but another inscription which said, "If thou were not a wicked person and of insatiable covetousness, thou would'st not disturb the mansions of the dead."

A giant eagle, having satisfied his own appetite, was unwilling to leave the rest of the carcass. He sank his giant talons into the flesh and with a mighty effort he was airborne, bearing the carcass with him. As he swept out over the sea his wings began to tire and he realized that the weight he was carrying was heavier than his wings could bear. Frantically he first shook one foot and then the other to try to dislodge the carcass but to no avail. Slowly and steadily he was borne down to the ocean waves. There was a splash and then suddenly the proud eagle disappeared, a victim of his own greed.

It is better to have less with contentment than to be abundantly rich without peace of mind. Contentment has to be worked at, and there are certain dangers to be avoided.

1. We must resist the impulse to try to keep up with the Joneses.

2. We must reject getting rich as the supreme goal of our lives.

3. The poor man must be liberal with what he has or before God he is as guilty of covetousness as a rich man who refuses to share his goods with the less fortunate.

Let it not be here assumed that it is a sin to be rich; far from it. It is the love of money that is the root of all evil, but money itself may be a great blessing in the right hands. For greatest good it must be shared. Adding land to land and bonds to bonds only increases the desire for more of what one already has. By contrast a sharing heart is a caring heart. By consistent, generous giving, covetousness is starved and will at last disappear.

Thus Christianity in essence is reciprocal giving. God gave His Son; we yield our lives to Him; He gives Himself to us and through us to others.

TWO MASTERS

No man can serve two masters: for either he will hate the one, and love the other; or else he will hold to the one, and despise the other. Ye cannot serve God and mammon. Matt. 6:24.

Christ and Satan are masters. Let there be no misunderstanding here. Christ would have the whole man or none at all. "I the Lord thy God am a jealous God" (Ex. 20:5). Again and again in Scripture He asserts this on the basis of His authority and His claim on the total affections of man. "Thou shalt love the Lord thy God with all thy heart, and with all thy soul, and with all thy strength, and with all thy mind" (Luke 10:27). As one man has put it, "God must be Lord of all or He is not Lord at all." This is also true of Satan. Despite the nature of his blandishments, he has but one objective—to dethrone God from the heart and to assume total control of the life. The approach may seem innocent enough. It is by this very means that he deceives his prey. Men play with sin as with a toy, unaware of its danger and its despotic nature.

It is said that a young woman at a time of religious interest sat down and wrote out all the reasons she could think of to help her decide whom she should serve. She wrote, "(1) Reasons why I should serve the evil one, (2) Reasons why I should serve the Lord." She was surprised that she could find no satisfactory reasons for the first, but very urgent ones for the second. She acted upon her reason and gave herself to God and was blessed.

A Hartford minister exchanged his pulpit with that of the chaplain of the Connecticut State Prison. As he arose in the desk he saw among the prisoners a friend of his youth. Their eyes met, and they recognized each other. At the conclusion of the service he sought the man to learn his history.

"We were boys together in the same neighborhood, went to the same school, and we sat on the same seat and my prospects were as bright as yours," said the prisoner. "At fourteen," he continued, "you embraced religion, but I chose the world and sin. You are now an honored minister of the gospel and I an outcast from society, committed here for life."

HOW TO CONTACT GOD

I love them that love me; and those that seek me early shall find me. **Prov. 8:17.**

Primary in our search for God is the matter of personal faith. "But without faith it is impossible to please him" (Heb. 11:6). God must be trusted. His credibility has been established. Nearly six thousand years of record exists of God's dealings with man. There is no logical reason why we cannot place our faith in Him. He has demonstrated His power to save, to heal, and to deliver. If we would have the blessing of His presence, we must believe in Him as Creator, Redeemer, and Friend. The poet Whittier wrote:

"Through the dark and stormy night
Faith beholds a feeble light
Up the blackness streaking;
Knowing God's own time is best,
In patient hope I rest
For the full day-breaking!"

Second in our search for God is repentance. "Except ye repent, ye shall all likewise perish" (Luke 13:3). Repentance literally means a change of attitude toward sin. We are born with a natural inclination to do wrong, and all have followed that inclination. "All we like sheep have gone astray" (Isa. 53:6). "For all have sinned, and come short of the glory of God" (Rom. 3:23). Sin separates man from God. There must come a change in man's attitude toward sin if contact is to be re-established. We must want to be free from our sins. There must be a reversal of will. Fellowship with Christ must be desired and actively sought. The deep movings of the Spirit of God will produce in us a revulsion toward our sins. There must be no resistance to this work, for by it the soul is brought into communion with God.

Then comes obedience. "And whatsoever we ask, we receive of him, because we keep his commandments, and do those things that are pleasing in his sight" (1 John 3:22). Obedience is active cooperation with God. It is allowing Him to mold the life after the revealed scriptural pattern. Obedience to God's will is the natural outgrowth of the faith-repentance relationship.

LOVE ONE ANOTHER

For this is the message that ye heard from the beginning, that we should love one another. 1 John 3:11.

The most neglected doctrine in all the Bible is that of brotherly love. I do not claim that it is not taught; rather that it is not generally practiced. In the fourth chapter of 1 John alone, we are reminded repeatedly, "Beloved, let us love one another. . . . He that loveth not knoweth not God. . . . Beloved, if God so loved us, we ought also to love one another. . . . If we love one another, God dwelleth in us, and his love is perfected in us. . . . If a man say, I love God, and hateth his brother, he is a liar" (verses 7-20).

Men will give their money to establish medical and educational facilities for peoples in lands afar and flatter themselves that they have given evidence of love, but when brought face to face with some of the peoples they have so generously helped, they find themselves uncomfortable in their presence. They are unable to break with tradition and convention and show a spirit of genuine fellowship and brotherly kindness. Such things as marriage, special invitations to one's home for birthdays, and other celebrations are personal, and one has the right and the privilege of inviting whom he will to such functions. However, in the general areas of basic fellowship and good will and service, all special privilege must yield before the love of God. It was this that moved Jesus to fellowship with the Samaritan woman at the well. He prolonged this conversation until the disciples returned, and of them the Scripture says they "marvelled that he talked with the woman." Basic good will and friendliness and genuine human kindness are a debt that we owe to all men without regard to race, color, religion, or circumstances of birth. The Bible does not say that we should love those who are like us or look like us but rather "love one another, as I have loved you" (John 15:12). The commandment to love goes even deeper than this. "Love your enemies, do good to them which hate you" (Luke 6:27).

Here then is the supreme test of love. Have we so emptied our hearts of self before the Lord in daily devotions that we can treat even our enemies with kindness and respect? This is a high calling indeed.

YOUR CONFIDENCE

Cast not away therefore your confidence, which hath great recompence of reward. Heb. 10:35.

A little orphan child was taken into a strange family, and when being put to bed the first night, knelt down to say her evening prayers, repeating the words her mother had taught her. Then she added a prayer of her own, "O God, make these people just as good to me as my own dear father and mother were. Please do it, Jesus." Then after pausing a moment she exclaimed, "Of course, You will." It is necessary to life that we maintain our confidence in God. In an increasingly materialistic, secular world where men would rule God out of human society altogether, cast not away your confidence.

1. We must have confidence in God's willingness to save from sin. Too many people in our world today neglect to ask forgiveness, fearing that God would not hear them. Their awareness of personal unworthiness stands like a block between them and the Saviour. When will men realize that Jesus Christ is a friend of sinners? Again and again He demonstrated this fact while walking among men. He permitted Magdalene to anoint His feet with oil. He conversed freely with the Samaritan woman who with her own lips confessed moral laxity, but His close association with Judas Iscariot should dispel all doubt as to His ability to fraternize with sinners for their salvation.

2. We must have confidence in His ability to save. The Bible says, "He is able also to save them to the uttermost" (Heb. 7:25) and that He "is able to keep you from falling" (Jude 24) and further that "if we confess our sins, he is faithful and just to forgive us our sins, and to cleanse us from all unrighteousness" (1 John 1:9). Finally, "Fear thou not; for I am with thee: be not dismayed; for I am thy God: I will strengthen thee; yea, I will help thee; yea, I will uphold thee with the right hand of my righteousness" (Isa. 41:10).

3. We must believe in His immediate availability. Christ is only a prayer away. His grace is not only adequate; it is available every hour. "Lo, I am with you alway, even unto the end of the world" (Matt. 28:20). Christ assures His followers, "I will never leave thee, nor forsake thee" (Heb. 13:5).

130

DIVINE SURVEILLANCE

God looked down from heaven upon the children of men, to see if there were any that did understand, that did seek God. Ps. 53:2.

God wants to be understood. Why else would He expose us to such a flood of information concerning Himself? The sixty-six books of the Bible are a revelation of God's love for man. Repeatedly He reassures us of this fact. The Creator recognizes that all of the misery that has come to man is a result of his own transgression. The devil has sought to represent the troubles that beset the human family as judgments from God and would thus misrepresent His character. Now, the problems that beset the human family are many and complex. They are problems of war and of peace, of disease and crime, of natural disaster and famine, plus a variety of related ills.

One young man said to me, "I cannot conceive of a God who would permit these things to continue while at the same time professing love for the human family." My answer was simple, "For God to destroy sin itself would involve the destruction of the sinner, and God loves that sinner and gives him time and opportunity to repent of his sins, but if God should rise up immediately and cut men off, He would be subjected to the charge that He did not love man or He would have given him more time to repent." Disasters and other ills are consequences of sin. Man brought this misery upon his own head by an arbitrary act of the will. Man reaps what he sows. The distress and trouble in the earth are permitted because God would withhold the ultimate justice until the good news of His saving grace penetrates to the ends of the earth. Our text pictures Him looking down from heaven upon His children to see if there were any that did understand.

The revelation of love contained in the gospel inspires men to seek after God. The knowledge that God loves us in spite of our waywardness and backsliding is enough to inspire the vilest sinner to reciprocate that love. It is thus that the weak become strong and broken lives are mended. "Be astonished, O ye heavens, and sing for joy, ye sons of earth; for salvation is created and an effectual door of hope is opened to the vilest sinner."

OF TIME AND PURPOSE

To every thing there is a season, and a time to every purpose under the heaven. Eccl. 3:1.

Man's allotted time on earth is threescore and ten years. He does not spend all that time doing any one thing. Our lives are generally made up of worship, work, and recreation. Our work concerns itself with the earning of a livelihood, our service to God, and our service to our fellow man. Our worship concerns itself with adoration to God alone. Our recreation usually involves physical exercise, mental relaxation, and social contacts. Undergirding all this are the years of preparation for all three. Our text states that there is a time and purpose for everything under the sun. In order to live balanced lives time must be allotted for all the various functions of man. Psalm 90: 12 says, "So teach us to number our days, that we may apply our hearts unto wisdom." It is important that all the various aspects of human activity be assigned their proper time, priority being given to that which is of prime importance. We are told, "Seek ye first the kingdom of God, and his righteousness; and all these things shall be added unto you" (Matt. 6:33). It would seem proper, then, that we begin each day with worship and with a seeking after God. Since we are enjoined to "pray without ceasing," it would appear that throughout our daily lives we may with profit consult God on every decision, major or minor.

But life is not all work and worship. There is a time and a place for wholesome recreation. Any activity that does not compromise one's spiritual welfare or endanger it is legitimate. There are some Christians who are afraid of laughter and enjoyment. The capacity to laugh and be joyous is a God-given gift. It is a release from the tensions that plague the human family. "A merry heart doeth good like a medicine." There is no tonic like mirth; however, this also has its limitations, and there is a time to be sober. The prayer of the heart should be, "So teach us to number our days, that we may apply our hearts unto wisdom." The Bible teaches that the fear of the Lord is the beginning of wisdom. To this high and holy purpose we need to apply our hearts.

MY ROCK

To shew that the Lord is upright: he is my rock, and there is no unrighteousness in him. Ps. 92:15.

There are many symbols used to depict various aspects of the nature of God. One of those symbols is the rock. It signifies stability and that which is unchanging in nature. It is also unshakable and indestructible. Christ Himself spoke of a man building his house upon shifting sands and of its being swept away by the raging storm. By contrast, the house built upon a rock withstood all that the raging winds and pounding tides could offer. There is clearly taught here the necessity of cementing one's relationship with Christ as the bedrock foundation for all spiritual exercise.

It should be understood that all activities that claim the time of the Christian are without merit before God except they be founded in this Creator-creature relationship. Indeed our obedience is an outgrowth of our personal experience with Christ. This is the meaning of Matthew 11:28: "Come unto me, all ye that labour and are heavy laden, and I will give you rest." Obedience becomes a restful experience when it is founded upon the rock of Christ Jesus. It thus becomes more than conformity to a set of rules and becomes instead a joyful expression of love to Christ. The rock also provides shelter in the time of storm. It is a defense against the breakers that roar against its immovable surface. Well may we pray, "Hide me in the cleft of the rock 'til these dangers be overpast."

The rock is also a symbol of permanence. Not only is it immovable and protective but it is enduring. "I am Alpha and Omega, the beginning and the end, the first and the last" (Rev. 22:13).

A young Welsh minister, going to a place exposed to the ocean, slept at a farmhouse on the highest point of land in the vicinity. After he retired to rest a wind blew in the tempest and the rain beat upon the house heavily, and he feared that it must fall. He could not rest. He arose and sat by the fire to prepare for the worst. His host did not even awaken. The next morning the minister inquired as to the reason for his calm. "Oh," he said, "I settled that when I built this house. You see, I built it on a rock."

SOUR GRAPES

What mean ye, that ye use this proverb concerning the land of Israel, saying, The fathers have eaten sour grapes, and the children's teeth are set on edge? Eze. 18:2.

Much of the sin of any given generation may be credited in part to the one preceding it. The sins of the fathers have their effect on the sons. It is literally true that either by memory of evil example or by transmitted traits the succeeding generation's teeth are set on edge by the sour grapes consumed by their fathers. I think of the preachments of the last century against the observance of the law of God. All the arguments come back to me now. "The law was nailed to the cross," or "The law is for the Jews," or "Nobody ever kept the law anyhow and nobody ever will," or "Grace has taken the place of law." These were the sour grapes that our fathers ate, and what we behold is the sad harvest of their children's teeth being set on edge. We see this in the new morality that is sweeping the land, which is in effect the old immorality. It is a breaking down of old guidelines or simply denying their existence or ignoring them.

Arrogant in their new-found misery, this generation proceeds from one excess to another and from one level of unhappiness to another. We are on the verge of total release from all semblance of restraint. Revolt has become a way of life. The older generation sowed the wind in disobedience. Their children are reaping the whirlwind of lawless living. But millions of men have broken the shackles of tradition and heredity by individually laying hold on the mighty arm of God by faith. Thus the cycle of sinful continuity is broken and His promise of mercy fulfilled.

A teacher was explaining to her class the words concerning God's angels, "Ministers of his, that do his pleasure." Then she asked, "How do the angels carry out God's will?" Many answers followed. One said, "They do it directly." Another said, "They do it with all their heart." A third said, "They do it well." After a pause a quiet little girl added, "They do it without asking any questions." How thought provoking are all these answers. Implicit obedience will counteract all inherited tendencies to evil.

THOUGH FEEBLE—NECESSARY

Nay, much more those members of the body, which seem to be more feeble, are necessary. 1 Cor. 12:22.

Twentieth-century living has brought about a change in concepts of industrial production. The assembly line is one of its typical operations. A man may stand in one place all day long just screwing on a particular bolt to the body of each automobile on the assembly line. Suppose at a given day he may underestimate the importance of what he is doing and deal with a slack hand? The purchasers of automobiles from that assembly line will be the ones to suffer.

The church has been compared with the human body. That all of the members of the human body are necessary to total body function is generally understood. The slightest disability will reflect itself in a faulty performance. And so it is with the church—the body of Christ. The most apparently insignificant member is necessary to the total body function.

A little boy only six years old who had developed a remarkable music precocity had been for some time on exhibition in various Eastern cities as a violinist, drawing crowded houses and eliciting hearty plaudits. His manager noticed indications of exhaustion and decided to give him a rest. While sleeping with his father, after a matinee at which he had been greatly excited, he was heard to murmur, "Merciful God, make room for a little fellow." These were his last words, and when the lights were brought, he was dead.

In the great plan of salvation God has indeed made room for little fellows. It is just this aspect of the gospel that appeals to so many humble peoples of the earth. In His own day it was said that "the common people heard him gladly" (Mark 12:37). The gospel emphasizes the dignity of the individual and the significance of every human being. A pagan and secular society is just the opposite. It favors the strong, the wealthy, and the refined. It would give first place to these. To this form of thought human life is cheap. Contrariwise, Christianity brought to civilized men a sense of the value of human life and in the great plan of God even little children play a prominent role.

THY KEEPER

The Lord is thy keeper: the Lord is thy shade upon thy right hand. **Ps. 121:5.**

Many people fail to follow Christ because they have great doubts about their ability to continue once they have begun. The question of the maintenance of a covenant relationship with Christ is a real one, and to desire reassurance on this point is only natural. We should admit at the outset that if the maintenance of our Christian experience rested solely with us, there would indeed be no need to start. Man is somehow incapable himself of traveling a straight course, because of his fallen nature consequent to the sin of Adam. Our faith, therefore, must be in another. The psalmist reassures us, "The Lord is thy keeper." "The Lord shall preserve thee from all evil: he shall preserve thy soul. The Lord shall preserve thy going out and thy coming in from this time forth, and even for evermore" (Ps. 121:7, 8).

Charles Spurgeon tells of two men in a boat approaching Niagara Falls. They found themselves unable to manage it and soon they were in the water and being carried swiftly down the current to that place where they must both inevitably be dashed to pieces. Persons on the shore saw them, but were unable to do much for their rescue. At last, however, one man was saved by a floating rope which he grasped. The same instant the rope came into his hand, a log floated by the other man. The thoughtless and confused bargeman, instead of seizing the rope, laid hold on the log. It was a fatal mistake. Both were in imminent peril, but the one was drawn to shore because he had the connection with the people on the land, while the other, clinging to the log, was borne irresistibly along and was never heard of afterward.

The consistent Christian has a living connection with Christ. This bears him up in the dangerous rapids and pulls him ashore safely at last. First attention, then, must be given to the building of a meaningful saving relationship with Christ. Faith and repentance must be man's daily spiritual exercise. God is not only a preserver of our souls but a lifeguard as well. He is pledged to our rescue.

LIGHT AT EVENTIDE

And after these things I saw another angel come down from heaven, having great power; and the earth was lightened with his glory. **Rev. 18:1.**

At this, the sunset hour of earth's history, there is promise of abundant light to guide God's people through the deepening darkness. In our text light is equated with the knowledge of God. In short, the revelation of God's character will literally blanket the earth before His second coming. We see herein pictured the triumph of the gospel. Every convert will become a convert maker and each church member will become a living witness. For this the world in ignorance suffers. To meet this commitment, what is our greatest need? "But ye shall receive power, after that the Holy Ghost is come upon you: and ye shall be witnesses unto me both in Jerusalem, and in all Judaea, and in Samaria, and unto the uttermost part of the earth" (Acts 1:8). We have often heard it said that the greatest need of the church is baptism of the Holy Ghost. I would like to amend that statement to read, "The greatest need of the church is for each individual member to be personally baptized of the Holy Spirit." You see, the need of the church is the sum total of individual human needs, and unless and until men enter upon this work individually the church can only do in a measure her assigned task.

An infidel in conversation with a Christian was overheard to observe, "If I believed what you say you believe, I could get no rest day nor night until everybody in my neighborhood, and indeed the city, became aware of what I knew." There are signs even now that the church is shaking off her lethargy. The seed-sowing potential of the Voice of Prophecy, Faith for Today, and many Bible schools across the nation is now becoming readily apparent in many of the giant reaping campaigns taking place across the world. Baptisms are on the increase. There is a strange stirring among the people of God. The Holy Spirit is arousing the church for her final task for a demonstration of power that will be awesome to witness. Evil long so dominant is yet to be struck its most telling blow. Demons will tremble, and saints rejoice. Hasten on, glad day!

SATAN TRANSFORMED

And no marvel; for Satan himself is transformed into an angel of light. 2 Cor. 11:14.

Demons often impersonate the dead. Our text admonishes us not to be surprised if Satan himself does this and pays us a visit. On the surface, this would seem to be but idle demon play, but there is something far more sinister involved here. As you know, the Bible teaches that when a man dies he is totally unconscious and will remain so until the resurrection morning. By imitating the dead the devil undermines confidence in the truthfulness of the Word of God. He paves the way for the teaching of unscriptural doctrines through these satanic imitators. Imagine with what force error may be propagated through a demon transformed as an esteemed departed relative! By using this avenue of approach, the devil may more readily gain control of the unsuspecting soul, turning the soul into a playground for devils. This type of demoniac activity is talked of much in the Scriptures. Such a masquerade paves the way for Satan's eventual imitation of Christ, which will be the master delusion. It will be the final masquerade. The song writer says:

"There are two guides for travelers, only two guides:
One's the good Shepherd, e'en through the death tides;
The other, the serpent, beguiling with sin
Whose beauty external hides poison within."

Satan has managed through the ages by devious methods to mask his poison, but after the last great deception of imitating Christ, he will then stand unmasked and proceed without the benefit of cover, and his true nature will be exposed. This happened once before on the hill of Calvary, where the Son of the living God withstood all the fury that hell could muster against a single individual. Were man a close observer he would mark this and be warned. The sufferings of Jesus Christ on the cross were more than an atonement for human sin. God further designed that we might discover once and for all the character of the enemy. His anger against Christ was so fierce that he could not restrain himself. In this we see a clear demonstration of the nature of evil and the power of love.

ABRAHAM'S SEED

And if ye be Christ's, then are ye Abraham's seed, and heirs according to the promise. Gal. 3:29.

The promise made to Abraham was that through him would all the nations of the earth be blessed; however, the Jews mistook the reasons for divine favor so lavishly conferred. They imagined themselves better than the Gentiles, who surrounded them, and shut themselves off behind a wall of seclusion, enjoying the blessings and benefits of the birthright in mercy conferred upon them and not sharing them with the nations round about. In consequence, with no overflow, they became a spiritually dead nation. And the invitation went out to all nations and men under the heavens, "Whosoever will, may come." Through Christ all men may become Jews spiritually and hence heirs to all the good things promised Abraham.

When the Jews revolted against the Romans and were finally crushed by Titus in A.D. 70, anything Jewish came under the scathing rebuke of Rome. This reacted unfavorably upon the church and accounts for the persecutions against Christianity in the early centuries. It became a byword among the Gentiles that anything Jewish was inferior and to be avoided at all costs. The Roman Church cultivated this anti-Semitic spirit in its war against the Sabbath and the law of God in general. Protestants who assign to the Jews those portions of Scripture to which they do not wish to bend the knee or surrender the heart inadvertently fall into this same spirit. Yet the Bible was written by Jews. The first preachers of the church were Jewish, and Jesus Christ our Saviour Himself was born of a Jewish mother. The names of the twelve sons of Jacob will be inscribed on the arches of the gates of the New Jerusalem. Jesus had the last words on this in John 4:22, "Ye worship ye know not what: we know what we worship: for salvation is of the Jews." Adoption into the family of Christ gives one the confidence to sing:

"My Father is rich in houses and lands;
He holdeth the wealth of the world in His hands!
Of rubies and diamonds, of silver and gold,
His coffers are full—He has riches untold."

139

ONCE TO DIE

And as it is appointed unto men once to die, but after this the judgment. Heb. 9:27.

Death is an enemy. It has been variously portrayed as a friend in order to ease its sting, but the sting of death is sin and this may be eased only through repentance and confession and faith in Christ's willingness and ability to save. So then, let us face death for what it is—an enemy; and second, let us face the fact that all men are appointed to die. Now, I well know that not all shall sleep, for some will be alive at the second coming of Christ. Nevertheless, it is appointed unto all men once to die whether or not they keep that appointment. But some will die twice. They will die the death appointed, which is the natural death consequent to sin, then they will die the second death, which is referred to by John in Revelation 21:8. John calls it "the lake which burneth with fire and brimstone: which is the second death." No one is appointed to this death. If he dies, it will be of his own choosing. The appointment is only that man once die.

I know of a physician who was a strong, stalwart Christian. From his sunny nature radiated good cheer to his patients. He had enough sunshine also for the frail little wife who needed all the vigor of his personality to sustain her. When the doctor suddenly passed away, friends said, "It will kill her. This will be the end of her." But the faith in God that the two had shared together did not fail her. By the doorway of the living room she hung the card that the doctor sometimes left during short absences on his office door. It read, "Gone out—back soon." She cherished that hope of being again with her loved one when Christ should come and gloriously resurrect the dead. What a challenging thought: "Gone out—back soon!" This is the Christian concept of death, and we approach our graves "like one who wraps the drapery of his couch About him, and lies down to pleasant dreams." This may be the experience of anyone who in this life cultivates his relationship with Christ. All fear of death is gone. Only hope of life in the hereafter radiates the soul and illumines the countenance.

SEND THEE HELP

The Lord hear thee in the day of trouble; the name of the God of Jacob defend thee; send thee help from the sanctuary, and strengthen thee out of Zion. Ps. 20:1, 2.

It was the day of a funeral. A heartbroken mother had to face the ordeal of seeing her son and daughter laid to rest on the same day. They had died about the same time on the same day and their funeral was at the Seventh-day Adventist church. She was an elderly mother, and the question on every heart was, "Will she be able to bear up under the pressure of grief?" I remember the day very well, for it was my lot to deliver the eulogy. This mother sat ramrod straight. Not a tear dropped from her eyes; in fact, there was a rather contented look on her face throughout the service. When it was over, I could not resist asking her, "How was it possible for you to bear such a staggering double load with such grace?" She answered, "If a person's religion is any good to him at all, it will certainly strengthen him in the day of trouble, and furthermore, Elder, I believe that Christ is coming. My hope is in the coming of the Lord. It is this that gives me strength to bear present burdens." I believe this woman's sincere testimony, that God literally sends help from His holy temple to every believing soul in the day of trial. His promise is, "I will strengthen thee; yea, I will help thee; yea, I will uphold thee with the right hand of my righteousness" (Isa. 41:10).

A little boy was observed patting his father's horse, which was standing in front of the house. A passer-by asked, "Can your horse go fast, my boy?" "No, not very," replied the little boy, "but he can stand fast." This world would be much better off if it had more people with strength to stand fast for the principles they know to be right.

Dwight Moody brought an eventful and Spirit-filled evangelistic meeting to its close. "Go home, my friends, and think it over, and we will come back Sunday and find out what you have decided," the evangelist said. Between the benediction and the next service Mrs. O'Leary's cow kicked over a lantern and large sections of the city of Chicago were destroyed. It changed Dwight Moody's preaching. Never again did he postpone a call to repentance.

IT IS FINISHED

When Jesus therefore had received the vinegar, he said, It is finished: and he bowed his head, and gave up the ghost. John 19:30.

The words of Jesus, "It is finished," signified that the divine human experiment for the salvation of man had been successfully completed. This the evil one had sought to prevent at all costs, for he realized that if Christ could live on this earth and die without sin, his own doom was sealed and the salvation of every believing Christian was assured. In this sense, then, the words, "It is finished," were a shout of triumph and not merely the reluctant last words of the dying. These words also signified that the atoning sacrifice for the sins of man was full and complete. The antitypical service that for more than three thousand years had required the continual slayings of lambs and the offering of their blood for atonement for sin had ceased. The true Lamb of God had at last been slain for the sins of the world. Henceforth men needed only to offer themselves in faith to Him who offered Himself in death for all. The words of our text also indicate that the second death is no longer a necessity, that lost men need die only once. In fact, the Saviour's death at Calvary was a substitutionary death for all our sins. By dying for me, He said in effect, "For you the fear of hell is finished. You need not experience it if by faith you accept My sacrifice for your sins." "It is finished" may mean to each of us the end of a life of sin, for His death provided blood—the symbol of new life—the balm that heals and saves from sin. Yes, there is a balm in Gilead, there is a Physician there. The wounded may be made whole. There is a cure for our delinquency.

> "Would you be free from your burden of sin?
> There's pow'r in the blood."

Men are overcoming sinful habits every day, some by the sheer exercise of the will power; yet others who are victims of compulsive habit are finding freedom and victory through faith in Christ. Thus drunkards become sober, philanderers become home-loving husbands, and thieves are made honest by the efficacious sacrifice of the only-begotten Son of the living God at Calvary for our sins.

MY SIDE

The Lord is on my side; I will not fear: what can man do unto me? Ps. 118:6.

As a little boy in my neighborhood in Chattanooga, Tennessee, I was often in danger of being attacked by juvenile gangs. Many mothers refused to send their children to the store unattended. More than once my journey on an errand was speeded up by one gang, which followed a policy of hot pursuit. One day I found a solution that should have been obvious all along. I asked my big brother to accompany me to the store. Now, my brother has always been rather large for his age. My assumption was that his bulging biceps would tend to discourage any belligerent youngsters from molesting me. One day I started to the store, walking well ahead of my brother. Knowing of my usual route, the gang had posted a lookout. Spotting me but not my escort, the gang sallied forth intent on watching me show my heels. It was then they discovered to their dismay that I was not alone. It was my pleasure to watch them show their heels.

In matters spiritual this is also true. Christ, our elder brother, has clearly demonstrated in times past His ability to cope with the enemy of our souls in any way on any battlefield. When there was war in heaven, it was Christ who was victorious over Lucifer, and when on earth Christ was confronted with the demon possessed, He expelled their evil spirits. The mark of the able fighter is not only his offensive tactics but his ability to take a punch. At Calvary Jesus clearly demonstrated that He could do just this, and it is grievous to contemplate when we remember that it was for us He suffered, bled, and died, and not for Himself. He could have delivered Himself. Instead, He took insult upon insult He did not merit. Such undeserved treatment made the Master's punishment almost unbearable, yet He bore it all for us.

We may then with confidence proceed against the enemy, for with Christ on our side, what have we to fear?

> "Be not dismayed whate'er betide,
> God will take care of you;
> Beneath His wings of love abide,
> God will take care of you."

THEM THAT OBEY

And being made perfect, he became the author of eternal salvation unto all them that obey him. Heb. 5:9.

Our text announces the good news that Christ is the author of our salvation in the sense that it is possible because of Him, and that it is possible for the Christian to live an obedient life because of this saving relationship. Few Christians wish to submit to the discipline of obedience. It is a sign of our times that men are restive under all disciplinary restraints. In the political world old social orders are yielding to the new. In economics time-honored principles of solvency are being surrendered in the highest and most respected economic circles to the new god of credit and get-rich quick. In the field of morals men are asserting a false liberty and erecting new standards by which to judge human behavior. In the realm of the spiritual there is an hypocrisy difficult to describe. Essentially it permits the Christian to profess ardent love for Christ and engage in all external religious forms while resisting the obedience to the law that grace demands.

In answer to this our Lord has said, "And why call ye me, Lord, Lord, and do not the things which I say?" (Luke 6:46), and "If ye love me, keep my commandments" (John 14:15). Obedience is a consequence of our love to God. It is a happy, willing relationship. It is an outgrowth of day-to-day companionship with our Creator, and the closer we get to God the more perfectly will our works reflect it.

A little boy is given an assigned task around the house. The parent expects defects in the job being done because of his son's age and lack of experience, but he can accept no lack of dedication and zeal on the part of the child. When the boy grows older and becomes more experienced, he is expected to improve in quality and quantity as far as his assignments are concerned. Familiarity with what his parents require and with the job itself will lead to progressive improvement in performance.

God cannot accept mistakes made in rebellion against Him, but what mistakes a Christian makes in the line of obedience He covers with His perfection. God says to His children, "I can tolerate your mistakes if I'm sure you are sincerely trying to do what I say."

JUSTIFIED

I tell you, this man went down to his house justified rather than the other: for every one that exalteth himself shall be abased; and he that humbleth himself shall be exalted. Luke 18:14.

Two worshipers are brought to view—one a Pharisee and the other a publican. They are indeed a study in contrasts.

Let us consider the Pharisee. He depended upon his performance of external forms. "I pay tithe." He boasted before the Lord. He compared himself with other men. "I am glad that I am not like other men," he said. The folly of comparing oneself with other faulty human beings is self-evident. Our only perfect pattern by which we may measure behavior is the absolutely perfect life of our Lord Jesus Christ. In spiritual things men who aspire to be like other men choose poor patterns, to say the least. The Pharisee depended upon his good deeds to qualify him before God. In a sense we may say that the Pharisee sought to buy God's favor in exchange for his own faithfulness in certain external forms. This churchman did not receive the blessing of God because his ostentatious worship was unacceptable.

Now, the publican typifies the true worshiper of God no matter how lowly. He knew his need. "God be merciful to me a sinner" (Luke 18:13) was his prayer. This is the proper attitude of worship. Such a soul will not leave the sanctuary without blessing. This worshiper had a measure of faith. He knew God to be a God of mercy, and his prayer was for God to be merciful to him. He believed he would be rewarded, therefore his confident petition. There was love in his heart. He was so sorry for his sins that he smote his breast. He had offended his Creator by some deed, some thought, or some word. His remorse was deep and genuine, and such remorse is born only of love. He had a strong desire to be free. "Be merciful to me," he pleads. "I have nothing to offer; I have nothing with which to commend myself. I throw myself on Your mercy, and I plead only Your merit. Do not judge me according to my works and do not give me my just deserts. Be merciful to me, a sinner." This humble plea won him clemency. He went down to his house justified, innocent, free from condemnation. Oh, that we might learn the grace of abasement.

THIS IS THE DAY

This is the day which the Lord hath made; we will rejoice and be glad in it. Ps. 118:24.

"Safely through another week God has brought us on our way." With what rejoicing the believer sings this old hymn!

The Bible states that the seventh day is the Sabbath. That Saturday is the seventh day few will deny, but the significance of this day is largely lost in the modern world. It is a memorial of Creation. We human beings are born surrounded by things that we did not make. They were here before our arrival. The Sabbath celebrates the finishing of the creation of the world and all that therein is. This is indeed the day the Lord hath made, the memorial of God's creative works. It is also an "emblem of eternal rest" for the Christian believer. Hebrews 4 uses the seventh-day Sabbath as an illustration of the heavenly rest that the Christian will enjoy in the heavenly Canaan. It is a day bright with promise of sweet rest with Christ throughout the eternal ages.

The Sabbath is also the day of physical rest in this life. It is appropriate that man work six days and rest at the end of his labors. The Sabbath day was placed at the end of the week that man might enjoy relaxation from the tensions of everyday living. I heard one housewife say, "I will be so happy when the Sabbath comes." I know what she meant, for no matter what was left undone when God's rest day came, it would remain undone until the first day of the week. The Sabbath is indeed the day of physical rest and spiritual refreshment. This is also the day of worship. We have the example of our Lord who "came to Nazareth, where he had been brought up: and, as his custom was, he went into the synagogue on the sabbath day, and stood up for to read." It is a day when God is worshiped in His holy temple; a day of fellowship with believers of like faith; a day of praise to God for all His wonderful works toward the children of men; and on this day we are to forsake not "the assembling of ourselves together, as the manner of some is; but exhorting one another: and so much the more, as ye see the day approaching" (Heb. 10:25).

Let us rejoice and be glad in this great sign of our allegiance—God's memorial day!

THEIR INVENTIONS

Thou answeredst them, O Lord our God: thou wast a God that forgavest them, though thou tookest vengeance of their inventions. Ps. 99:8.

The Bible says that "God hath made man upright; but they have sought out many inventions" (Eccl. 7:29). By implication these inventions have to do with transgression. Man has strayed from the uprightness of character with which he was originally infused, and his inventions in evil-doing will call forth the judgments of God. Since Adam and Eve partook of the forbidden fruit in the Garden of Eden, sin has assumed many diversified forms. It is difficult to conceive that there was a day when sin was nonexistent on this planet, that the one great test of man's allegiance to God was a tree that stood in the midst of the Garden which they were forbidden to touch. Partaking of the forbidden fruit was the original sinful invention. This opened up to man a whole encyclopedia of transgressive conduct until today, six thousand years later, man has literally run out the string, and simply bores himself by going over and over beaten sinful paths. When will the day come when man will understand that his only hope for happiness and lasting peace of mind lies in the realm of obedient faith? When the life is disciplined to the requirements of the divine will, there is a heavenly peace that pervades the soul that no earthly thing can destroy. The problems consequent to these sinful inventions have become more grievously complicated, producing in man new depths of unhappiness, frustration, and misery.

I talked with a well-known entertainer who gave up show business for Christ. I mentioned to her that while in the world she had given evidence of great happiness with a smile that was literally sunshine in itself. "How do you explain this?" I asked. "Oh," she answered, "that was my professional smile. I did it during my acts, and for photographers, but you may be sure that there was little genuine joy in my heart. I was a chain smoker, I drank stimulants to relieve my tensions, and took sleeping pills to go to sleep at night. That smile? Well, that was how I made my living, but if I had been as happy as that smile would indicate, I would never have left show business."

HUMBLE YOURSELVES

Humble yourselves therefore under the mighty hand of God, that he may exalt you in due time. 1 **Peter** 5:6.

The secret of Christ's power with men was His humility. This grace seems to be foreign to the natural human heart. We usually associate power with rippling muscles and bulging biceps, or in a military sense with an adequately stocked atomic arsenal, or in the language of the automotive industry with one of the $16,000 to $50,000 "bombshells" that race at Indianapolis once a year, or in pugilistic circles with the man who has a knockout punch. These are carnal concepts. According to the Scriptures spiritual power is generated when the human heart is surrendered fully to the will of Christ. This requires humility. There can be no self-assertiveness in man's relationship to God. Cooperation with Him must be total and entire. Surrender must be without condition.

There are two ways to develop genuine humility. First, through trial. This incidentally is the usual method by which God humbles men. Remember the encounter of Christ with the apostle Paul on the road to Damascus. The encounter cost the apostle Paul his sight for three days and nearly his life. It is dangerous to delay humbling oneself until God lays His disciplines upon us. The case of Nebuchadnezzar is one in point. You will recall that not until he was deprived of reason for seven years, was he sufficiently humbled to acknowledge the God of heaven, the Most High who ruleth in the kingdoms of men.

To humble us, God may bring us into a state that may prove totally discouraging. Take the case of Jonah. He almost lost his life by not submitting to the will of God. In the belly of the "great fish" he was humbled to promise God that he would cooperate with His blessed will if extricated from his predicament. But developing humility under duress is doing it the hard way. The second way is a better one. It is found in the counsel of the apostle James: "Submit yourselves therefore to God. Resist the devil, and he will flee from you" (James 4:7). Yes, it is by voluntary submissiveness through prayer and exercise of the will to the disciplines of our daily routines that a man humbles himself.

148

IT IS BETTER

It is better to trust in the Lord than to put confidence in man.
Ps. 118:8.

Some explorers were high in the mountains, seeking a rare flower. Gazing down the mountainside, on a precarious ledge one of the scientists saw the flower they sought so eagerly. But how to get it was the problem. Of course, they had rope, but there were not enough men to allow one of them to descend in safety. A little boy, obviously a resident of the area, sat studying them quizzically as they debated just what to do. Suddenly one of them thought of the little fellow and approached him, asking, "Little boy, allow us to tie this rope around your waist and lower you to yonder ledge so you can get us the flower." The boy peered cautiously down the precipice to the ledge and said, "Wait just a minute," and disappeared in the bush. A few minutes later he returned holding a large man by the hand. "All right, you can strap me in," he said.

"Who is this?" the scientist asked.

"Oh, this is my father," replied the boy, "and I don't mind going down the precipice so long as his hand is on the rope."

A train was speeding along the tracks at ninety miles an hour. Some of the passengers were uneasy, but a little girl was noticed gazing placidly out the window. Someone asked her, "Little girl, aren't you frightened at the train traveling at such speed?"

"No, I'm not afraid," she said. "My father is the engineer."

A boat was slowly threading its way through the fog. The passengers down on the deck huddled together, wondering whether each moment would be their last. One passenger was serenely reclining in a deck chair. Someone asked him, "Sir, do you know where we are?" "No," he said, "I guess I don't." "Aren't you worried about what might happen in this fog?" "Well, no," he replied, "I'm afraid I'm not worried at all, for up there on the bridge this boat has a captain, and he knows where we are. I trust him."

Men are fickle and often untrustworthy, but Jesus Christ is the same today, yesterday, and forever. And to all who trust Him the promise comes, "I will never leave thee, nor forsake thee."

TALK YE

Sing unto him, sing psalms unto him: talk ye of all his wondrous works. **Ps.** 105:2.

"People will talk," and much of our state of mind is produced by what people say. It is true that out of the abundance of the heart the mouth speaketh, but it is equally true that what the mouth speaketh influences one's state of mind. How important it is then that we talk and sing of the wondrous works of God. This will cheer up our spirits, firm up our courage, and make us living advertisements of the joy that comes from serving God.

In a certain country I got up early in the morning and went walking while the day was still cool. There were people sleeping on the sidewalks. As I threaded my way among them I came upon the form of a man who was covered by a blanket from head to toe. The sidewalk was his bed but from beneath that blanket I heard a cheerful little tune being sung. I was rebuked in my heart, for is it not true that many of us with material advantages are unthankful and unhappy and often fretful, and yet this man with only a blanket over him and the concrete sidewalk under him had a song in his heart and on his lips. "O give thanks unto the Lord; for he is good: for his mercy endureth for ever" (Ps. 106:1).

Dr. Spurgeon says, "There is nothing like singing to keep your spirits alive." When we have been in trouble we have often thought ourselves well-nigh overwhelmed with difficulty, and we have said, "Let us sing a song," and we have begun to sing. Martin Luther said that the devil cannot bear singing. That is about the truth. He does not like music praising God. It was so in Saul's day. An evil spirit rested on Saul, but when David played on his harp the evil spirit went from the king. This is usually the case. If we can begin to sing, we can remove our fears.

Hugh Thompson Kerr has said, "Christianity came into the world on the wings of song." Infidelity never sings. Unbelief has no music, no anthems, no hymns, no oratorios, no symphonies. When Robert Ingersoll died, the printed notice of his funeral said, "There will be no singing." Thank God for the triumphant songs of the gospel.

150

MUCH BETTER

Behold the fowls of the air: for they sow not, neither do they reap, nor gather into barns; yet your heavenly Father feedeth them. Are ye not much better than they? Matt. 6:26.

To every life there comes a crisis at some time or another. In our immediate text the reference is that of physical need. The tendency of man to worry when there is an acute shortage of material things is here dealt with. The suggestion in this verse is that if the fowls of the air neither reap nor sow nor gather into barns and yet are fed, why should not man, who works for his living, trust God to make up the difference between need and supply out of His boundless resources.

The futility of worry is pictured in verse 27: "Which of you by taking thought can add one cubit unto his stature?" Here is no injunction to be mentally lazy. Rather it is an encouragement that we mark the difference between what can be helped and what cannot.

W. M. Punshon was quoted in the book, *Six Thousand Sermon Illustrations,* "It is a beneficent arrangement of Providence that the divinity which shapes our ends weaves our sorrows into elements of character and that all disappointments and conflicts to which the living are subject—the afflictions, physical and mental, personal and relative, which are the common lot—may, rightly used, become the means of improvement and create in us sinews of strength. Trouble is a marvelous mortifier of pride and an effectual restrainer of self-will. Difficulties string up the energies and intensity is gained from repression. By sorrow the temper is mellowed and the feeling is refined. When suffering has broken up the soil and made the furrow soft, there can be implanted the hearty virtues which outbrave the storm."

So when plagued with shortages of material goods and trouble of any kind, let us recognize in these things the Hand of divine providence, purging the dross, purifying the metal, and that if we trust in God He will bring us out more than conqueror.

There is a Negro spiritual that says, "Leave it there, leave it there. Take your burden to the Lord and leave it there. If you trust and never doubt, He will surely bring you out. Take your burden to the Lord and leave it there."

OUR DEBTS

And forgive us our debts, as we forgive our debtors. Matt. 6:12.

In this portion of the Lord's Prayer, we acknowledge that God's forgiveness is conditional on our own. How indeed may we expect Him to forgive us when we refuse to forgive our fellow men their debts? The Bible tells of a man who owed his master much but who was graciously forgiven. This same man turned on his debtor who owed him much less and had him thrown into prison for his failure to pay, and upon his head came the wrath of his own master, who repaid such base ingratitude by inflicting upon him the full penalty of the law. The principle is, freely you have been forgiven, freely forgive.

Necessary to this attitude, however, is the spirit of humility. When one recognizes his own frailty, he will not be so exacting on another. It is the cruel spirit of the Pharisee against which this portion of our Lord's Prayer is directed. Sinful man is a more exacting judge than is a sinless God. Witness the men who dragged the poor woman before Jesus, saying she was caught in adultery. Their desire was to stone her forthwith. Hypocritically they sought the advice of Jesus. He simply began to write in the soil. One by one the woman's judges silently slipped away. Inspiration tells us that He was recording some of their own sins. Their uncompromising spirit, lack of forgiveness, and cruel heartlessness disqualified them from being effective petitioners. There is no forgiveness for the unforgiving.

A boy who had done a wrong and confessed it was put on bread and water for three days as punishment. On the morning of the third day, his father asked him how he liked his fare. The child answered, "I can eat it very well, Papa, but I don't much like it." After a moment's silence, he asked, "Can't you forgive me, Papa?" The father answered, "No, son, I cannot. My word has passed, and you must take your punishment." The boy then said, "Papa, then how could you say the Lord's Prayer this morning?" Struck with the child's reproof, the father ordered the bread and water removed, and said with evident emotion, "My boy, you've preached me a better sermon than I ever preached in all my life."

THE WOMAN

And the dragon was wroth with the woman, and went to make war with the remnant of her seed, which keep the commandments of God, and have the testimony of Jesus Christ. **Rev. 12:17.**

The woman referred to here is the church. Her identifying marks are clear: she has the testimony of Jesus Christ, and she keeps His commandments. All religion may be measured by this twofold yardstick and the true separated from the false. Salvation by grace through faith in Christ is the testimony of Jesus that must be on every saint's lips. The keeping of the commandments of God manifests the reality of this testimony. We thus have the measuring stick by which we may determine the true church from the false. The lines are clear and distinct. The true church will accept Christ as Saviour and uphold His law.

In a search for the true church, there are those who look for a communion of believers who are without fault. That this is a false measurement is clearly evident from the fact that if this rule were used on the early New Testament church, it would not pass the test. Paul's admonitions prove them to have been faulty. The same is true of ancient Israel, the Old Testament church. There were times when the members themselves were anything but exemplary in their conduct. In short, there have been hypocrites in all ages, and the tares will grow with the wheat until the harvest, or the end of the world. However, in every era there have been those who have been true and faithful to the testimony of Jesus Christ and obedient to the Ten Commandments. These have ever been the salt of the earth, for they embody in their lives what they profess with their lips. Members of the true church may expect the unmingled wrath of Satan to be directed against them in these last days. He will attack doctrine, besmear reputations, and insinuate doubt concerning the church's mission in the earth. But unswerving loyalty will mark every believer.

As spiritual apostasy progresses, the line between those who serve the Lord and those who serve Him not will become more clearly distinguishable until that day when every honest heart has joined the people of God and every hypocrite has shown his true colors.

FOLLOW THOU

Jesus saith unto him, If I will that he tarry till I come, what is that to thee? follow thou me. John 21:22.

The apostle Peter was a man of extremes, as is indicated by his preconversion declaration that though all men should forsake the Lord, he would be faithful, and after his conversion showing concern about John, his fellow disciple. Christ had just signified prophetically that Peter would die by crucifixion. Observing John standing nearby, Peter inquired as to just what his end would be. "Lord, and what shall this man do?" he asked. Christ assured him that it was none of his business and that if He willed that John should live until the Second Coming, Peter's first concern should be to follow Christ himself: "Follow thou me."

While it is true that a Christian is responsible for the example he sets before others, it is equally true that his primary concern must be that he order his own footsteps aright. We are accountable to and for others only to the extent that we lead them astray or fail to share with them the light that we have. Curiosity as to their destiny or to the role they are to play in the plan of God is primarily their own business and God's. This lesson He sought to teach the apostle Peter. He said to him in effect, "Peter, you have your hands full fulfilling your own destiny. Leave John to Me, and if I will to minister differently through him than through you, what business is it of yours? Follow thou Me." And we may thank God that Peter did just this. He followed Christ all the way to his own martyrdom.

Samuel Salter has said, "That flower that follows the sun doth so even in cloudy days when it doth not shine forth, yet it follows the hidden course and motion of it. So the soul that moves after God keeps that course even when He hides His face, and is content, yea is glad, at His will in all estates or conditions or wants."

Our pledge must be the words of the song: "Where He leads me I will follow, I'll go with Him all the way." And the further pledge of another song: "If Jesus goes with me, I'll go anywhere," for anywhere He leads us we can safely go. Can anyone safely follow in your steps?

PENTECOST

And when the day of Pentecost was fully come, they were all with one accord in one place. Acts 2:1.

Morris has said, "Next to the day of Christ's death the Day of Pentecost was the greatest day that ever dawned on our world. It was the first day of the last and best dispensation of revealed religion. It was, as it has been called, the birthday of the Christian Church. It was the first day of the new creation in which the elements which had previously existed in a state of chaotic confusion began to be fashioned and arranged by the plastic power of the Spirit of glory and of God." Yes, on Pentecost the power came to the church in fullest measure. The disciples met the condition of the reception of the Holy Ghost, for "they were all with one accord." They confessed their faults one to the other, asked forgiveness for offensive words and deeds, making way for the outpouring of the Holy Ghost.

While it is true that the Holy Spirit is responsible for man's most primitive impulses toward God, it is our happy privilege to crave more and more of this power in our lives, and we have the assurance that if we meet the conditions, the Spirit will come.

"By prayer and confession of sin we must clear the King's highway. As we do this, the power of the Spirit will come to us. We need the Pentecostal energy. This will come; for the Lord has promised to send His Spirit as the all-conquering power."—*Testimonies,* vol. 8, pp. 297, 298.

And so it was with the church at Pentecost. The full revelation of the availability of divine power at last dawned upon their waiting hearts, and they claimed this power by faith unexcelled in succeeding time. The preaching of the Word was incandescent.

How long we have been living beneath our privileges! What a difference it would make if we would but realize that there is power available for all our needs. When a man knows that, he can mount up with wings as the eagle. He can run and not be weary; he can walk and not faint. He deals boldly with life.

Have you surrendered your life to Christ? Once this happens you will release Pentecostal power in your life.

155

UPSIDE DOWN

The Lord preserveth the strangers; he relieveth the fatherless and widow: but the way of the wicked he turneth upside down. Ps. 146:9.

Christians have been known to envy the wicked for their apparent prosperity. On the surface it would appear that there is a higher premium on wickedness than on righteousness, for the righteous are often persecuted in this world. However, Isaiah 57:21 is clear: "There is no peace, saith my God, to the wicked." Sin is deceptive. It remains attractive just long enough to ensnare its victim, then suddenly his world is literally turned upside down. He must keep up a constant round of activity to quiet the voice of his conscience.

Spiritually the sinner is lost. His world is upside down whether he knows it or not. His habits of life are inverted. If he is ever to be saved, he will need to be born again. His eating, drinking, and recreational habits are all out of line with Bible principles, and his devotional life is literally starved from neglect. His "cup" will need to be righted before he can be of service to God and fellow man. In another sense God turneth the sinner upside down. By living contrary to the elementary laws of morality and nature, man calls upon his own head the retributive hand of God, and so it is that in this life the sinner's castle begins to collapse. Not alone in this world but in the judgment to come he will find himself literally turned upside down. It is a portion of the wages of sin, and for sin there is but one remedy: "Repent ye therefore, and be converted, that your sins may be blotted out, when the times of refreshing shall come from the presence of the Lord" (Acts 3:19).

But what does it mean to repent? Francis Fuller says, "To repent is to accuse and condemn ourselves; to charge upon ourselves the desert of hell; to take part with God against ourselves; and to justify Him and all that He does against us; to be ashamed and confounded for our sins, to have them ever in our eyes and at all times upon our hearts." Another has said, "Repentance is sorrow for sin so deep that it discontinues the same," for when a man makes a rightabout-face, his vision, his horizon, his entire outlook is altogether different.

156

THE LORD'S DOING

This is the Lord's doing; it is marvellous in our eyes.
Ps. 118:23.

"It is not the capabilities you now possess or ever will have, that will give you success. It is that which the Lord can do for you. We need to have far less confidence in what man can do, and far more confidence in what God can do for every believing soul. He longs to have you reach after Him by faith. He longs to have you expect great things from Him. He longs to give you understanding in temporal as well as spiritual matters. He can sharpen the intellect. He can give tact and skill. Put your talents into the work, ask God for wisdom, and it will be given you."—*Colporteur Ministry,* p. 119.

In the strictest sense man is responsible for little good that he accomplishes in his lifetime, "for in him we live, and move, and have our being" (Acts 17:28). That man has come closest to discovering the secret of life who recognizes Christ as the giver of every good and perfect gift. This covers everything from talents to the rewards of what man calls his own labor. With every success there should be the acknowledgment of the Lord's doing, "marvellous in our eyes."

Men can seldom resist the temptation of taking credit to themselves for things that others do. It is even more difficult when the deed in question involves our own efforts. To give God glory for all the good we have accomplished in the world by His grace is to achieve true humility.

A young man said to me once, "Look at all that man has achieved without God," and he referred to the great space program, citing the fact that many of the men who worked in it did not believe in God. Then came the tragic fire that consumed the lives of three astronauts. At the funeral Christian hymns were sung and a chaplain read from the Word of God as their bodies were lowered into the earth. Mistake-prone man at his best is never foolproof, and it is clear that man needs God all along the way, whether it be in scientific fields or the day-to-day problems of everyday living. The devotional heart ever sings:

"I need thee every hour; teach me Thy will,
And Thy rich promises in me fulfill."

HIM THAT HATH THE POWER

Forasmuch then as the children are partakers of flesh and blood, he also himself likewise took part of the same; that through death he might destroy him that had the power of death, that is, the devil. Heb. 2:14.

This text is indeed a strange one but true nevertheless, for it states that by subjecting Himself to the death on the cross Christ destroyed the power of the devil. In short, by allowing Himself to be maligned, insulted, and beaten, and finally crucified, Christ revealed the true nature of Lucifer to the universe and thus sealed his doom. It must be remembered that Christ might have destroyed Lucifer when he first committed sin, but for the angels. You see, so deceptive were Lucifer's workings that there were those angels who were not sure but that he had a point. Though still loyal to God, they did not fully and completely understand His love until His sacrifice on Calvary. And there Christ was "wounded for our transgressions, he was bruised for our iniquities: the chastisement of our peace was upon him; and with his stripes we are healed." It was there that Lucifer bared his fangs. He could not contain himself, thinking that he had the Son of man in his grasp at last. He was determined to make sure of his prey, and so he unleashed all the hellish fury of his wrath.

He had previously represented himself as being interested in improving the government of God. He implied that by easing the restrictions of the law, God would be exercising a trust in the angels that would move them to deeper loyalty, but at Calvary his true colors were revealed.

Let us go back to Pilate's judgment hall; see the demon-inspired frenzy with which the mob cries for His blood; see the Son of God subjected to scourging, a cruel Roman custom calculated to debase and degrade and to rob a man of the sense of his humanity; then see Him crowned with a crown of prickly thorns; see the rivulets of blood run down His face and understand that this is the innocent Son of God being subjected to the demoniacal fury of one who would amend the constitution of the universe for man's so-called benefit. Make Christ your choice today.

THE LOINS OF THE MIND

Wherefore gird up the loins of your mind, be sober, and hope to the end for the grace that is to be brought unto you at the revelation of Jesus Christ. 1 Peter 1:13.

Our text suggests that we perfect our hope of the abundant life here and of life in the world to come, both of which are predicated on the revelation of Jesus Christ to each of us personally. The phrase, "gird up the loins of your mind," suggests an individual preparing for travel, wearing the toga that was customary in the Roman Empire. He would gather the folds of the garment about him, making it secure around his body so as not to impede his movements. That the mind is mentioned in this text is significant, for out of it are all the issues of life. The mind is the seat of reason. "For as he thinketh in his heart, so is he" (Prov. 23:7).

We are admonished to adjust the loins, or the creative portions, of our mind to standards of sobriety and thus cultivate the hope of life abundant here and hereafter. This calls for an exercise of the will. Men have been known to overcome very strong habits by daily self-discipline. In short, "the blessed hope" is more to them than mere hope. It is a day-to-day experience to be worked at. It requires the exercise of man's highest mental faculties and a total subjugation of his evil propensities to the laws of the mind. This is impossible without conscious effort. There are those who believe that faith in Christ will somehow accomplish this in them and for them. It should be understood that this is true only when there is positive, active cooperation on the part of man. There must be a willingness to reform, a desire to change, and active participation with Christ by His grace in the work of change.

The expression is often heard, "Something must be done to hold our young people." The fact is, little can be done to "hold" any church member, young or old. There must be a personal realization on the part of every lover of the Lord of the necessity of girding up the loins of the mind. Fully girded, the Christian warrior wears a shield of faith, a breastplate of righteousness, a helmet of salvation, and a girdle of truth (Eph. 6:13-17).

159

WHO HATH BELIEVED?

Who hath believed our report? and to whom is the arm of the Lord revealed? Isa. 53:1.

Isaiah 53 is the gospel in capsule. It speaks of the fearful price that our Lord was to pay for the sins of men. It tells of the length to which Christ would go to portray to man the love of God. Perhaps the most poignant thing mentioned in the entire chapter is the statement, "He was numbered with the transgressors; and he bare the sin of many" (verse 12).

One of the most difficult things to bear as a little child is to be punished for another's sin. We read of men who have been imprisoned for crimes they didn't commit. To be numbered among transgressors when one is not a transgressor is exceedingly grievous. Yet this indignation He bore for us, and willingly, for His great heart yearned only that man would believe and be saved.

But the question is a pertinent one: "Who hath believed our report?" The sad truth is that there are millions of people around the earth who have never heard the report because there are so few to tell the story. Yes, it is a fact that the population explosion has literally telescoped the membership of the church to the point that one man will indeed have to chase a thousand, and two will have to put ten thousand to flight if the work of God is ever to be finished. In view of the glorious truth of the gospel plan there is an astonishing lack of enthusiasm on the part of many believers.

In Israel's experience, when the lepers made a discovery of abundance while the people in the city were starving for the elementary necessities of life, one of them said to the other, "We do not well." This is the dilemma of our times; namely, that men who possess great light refuse to share it with those who know it not. Then there are those to whom the gospel has been reported but who deem it fashionable to turn a deaf ear. I do not find this discouraging in the light of sacred history, for many heard the Master Himself and walked away. I preach to an estimated 200,000 people a year. Much of my joy stems from the fact that the good news of salvation is being spread, and that thousands of men and women are being exposed to its beauty.

160

THIS IS THE HERITAGE

No weapon that is formed against thee shall prosper; and every tongue that shall rise against thee in judgment thou shalt condemn. This is the heritage of the servants of the Lord, and their righteousness is of me, saith the Lord. Isa. 54:17.

One of the joys of being a Christian is the realization that even our curses are blessings and that all things work together for good to them that love the Lord and are called according to His purpose. No human philosophy or competing religious faith offers this type of assurance to its adherents. It is this realization that makes the Christian invincible. Living by it enables one to endure the utmost trial, knowing that the outworking of this experience will be for his own best good. It was this revelation of God's grace that enabled millions of martyrs to seal their faith in Christ with their own blood. They knew that if not in this life, then certainly in the life to come, their faith would be vindicated and even their death on this earth would serve best the purposes of a loving Saviour. Hence, whatever suffering life brings the Christian, he bears with fortitude and strength, and he fights the good fight of faith. Moses and Elijah are perfect examples.

Let us consider Elijah first, for he symbolizes those thousands of men and women who will not see death but will witness in their lifetime the coming of the Lord. Like all other human beings, Elijah's life was a mixture of joy and sorrow, success and frustration. From his victory on Carmel he fled in terror from Jezebel's wrath, but he lived to see that "no weapon that is formed against thee shall prosper," and profited even from his momentary panic at Jezebel's warriors. His triumph came when he was escorted to heaven in a fiery chariot.

Then there is Moses, a man who was not allowed in this life to see the ultimate outworking of the promise in our text. He is symbolic of the thousands of Christians who will die in faith with their hopes yet unfulfilled in this life but who will assuredly find that fulfillment in the life to come. Standing on the mount, he was permitted to view the Promised Land and the ultimate triumph of Israel. As a tired warrior he was laid to rest by an angel, and in his resurrection typified the resurrection of the saints at Christ's second coming.

TAKEN AWAY

The righteous perisheth, and no man layeth it to heart: and merciful men are taken away, none considering that the righteous is taken away from the evil to come. Isa. 57:1.

It has been my solemn responsibility over the years to comfort many wounded hearts whose mates have been snatched from them by the icy fingers of death, and words at such times do not come easy, for deep within us is the realization that ultimately only the true Comforter can comfort. But somehow words must be found, for sympathy does soothe the wounded heart. What more perfect assurance is to be found in all the Scriptures than that in our text—that when a good man dies it is an act of mercy, and Christ literally removes him from the earth, "from the evil to come." It is in this sense that the dead who have died in the Lord are blessed.

It is natural that man should will to survive. Very few men really want to die, and those visited by the Grim Reaper usually fight stubbornly before yielding up their lives. But when that day comes, it is good to know that there is a divine purpose in it all and that far from neglecting and ignoring His children, Christ is there to move with them into the valley of the shadow of death. Hannah More said: "No man ever repented of being a Christian on his death-bed." Therefore, "Turn you to the strong hold, ye prisoners of hope" (Zech. 9:12). With these heartening words, death loses some of its sting, and the grave at best achieves a hollow victory. There is no satisfaction among devils over the death of a righteous person, for in death the Christian has at last escaped even the temptations of the evil one. In short, through death he is beyond Satan's power. In this sense also those that die in the Lord are blessed. Add to this the hope of life in the hereafter, the certainty of the resurrection, and we may in truth "comfort one another with these words" (1 Thess. 4:18).

Reading this lesson this morning are thousands of men and women whose family circles have been broken by the death of a loved one. May you find comfort and assurance today in the marvelous grace of our loving Lord. He is the hope of the bereaved and the dispossessed.

THE DAYS ARE EVIL

*See then that ye walk circumspectly, not as fools, but as wise,
redeeming the time, because the days are evil.* Eph. 5:15, 16.

It is meaningless to quote last year's crime statistics, for they are
being revised upward by the day. It is a fact that it is now dangerous
to walk the streets of the large cities of the earth. Every form of
violence and immorality known to man stalks earth's inhabitants. The
arsenals of the nations contain the most awesome weapons, and the
creation of weapons for biological warfare is as fearful as the stockpiling
of atomic weapons. Human philosophy seems dedicated to expelling
the knowledge of God from the minds of men. Atheism is even more
pernicious in its influence. Sins long concealed in certain areas of the
cities of the world now walk the streets and flaunt themselves boldly
before the public eye. Base immoral practices are seeking recognition
and even approval in respectable circles, and are achieving it.
Trouble stalks the earth in crimson boots.

Our text says, "See then that ye walk circumspectly, not as fools,
but as wise, redeeming the time." Civilization's hour is growing late,
and her sun is rapidly setting. By circumspect living we may make the
best use of remaining time, for it is a fact that hypocrisy has its effects
upon the hypocrite as well as upon all whom it deceives. The genuine
Christian life is a great blessing to society as well as to the one who
lives it.

I am told that there are some varieties of trees that breathe out
poison, and woe betide the traveler who is ignorant enough to rest
under their shade. It is said that on the hills and slopes of Chile there
is a tree which the natives look upon as being possessed of an evil
spirit. Many cases have occurred where innocent travelers have crept
under its branches during the heat of the day and paid for its shade
with their lives. After a traveler rests under one of these trees for a
short time, his hands and face swell, as in the case of snake bites, and
the surface of the skin is covered with boils. Many visitors in Val-
paraiso have succumbed to the influence of this poisonous tree. So
is it with spiritual influence. We either bless or we curse by the lives
we live, and in evil times like these, the wise walk circumspectly.

THE PROPHETS

God, who at sundry times and in divers manners spake in time past unto the fathers by the prophets, hath in these last days spoken unto us by his Son. Heb. 1:1, 2.

The prophetic gift is only one of many manifestations of the love of God for man. It is an effort on the part of God to establish communication with man. There can be no genuine love without communication, and the prophets are instruments of divine communication—God to man.

As we look back through the ages, God's people have at no time been left without a messenger through whom He could communicate His will. The Bible is replete not only with names but with case histories of Spirit-filled men fierce in their loyalty to God but equally strong in their love for people. Their inspiration often took the form of a vision or a dream or the voice of God talking to them directly. In this sense, "all scripture is given by inspiration of God."

It is also clear that the prophets were "God's penmen, not His pen." This simply means that the choice of words was often left with the prophets but what God said had to be faithfully recorded. That is why many translations of the Bible are a blessing, for not all are familiar with the original languages in which the Scriptures were written and therefore as many languages and dialects as possible should be employed in spreading the Word of God to earth's teeming billions.

In these last days Scripture indicates that the gifts of the Spirit are to be no less pronounced in the twentieth-century church than in the first-century church. Joel 2:28 indicates that the prophetic gift is to be among those who name the name of Christ in the last days. The writings of Ellen G. White have withstood the attacks of critics and survived the genuine testing of God-fearing men and have taken their place in the annals of Christian literature as being an inspired commentary on the Holy Scriptures. Her writings bear the relationship to the Scriptures as the moon does to the sun. They are the counsels of Christ to this modern generation. "Believe his prophets, so shall ye prosper" (2 Chron. 20:20).

HIS SON

While he yet spake, behold, a bright cloud overshadowed them: and behold a voice out of the cloud, which said, This is my beloved Son, in whom I am well pleased; hear ye him. Matt. 17:5.

The Jews were largely tradition-minded, and they idolized Moses and the prophets. They would respond to any impugning of their knowledge of tradition and history by referring to Moses and the prophets. Our text does not belittle the value of the prophets and their writings, but it does announce that a new era had dawned; that He who had been the subject about which the prophets had spoken and scribes had written was now here and that shadow had now become substance. "Hear ye him," was the burden of the voice. What He stood for transcended all else, and what He taught must be regarded as primary and all else secondary. Significantly He appears between Moses, to whom He gave the Law, and Elijah, symbolizing the prophets. For nearly four thousand years the Law had been pointing men to Christ, the coming Messiah. In short, the Law and the prophets were the teachers, and Christ was the subject matter, or Textbook.

But now the situation was changed. Christ was here. In the flesh He spoke His word. A new emphasis was to be sounded. "For what the law could not do, in that it was weak through the flesh, God sending his own Son in the likeness of sinful flesh, and for sin, condemned sin in the flesh: that the righteousness of the law might be fulfilled in us, who walk not after the flesh, but after the Spirit" (Rom. 8:3, 4). He who for nearly four thousand years had been Textbook had now in the flesh become Teacher, and that which had been for nearly four thousand years Teacher now became Textbook. The law taught about Christ and Christ taught the law. He gave men deeper insights into its true meaning. The adulterer was not merely one who broke the law by committing an act but one who in his heart desired to do the same. The murderer was not only one who committed an act of murder by striking down his victim but one who hated his victim in his heart though he never struck him.

Thus in these last days hath Christ spoken unto us by His Son.

AMONG YOU

But Jesus called them unto him, and said, Ye know that the princes of the Gentiles exercise dominion over them, and they that are great exercise authority upon them. But it shall not be so among you: but whosoever will be great among you, let him be your minister. Matt. 20:25, 26.

Originally the people of God were to be ruled as a theocracy, meaning that God Himself would be leader and all others followers. That is how things started out under the most ideal situation. In the Garden of Eden, Adam and Eve were coequal members of the first church, and Christ was pastor. With the advent of sin, however, face-to-face communion became impossible. However, the love of God would not permit Him to break off all relationships with man, so He chose men through whom He could communicate His will to His people. These men became known as prophets and judges. As time passed, the children of Israel were dissatisfied with this arrangement and appealed to their leaders that they might have kings to rule over them as did other nations. It was a regime that God permitted to teach them the folly of their self-dependence. The sad story of their apostasy certainly pointed up the lesson the Saviour would teach them here.

With the advent of the New Testament the Lord provided bishops, pastors, prophets, and businessmen to administer the affairs of the church, but it has been His will throughout that no man become master in the church of the living God. The Seventh-day Adventist Church is organized so as to prevent this type of thing. Its affairs are managed by the committee system, which constitutes a safeguard against any one man wielding undue personal power. The entire arrangement is conducive to the greatest among us becoming servants. The pastor is servant to his congregation, not its lord. The conference president is the servant of the pastors, and not their lord. Likewise the union and division presidents, and the General Conference presidents are servants of those of whose labors they are overseers. The great among us are our ministers, or servants like Christ, the great loving Shepherd of all the sheep, who is still the head of the church.

166

THE DAYS OF NOE

But as the days of Noe were, so shall also the coming of the Son of man be. Matt. 24:37.

But how were the days of Noah? Three conditions marking those days attracted the attention of the God of heaven, bringing upon the heads of the antediluvians His unmixed wrath. Note them carefully: "For as in the days that were before the flood they were eating and drinking, marrying and giving in marriage, until the day that Noe entered into the ark" (verse 38). Enlarging the perspective a bit, the days of Noah were days of unbridled appetites and unrestrained self-gratification. In terms of diet, gluttony was the order of the day, and men ate anything that would walk, crawl, swim, or fly. The counsel of God with reference to these matters was ignored (see Gen. 1:29). Certainly it was known that unbridled appetite is a sin, as is clearly taught in the New Testament, for "Whether therefore ye eat, or drink, or whatsoever ye do, do all to the glory of God" (1 Cor. 10:31).

It is clear, then, that the will of God should be consulted in such everyday matters as our eating and drinking habits. I need not point out that gluttony is a sin of this age and that eating houses do a thriving business twenty-four hours a day. Men are still eating gross foods that dull their finer sensibilities. And as for drinking, John Barleycorn is again having his day! Taking an "eye opener," "one for the road," and "a nightcap," has become as common as eating.

The days of Noah were also days of unrestrained immorality, "marrying and giving in marriage." There were giants in the land in those days, and violence was common as men set their hearts upon mates belonging to other men and took them by force. The moral bankruptcy of Noah's era is being repeated again today. Unrestrained violence, personal and international, is the order of the times. An assault against time-honored standards of decency and morality threatens the very basis of civilized society—the home. These are all signs of the times, and as in Noah's time "the flood came, and took them all away; so shall also the coming of the Son of man be" (Matt. 24:39).

YOUR ENEMIES

But I say unto you, Love your enemies, bless them that curse you, do good to them that hate you, and pray for them which despitefully use you, and persecute you. Matt. 5:44.

A man in a fit of anger hurled a stone at his dog. The stone struck the dog's leg and broke it. The dog lay motionless for a moment, then he dragged himself to the feet of his master and licked the hand that had hurled the merciless stone at him. The owner of the dog felt rebuked, as well he might.

To love one's enemies is beyond normal human capacity. Required here is divine love—a love that God imparts to unregenerate human nature. That Christ after His terrible ordeal on earth could pray, "Father, forgive them; for they know not what they do," clearly demonstrates that such a love is possible to human flesh.

It is said that during the Korean war a South Korean Christian was arrested by the Communists and ordered to be shot. But when the young Communist leader learned that the prisoner was in charge of an orphanage caring for small children he decided to spare him and kill his son instead, so they shot the nineteen-year-old boy in the presence of the father. Later the fortunes of war changed and the young Communist leader was captured by the United Nations forces, was tried and condemned to death, but the Christian whose son had been killed pleaded for the life of the killer. He declared that the young man didn't really know what he was doing. "Give him to me," said the father, "and I will train him."

The United Nations forces granted the request and that father took the murderer of his own son into his home and cared for him. Today that young Communist is a Christian pastor. Such is the power of divine love. But such love must be sought, for it is not inherited. "Ask, and it shall be given you; seek, and ye shall find; knock, and it shall be opened unto you" (Matt. 7:7).

To every earnest seeker there is promised an abundant supply of love. "And hope maketh not ashamed; because the love of God is shed abroad in our hearts by the Holy Ghost which is given unto us" (Rom. 5:5).

SAVED

Look unto me, and be ye saved, all the ends of the earth: for I am God, and there is none else. Isa. 45:22.

Sam Hadley in his book *Down in Water Street,* tells of an old colonel who wandered into the mission room one night. He was over six feet tall, and about fifty years of age, but he looked at least a hundred. His eyes were bleary and the hue of his face showed that he had long been a stranger to water. He wore an old ragged overcoat fastened with a nail. Whisky had brought him to this sad condition. After graduating from college he had studied law in the office of Lincoln's great Secretary of War, E. M. Stanton, but down on Water Street Christ took hold of him and he cried, "O Lord, if it is not too late, forgive and save this poor old sinner." After seven nights of intercession he arose and calmly said, "Brother Hadley, I am saved." From that instant he loathed rum, God restored his intellect, and he was a dignified Christian gentleman until the day of his death.

Christians who talk about the saving power of Christ are not telling idle tales. The experience of salvation is real. Drunkards become sober, liars become truthful, and the immoral become good husbands and wives. Superficial experiences, however numerous, fail to dim the luster of the Christ-changed life.

After one of Gypsy Smith's meetings a Christian was trying to lead another to Christ. He read John 3:16, Romans 10:9, and 1 John 1:9 to him and asked him whether he believed what he read. The man said he did. The Christian said, "Then you are saved."

"No, I am not," said the man; "read Isaiah 55:7."

The man with the Bible did as he requested. "Now," said the other, "I am the wicked man, I am unrighteous, I have to forsake sin and wicked thoughts and I must come away from my own way to God's way. In my heart is a sin. I am hugging it and am not willing to give it up. My own common sense tells me that I cannot be saved until I surrender."

Gypsy Smith said, "This is the best sermon on repentance I have ever heard in my life."

REST

Come unto me, all ye that labour and are heavy laden, and I will give you rest. Matt. 11:28.

William Dawson once told a story of a little Methodist lad who went home to his mother and said, "Mother, John is under deep conviction and seeking peace but he will not find it tonight."

Asked mother, "Why, William?"

"Well," answered her son, "because he is only down on one knee, Mother, and he will never get peace until he is down on both knees."

This young boy's expression illustrates the dilemma of many Christians today who are seeking peace on "one knee." They are operating from half-surrendered lives. They know not the joy of total commitment.

During a test a submarine remained submerged for many hours. When it had returned to the harbor the commander was asked, "Well, how did the storm affect you last night?"

The commander looked at his questioner in surprise and said, "Storm? We knew nothing of any storm." They had been down far enough below the surface not to feel any effect of the storm. It is even so with a repentant heart. We may live lives so fully surrendered to God that our souls are at rest in moments of turbulence.

Necessary to this restful experience is absolute faith in God. A little boy was playing with his neighbor and stayed until the sun went down. His home was quite a distance through the woods and he was naturally afraid to go home alone. He telephoned his home and his father answered.

"Daddy," the little boy said, "I want to come home but I am afraid to come through the woods alone."

"Wait for me," the father answered, and not long thereafter the boy heard a knock on the door. "Follow me," said his father, with giant strides moving into the woods carrying a lighted lantern.

"Daddy," the little boy called, "I can't keep up with you."

"It is not necessary, son, that you match strides with me but just follow the light, and as you follow the light you follow me."

REVENGE

Dearly beloved, avenge not yourselves, but rather give place unto wrath: for it is written, Vengeance is mine; I will repay, saith the Lord. Rom. 12:19.

The natural tendency to even the score is common to all men. It is evident in the early years of childhood when it is considered the mark of cowardice not to fight back. "The survival of the fittest" is not only the law of the jungle but the law of unregenerate man, and the deciding factor in international situations is that "might makes right." No one wants to lose face by appearing to back down or to retreat. Jesus Christ teaches a different philosophy in contrast to the "fight fire with fire" human ideal. Christ teaches that His followers show kindness in the face of insult, patience in the face of provocation, and love when confronted with hate. There are two basic reasons for following this counsel:

1. God can always do a better job in balancing accounts than we can, and when men take up the cudgel in their own defense, they are more likely to sow the seeds for new wars and antagonisms. Is this not the history of the human family written in blood?

2. There is the possibility that a display of love will soften the heart of one's tormentor and thus lead him to Christ.

As a little boy on the ball diamond, I saw a clear demonstration of the Christian philosophy of love in the face of hate. My father was umpire of a ball game. He called a strike which the batter thought was a ball. The batter happened to be a seventeen-year-old youth. He immediately swung around and stood face to face with my father, cursing violently. With remarkable calm and self-restraint, my father stood and looked him in the eye. The boy waved the bat menacingly. My father simply stood there. Finally the cursing died away in embarrassment, since there had been no reply from my father. Then I saw him walk away. Even as I recite this incident, I can recall the disappointment I felt that my father had not settled the score there. We were fully prepared to help him. Later, while discussing this with him, my father said to me, "God will do a better job than I ever could, son."

171

DIVINE COVERING

But put ye on the Lord Jesus Christ, and make not provision for the flesh, to fulfil the lusts thereof. Rom. 13:14.

There is a strange preoccupation in our world with the lusts of the flesh. Men are largely occupied in making provisions for creature indulgences. From these excesses we are called away: "Let us walk honestly, as in the day; not in rioting and drunkenness, not in chambering and wantonness, not in strife and envying." The Lord Jesus Christ satisfies the deepest needs of the soul. The lusts of the flesh are symbolic of depraved human nature, mankind desiring the forbidden fruit. Put ye on the Lord Jesus Christ. Trust in His sufficiency in all things. He is as protective as a garment against the extremes of weather. He diffuses divine energy to the soul as does the sun to all things living. He gives guidance to the human mind as do the stars to those who do business in great waters. The thirsty find Him the source of living waters whose refreshing streams forever flow. The hungry see Him as the living bread, satisfying the deepest needs of the soul. The sin-sick sinner sees in Him the balm in Gilead.

Those who put on the Lord Jesus Christ feel no lure in the lusts of the flesh. They find happiness with their feet in right paths and need not the artificial stimulation that sin affords. The laughter of the Christian is the mirth of the soul. He is at rest with God and man. His conscience is clean. His thoughts are pure. He has put on the Lord Jesus Christ. This must be done daily. Through prayer and the daily study of the Word of God our relationship with Christ is strengthened. It is thus that we put Him on.

When you see a dog following two men, you know to which of them he belongs when they separate, for he will follow his master.

Dante, in one of his poems, tells of Buonconte, who fell mortally wounded at the battle of Campeldino. As he lay dying he thought of his sins, and fashioning a rough cross from two pieces of wood, he held it before him while his soul yearned to repent. At last a single tear of true repentance fell upon it as he died. The poet describes how a demon claimed Buonconte for hell but the virtue of a single tear answered him: "Never."

THE SUM

Now of the things which we have spoken this is the sum: We have such an high priest, who is set on the right hand of the throne of the Majesty in the heavens. Heb. 8:1.

While on earth, Jesus said, "No man cometh unto the Father, but by me" (John 14:6). Our approach to God is made only through the priesthood of Christ. It is through Him that we are admitted into the immediate presence of God. Through His priestly ministry He interprets the needs of our souls to the Father—those needs we express to Him through prayer. It is through Christ's presence at the right hand of the Father that the benefits of divine grace are bestowed. Pardon, cleansing, power, are ours through Him. It is small wonder, then, that the apostle speaks of Christ's present position and occupation before the Father as being *the sum.* Every act of grace toward man on the part of God was implemented by Christ, who made available all the benefits of His atoning sacrifice.

The *Homiletic Commentary* reads thus: "'This is the sum' does not mean that this is a brief recapitulation. It means 'this is the chief point,' 'this is the most important thing,' 'this is the consideration upon which attention should be most anxiously fixed.'"

The merit that Christ has built up through His long ministry for fallen man, covering a period of nearly six thousand years, is now available to us as a gift of free grace. There is no limit to what He can do for us or how. He requires only that we accept Him as Saviour, that we embrace Him as companion and friend, that we obey Him as Father, that we believe and trust in Him as a child would his mother. We may, therefore, come boldly to the throne of grace secure in the assurance of help in time of need.

About twenty-five years ago I sat in a courtroom witnessing a trial. The man against whom the complaint was lodged was too poor to hire a lawyer. He decided to defend himself. He was an eloquent man but should have known that without a representative at the bar his case was hopeless. Needless to say, he was convicted. Before the great tribunal of the universe no man is worthy to try his own case. We need a counselor. Thank God we have one in Jesus.

173

FOR ONE ANOTHER

Confess your faults one to another, and pray one for another, that ye may be healed. The effectual fervent prayer of a righteous man availeth much. James 5:16.

That man's extremity is God's opportunity has been common knowledge through the years, but how many people would be alive today if they simply believed the words of this text. To be sure, there are extremists who read in this a prohibition against physicians. Nothing could be further from the truth. Consecrated physicians are God-ordained ministers of health. I owe my life to God and just such a doctor. However, there comes a time when the best physician shakes his head and admits that there is nothing more he can do. It is then that the patient can ask for anointing and appeal to God as the only source of life and strength.

That God is still healing human bodies as He did while living among men on earth is a fact easily substantiated. The writer had an experience in this regard. I was a visitor in Seoul Sanitarium and Hospital. A nurse was guiding me through the wards when suddenly she said, "I would like for you to pray for the little dying boy in this room. He has cancer and is so far gone that there is nothing the physicians can do for him." I remember the dimly lighted room and the little orphan sister sitting weeping silently as we entered. We both knelt in prayer by this dying boy's bed. We presented him to God as a little boy who hadn't had a chance to live. Why then should he die so early? We acknowledged to God that, being human, we were shortsighted and that His wisdom would dictate the best course to follow in this case. However, we appealed for mercy, for healing power. We rose from our knees and left the room. At that point there was no evidence that our prayer had been answered. Upon my return to the States a few months later, a letter written in Korean by this little boy was translated for me. In it he revealed that his body had been healed. He was back in school, and he looked forward to the day when he could become a gospel minister. Thirteen years have passed since then. The young man is now happy in the work of God.

BY FAITH

Therefore being justified by faith, we have peace with God through our Lord Jesus Christ. Rom. 5:1.

> "In vain we seek a heaven below the sky,
> The world has false but flattering charms,
> Its distant joys show big in our esteem,
> But lessen still as they draw near the eye.
> In our embrace the visions die,
> And when we grasp the airy forms,
> We lose the pleasing dream."

To be justified means to be put right with God. It means to receive a new standing before God. It is to be declared righteous by faith in Christ.

Justification includes freedom from guilt and divine acceptance. This is possible only on the merits of the Son of God Himself, and we receive this precious gift by faith in Him. Thus are our hopes well grounded, and we grasp not as at elusive dreams, as pictured in the poem above. Self-justification is the vanity of seeking a heaven below through our own merits. Our hope is in Christ alone.

In this connection, let us consider the case of the French military officer, Captain Dreyfus. You remember that he was charged with selling French military secrets to the German Army and court-martialed for it. Because he was a Jew, his hearing was utterly unfair, and in the face of the evidence, he was accounted guilty and banished to Devil's Island. But there were friends who kept agitating for a second trial, and when this was held, again he was found guilty. Now the president of France, to save the face of the nation, pardoned him, and Captain Dreyfus was free, but he was not satisfied with pardon, nor were his friends. They continued to press for satisfaction. The whole world indeed had awakened to the unfairness of the judgment and cried out for a clearing at court. The third trial was granted, and at last Captain Dreyfus was justified. He received something better than a pardon—he was now regarded as one who had never committed a crime. This is justification. This is our privilege by faith in Christ.

175

STRONG DRINK

Woe unto them that are mighty to drink wine, and men of strength to mingle strong drink. Isa. 5:22.

I hate the liquor traffic. It killed my uncle. Week after passing week I saw him die the slow death of a man poisoned. How often have I stared into his glassy, bloodshot eyes, eyes appealing for help that God alone could give, but somewhere back in his brain was a will, a will that had grown enfeebled by repeated transgression, and finally it was paralyzed though still alive. This former faithful lay activities secretary, a gifted man, an artist, and an orator, was as the living dead. Demons must have added their unquenchable thirst to his own, and he died a slave, hair prematurely gray, enlarged heart, impaired liver, and weakened mind—a physical wreck.

I shall not ever forget the last sight of him alive. I visited the jail where he was incarcerated, spoke to the jailer, identified myself, and told him whom I wanted to see. His eyebrows arched in surprise, and then he turned to find my uncle. I was quite unprepared for what I saw. His handsome face was now lined with evidence of his physical deterioration. He could only numbly embrace me and cry. I prayed a prayer for him that day, standing in that lonely jail, and months later was not surprised to hear the news that my uncle was dead. Murdered by an enemy as real as the devil. I traveled south into the Tennessee Valley to preach his funeral service. It was at a funeral home, and there were a few derelicts and drunks who had been his last companions who came to bid an old partner in doom a fond farewell. But to my surprise, one hundred church members came to that funeral, for like me, they remembered. They remembered better days when a bright-eyed young man used to stand before them and urge them to communicate the light of the gospel to their sin-sick neighbors. He would fill his automobile with those who cared to go, and before going home to dinner on the Sabbath, they would distribute literature in the neighborhoods of the town.

Sadly I stood and recalled tender memories of the pride I had had in this man now destroyed by strong drink. Read this story and be warned, "Wine is a mocker, strong drink raging."

THEY COME OUT

And they were all amazed, and spake among themselves, saying, What a word is this! for with authority and power he commandeth the unclean spirits, and they come out. Luke 4:36.

Christ had come down to Capernaum, a city of Galilee. In the synagogue was a man with the spirit of an unclean devil who came to him, "Saying, Let us alone; what have we to do with thee, thou Jesus of Nazareth? art thou come to destroy us? I know thee who thou art; the Holy One of God" (Luke 4:34). Here we are faced with a startling admission—the devil himself acknowledging that Christ is the Holy One of God. Those who deny the divinity of Christ declare themselves less discerning than the devil himself, for Lucifer knew Christ. He knew Him as Creator. The demon acknowledged Christ to be the Holy One. Christ rebuked him and commanded that he come out of the man. He obeyed, and those who beheld this miracle testified, "And they come out" (verse 36).

We are here confronted with the power of God over demons. 1 John 4:4 says, "Greater is he that is in you, than he that is in the world." It is comforting to know that we are not at the mercy of the powerful fallen angelic beings that surround us. It is also important that we understand that there is such a thing as demon possession. Much of the crime and erratic behavior in human beings today may be accounted for by this fact. However, no one need fear his soul will be taken over by these evil forces, for their abode in the soul is dependent wholly upon the exercise of one's own will.

In Port of Spain, Trinidad, there was a young man who was possessed of a demon. He walked by night and slept by day. This made it impossible for anyone else in the house to sleep. In desperation the mother brought the boy to the Adventist church for prayer. Forty-six of us knelt around him and prayed simple prayers for the deliverance of this young man. While we were on our knees God answered our petitions. The young man was set free. Today he is living a normal life and his mother is a baptized member of our church. Yes, when the authority of Christ is brought to bear, devils come out, for the will of God is omnipotent.

HE COMETH

Our God shall come, and shall not keep silence: a fire shall devour before him, and it shall be very tempestuous round about him. Ps. 50:3.

During the recent war, after a German attack, an American boy who came back to our lines discovered that his pal with whom he had fought side by side was missing. Immediately he asked permission to go back over the field and get him. His officer advised him not to go and said, "If you do, it will not be worth while. Go at your risk, but it will cost you your life." The boy went out and found his friend badly hurt and brought him back near the line. At that point the wounded soldier died and the rescuer himself was shot. Dying he was able to crawl back within the line. The officer, leaning over him just before he died, said, "I told you you would lose your life. Was it worth while?" "Yes, sir," answered the dying soldier. "My buddy said he knew that I would come."

And so it was with Christ at His first coming to the earth. At the risk of His own life He came to save us. At the end of thirty-three years of selfless ministry He paid with His life for His love. Were we to ask Him, "Was it worth it?" I'm sure His answer would be "Yes." Yes because of the thousands of men and women around the earth who have accepted by faith His sacrifice and are living His life because He died their death. We know that He ascended unto God, but He promised to come back to this earth to receive all who put their trust in Him. He will come again.

I can remember when I was a little boy that a loving uncle, every Christmas, visited his nephews and brought them presents. I can remember with what excited anticipation we awaited his coming on Christmas Eve, and when his footsteps were heard climbing the stairs and his knock was heard on the door, our joy was unbounded. We could hardly contain ourselves. It was for me an experience of pure ecstasy that I can feel even now as I remember it. But what will it be like when Jesus comes? Many have been long expecting Him, desiring His coming. Will you join the growing ranks of them in all the earth?

HIGH CALLING

I press toward the mark for the prize of the high calling of God in Christ Jesus. Phil. 3:14.

An expert had come to see what was wrong with the kitchen range. "The fault is in the chimney," he said. "A stove has, of course, no draft in itself. It is only its connection with the flue that makes the fire burn and the smoke ascend, and the higher the chimney the stronger the draft. At foundries where fierce fires are needed, the stacks run up to a great height. Your stove smokes because your chimney is too low. You must build higher."

An inspired writer has said, "Higher than the highest human thought can reach is God's ideal for His children. Godliness—God-likeness—is the goal to be reached." Our faith must match our calling if we are to become overcomers. We must build higher.

The story is told of a dying Indian chieftain who wanted to choose one of his three sons to succeed him as head of the tribe. Pointing to a nearby mountain, he said, "My sons, I want each of you to climb the mountain, and the one who reaches the topmost peak will be my successor." Soon one of his sons returned with a beautiful flower. "I have climbed to the topmost peak, Father," he said, "and I bring you this flower in evidence."

"Stand aside," said his father.

Shortly the second son returned with a green branch from a tree. "My Father, I have scaled to the utmost peak of the mountain, and I bring you this green branch in evidence."

"Stand aside," said the father.

Soon after, the third son appeared, tired, haggard, his feet bruised by sharp stones but with nothing in his hand. "I have climbed to the utmost peak, my Father, but I brought nothing, for where I've been nothing grows. But," he said, his eyes lighting up, "I saw the sea."

"Come hither, my son," his father said. "You are the chief of the tribe. For I too saw the sea." Vision is paramount in a leader.

It may require all we have to reach the divine standard, but the vision of God we obtain on reaching it makes it worth it all.

179

MY HOME

These all died in faith, not having received the promises, but having seen them afar off, and were persuaded of them, and embraced them, and confessed that they were strangers and pilgrims on the earth. Heb. 11:13.

The dream of a better world than this has encouraged Christians in all ages to be faithful to their trust. Jesus assured us that there is just such a better world. He called it, "My Father's house." Paul, writing to the Hebrews, said of Abraham, "For he looked for a city which hath foundations, whose builder and maker is God." The apostle John wrote, "I John saw the holy city, new Jerusalem." And he describes that city in much of its minute detail. In the twenty-first chapter of Revelation he states that there are twelve gates to the city, and they are pearl; that the walls are jasper and the streets gold. Yes, there is ample Biblical evidence that there is a city out there in space that will one day be occupied by the saints.

Living in today's world, it is difficult not to hear the preachments of the faithless. To many of them heaven is a state of mind and so is hell. An increasing number of theologians have labeled as myth the reality of the city of God. Somehow they never give up, despite the fact that a hundred years ago men were proclaiming the kingdom of God on earth through church-state cooperation and that somehow the spirit of the church would so permeate the state that men might produce a utopia here with God's help. You have but to look around you to see the sad utopia that man has produced, and you will have to conclude that God must have a better place.

A little girl was running along a path leading through a burial ground. She was asked if she was not afraid to go through the cemetery at night. "Oh, no," she said. "I am not afraid, for my home is just beyond." And so it is with all of us who by faith accept Jesus Christ as Saviour. All such may truly say,

> "In that bright city, pearly white city,
> I have a mansion, a robe, and a crown.
> Now I am watching, waiting, and longing
> For that white city John saw coming down."

AGAINST GOD

There is none greater in this house than I; neither hath he kept back any thing from me but thee, because thou art his wife: how then can I do this great wickedness, and sin against God? Gen. 39:9.

Joseph was in the house of Potiphar. This great Egyptian trusted him and made him overseer of all his goods. Potiphar's wife desired Joseph and tempted him to break the seventh commandment, but he resisted steadfastly, and his words are interesting. "How then can I do this great wickedness, and sin against God?"

We live in a day of restiveness under authority, both human and divine. Rules are resented just because they are rules, and the new attitude is that rules exist to be broken. As to the law of God, men have long ago declared it null and void. They have exalted human reason as the measure of right and wrong. They would allow man to be his own judge and thus cast off all divine restraint. Joseph in his answer to Potiphar's wife brings the law of God into true perspective. To him the violation of the seventh commandment was more than just breaking a rule. He regarded the commandments of God as existing to safeguard his relationship with God. To break the commandment was to sin against the person of God. It would strain the relationship existing between them, and if cherished, sin would finally sever that relationship altogether. When this happens, one has sinned against the Holy Ghost. This is the sin called by David "the great transgression." Men who have this insight into divine law regard their relationship with Christ as being sacred, and the commandments as blessed guidelines into right paths.

Dr. Clay Trumble used to tell of the secret of Napoleon's power over his soldiers. Happening to meet a French veteran who served under him, Dr. Trumble asked, "Did Napoleon's soldiers like him?"

"Like him!" exclaimed the old man. "We believed in him! If Napoleon said, 'Go to the moon,' every soldier would start, and Napoleon would find a way."

Every child of God thus serves his Master. Fidelity, trustworthiness, moral purity—what noble virtues are these.

THE LORD'S WILL

For that ye ought to say, If the Lord will, we shall live, and do this, or that. James 4:15.

Human life is so uncertain that we cannot plan a day ahead on our own. There are always unforeseen circumstances that only God can know exist. Therefore, it is best when planning for us to say, "If God wills." This statement acknowledges wisdom above ours. It says that we are subject to the will of God in all things and we will make no demands of the future that He cannot approve.

We say, "If God permits." Here we are cognizant of His permissive care. Balaam was not allowed to go farther until he had decided to bless and not curse Israel. The apostle Paul spoke of himself being hindered by the Holy Ghost from entering a certain city. The Wise Men from the East who came in search for the Son of God were forbidden to go back by the way they had originally intended. Yes, we must surrender ourselves to the sovereign will of God in all things.

Thus Cyrus, king of Persia, went under the pretense of hunting. He designed an expedition into Armenia in which a hare started and was seized by an eagle. He said to his friends, "This will be prosperous hunting to us if God will." And Socrates says, "But I will do this and come unto thee tomorrow if God will." And it is reported of the Turks that they submit everything to divine will, as the success of a war, a journey, or anything of the least moment that they desire to be done, and never promise themselves or others anything but under this condition, "Inshallah"; that is, "if God will." It is an example of trust in God to refuse to do anything without first acknowledging Him as sovereign in all our affairs.

A properly trained child is taught to consult the will of his parents while a minor. The reason is that he is a dependent and his judgment is not mature enough to make full decisions on his own. Even so with God's children; we are all dependent on Him, and His wisdom is greater than ours, hence we should seek His will in all things.

HELP US

And a vision appeared to Paul in the night; There stood a man of Macedonia, and prayed him, saying, Come over into Macedonia, and help us. Acts 16:9.

An old Mesopotamian said to his teacher, "Ten years ago I went on a pilgrimage to Arabia. There in the market place I bought this little book from a stranger. As I traveled home, I read how God sent His Son into the world and how He died and rose again. The journey did not seem long to me. Then I prayed, 'O God, send me a teacher that I may understand these things.' And for ten years I waited. Now the teacher has come. Teach me."

In unnumbered hearts there is this deep longing for spiritual help. The call from Macedonia may be nearer than we think. In 1965 I was conducting a campaign on Long Island in New York. One of my Bible instructors had been out visiting and was making her way to the tent. Suddenly there was a collision. Another automobile had come up from apparently nowhere and struck the front end of her car. Resisting the impatience that comes naturally at a time like this, she whispered a prayer and got out and confronted a bewildered young man. She spoke to him kindly, and after dealing with the business connected with the accident, referred him to our meetings. It was not long before we discovered that this was indeed one of the hungry young souls out there who needed guidance and light. I baptized him in that campaign, and he is now in Oakwood College training for the gospel ministry. An automobile collision is a strange appeal for help, but God used it to His purpose.

About fifteen years ago in Orlando, Florida, an automobile had stalled in front of my tent, and all the frantic work of the driver could not start it. He accepted my offer to give him a push. After his engine had started, he offered to pay for my services. I declined pay but urged him to attend my meetings in the tent that night. Sure enough, he came, bringing his mother, father, wife, and three children. In the course of time, they were all baptized into the church. In this instance a stalled car and a cry for help were one and the same.

UNTO DEATH

Fear none of those things which thou shalt suffer: behold, the devil shall cast some of you into prison, that ye may be tried; and ye shall have tribulation ten days: be thou faithful unto death, and I will give thee a crown of life. Rev. 2:10.

At the close of the first day of the battle of Shiloh, a day of severe Union reverses, General Grant was met by his much-discouraged chief of staff, Macpherson, who said, "Things look bad, General. We've lost half our artillery, and a third of our infantry. Our line is broken. Our backs are to the river. What shall we do?"

"Do?" answered Grant. "Why, re-form the lines and attack at daybreak. Won't they be surprised?"

Surprised they were—and routed before nine o'clock.

In too many of us there is a tendency to be discouraged and to fall back. Life with all its complications can get threatening at times. The strongest Christians have endured moments of frustration and heartbreak and survived the ever-recurring temptation to back away from life's issues. To all these at such times comes the admonition, "Be thou faithful unto death."

Of Christ it was said, "He shall not fail nor be discouraged." We pause to think of Him now. His life was almost a constant round of tests and confrontations. Precious little sunlight came His way from other human beings. Nearly all of His encouragement came from daily communion with His Maker. Only once did the cup tremble in His hands. Even then His recovery was rapid and complete. "Nevertheless not my will, but thine, be done," He said. And so our Lord pressed on until that triumphant day when He could say, "It is finished." So may it be with us. We may drink from the cistern that never runs dry.

In my hometown of Huntsville, Alabama, years ago the center of attraction was a spring down in the very heart of the city. Its cool refreshing waters sprang continually from an apparently inexhaustible supply. Those who drank there would return to drink again. Likewise, those who are constantly drinking at the fountain of life will find refreshment and strength with which to help others.

184

SEEST THOU A MAN?

Seest thou a man diligent in his business? he shall stand before kings. Prov. 22:29.

A stooped, grizzled man, employed by an automobile factory in Toledo, Ohio, does not look like a very important part of this big factory, but the president of the company says that Magnet Bill saves his salary a dozen times over every day he works. Rain or shine, summer or winter, Magnet Bill may be seen walking slowly about the plant, his eyes almost constantly cast on the ground. He gets his nickname from the fact that his tools consist solely of one tin bucket and a big steel magnet strapped to the end of a shovel handle. He saves automobile tires by removing from the roadway every nail and bit of iron, brass, or steel that might cause a puncture. Thousands of cars are run over the roadway to the testing place, and without the work of Magnet Bill the cost for cut and punctured tires would be great.

There are many who perform important tasks in quiet, obscure corners of the world who sometimes get discouraged because they are out of the limelight. But society is built on people who often perform the most vital duties in undistinguished places.

We saw an illustration of this in the flash fire that destroyed the lives of the three American astronauts at Cape Kennedy. Hearings were held before a Senate subcommittee as to the cause of the fire. In the charred remains of the space capsule, damaging evidence of negligence was readily apparent. Some unidentified workman had left a wrench lying loose in a strategic spot. Whether this caused the fire is as yet undetermined. What is clear is that every man working on the space project is important, from the astronaut to each workman responsible for the construction of the capsule.

Likewise in the church of God, in the home, and in our social structure we must come to understand the importance of the individual. In this computer age it is easy for us to become impersonal, but when we remember that our Lord notices even the sparrow's fall, we can be sure He looks with even greater concern upon those dear souls who live their lives in the shadows.

OUR HELP

Our help is in the name of the Lord, who made heaven and earth. Ps. 124:8.

An artist once drew a picture representing a night scene. A solitary man is rowing a little skiff across the lake. The wind is high, and the billows, white and crested, rage around his frail bark. Not a star, save one, shines through the dark and angry sky above. But upon that lone star the voyager fixes his eye and keeps rowing away, on and on and on through the midnight storm. Inscribed beneath the picture are these words, "If I lose that, I am lost."

When Peter was walking on the sea, as long as he kept his eye on the Master, he was safe. Losing sight of Him for an instant, the disciple began to sink. His desperate cry, "Lord, save me," reflects the desperation of a man who knows that if he loses Christ, he is lost. "Neither is there salvation in any other: for there is none other name under heaven given among men, whereby we must be saved" (Acts 4:12).

In the 121st psalm, David contrasts the sources of help available to man in interesting language. In the original language verse 1 would seem to pose the question "Shall I lift up mine eyes unto the hills? Whence cometh my help?" In the groves and on the high hills, Israel, in apostasy, erected altars to heathen deities and looked unto these in vain for their help. In verses 2, 3 David contrasts this fruitless search for assistance with his own profitable venture. He says, "My help cometh from the Lord, which made heaven and earth. . . . He that keepeth thee will not slumber." Here again is an indirect reference to the impotence of man-made gods. They are as one that slumbers. They are not creative. They are powerless.

Pastor R. Cecil once fell into the hands of four highwaymen. As soon as he perceived his danger there flashed into his mind the admonition, "Call upon me in the day of trouble." He silently prayed for deliverance. The leader of the band asked him who he was. Mr. Cecil told him his name and business. The leader said, "I know you, sir, and have heard you preach. Men, let the gentleman's horse go. We wish you good night."

186

YOUR ADVERSARY

Be sober, be vigilant; because your adversary the devil, as a roaring lion, walketh about, seeking whom he may devour. 1 Peter 5:8.

One of the difficulties in the war in Vietnam is that from the American point of view the enemy is often difficult to distinguish from the nationals, for the Viet Cong are also Vietnamese. One American killed five Vietnamese. At his trial he stated the difficulty. Said he, "I thought they were the enemy."

In spiritual matters this can be tragic. There are millions of people in this world who have mistaken the adversary for a friend. They literally blame God for the reverses they have met in this life. Lucifer has so skillfully misrepresented the character of God that the majority of the world's population neither worship nor obey Him. Skeptics use the existence of such calamities as war, sickness, death, famine, pestilence, and other distresses as evidence that there is no God, or if there is one, He is asleep or on sabbatical leave. This misapprehension pictures God as an adversary rather than as a friend and father to the human family and as a consequence questions His love. Our text assures us that our adversary is not God but the devil, and therefore all our human woes are in consequence of sin, for which the devil must accept full responsibility. This evil one is the enemy of man. He is our adversary. God is our friend. What greater pledge of friendship can we require than that He would take on human flesh and dwell among us as a man for thirty-three years and finally pay with His own life the supreme price for our redemption. It is the most valid evidence of love the world has ever witnessed.

Augustus Hare tells the following story: "In the frescoes of Signorelli we have 'the teaching of the anti-Christ,' no repulsive figure but a grand person in flowing robes and noble countenance, which at a distance might easily be taken for the Saviour. To him the crowd are eagerly gathering and listening, and it is only when you draw close that you can discover in his face a cynical expression and a small evil spirit whispering in his ear that it is not Christ."

187

THEN SHALL WE KNOW

Then shall we know, if we follow on to know the Lord: his going forth is prepared as the morning; and he shall come unto us as the rain, as the latter and former rain unto the earth. Hosea 6:3.

There are those who have only a superficial knowledge of God and of His dealings with the human family, all because they do not study to follow Him in all His ways. Our text reveals the secret of gaining a deeper experience with Christ. We have to follow on to know.

At different stages of our spiritual development there are mysteries to be encountered on every hand. For instance: A Christian may not know why he, as a Christian, is brought into a strait place, whereas sinners seem to be prospering, without a care in the world. The true follower of Christ never denies that there are mysteries all along the way, but he follows on, knowing that understanding will come with experience. How else can we explain Joseph's steadfastness under intolerable pressures? Joseph was thrown into a pit, sold into slavery, and then placed in a dungeon for keeping God's commandments. But upon his emergence, and eventually Christians do emerge, he made this statement to his brethren, "God sent me before you to preserve you a posterity in the earth, and to save your lives" (Gen. 45:7).

Yes, somehow, if we have the patience to follow on, we understand.

It is said that in the winter there are periods when a thick mantle of fog covers the city of Geneva, Switzerland. When on such a dismal day one mounts the side of Mount Salève, he comes after a time to a cross erected alongside a precipitous slope and overlooking the entire valley of the Rhone River. Here at the same time comes the lifting of the fog. A farmer recently told a tourist who wondered at not being able to see the sun, "Sir, you must climb to the cross, and there you will find the sunshine." And indeed, it is so. When the city, the lake, and a good part of the valley are hidden from view, the cross is bathed in unclouded light.

LET US WATCH

Therefore let us not sleep, as do others; but let us watch and be sober. 1 Thess. 5:6.

Our text is written against a context of death. Verse 3 pictures sudden destruction coming upon the earth. We are reminded that as Christians we're not children of darkness but children of the day. Our text admonishes us to walk as children of the day, not to sleep as do others but to watch and be sober. The reason for this counsel is not difficult to see. We're told to watch and be sober in view of (1) the uncertainty of the period when death should arrive, for it will come as a thief; (2) the fact that it is our manifest duty.

A sentinel posted on the walls sees a hostile party advancing. He does not attempt to make a thrust against them himself but informs his commanding officer of the enemy's approach and joins him in combat against a common foe. So it is with a Christian. After discovering the enemy's approach to the soul he does not attempt to do battle in his own weakness but calls upon God for divine strength, and in His imparted might turns to meet the foe.

"If I had not been in the crowd, I wouldn't have done such a thing," someone has said. But watchfulness demands that we discern the enemy's approach prior to temptation. It is possible only to one with a conscience cultivated by daily prayer and the study of the Word of God. The approaches of the soul must be guarded. "Eternal vigilance is the price of freedom." This is certainly true of spiritual freedom. The enslavement of our sensibilities is seldom a sudden and dramatic thing. Usually habits have been secretly practiced and ideas cherished over the years until one ceases his resistance to evil and yields to the powers of the night. Our vigilance then involves a sensitivity to every approach of sin to the sacred precincts of the soul, and to resist the evil one unto death.

America for years has operated on the theory in warfare that it is better to fight on an extended battle line on other territory than to wait until our own nation becomes the battleground. It is certainly better to stem the tide of evil before its waters reach the soul. In sobriety and vigilance lies our hope of spiritual survival.

OF ANGER AND CLAMOR

Let all bitterness, and wrath, and anger, and clamour, and evil speaking, be put away from you, with all malice. Eph. 4:31.

John the patriarch of Alexandria had a controversy with Nicetas, a chief man of that city, which was to be decided in a court of justice. In the controversy John defended the cause of the poor, and Nicetas refused to part with his money. All efforts to adjust met with rebuff as angry words passed between the men. When Nicetas had gone, John began to reflect on his own stubbornness. With tear-filled eyes, he asked himself the question, "Shall I suffer the sun to go down upon my wrath?" Seizing a pen, he wrote these words to Nicetas: "Oh, sir, the sun is going down." Upon receiving the message, Nicetas was very much affected. He hastened to the patriarch, and saluting him in a most gentle manner, exclaimed, "I will be ruled by you in this and in any other matter." They embraced and settled the dispute instantly.

Bitterness and wrath are to be put away from us, according to the words of our text. In Job's experience we are told that God "turned the captivity of Job, when he prayed for his friends." The Chinese rendition of this passage reads, "When Job prayed for his friends, the bitterness left his soul." It is difficult to harbor ill thoughts concerning another and pray for him at the same time. Kindness begets kindness and interest begets interest. Much of the clamor that prevails in the streets and in our homes and in the churches would disappear if this text were obeyed.

There is so much of misunderstanding in our world that could be solved if men would simply sit down quietly as Christians and mature human beings and quietly discuss their differences, but so many are moved from impulse and by the inflammatory statements of demagogues, some of whom have a vested interest in confusion and trouble. The heart of a Christian should be an island of calm in a sea of stress, an oasis of love in a desert of hate, but man of himself is incapable of rewarding good for evil and showing kindness in the face of anger. This gift is God bestowed. We must seek it persistently and faithfully through prayer and the study of the Word.

HIM THAT COMETH

*All that the Father giveth me shall come to me; and him that
cometh to me I will in no wise cast out.* John 6:37.

It is a characteristic of human pomp and vanity that often important people are unavailable to the masses. They barricade themselves with so many secretaries and so much red tape that the fainthearted seeker is discouraged. Christ has made Himself accessible to
all men at all times, and He goes further to promise that "him
that cometh to me I will in no wise cast out." Christ says that not
only may we see Him, but if what we seek is for our best good, we
will receive it. Here we deal with two primary fears of the human
heart: (1) God will not hear me; (2) He will not regard my case
as important and will cast me out. These two deterrents have hindered more Christians from seeking Christ and His free salvation than
any other.

In His earthly ministry Christ repeatedly demonstrated His deep
interest in the human family. All classes of men were welcome in
His presence. There was the sophisticated Nicodemus and the lowly
cripple at the pool of Bethesda; and what of Zacchaeus, the tax
collector? And by contrast, the guests at the wedding at Cana?
None were ignored. Their minutest needs were attended to.

The custom prevailed among some pagans of casting out their
sick and dying friends and leaving them in a desolate place lest
their houses be defiled with the bodies of the dead. The helpless
were thus left to suffer cruel agonies. A little girl who had been
torn by wolves was cast out by her parents to die. She thought of a
missionary's well-known kindness and resolved, "I will try to creep
to his house, for he is kind and will let me in." Slowly she made her
way to his door. He received her with great tenderness and bound
up her wounds and tended her carefully until they were healed.
Then he asked her if she would go back to her parents. She answered, "Oh, no, they cast me out. You took me in, and I will stay
with you." She also found Christ, and He received her. It is comforting to know that both took her in. God will never cast out any who
seek Him diligently.

IN HONOR

Be kindly affectioned one to another with brotherly love; in honour preferring one another. Rom. 12:10.

It is said that General Grant had been for several months in front of Petersburg apparently accomplishing nothing, while General Sherman had captured Atlanta and completed his grand march to the sea. Then arose a strong cry to promote Sherman to Grant's position as lieutenant general. Hearing of it, Sherman wrote to Grant, "I have written to John Sherman [his brother] to stop it. I would rather have you in command than anyone else. I should emphatically decline any commission calculated to bring us into rivalry." To which Grant wrote in reply, "No one would be more pleased with your advancement than I, and if you should be placed in my position and I put subordinate, it would not change our relations in the least. I would make the same exertion to support you that you have done to support me, and I would do all in my power to make your cause win." Small wonder these two great generals combined to succeed where others had failed. They were each solicitous of the other. Brotherly love is the key to such a spirit.

It is natural for us to seek our own welfare first. The old slogan, "Look Out for Number One," is universally accepted. When another is preferred instead of ourselves, it is an opportunity to grow and mature, and the warmth of love floods the soul. The man who pushes himself reveals the natural selfishness of the human heart. All his good is done with a view of some gratuitous return. His heart is covetous of glory, honor, and praise. Basic to a change of attitude is a change of heart. Christ must be accepted into the heart by faith. His love must be invited to fill the soul. The love principle must guide the life. Day by day we must surrender our proud hearts to it. Then only can we in honor prefer one another.

Kind and unselfish deeds disarm mistrust and suspicion. But they must be done with pure motives, for doing them with expectation of reward puts the action in the category of a cheap expediency. For Christians to share their griefs and bear one another's burdens is the greatest testimony that they have passed from death unto life.

THEIR DUES

Render therefore to all their dues: tribute to whom tribute is due; custom to whom custom; fear to whom fear; honour to whom honour. Rom. 13:7.

Both moral and civil responsibilities of the Christian are important. There are those who think themselves free from the obligations of modern-day society. They have the mistaken notion that a brother-to-brother relationship is only for their church circle, but Christianity demands deference to those in authority in business and community affairs, and friendly cooperation with our neighbors and fellow workers. Jesus admonished us to "render therefore unto Caesar the things which be Caesar's" (Luke 20:25).

Jesus said that His kingdom was not *of* this world. He did not say that it is not *in* this world. Indeed, the kingdom of grace is set up within every believing heart that accepts Jesus Christ as Lord and Saviour. There are, therefore, in consequence civil obligations that the Christian must meet. Being a part of society he must never be caught driving a nail in his fellow man's coffin or strengthening the chains that would enslave him. In civil affairs the Christian must make every man's load as light as he possibly can. "Be ye kindly affectioned one to another" is the injunction of Romans 12:10.

I have heard it said that the brotherly love required of Christians is love without affection. The words of Romans 12:10 would indicate otherwise. In the early days of Christianity those who belonged to the Christian church were accused by its very membership of being traitors to Caesar. Because they sought recruits for the kingdom of heaven, they were thought to be disloyal to earthly rulers. Our text suggests the contrary. Christians should be the best of citizens, obedient to law, peaceful neighbors, and interested in every community project for the common uplift.

Men hesitate not to do obeisance in the presence of a king or give honor to some rich, wise, or powerful personage, but let it be understood that the most noble may be among the poor. Let not the tattered garment occasion disrespect. While giving honor to wealth, power, and wisdom let us also pay tribute to the good.

POOR YET RICH

There is that maketh himself rich, yet hath nothing: there is that maketh himself poor, yet hath great riches. **Prov. 13:7.**

A man of vast fortune sent for a friend to settle some affairs. While they were together, he walked to the window, and as he looked out he observed a little chimney sweep's boy with his sack, passing by. The little boy was whistling a merry tune. The friend was surprised to see tears burst from the eyes of the rich man, as clasping his hands, he exclaimed, "I would give every penny I am worth in the world to change places with that little chimney sweep."

Yes, it is possible to have a vast fortune and to be rich in this world's goods while at the same time experiencing poverty of spirit.

Stephen Girard, of Philadelphia, the infidel founder of Girard College, into which all clergymen are forbidden to enter, when surrounded by immense wealth and supposed to be taking supreme delight in its accumulation, wrote these words to a friend: "As to myself, I live like a galley slave constantly occupied and often passing the night without sleeping. I am wrapped in a labyrinth of affairs and worn out with care. I do not value fortune. The love of labor is my highest emotion. When I arise in the morning, my only effort is to labor so hard during the day that when night comes I might be enabled to sleep soundly." This is the poverty toward which the Christless life tends. By contrast there is he that "maketh himself poor, yet hath great riches." This is the man who embraces Christ as Saviour and Lord, who day by day puts his trust in God. He may be poor in this world's goods, but his heart is daily filled with singing. He literally enjoys being alive. Day by day his spiritual strength is renewed.

I awakened early on a chilly spring day and sat reading my Bible, reflecting on the beauty of its language, when suddenly I was startled by the beautiful song of a bird coming from my chimney. The sooty condition of his environment did little to dampen his spirits. That bird had its little heart filled with heavenly implanted joy, and its music reflected its mood. So may it be with us. We may boast of little in terms of material riches, but it is the privilege of every man to be eternally rich with the abundant grace of God daily.

A TREE OF LIFE

Hope deferred maketh the heart sick: but when the desire cometh, it is a tree of life. Prov. 13:12.

Thousands of voices like the sound of many waters crashing against the turf blended in voicing the hope of humanity,

"We have this hope that burns within our hearts,
Hope in the coming of the Lord.
We have this faith that Christ alone imparts,
Faith in the promise of His Word."

Yes, the hope of the Christian is the coming of Christ. When He went away He promised, "I will come again," thus causing hope to spring up in His loyal followers. For nineteen centuries the eyes of the Christian have lifted wearily skyward in anticipation of his coming Lord. The anxious inquiry from every devout heart is "Will He not come soon?" But hope has been deferred. The Lord's coming has indeed been delayed. Not by the lack of faithfulness on His part but because men on earth have been tardy in following on to know Him. And so in mercy the coming of the Lord is deferred, and the Christian's heart is sick. There are those on this earth who sigh and cry for the abominations that are done in the land. There are those who are not happy to be here and who are not satisfied with things as they are. Bowed down with care, countless thousands around the earth pray daily, "Even so, come, Lord Jesus" (Rev. 22:20).

Then there are multiplied thousands on this globe who love the Lord but do not wish for His coming. They would rather He would not come now. It is these who delay the fulfillment of His wonderful promise that His coming is near, even at the door. While He tarries let us not be deceived by the apparent prosperity of the wicked nor by the apparent advancement in civilized society. We know that the times are corrupt with moral and spiritual erosion. The accumulated decay of six thousand years of human degeneracy is upon us. The true Christian wants to get away from it all. The true believer longs for the coming of the Lord, and to him the fulfillment of that hope will be a "tree of life."

Do you really want Jesus to come? Are you ready for Him?

ANY PEOPLE

Righteousness exalteth a nation: but sin is a reproach to any people. **Prov. 14:34.**

It is a fact of Biblical history that nations conscious of their destiny in God's plans, and that order their affairs after His leading, have enjoyed unparalleled prosperity. But when the seeds of apostasy set in, there is a corresponding decline in national prestige and power, with a forsaking of spiritual guidelines. Students of the Word of God are aware that there is a Divine Hand on the wheel of history and that whether man likes it or not, he is not the master of his fate nor the captain of his own soul. What is true of nations is true of individuals. As human beings we are exalted when we are at the center of the will of God.

The greatest types of spiritual excellence are reached when we are following Christ's purposes for us, acknowledging His leadership of us, and allowing Him to do His perfect will in us. We stand reproached by our own apostasy when we despise His matchless love. To walk after our own ways, to succumb to the temptation of demons, to plead the overmastering influence of environment, or to blame the inevitable toll of heredity for our failure is to sin and come short of the glory of God. We are reproached as we behold by faith the awful price paid by the Lamb of God at Calvary for our sins. For us He was scourged with a cat-o'-nine-tails, the Roman whip especially designed for such occasions. For us He bore the cross to the hill. For us He was nailed to that cross, and for us He suffered in agony the rejection that would come from the unrepentant. We are reproached by our own unconfessed sins in the light of His matchless sacrifice, His undying love.

Pilate washed his hands but he could never be rid of the guilt that was consequent to his crucifixion of the Son of God. The reproach of his sin was ever upon him and haunted him to his grave. Repentance might have broken this cycle, but power-hungry Pilate would not repent. This was his reproach, and it cast shame and obloquy on the authority of the Roman Empire, whose insigne, SPQR, "the senate and people of Rome," was inscribed on the back of Pilate's seat.

TILL DEATH

For the woman which hath an husband is bound by the law to her husband so long as he liveth; but if the husband be dead, she is loosed from the law of her husband. Rom. 7:2.

Marriage is for life. The pledge between husband and wife is clear on this point: "in sickness and in health, in prosperity or adversity." Yes, they are pledged to keep only to each other as long as they both shall live. What marriage is becoming in this world is another story. Erosion of the marriage relationship is not a new thing. It has been under assault since the advent of sin, so that today death has been supplanted by a hundred other man-made reasons for divorcing a mate. The fact is, marriage is a divine institution, and its success depends heavily upon divine principle. God is the author of marriage, and whenever a marriage is a valid one, it is a God-endorsed marriage. Christ literally inserts Himself, His character, into two hearts and binds them together for a common purpose.

There are rules that govern marriage just as there are rules that govern the growth of the body. If muscles are to be developed and the body health to be maintained, there are certain things that just must be done. So it is with a healthy marriage.

1. The early attentions and courtesies extended during courtship must be continued through marriage.

2. The tendency to argue and contend must be earnestly resisted for the sake of the marriage partners as well as for the children.

3. There must be an exercise of mutual agreement with reference to things financial. There can be no selfishness here. The needs of the individual must be subordinated to the greater good of the family or there will be disaster—financial and marital.

4. There must be frequent family conversations and consultations with reference to the direction in which the affairs of the family are headed. There should be as few surprises sprung on each other as possible.

5. There should be a rich spiritual emphasis both in home devotions and in church attendance. Prayer is the cement that binds a family to God and to one another.

197

SOFT ANSWER

A soft answer turneth away wrath: but grievous words stir up anger. **Prov. 15:1.**

Bishop Runnels has said, "Though men were as hard as rocks, the Word is a hammer that can break them; though as sharp as thorns and briars, the Word is a fire that can devour and torment them."

Anger feeds on harsh words. It is a fact that it takes two to make an argument. A clash of words produces tension and tension kills. My father once said, "When you're in an argument, suddenly strike silent. When your mouth is not running, your temper can cool. It will not be long until the other fellow understands that a monolog is foolish." Try the soft answer. The Bible says it turns away wrath.

I was driving an automobile through a little town in the State of Georgia. A fellow minister and I got into a heated discussion over some Biblical point, and without being aware of it, I was driving five miles over the posted speed limit. There was a wailing of sirens, and suddenly I realized my problem and pulled to a stop. Getting out of the car, I approached the officer. "Where is the fire?" he shouted. I gave him a soft answer. He decided to give me another chance without fining me. How much more peaceful the world would be if world leaders gave soft answers. Fewer marriages would end in divorce courts if one of the contending parties would give the soft answer.

Back in 1917 my father was court-martialed for not bearing arms. Quickly the word spread among the soldiers that Cleveland would not bear arms. They decided to give him a sand bath. Now, this is a very painful treatment, during which the man is stripped to the skin and repeatedly rubbed very hard with sand. My father sat studying his Bible and then was moved to get on his knees. Suddenly he heard the footsteps of possibly thirty soldiers climbing the stairs, intent on giving vent to their wrathful feelings on one man's body. My father continued on his knees in prayer. This was his soft answer. Suddenly they stopped, and they stood silently watching him. He continued in prayer as if they were not there, then slowly one by one they tiptoed down the stairs and away. Their wrath was spent.

UNDERSTANDING

He that refuseth instruction despiseth his own soul: but he that heareth reproof getteth understanding. Prov. 15:32.

Compliments are easy to absorb, but criticism is much more difficult. However, one's best friend will tell him the truth no matter what the consequences, and to reject constructive criticism is the height of folly. Such an attitude bespeaks pride. Some of the prophets of Israel suffered because the king wanted to hear only pleasing things. Prophets were promoted to positions of favor who could outdo others in predicting rosy futures. Conversely, those who told the truth, no matter how severe, were remanded to dungeons or exiled. The king always suffered the consequences of his own folly. By contrast there was King David, who, when rebuked by faithful prophets of God, repented of his sins, bedecked himself in sackcloth and ashes, and literally groveled before the Lord. This man loved his own soul. This man got understanding.

A good listener must have the spirit of meekness or he will never hear the voice of reproof without resentful reaction, and meekness is a very rare quality in our world. Jesus said, "Blessed are the meek: for they shall inherit the earth" (Matt. 5:5). Meekness is a quality that has to be cultivated. One must deliberately, by an act of the will, humble himself before God daily, acknowledging his sins. Some of the prayers of David are beautifully interspersed with confessions of unworthiness. Meekness is also often the product of suffering.

Peter in his earlier years was brash, impulsive, and quick tempered, but in that courtyard scene when the rooster's voice three times signaled the folly of human resolutions unaided by divine power and the piercing eye of the Son of God searched his soul, driving him to Gethsemane and to his knees, a different Peter emerged—a Peter meek and powerful. To say it better: His meekness was his power.

Most of the strife in our world may be traced to misunderstanding. There are too few people with the gift of being able to sit down and analyze a situation without emotion. The prayer of Solomon was for a wise and understanding heart. His prayer was answered, and today, thousands of years after his death, his wisdom is a legend.

FROM ABOVE

Jesus answered, Thou couldest have no power at all against me, except it were given thee from above: therefore he that delivered me unto thee hath the greater sin. John 19:11.

All power is from above. This was the message of Jesus to Pilate. This haughty Roman governor considered himself empowered of Caesar to administer the territory. To him Christ was just another problem to be dealt with. Pilate had said to Him, "Knowest thou not that I have power to crucify thee, and have power to release thee?" (John 19:10). It was in reply to this bold assertion that Christ provided this interesting revelation, "All power is indeed from above."

I think of the powers granted to us—the power to think, the power to act, the power to speak. These are simple capacities that men take for granted day by day, little realizing that there are countless thousands deprived of one or more of these powers. All power is from above. This is the basis for prayer and the study of the Word of God. These powers are gifts from God. In gratitude to Him for His beneficence, grateful hearts everywhere are uplifted to Him in prayer and thanksgiving for His wonderful works.

The Saviour's words must have impressed Pilate or frightened him, for the Bible says that from that time Pilate sought to release Him.

According to Harold E. Nicely, "Rufus Jones has pointed out that man lived for thousands of years before he discovered that electrical energy fills all space and touches our lives at every point. It is closer than the air we breathe, but it is revealed only when matter is so organized as to let it come through and operate. What a discovery that was. Likewise, a man makes a great discovery when he knows that the deeper forces of the universe are spiritual and can so organize his life as to let them come through and work in him. The Christian has found that secret. The universe works with him; is on his side; conspires for his well-being; furthers his undertakings and secures his hopes. There is power available for all of our needs. It is the power of God. When a man knows that, he can mount up with wings as the eagle. He can run and not be weary. He can walk and not faint."

SPIRIT OF ADOPTION

For ye have not received the spirit of bondage again to fear;
but ye have received the Spirit of adoption, whereby we cry, Abba,
Father. Rom. 8:15.

Sinful man has every natural reason to fear facing his Creator. The awfulness of transgression should not be lost on us, and the hatred of God for the sins of man is terrible beyond description, but through Jesus Christ all of this is changed. To the soul that accepts by faith the life of Christ as his own, the bondage of fear is immediately removed. Was it not prophesied that He would set at liberty the captive? This is true, gloriously true, and instead of the bondage of fear, we have received the Spirit of adoption. What a beautiful word! It signifies that though of a different family by nature we are recipients of divine love and have been transplanted into the kingdom of heaven by an act of free grace. "Marvelous grace of our loving Lord, Grace that exceeds our sin and our guilt, Yonder on Calvary's mount outpoured, There where the blood of the Lamb was spilt."

An adopted one does not earn his way into the affection of his parents, nor is there anything to recommend him as a member of the family by nature. He was and is, according to Scripture, an alien from the commonwealth of Israel, without God and without hope in the world. He has no merit of his own to qualify him for adoption. His only hope is in divine favor unmerited and undeserved, and this is how it came; this is the Spirit of adoption, this is the Spirit of Christ. What else could have made Him leave heaven and all its glories to walk in the valley of the shadow of death for thirty-three years? What else would make Him persevere to drink the cup when He could have shunned it and returned to His kingly throne? It was the Spirit of adoption, Christ's love for man, that led Him all the way to the cross.

When the missionaries stationed at Malahra set some of their converts to translate a catechism, they came to the revelation that through adoption we become sons of God. One of the translators was so startled that he dropped his pen, exclaiming, "It is too much. Let me rather render it, 'They shall be permitted to kiss His feet.'"

201

UNAWARE

The lord of that servant shall come in a day when he looketh not for him, and in an hour that he is not aware of. Matt. 24:50.

I visited old Pompeii. The ruins of the city speak of a tragedy that could have been avoided. Vesuvius, that giant volcano, stood quietly but majestically silhouetted against the sky, but hundreds of years ago tragedy spoke from its open heart. For days Vesuvius had been rumbling threateningly. Occasionally volcanic ash would be thrown into the air. The inhabitants of the city, undoubtedly trusting in the fact that they had seen these things before, paid little attention. Theirs was a constant round of revelry and mirth. They knew not that within a few hours they would be summoned to a judgment for which they were unprepared. The noises in that giant mountain of molten lava grew louder and louder day by day. This only increased the revelry and the fun, and then one day the very bowels of the earth erupted through the open mouth of that volcano. Fiery volcanic ash was belched into the air and descended like rain on the stricken inhabitants. In terror they ran for their lives, but too late. That which need not have overwhelmed them came in a surprising hour.

On the day of my visit in the museum that stands on the ruins of this old city, I saw the forms of men and women just as they had died. You see, someone visiting the ruins discovered holes in the ground. Into these holes they poured plaster of Paris, and when it hardened they dug the very shapes of the forms of human beings just as they had fallen. It will be so in the day when the Son of man shall come.

The Bible speaks of man going about his duties as usual as though unaware of impending catastrophe. Then suddenly the Son of God will break upon the world. The shocked inhabitants will run to the rocks and to the mountains, seeking shelter from the face of Him whom they have rejected and crucified and ignored. There will be another class, who will look up in that day and say, "This is our God; we have waited for him."

"There's life in a look at the sacred cross. Jesus has said, 'Look unto Me.' "

May we daily seek His face and make our peace with Him.

YOUR REST

Arise ye, and depart; for this is not your rest: because it is polluted, it shall destroy you, even with a sore destruction. Micah 2:10.

A few years ago I was climbing one of the giant pyramids outside Cairo. After ascending sixty feet, I sat down to rest. My Arab guide sat down, eying me quizzically. He said to me, "Do you think you can make it?" I said, "Perhaps we should turn back."

"Oh, but there is much more higher up," he said. With the promise of better things to come, I resumed the climb toward the top, but I soon got winded again and sat down in discouragement. My guide sat down and eyed me once more. "Just sixty more feet to go," he said, "and the giant stones—alabaster stones—that you will see will make the journey worth it all." With this promise I stood, and with aching muscles and faltering footsteps, made my way at last to the summit of the pyramid, there to behold the glories that had lured me from the earth. As I stood there I thought of the things that I had nearly missed. During those two rest stops I had almost given up.

I think of the Christian in his journey from earth to heaven. Often the path is steep and difficult to climb. With tired muscles and heavy hearts many are tempted to settle for less than the glories of the world beyond. To all such our text speaks today.

The Finnish people struck a coin on which they put the words *Ne Plus Ultra,* "no more beyond," but an enterprising explorer went farther than the others had gone and when he returned, he described the glories of his exploration. They struck another coin, *Plus Ultra,* "more beyond."

An hour of expectancy hung over our household. We had lived in the same house for about fifteen years and now we were going to move. The top of the hill marked the boundary line between our neighborhood and a better one. Up there the streets were paved and the houses were not substandard. What restlessness was ours as little boys as we loaded the furniture on the truck and made our way to the new and better location. Soon it will be moving day to the kingdom of God. How exultant we should be!

I AM FULL

But truly I am full of power by the spirit of the Lord, and of judgment, and of might, to declare unto Jacob his transgression, and to Israel his sin. Micah 3:8.

I grew up in the heart of the fertile Tennessee Valley. The power that floods that valley, bringing light to homes and moving the giant machines of industry, has its origin in the giant dynamos of the TVA. As one witnesses the evidence of the power that flows through the valley, he remembers its mighty source.

By a miracle of love, God has made it possible for the Christ life to be lived in human flesh. As men live victoriously by this power, their lives stand out as lights in a sin-darkened world. Since this is true, we would do well to remember the Source of divine power. The text says it is "by the spirit of the Lord."

According to James Smith, "Chemistry has performed many wonderful feats of transformation. What is more black and dirty and unpromising than coal tar? Yet it has been changed into the most beautiful and useful colors. The grace of God has wrought still more marvelous wonders. What could be more filthy and unpromising than a God-hating, blaspheming sinner steeped as in a cesspool of iniquity and possessed by the spirit of the devil? Yet the grace of God as by spiritual chemistry has transformed such depraved and hopeless characters into the most beautiful and useful lives."

And for what purpose? Micah recognized that the imparted power of God was given that we may bear to the world by word and deed the message of the saving grace of the Lord Jesus.

When the prophet Isaiah caught his larger vision of the Lord and was baptized with power, his response to the divine visitation was, "Here am I; send me" (Isa. 6:8). To which the God of heaven responded, "Go, and tell this people" (verse 9). And that is God's message to us today. This power is not given by measure but according as we need it in ministering the Word of truth for the salvation of others. To be filled with all the fullness of God should be our soul's deepest yearning, and to convey to others a knowledge of the blessings our own hearts have felt is our first response to the promised blessing.

WHOM HE RECEIVETH

For whom the Lord loveth he chasteneth, and scourgeth every son whom he receiveth. Heb. 12:6.

Christians have often wondered why it is that sinners seem to enjoy prosperity in this life while the child of God is often in stress and difficult circumstances. The Bible has not fully answered this question. David was concerned in the thirty-seventh psalm with this same problem. He wondered why the wicked prospered and spread like the green bay tree. The only assurance he got was that the wicked would eventually receive their due, and he was admonished, "Trust in the Lord with all thine heart; and lean not unto thine own understanding" (Prov. 3:5).

"God dealeth with you as with sons; for what son is he whom the father chasteneth not?" (Heb. 12:7). As a little boy I was frequently called to judgment. My father would patiently explain to me the nature of my transgression. He would assure me of his love before administering corporal punishment, which, he explained, was given because of that love.

A young man was thrashing about in the water drowning. His rescuer swam to his side and administered a firm blow on the jaw, knocking him senseless, and brought him to shore safely. When he awakened the young man said, "But why did you hit me so hard?" His rescuer answered, "I had to knock you out to save you."

The chastening of the Lord is for our salvation. Let us endure it with patience. Henry Ward Beecher has said, "Some have floated on the sea, and trouble carried them on its surface as the sea carries cork. Some have sunk at once to the bottom as foundering ships sink. Some have run away from their own thoughts, some have coiled themselves up into a stoical indifference, some have braved the trouble and defied it, some have carried it as a tree does a wound until by new wood it can overgrow and cover the old gash. A few in every age have known the divine art of carrying sorrow and trouble as wonderful food, as an invisible garment that clothed them with strength, as a mysterious joy so that they suffered gladly, rejoicing in infirmity and holding up their heads with sacred prestiges, whenever times were dark."

STRAIGHT PATHS

And make straight paths for your feet, lest that which is lame be turned out of the way; but let it rather be healed. Heb. 12:13.

The Bible declares, "None of us liveth to himself, and no man dieth to himself." Modern communication has made isolationism obsolete. The fact is every man that walks the earth influences somebody else. It is in this sense that the Christian is the salt of the earth, the light of the world. How often as a Christian minister have I heard sinners say, "Why should I join the church when So-and-so, who is a member of the church, does the same things that I do?" Thus the hypocritical Christian turns the lame out of the way. Conversely, I will never forget the testimony of a man who had been married to a Christian woman for thirty-five years before I baptized him. His testimony to me was, "Had it not been for that good woman who lived the life before me day by day, I would not be a Christian even now. I am one because of her." Christian, make straight paths for your feet, for the lame are watching you.

Farmers plowing a furrow in a field follow the focus of their eyes on a distant fixed objective. We, too, must have clear spiritual objectives if we would walk acceptably before God.

It is a fact that "you, Christian, are the only Bible that some soul will ever read. You are some sinner's gospel. You are some sinner's creed." As we journey through life our footsteps carve a path over which some lost soul will travel. Let us make straight paths for our own soul's sake and for the sake of those who follow after. Of course, it is impossible for man to correct his own delinquency, for his defection is rooted in the basic weakness of human nature, but grace is sufficient and divine power adequate to effect whatever changes are necessary. "For the grace of God that bringeth salvation hath appeared to all men, teaching us that, denying ungodliness and worldly lusts, we should live soberly, righteously, and godly, in this present world" (Titus 2:11, 12).

Divine grace is enabling power and by it we may become more than conquerors in this life and citizens of the world to come, through Him who has redeemed us.

LOVE NOT THE WORLD

Love not the world, neither the things that are in the world.
If any man love the world, the love of the Father is not in him.
1 John 2:15.

Christians should find little difficulty distinguishing between that which is of God and that which is of the world, for the evidence is clear. "For all that is in the world, the lust of the flesh, and the lust of the eyes, and the pride of life, is not of the Father, but is of the world" (verse 16). Lust is defined in Galatians 5:19-21: "Now the works of the flesh are manifest, which are these; Adultery, fornication, uncleanness, lasciviousness, idolatry, witchcraft, hatred, variance, emulations, wrath, strife, seditions, heresies, envyings, murders, drunkenness, revellings, and such like: of the which I tell you before, as I have also told you in time past, that they which do such things shall not inherit the kingdom of God."

The sad fact is, we are born with human nature, and there is in us all a natural tendency toward the things listed above. The command to "love not the world" contains an enabling promise. This is true of all God's commands. To the unregenerate soul the words, "Do not commit adultery," are a command, but to the regenerate Christian, "Thou shalt not commit adultery," implies a promise. God is literally saying, "Now that you have accepted Me as Saviour and Lord, the love of these things will not be in you."

What, then, is the secret of the new life? What is the key to victorious living? It is daily submission to the will of God through prayer and the study of the Word of God. New appetites are cultivated and old appetites are repressed. Under the influence of divine love the new life is born and men behold in us an increasing likeness to our Lord and Master. Let us surrender our lives to Him today. And it will be with us like entirely and wholly refitting an old ship and employing it in the service of a new and better master. Now when Christ meets and apprehends a man in conversion, he takes possession of the ship, puts in a new pilot, a new compass, and turns its prow another way; and all of the cargo the ship contains that he dislikes he throws overboard and fills it with better products.

SELF-DECEPTION

*For if a man think himself to be something, when he is noth-
ing, he deceiveth himself.* Gal. 6:3.

Wilbur Chapman tells the story of an Indian and a white man who
attended the same meeting of a missionary, and both were convicted of
their sinfulness. In a short time the Indian was rejoicing over the grace
of God which he had experienced. The white man was long downcast
and full of despair even though the sun of righteousness shone in his
heart also. Some time later he said to the Indian, "How was it that
you could rejoice in Jesus so soon while I had such a hard struggle
before peace entered my heart?"

"Brother," said the Indian, "I will answer you. Suppose a chief
would approach us both and say, 'I will give you new clothes.' You look
at your own, which are pretty good, and say, 'Mine will do for a while,
thank you.' But I look at my soiled and torn clothes, and I say, 'I need
others badly enough. I accept your gift immediately.' That is the difference, my friend. I am happy now, for I realize that my righteousness is as filthy rags. Until that fact dawns on you, you will continue
to be miserable."

Before we can become Christians we must literally love self less.
Christ refuses to compete with man for the possession of his heart.
There must be willingness on the part of man to surrender the whole
heart and life. Indeed, we must be willing to be made willing.

A little boy was seen by his mother playing in the dangerous
streets. "Come in, Johnny," she shouted.

The little boy answered, "I don't want to."

"But it's dangerous out there," the mother answered. "Why don't
you want to?"

To which the little boy replied, "Well, Mamma, I don't want to
want to."

We must want to *want* to be saved. This involves an act of the
will; a conscious commitment of the life. Until this is done we will
serve our Lord as slaves would serve a taskmaster.

May the prayer of our heart today be, "None of self and all of
Thee."

THE TIME IS COME

The time is come, the day draweth near: let not the buyer rejoice, nor the seller mourn: for wrath is upon all the multitude thereof. Eze. 7:12.

God had selected Israel from all nations of the earth to be a kingdom of priests to represent His grace to a heathen world. He had conferred upon them every beneficence of a loving Father. He had parted rivers, caused water to flow from the rock, rained food from heaven to sustain their needs. He fought their battles and vanquished their enemies and at last secured them in the land of Canaan. He blessed their kings to build their cities and to establish the greatness of the kingdom under the whole heaven. But when Israel prospered they disgraced God. They went after gods of wood and stone, those that were worshiped by the nations that surrounded them. God's commandments were put at naught, His grace was despised, and they were as those who had never heard of the coming Messiah and His promised redemption. The day of recompense came, and the seventh chapter of the book of Ezekiel details the judgments of God upon His backslidden children. "The time is come, the day draweth near," said the prophet, and the wrath of God is upon the multitude.

Dwight Moody was in Chicago during the great Chicago fire. He states, "As the flames rolled down the streets, destroying everything in their onward march, I saw the great and the honorable, the learned and the wise, fleeing before the fire with the beggar and the thief and the harlot. All were alike. As the flames swept through the city, it was like judgment day. The mayor, nor the mighty men, nor the wise men could stop these flames. They were all on a level then, and many who were worth thousands of dollars were paupers that night. When the day of judgment comes, there will be no difference. When the deluge came, there was no difference. Noah's ark was worth more than all the world. The day before it was the laughingstock, and if it had been put up for auction, you could not have gotten anybody to buy it except for firewood. But the deluge came, and then it was worth more than all the world together. And when the judgment day comes then Christ will be worth more than ten thousand worlds."

PREPARE YE THE WAY

For this is he that was spoken of by the prophet Esaias, saying, The voice of one crying in the wilderness, Prepare ye the way of the Lord, make his paths straight. Matt. 3:3.

It is said that a heathen king wounded in battle sent in his dying hours for his trusted servant and said to him: "Go tell the dead I come." The soldier's servant, without hesitating for a moment, drew his sword and stabbed himself to the heart that he might precede his master in death. The spirit of this mistaken servant challenges the Christian in his mission for Christ. As in the case of John the Baptist, the voice of the Christian is the voice of one crying in the wilderness, "Prepare ye the way of the Lord, make his paths straight."

It was an ancient custom that when a king was to traverse the streets, a crier would go ahead of him shouting, "The king cometh, the king cometh," thus preparing the way. Often the citizens would spread their garments on the road over which the king would travel.

Christians today are God's criers, His forerunners. They are to go before Him announcing His coming and urging men to prepare to meet Him. Gladly should we spread our plans before Him, anxious over them, for unless they find His approval they cannot flourish. The responsibility of the church in this regard is indeed a serious one, for it is charged in this day of His preparation with the twin obligation of witnessing to souls in lands afar as well as to neighbors at home. Each of us has a part in the program. With our means we send missionaries to those abroad, but our consecrated energies must be employed individually in witnessing at home. Neither pride nor fear must stand in the way. The word must go out. "Christ is coming soon." Will you lend Him your hands, your feet, your voice?

In 1932 the President of the United States visited Chattanooga, Tennessee. I shall never forget the excitement in our city on this occasion. Streets were given a special cleaning, flags were hung, and schools dismissed for the day. I stood in the crowd along Market Street as the open limousine passed and the big friendly face of the American President was seen. For days ahead men had been in the city preparing his way. Can we do less for our Lord?

CALL FOR THE ELDERS

Is any sick among you? let him call for the elders of the church; and let them pray over him, anointing him with oil in the name of the Lord. James 5:14.

The Christian physician is a God-ordained blessing to the world. His work is responsible for the saving of countless lives. But even the wisest among men of medicine admit that there are cases that are beyond their capacity. It is well to pray even when the situation is under control, but when the Grim Reaper hovers ominously near, our chief resource is divine intervention. We are instructed to "call for the elders of the church."

While on earth Christ exhibited a deep interest in the healing of the sick. Lepers were cured, the lame were made to walk, the dumb to talk, the deaf to hear, and even the dead were raised to life. We cannot ignore the manifest interest of Christ in man's physical well-being. The sad fact is that many Christians assume that because Christ is not present in the flesh today His work of healing bodies has been discontinued. Nothing could be further from the truth. In our own day there have been many miracles of physical healing. Men have taken their ills to Christ in prayer, and He has heard and answered.

A remarkable instance of simple faith took place in Africa. The day was a typical scorcher on the grasslands. A teen-age native boy lay dying of a fever. His mother asked prayers for the ice she was told he needed for recovery. Half doubting, the native pastor made the prayer. A sudden hailstorm furnished hailstones as large as hens' eggs. Cold packs were made and the boy was saved. The Lord asks, "Is there any thing too hard for me?" (Jer. 32:27).

If Divine Providence should see fit to heal the body, and we want to give the rest of our days to the promulgation of the gospel, His cause should be our first concern. The Bible declares, "The effectual fervent prayer of a righteous man availeth much." If this be so, we are living beneath our privileges when we fail to pray for good health.

And for those who seek prayer for their physical illnesses there is this word of caution: there are many false prophets in the land today praying for healing of the sick. Let us "try the spirits" (1 John 4:1).

211

MY CHURCH

And I say also unto thee, That thou art Peter, and upon this rock I will build my church; and the gates of hell shall not prevail against it. Matt. 16:18.

Of all the religions of the earth only Christianity claims a church. The church is a body of called-out ones—believers in the Lord Jesus Christ. If the knowledge of God was to overspread the earth, the church was a necessity. Hence the diligence with which Christ built it. The true church of God in these last days may be clearly distinguished from other religions and churches by two outstanding characteristics, set forth in Revelation 14:12: "Here is the patience of the saints: here are they that keep the commandments of God, and the faith of Jesus."

Having discovered the church of the living God, the adherent should find it important to enter fully into all the privileges of worship, fellowship, and service that the church affords. Thus alone is the church meaningful to one's spiritual development. The church should be taken seriously or let alone, for Christ calls it His church. He founded it and established it and has promised that "the gates of hell shall not prevail against it."

The church can be exceedingly dull if one pledges only half-hearted allegiance to it, but it can be the most exciting institution on earth when one makes it the center of his life activity. For you see, the church is charged with the supreme mission of reconciling man to God and man to his fellow man. In this vast twofold program there is plenty to claim the earnest attention of all.

There are some who, when they discover that they have not overcome all their weaknesses, stay away from church services and regard attendance under such circumstances as hypocrisy. This is an unfortunate conclusion. It is not the man who is well who needs the physician, but the sick. The church provides spiritual remedy for sin. For one to absent himself from the sacred environs of the church is to separate from the only cure for his illness. The suggestion is then that we forsake not "the assembling of ourselves together, as the manner of some is," but press in so much the more as our soul needs become apparent.

HE WHICH CONVERTETH

Let him know, that he which converteth the sinner from the error of his way shall save a soul from death, and shall hide a multitude of sins. James 5:20.

Of course, Christ alone converts a soul, but human beings are the instruments of conversion. Every convert must become a convert maker. It is the solemn duty of those who possess great light to share it with others. The benefits of such a course are many. Our text states that we save a soul from death and thus hide a multitude of sins.

Under the terms of conversion sins are covered. They are cast "into the depths of the sea." That man who is saved from sin has his sins covered, and therefore they no longer rise to condemn him.

The power of man over other men must not be underestimated. It is probably because of this that God committed to man the responsibility of reaching other men with the saving knowledge of the grace of God.

A ship was wrecked offshore, and a young man kept diving in to rescue those who were sinking. Again and again he went into the icy waters and came back shivering with a passenger in tow. Finally, those who stood on the banks noticed his fatigue and warned him, "You'd better not go out there again; you'll never get back."

His answer was, "I don't have to come back, but I do have to go." One more trip into the icy waters, and the story says that he brought back his own blood brother.

Soulsaving also strengthens the spiritual muscle of the evangelist. Someone has said, "If you would save yourselves, save others." We are builders of the kingdom of God. Our talents are tools in the hand of the Almighty for the salvation of our fellow man. John Knox of Scotland cried, "Give me Scotland or I die." Not until we identify others' soul interest with our own are we truly Christian.

We are often overwhelmed with problems, but when we become involved with others we discover that many of them are in such dire difficulty that our own troubles appear as nothing. This is one of the blessings of involvement. We forget ourselves as we reach for solutions for our fellow man, and thereby often find them for ourselves.

THE GLORY

Whether therefore ye eat, or drink, or whatsoever ye do, do all to the glory of God. **1 Cor.** 10:31.

True religion does not confine itself to the heart but expresses itself in thoughts, words, and actions. It even influences the daily habits of life, such as eating and drinking. As in all other areas of Christian requirement, restrictions on diet are for man's best good. God does not prohibit just for the sake of withholding. The health laws of the Bible relative to eating are merciful provisions of divine grace for man's physical, spiritual, and mental well-being. As to drinking, alcoholic beverages and those with narcotic content should be excluded from the Christian's diet.

The evils of smoking have been clearly demonstrated in scientific research laboratories. They need not be recited here. We need only point out that one cannot smoke and use narcotics to the glory of God.

The Christian religion also relates itself to man's eating habits. There are animals classified in the Bible as being unclean and therefore forbidden. There are others that the Bible grants man permission to eat. It is abundantly clear, however, that the present diseased state of the animal kingdom makes the continued consumption of flesh food exceedingly hazardous. When the world stood in its most ideal state, flesh foods were not an article of diet. This light on diet God has gone to great pains to share with His people. Is it not high time that as Christians we aimed our footsteps toward the light?

Whatever we do, may we resolve today to make the glory of God our primary concern. One of the great dangers in all reformatory practice is that our motives shift from the glory of God to the glory of ourselves. There are those who practice abstemiousness and pride themselves that they are not like other men. These saints use the health reform program as a lash with which they reproach other Christians, with obvious self-approval. This is not to the glory of God, but is rather the outworking of pride that lies unrecognized within the human heart. The closer to God one gets, the more humble he becomes; and the nearer his habits resemble those of his Saviour, the more considerate he is of others. This is transformation through reformation.

THROUGH GOD

Through God we shall do valiantly: for he it is that shall tread down our enemies. Ps. 60:12.

Thinking Christians view with alarm the dark history of persecution during the Dark Ages. They see in this history a foretaste of the future. Add to this the definite predictions of prophecy, "There shall be a time of trouble, such as never was since there was a nation even to that time," and the picture is indeed foreboding.

But there is a bright note to this prophecy. We find it in Daniel 12:1: "And at that time thy people shall be delivered, every one that shall be found written in the book." And "through God we shall do valiantly: for he it is that shall tread down our enemies." The assurance that we will not be alone in the time of trouble comforts our hearts.

Many have read the passages of warning in *The Great Controversy* and secretly long to be laid to rest before that time comes. They need have no fear, for the God who shepherded His church through the first-century persecutions will be with us then. Did He desert Daniel in his ordeal in the lions' den? The answer is a simple No. Did He desert the Hebrew boys in their trial by fire? The answer is No. Did He desert Elijah in his wilderness escape from Jezebel? The answer is No. Angels were there to minister to his physical needs. We need have no doubt that the God of Abraham, Isaac, and Jacob is ours and will in the day of utmost necessity be to us a shelter and a refuge from the storm. These men who stood almost alone in time of spiritual peril prove that one with God is a majority.

I was sent to the city of Port of Spain, Trinidad, to conduct an evangelistic campaign. It was the rainy season, and the predominant religion is one that makes the progress of Adventism difficult. Furthermore, there were forty-six ministers there as part of the evangelistic team. Their eyes would also be upon me. My heart cried out to God: "Who is sufficient for these things?" Paul supplies the obvious answer, "Our sufficiency is of God" (2 Cor. 3:5). And God indeed came mightily to our help. A great victory was won in that city. Through Him we did valiantly.

MY SALVATION

Truly my soul waiteth upon God: from him cometh my salvation. Ps. 62:1.

A young man who had trouble with his eyes consulted his doctor, who said: "There are two cataracts growing over your eyes and your only hope of preserving your sight is to visit a specialist. I would advise you to go at once, and don't forget to take many dollars in your pocket, for you might find the fee heavy."

The working man had eighty dollars in the bank, and drew it all out. The specialist examining his eyes said, "I am not sure whether you can pay the fee. I never take less than three hundred dollars."

"Then," said the working man, "I must go blind and remain so."

To which the specialist replied, "You cannot come up to my terms and I cannot go down to yours, but there is another way open. I can perform the operation free." This is exactly salvation's terms. Man cannot reach God's terms of himself. Nor can God bend to meet man's. There is another way.

A Christian woman visited a poor, sick neighbor woman. After conversing with her for a while she asked if she had found salvation. "No," said the sick woman, "but I am working hard at it."

"Ah," said the other, "you will never get it that way. Christ did all the working, and when He suffered and died for us and made complete atonement for our sins, this was all the work required. You must take salvation solely as a gift of unmerited grace or you can never have it."

God is the sole source of saving grace. The words of my text provide the key for tapping this boundless resource. "Truly my soul waiteth upon God." Good works are an outgrowth of the saved experience. Salvation is solely the work of God on the human heart. Repentance, confession, and faith are the conditions for this operation. All who possess these possess Christ and are truly saved from their sins in this life. This is the basis of all true obedience. Conformity to the law of God based on a true heart experience such as is here described can never be termed legalism. It is the natural outworking of grace in the heart of the believer. Obedience becomes the barometer of man's inner state of grace. By it we know if a man knows God.

216

THE WAGES OF SIN

For the wages of sin is death; but the gift of God is eternal life through Jesus Christ our Lord. Rom. 6:23.

A woman caught a small creature which she thought was a chameleon and attached it by a short chain to her collar so that it could crawl about on her shoulder. The chameleon is a harmless little reptile which changes its color from gray to green or red; it is considered beautiful by some people. Instead of a chameleon, however, this creature was a poisonous kind of lizard, and it bit her and caused her death. What this woman did with this apparently harmless animal, millions of people are doing every day—fondling a viper called sin.

> "There are two guides for travelers, only two guides:
> One's the Good Shepherd, e'en through the death tides,
> The other, the serpent, beguiling with sin
> Whose beauty external hides poison within."

The danger in sin is not always apparent to the naked eye, for like the chameleon, it has the mysterious property of changing color according to its environment. Sin is safe only when it is let alone.

The story is told of a circus performer who did his act with a snake he had raised from babyhood. One evening as he allowed the giant serpent to coil around his body he discovered to his horror that the python was tightening his body in the death grip. In horror he cried out, but the audience thought it was a part of the act. They awakened to the truth only when, mid the breaking of bones and oozing of blood from his nose, they realized that the pet had become the killer of his master.

Someone leaving the scene was heard to observe, "No matter how long you know it or how familiar you get, a snake is still a snake." And may I add, no matter how familiar you get with it, sin is still sin, and the wages of sin is death. Our text, however, ends on a high note; it says: "But the gift of God is eternal life through Jesus Christ our Lord." There is one antidote to sin, and that is the blood of Jesus Christ. Those who deal with snakes carry with them a snake serum so that if bitten they can use the hypodermic and set up a resistance to the poison. The antidote to sin is free grace.

217

TRUST IN HIM

Trust in him at all times; ye people, pour out your heart before him: God is a refuge for us. **Ps. 62:8.**

The celebrated Dr. Guthrie gives us an insight to travel in the Alps. He says, "I have known a timid traveler whose route lay across the higher Alps along a path no broader than a mule could walk that skirted a dreadful precipice from which could be discerned the river far below, diminished to a silver thread. On this dizzy precipice I have known a timid traveler who fancied it safest to shut her eyes and not attempt to guide the horse or touch the bridle. A careless touch would have thrown the steed and rider to a horrible death."

The rider must trust in his animal at all times. Panic that comes from fear must be steadfastly resisted. This is even more so as we face life's problems. We must be aware that at all times God knows the road we follow, the dangers we face, and that He is there to meet our every need. Most of us trust in God spasmodically. He appeals for deep, abiding, and constant reliance upon Him. This precludes all worry. We cannot, reasons the Bible, by taking thought add one cubit to our stature. The obvious question is, then, Why worry?

I have seen men whose vocation is that of walking tightropes high above the earth. I have seen one such act in which three people balanced themselves upon a fourth and performed their act. Their confidence in one another must never fail lest catastrophe ensue.

Several German princes were extolling the glory of their realms. They boasted of their vineyards, their hunting grounds, their mines. Abelard interrupted them: "I own that I am a poor prince and can vie with none of these things, nevertheless I too possess a noble jewel in my dominion, for were I to be without attendants, either in the open country or wild forest, I could ask the first of my subjects whom I met to stretch himself upon the ground and confidently place my head upon his bosom and fall asleep without the slightest apprehension of injury."

This is an excellent example of trust by the Christian who can rest his head and heart in the lap of God's providence with perfect assurance that neither man nor devil can touch him there.

IDOLS

Little children, keep yourselves from idols. 1 John 5:21.

An idol is a poor substitute for the living God. It may assume any form other than that of God. An idol may be an angel, a human being, or a material object. By this definition, idolatry may be correctly understood as being widespread, and I should add that some men worship themselves. Gold, silver, brick and mortar, steel and concrete, are the new idols of this age, but idols endanger the relationship between man and his Maker. "For I the Lord thy God am a jealous God" (Ex. 20:5). He will share His glory with none other. It is said that at the grave of Medzumi Kozo, who was a famous pickpocket, incense is always found burning. Who offers this incense? All the pickpockets of Tokyo burn incense there. He is the god of the pickpockets. When I was traveling in the southern part of the island of Kyushu, one day I found a certain temple with a great many flags and banners flying from it. I asked what kind of temple this was. It certainly must be one of a famous god. The man answered, "It is the god of the gamblers. All these flags and banners were offered by gamblers from all parts of the country. And if you have faith in this god, you will win all the games whether in gambling, in stock speculation, or even in wrestling and fighting."

Idols are a poor substitute for the living God. They can neither reward nor punish, bless nor curse. They are but cruel extensions of the human personality. Through them man worships himself. The God who created heaven and earth tolerates no competition. He will have all of us or none. He is outraged that man, the highest created creature on earth, would turn from worship of the high and Holy One who inhabits eternity to the adoration of images; yet millions of sincere worshipers bow down to gods of wood and stone, seeking relief from the day-to-day abrasive problems that plague mankind. Would to God that the pointlessness of their idolatry could reach them and that their hearts could be turned to the worship of the true God. This is the mission of every Christian. May we be about our Father's business. Any interest or appetite or passion that weakens our relationship with God is idolatrous.

HE WROTE OF ME

For had ye believed Moses, ye would have believed me: for he wrote of me. But if ye believe not his writings, how shall ye believe my words? John 5:46, 47.

The Scriptures cannot be broken. There are those who have been trying to do it though for many years. Abroad in our world is the doctrine that the New Testament is the only rule of faith and practice for the Christian but that the Old Testament is good only for history and for reference. Jesus thought to dispel this and other related superstitions. He validates the writings of Moses by assuring His listeners that he (Moses) wrote of Him (Jesus). We may, therefore, trace the life of Christ in the writings of the Old Testament. We may find there the story of His mission to the earth and of His teachings. Someone has said that the Old Testament is the New Testament concealed, and the New Testament is the Old Testament revealed. In any event, Moses is freely quoted in the Scriptures, and the Old Testament is the only scriptures the apostles had from which to preach. Indeed, it was from Old Testament writings that the apostles proved that the Christ of the New Testament was indeed the Son of God and the promised Messiah.

The wisdom of the Bible is attested to in all ages by many interesting events. The fact that the Standard Oil Company discovered oil and is operating wells in Egypt is generally known, but the reason for its going to the ancient land to look for oil is probably not so well known. It is asserted that one of the directors of the company happened to read the second chapter of Exodus. The third verse caught his attention. It states that the ark of bulrushes which the mother of Moses made for her child was "daubed . . . with slime and with pitch." This gentleman reasoned that where there was pitch there must be oil, and if there was oil in Moses' time, it was probably still there. So the company sent out Charles Whitshact, its geologist and oil expert, to make investigations, with the result that oil was discovered. There are now wells in operation there, with more to be opened.

Yes, the message of God is to be found in the Book. The wisdom of God it enfolds has been attested to even by skeptics who approached it without belief.

220

MARVEL NOT

Marvel not at this: for the hour is coming, in the which all that are in the graves shall hear his voice. John 5:28.

There is life in the voice of God. When Adam and Eve sinned, God came walking in the cool of the evening, saying, "Adam, where art thou?" His voice brought assurance to the stricken couple and gave them hope of life. It was the voice of their Creator. It was the voice of God that gave birth to this universe and to our planet. "By the word of the Lord were the heavens made; and all the host of them by the breath of his mouth. . . . For he spake, and it was done; he commanded, and it stood fast" (Ps. 33:6-9).

It was the voice of God that calmed the wind and the waves on the Sea of Galilee, and brought sight to the blind and health to the lame. It is that voice which will sound from heaven at the end of the age, penetrating the earth to the very ears of the righteous dead. The Bible says, "All that are in the graves shall hear his voice, and shall come forth." It is important that we get familiar with the voice of God now. He speaks to us through the Bible, the Word of God. He speaks through nature. He speaks to us through dreams and visions. He speaks to us by impressions. Yes, "He speaks, and the sound of His voice Is so sweet the birds hush their singing; And the melody That He gave to me, Within my heart is ringing."

A youth bent on a night of pleasure was picked up by a young woman driving an automobile. He got into the automobile, and after making a few flippant remarks, was suddenly aware that this was not an ordinary girl at all. He said that it seemed she was talking to him and yet the words coming from her lips were not hers but another's, and they burned more in his soul than in his ears. Her conversation was on heavenly things and his whole life was reviewed before him so that he was made ashamed of his course of sin. With troubled mind he got out of the automobile, and at four o'clock in the morning knocked at the door of a minister of God, who led him to the foot of the cross. You cannot convince this young man that the voice he heard was not the voice of God. "The words that I speak unto you, they are spirit, and they are life" (John 6:63).

221

HE HEARETH US

And this is the confidence that we have in him, that, if we ask any thing according to his will, he heareth us. 1 John 5:14.

One of the most terrifying feelings about being lost is to shout without a knowledge of being heard. Men have been known to panic and die of fear from the grim realization that their voices were not being heard. To know that prayers uttered here on earth are heard in heaven is comforting assurance.

A little boy fell into a well. For hours he screamed without anyone coming to his rescue. Suddenly his uncontrollable sobs were interrupted by a voice at the mouth of the well. It was the voice of his father. "Tommy, is that you down there?" Hope sprang up in his young heart when he knew that he would be saved.

Perhaps the greatest producer of misery in our world is loneliness. The human heart by nature craves communication. We just must talk to somebody at some time. How sweet to know that the Lord's arm is not shortened that it cannot save, nor is His ear heavy that it cannot hear. One of the most inspiring things about the God we serve is His sensitivity to human need. People that men walked by and ignored on earth, Christ comforted with a word or applied a healing hand.

On the road to Jericho a little man crouched in curiosity on a limb, wanting to see Jesus when He passed. Who noticed this tax collector as he sat there among the leaves? Christ did. "Zacchaeus, make haste, and come down; for to day I must abide at thy house" (Luke 19:5). And He turned aside to this despised young man and taught him the way of life. This is the confidence that we have in Him, that if we ask anything according to His will, He heareth us. This is the lesson of the woman with an issue of blood for twelve years. She merely touched the hem of His garment and was made whole. "The healing of His seamless dress is by our beds of pain."

But not all of God's answers give us what we ask. However, He always supplies our deepest need. Therefore, His every answer, whether yes or no, is in our favor. All things therefore work together for good, and when He denies our request, the comforting thing is, we have been heard when we conversed with Him.

CONTENTMENT

But godliness with contentment is great gain. 1 Tim. 6:6.

Few people are contented with anything. Man is forever reaching out for what he doesn't have. Whether what he seeks is good or bad depends upon the man. The fact is, the basis of all genuine contentment is godliness. Without it there can be no soul satisfaction. On the other hand, some of the happiest people on the face of the earth are without an adequate supply of life's necessities. This is one of the great mysteries of life. It is a fact that there are those left with all that money can secure who are miserable in their innermost souls.

Riches and poverty in themselves, then, do not necessarily produce misery, for there are many rich and poor who have found peace and contentment of soul. The presence of Christ in the life makes the difference. "Come unto me, all ye that labour and are heavy laden, and I will give you rest" (Matt. 11:28), said Jesus. Contentment is a gift of God. It should be understood, however, that the peace of mind referred to in our verse refers not to satisfaction with mediocrity. There must ever beat in the bosom of the believer an aspiration for betterment—spiritual, physical, and mental. This is no encouragement to rest on one's laurels, for whatever achievement. We must ever remember that nothing we have done, however efficient, is enough.

The warning of our text is against competitive ambition—the tendency to want to "keep up with the Joneses." Contentment does not need to impede progress; rather it should enable one to enjoy life as it is as one presses on to life as it may become. We will travel this way but once. We owe it to ourselves to live and die happy. This is our privilege. The text assures us of this, and tells us how to achieve it. There is a feverishness associated with discontent, a restlessness that keeps a person ever on the move. The root of restless discontent is sin. "There is no peace, saith my God, to the wicked" (Isa. 57:21). "O that thou hadst hearkened to my commandments! then had thy peace been as a river, and thy righteousness as the waves of the sea" (chap. 48:18).

The restful calm of a still sea is a perfect picture of the contented saint who reflects the peace in the face of the Master he loves.

UNTHANKFUL

This know also, that in the last days perilous times shall come. For men shall be lovers of their own selves, covetous, boasters, proud, blasphemers, disobedient to parents, unthankful, unholy. 2 Tim. 3: 1, 2.

The focus of this thought today is on the word "unthankful." This is in truth a sign of our times. Parents who have spent their lives sacrificing for their children awaken to the shock of their ingratitude in later life when many of them are allowed in old age to fend for themselves, with not a letter or even a visit from the child.

It was a September day, 1860, that *Lady Elgin,* an overloaded steamer, floundered off the shore of Lake Michigan just above Evanston. Spectators gathered on the shore. One of them, Edward W. Spencer, a student in Garrett Biblical Institute, saw a woman clinging to some wreckage far out in the breakers. He threw off his coat and swam out through the heavy waves, succeeding in getting her back to the land and safety. Sixteen times during that day young Spencer fought the heavy waves, rescuing seventeen persons, then he collapsed in exhaustion. While tossing in delirium that night, he cried over and over to his brother, "Did I do my best? Oh, I'm afraid I did not do my best!" When his brother tried to quiet him by saying, "You saved seventeen lives," he would reply, "Oh, if I could have saved one more!"

Ed Spencer slowly recovered, and finally died at eighty-one. In the newspaper account of his death it was stated that not one of the seventeen people had returned to say thanks for his having saved their lives.

With indignation we read of the ten lepers who were healed by Christ and only one returned to give Him thanks. Are we thankful day by day for the blessings God bestows upon us? And do we pause to say thanks to our fellow man for little kindnesses rendered?

Our thoughts turn to a lonely hill where on a cross hung the Son of the living God. As He surveyed the multitudes wagging their heads and hurling insults in His face, perhaps the most difficult thing for Him to take was their ingratitude, for these were souls He came to save. God forbid that we should be among those who despise Him.

WE SHALL REIGN

If we suffer, we shall also reign with him: if we deny him, he also will deny us. 2 Tim. 2:12.

Humanity naturally recoils from suffering. Pain is no pleasure, and yet in the history of the Christian church more blood was shed than in any of the great wars of history. Christians willingly went to their death as the comforting power of God was manifest in their souls and on their countenances. We read of the martyrs of the Middle Ages. Many of them died singing while flames consumed their bodies. Others were thrown to lions, placed on the rack, and tortured in dozens of fiendish fashions, and yet they never faltered. They were willing to die for Him who had died for them.

Persecution is one of Satan's chief weapons. Knowing man's natural love for life, he naturally seeks to gain decisions for apostasy by threatening.

Twenty years ago in an Alabama city I baptized a young high school girl. From the day of her baptism her life became a hell on earth in her home. She was beaten, threatened, and harassed in dozens of ways. She finally made good her escape from home and attended an Adventist college and married a young Seventh-day Adventist hospital attendant. The fury of her parents turned to pride as they saw the course that she took led to an honorable marriage and a Christian home. But if we deny Him, He will also deny us the scripture says.

I think of Pontius Pilate, who had a marvelous opportunity when he met the Lord to demonstrate not only his fairness as a judge but his basic integrity as a human being. Again and again he confessed that he could find no fault with Christ, but for reasons of his own he refused to set Him free. When he washed his hands he denied the Lord. Tradition has it that he sought to save his own position but in the end he lost it and became a hopeless maniacal wanderer.

Those who refuse to fall on the stone and be broken will be fallen upon by the stone and ground to powder. The apostle Peter denied the Lord, but in a moment of abject repentance he made the full cycle swing from despondency to spiritual ecstasy. Better to suffer and reign with Him than to deny Him and be denied in the latter day.

THE SERVANT OF THE LORD

And the servant of the Lord must not strive; but be gentle unto all men, apt to teach, patient. 2 Tim. 2:24.

We live in an age when might makes right. The tendency to retaliate and defend oneself is well-nigh universal. To absorb mistreatment in silence is a sign of meekness. To suffer for Christ's sake is glory and to do it as He did it is a sign of strength. It is indeed the only true evidence of the meekness that Christ said would inherit the earth. The tendency to defend oneself is natural. When one has the new nature he is less defensive. It should be made abundantly clear, however, that there is a difference between defense of self and defense of principle. To sit in abject silence in the face of offended principle is not a virtue; it is a sign of weakness. Nothing illustrates this more clearly than the life of Jesus Christ and the lives of His apostles. When attacked Himself, Christ stood meekly as a lamb. He was led to the slaughter. On the cross He was challenged by the two thieves to come down to save Himself and them. To this He answered not a word, but when the sanctity of the Temple was threatened, He took a whip and drove out the moneychangers. When the character of His Father was impugned, He literally baffled His detractors in daily debate with the Pharisees and Sadducees.

Yes, the Christian may be at the very forefront of the battle in defense of principle and his fellow man, but when attacked personally, if he defends himself it will be with meekness and sobriety. He will avoid strife and in patience try to teach. But he will above all try to maintain his spiritual balance.

Violence is outside the realm of the Christian's thinking. He would rather die himself than inflict physical injury on someone else. Nevertheless, within the realm of Christian principle, assertiveness is not condemned. The apostle Paul asserted his rights as a Roman citizen when his civil rights were violated and yet submitted to the authority of civil government in the process, but in matters of Christian principle he would have died rather than compromise. Humility is the most powerful weapon in the world, for it acknowledges that vengeance belongs to God (Rom. 12:19).

NOT BOUND

Wherein I suffer trouble, as an evil doer, even unto bonds; but the word of God is not bound. 2 **Tim.** 2:9.

The messenger was in chains, falsely accused and under arrest. He assures us, however, that that which he represents is not chained; indeed, that it cannot be chained. "The word of God," he says, "is not bound." How true this is. From one end of the earth to the other, in dozens of languages, men are able to read the Word of God for themselves. This was not always so. There was a time in our world when it was a crime to possess the pages of the Holy Bible. During the Middle Ages soldiers swarmed over the country in search of heretics who might possess a few pages of Holy Writ.

I have heard it said that the gray heron has a very singular mode of defense. When attacked by the eagle or the falcon it simply stands quiet and firm, using its bill as a sword, allowing the enemy to pierce himself through by his own force. The Word of God is a sword of defense to the Christian. You need not wield it so energetically; just stand firm and allow the enemy to batter himself senseless against its sharp edge. All over the earth the unbound Word of God is accomplishing its righteous purposes in human hearts. Drunkards are being sobered, philanderers are being rendered moral, thieves are becoming honest under the persistent hammering of this Holy Book. There is a divine power that accompanies the reading of the Bible. This few people will deny. Evidence of its burning words can be seen from one end of the earth to the other. From the king's palace to the aborigine of the New Guinea forest, men by reading it become aware of their own dignity and begin to walk as children of God.

Thank God the Word is not bound and that men of every nation, kindred, tongue, and people may read and understand!

Among the dead on one of the battlefields near Richmond, Virginia, was a Rebel soldier who lay unburied days after the conflict. Already the flesh had been eaten from his fingers by worms, but underneath the skeleton hand lay an open Bible, and the fingers pressed upon those precious words of the twenty-third psalm: "Thy rod and thy staff they comfort me."

SOUND WORDS

Hold fast the form of sound words, which thou hast heard of me, in faith and love which is in Christ Jesus. 2 Tim. 1:13.

A new and grave danger threatened the Christian church. The apostle Paul himself had predicted that men would "heap to themselves teachers, having itching ears" (2 Tim. 4:3), and "that after my departing shall grievous wolves enter in among you, not sparing the flock. Also of your own selves shall men arise, speaking perverse things, to draw away disciples after them" (Acts 20:29, 30). Knowing this to be true, he exhorted them to hold fast the form of sound words.

Sound words, as they relate to Christianity, are Bible-based words. This is the secret of their soundness. When men lead other men astray by human philosophy and vain reasonings they are not delivering sound words.

One day John Randolph had a clergyman as his guest, and the family Bible became a topic of the conversation. The eccentric orator said, "I was raised by a pious mother, who taught me the Christian religion and all of its requirements, but, alas, I grew up an infidel, and if not an infidel completely, yet a decided deist. But when I became a man in this as well as political and other matters, I resolved to examine for myself and never to pin my faith to any other man's sleeve, so I bought the Bible and pored over it. I examined it carefully. I sought and procured those books that were for and against it, and when my labors were concluded, I came to this irresistible conclusion: The Bible is true. It would have been as easy for a mole to have written Sir Isaac Newton's treatise on optics as for uninspired men to have written the Bible." The Word of God is indeed inspired and its counsel sound.

In a far-off heathen village the Bible was being translated into the native tongue, and the translator paused, looking for a word to express trust. Finally a young man said to him, "Why not use the word that means to do what you are doing?"

"What am I doing?" said the missionary.

"Oh," he replied, "you are resting your full weight on the chair."

So this version of the word faith was placed in that translation.

228

PERSECUTION

Yea, and all that will live godly in Christ Jesus shall suffer persecution. 2 Tim. 3:12.

The Christian life is just the opposite of that of the sinner. In a sinful world such as this, the Christian may be likened to a swimmer who is trying to swim against the tide. People do not appreciate those who are different from themselves. Friction naturally results with men opposite in their viewpoints. The conscience of the wicked is stirred by those who make him aware of his unfulfilled duty. It infuriates him. In the example of Cain and Abel, Cain followed his own preference, and when our God honored the offering of Abel, and rejected his own, he rose up in wrath and slew his brother. What had Abel done to him? Nothing. Cain was infuriated by the obvious contrast between his disobedience and Abel's righteousness. The wrath of guilty sinners is inflicted upon Christians because they resent the contrast in their ways of life. Persecution is the common lot of the godly. The righteous must anticipate and prepare for persecution.

Daniel was prime minister of the kingdom of Media and Persia. His associates plotted against him because of the purity of his life. They induced the king of Persia to sign a decree that no man was to worship any other god than himself for thirty days. Knowing full well that Daniel would disobey the law, they surmised that by doing this they would be rid of him forever. For being true to God, Daniel was thrown into a den of lions. He was not devoured by the lions because God was with him. He was delivered and lived to write some of his sublimest prophecies.

A young Christian soldier in the army was often assaulted by his tent mates while at prayer at night. On the counsel of his chaplain he omitted his usual habit of praying. His ardent heart could not long endure this, however, and he resumed his old way, risking persecution. The result was that after a time all of his ten or twelve tent companions knelt in prayer with him. In reporting to the chaplain, he said, "Isn't it better to keep the colors flying?"

Truly, persecution should only strengthen us in those habits that are our duty to God and our fellow men.

THE OPERATION OF GOD

Buried with him in baptism, wherein also ye are risen with him through the faith of the operation of God, who hath raised him from the dead. Col. 2:12.

Baptism is indeed a burial. The old man, having been killed by the Sword of the Spirit, which is the Word of God, is now submitted to burial in the public baptismal font. The resurrected saint recognizes his life to be in Christ henceforth. He can claim credit for no goodness. He must acknowledge all to be the product of the divine-human relationship. This rising from the dead is descriptive of the transformation that takes place at conversion. The "operation of God" is that act whereby He literally gives man a new nature. He does not supplant the old nature with the new but rather superimposes it and with it subdues the old nature. Christ reigns from the throne room of the heart. The new man is His lawful subject.

The operation of God in this transformation is as mysterious as it is wonderful. No man can tell exactly what takes place at the new birth, but that a great change does take place is undeniable. Slaves of the vilest habits have been known to give them up, and their whole pattern of living has become a witness for God. What better evidence have we of the genuineness of the experience of conversion?

Afrikaner, the notorious Hottentot chief, was the terror of the whole country. He carried on a cruel and constant warfare with his neighbors, stealing cattle, burning kraals, capturing women and children, and killing his enemies. When Robert Moffatt, as a messenger of the Prince of life, started for Africa, friends warned him that the savage Afrikaner would make a drumhead of his skin and a drinking cup of his skull and that no power could change such a man. But when Moffat went to the chief and spoke to him the Word of life, it entered the heathen heart, and Afrikaner was delivered from his evil ways. He left the environment of death, was loosed from the bands of the grave, and became a Christian chief. When a Dutch farmer whose uncle Afrikaner had killed saw the converted Hottentot, he exclaimed, "O God, what cannot Thy grace do! What a miracle of Thy power!"

THE RICHES OF THE GLORY

To whom God would make known what is the riches of the glory of this mystery among the Gentiles; which is Christ in you, the hope of glory. Col. 1:27.

It is to the saints that God would make known the riches of the glory of this mystery of the Gentiles, "which is Christ in you, the hope of glory."

A man was seen to put an iron rod into the fire. He let it remain there until it literally glowed. An atheist friend who stood nearby said, "Christian, how is it that you speak of Christ being in you and at the same time you say that you're in Christ?"

Holding up the iron that was now glowing red with heat, the Christian asked, "Is this fire in the iron?"

The skeptic answered, "Yes."

Then he pushed the iron into the fire, and he said, "Is the iron in the fire?"

The skeptic answered, "Yes."

"You have your answer, sir. I am in Christ and Christ is in me just as this rod is in the fire and the fire is in the rod."

John Malcolm Shaw relates that he was sent for to minister to a man dying of pneumonia. He had been an old pilot of the Hudson River Line. Shaw says, "I stepped up to the old man's bedside and began to talk to him tenderly of the love of Jesus, but with no effect. Desperate, I began to pray, and seemed to hear the Spirit say to me, 'Present Jesus to him as the pilot's Pilot, and you will reach him.' Using the hint, I looked him straight in the eye, took hold of his calloused hands already clammy and cold with the touch of death, and said, 'How many times, my friend, when the fog was on the river and the current against you, the only thing that kept your boat off the rocks was your clear eye and your steady nerve? Now you are in the strait of death and the tide is against you and the mist hangs heavy over all. You need a pilot, and Jesus is the pilot's Pilot. Accept Him.'

"Gathering up his last ounce of strength, the old pilot said, 'I will,' and died. I somehow have the assurance that Christ accompanied that man through the valley of the death shadow."

231

YOUR CHILDREN

Fathers, provoke not your children to anger, lest they be discouraged. Col. 3:21.

Children are the heritage of the Lord. They are lent to us as parents that we may have the high privilege of raising them in the admonition of the Lord. Our children are not ours but His. We should be careful how we treat God's property. Some parents consider it their duty to beat their children. They little understand human nature. Frequent beating hardens the attitude of the child toward the parent, makes him resent doing what is right, and may produce a frustrated, neurotic child. Yet other parents have the custom of shouting at their children. Aside from making the child nervous, this suggests to the child that the parent is out of control. When you were young and found that you could "needle" a playmate and make him react violently, you delighted to pick on him. Many parents are asking for trouble by picking on their children. There are other parents who are harsh and restrictive. They will permit their children little or no liberty. This also tends to anger an independent spirit. Such lack of wisdom in parents can easily discourage a child, and there is nothing more tragic and pathetic on earth than a discouraged young person. He begins to doubt himself and retires into a shell for defensive purposes. Such parents are fortunate if this young man meets some person in whom he can have confidence and can express himself.

Parents need to analyze their own feelings when punishing a child. Some see in the child a reflection of themselves, and because they do not like themselves, they take vengeance on the child, who is their living replica. Parents, better to give yourselves a spanking than to forge a dagger with which to pierce your little one's heart.

Socrates once said, "Could I climb to the highest place in Athens, I would lift my voice and proclaim, 'Fellow citizens, why do you turn and scrape every stone together for wealth and take so little care of your children to whom one day you must relinquish it all?'"

Jesus taught His disciples, "Except ye be converted, and become as little children, ye shall not enter into the kingdom of heaven" (Matt. 18:2).

ALL HIS COMMANDMENTS

The works of his hands are verity and judgment; all his commandments are sure. Ps. 111:7.

The eternal nature of the commandments of God is under serious dispute in our world. It is claimed variously that "the law was nailed to the cross," or that "the Ten Commandments were for the Jews," or that "the Ten Commandments were binding in another dispensation but not this." The Bible clearly states that "all his commandments are sure. They stand fast for ever and ever" (Ps. 111:7, 8).

When Adam and Eve sinned, God had three choices: (1) He could have destroyed man immediately and thus justified Himself and vindicated His law, but this His great heart of love would not permit. (2) He could have changed His law and made it to condone Adam's misdeed rather than condemn it. Had He done this, every sinner in all succeeding time would be able to claim Heaven's indulgence, and if such were granted for every sinner, God's law would have been a capricious thing without valid authority. This left the third alternative, and it is this course that our Lord followed. (3) He took man's place before the offended law and suffered that man might escape.

And so it is written, "For God so loved the world, that he gave his only begotten Son, that whosoever believeth in him should not perish, but have everlasting life" (John 3:16). The offended law called for the death of the sinner. Christ took the transgressor's place and was "wounded for our transgressions, he was bruised for our iniquities" (Isa. 53:5). This act of grace satisfied the claims of the law and expressed most fully the love of God for man. Thus the great heart of God was satisfied. A great and effectual door of opportunity was opened to lost man. He who was by nature an alien from the commonwealth of Israel, without hope or God in the world, could now look and live.

On rugged Mount Rushmore in South Dakota the faces of familiar American presidents have been carved in the cliffs by a celebrated sculptor as a permanent tribute to their fame. The Ten Commandments, first etched in stone, are now, by the miracle of grace, written in the hearts of men. Both memorials are symbols of perpetuity.

LIKE UNTO THE LORD

Who is like unto the Lord our God, who dwelleth on high!
Ps. 113:5.

To this vital question God has given His own answer: "Look unto me, and be ye saved, all the ends of the earth: for I am God, and there is none else" (Isa. 45:22).

It is clear that in this universe God stands alone. He bases this unique position upon:

1. Creation: "For thus saith the Lord that created the heavens; God himself that formed the earth and made it; he hath established it, he created it not in vain, he formed it to be inhabited: I am the Lord; and there is none else" (verse 18). The creature can only make, he cannot create. He must take what he finds here and fashion new forms of existing matter. God can take nothing and make something of it.

2. God is man's redeemer: "In whom we have redemption through his blood, even the forgiveness of sins" (Col. 1:14). After man's transgression he was helpless to deliver himself. Being a sinner, he could not be his own redeemer. Nor could the angels, for they had taken no part in his creation. God alone could redeem man by taking his place before the offended law and offering Himself as a sacrifice for sin. "What? know ye not that your body is the temple of the Holy Ghost which is in you, which ye have of God, and ye are not your own? For ye are bought with a price: therefore glorify God in your body, and in your spirit, which are God's" (1 Cor. 6:19, 20).

It is said that in the time of ancient Rome there were two brothers, one of whom was brave as a soldier and lost both his hands in battles for his country. The other on one occasion was a criminal. In due time he was brought before the judge to receive a sentence for the grievous crime of which he had been found guilty. Just as sentence was to be pronounced on the culprit his brave soldier brother rushed hastily into court, and going right up before the judge, held up those wounded and disfigured arms as the best plea he could make for his guilty brother. They seemed to say: "Spare him for what I have done." And the guilty one was pardoned for his brother's sake.

234

IF YE WERE BLIND

Jesus said unto them, If ye were blind, ye should have no sin: but now ye say, We see; therefore your sin remaineth. John 9:41.

A just God could never punish a man for sin committed in ignorance. Acts 17:30 says: "And the times of this ignorance God winked at; but now commandeth all men every where to repent." This is the purpose of the preaching of the gospel, that there may be a universal awareness of the terms of God's saving grace.

There are two ways in which men displease God:

1. Sins of omission. Specifically this refers to one who knows the will of God but will not do it, for whatever reasons, and we must understand that God does not accept excuses.

2. Sins of commission. Under this definition a man knows what he is not supposed to do but does it anyhow. This is transgression—deliberate and overt. In any event knowledge must be involved or one must have had access to knowledge and deliberately neglected it. In any event, God is displeased, His law transgressed, and our sins remain.

There is a text that says "my people are destroyed for lack of knowledge" (Hosea 4:6). This text, however, refers to willing ignorance—having access to the will of God through the Word of God, but deliberately refusing to accept light lest it involve accountability. But all who turn a deaf ear to God's voice are accountable anyhow, for unwillingness to seek light leaves sin unremitted.

There are others whose lives are dictated by social pressures. They have not the will power to stand for the right though the heavens fall.

A large crowd of people in New York's Union Station were waiting to go to Boston. Everybody had to show his ticket as usual as he passed through the gate. Some who could not find their tickets made appeal to the gatekeeper, but he was adamant, "You must show your ticket." There was grumbling and swearing. A gentleman standing by said to the ticket collector, "You're not very popular with this crowd."

He cast his eyes upward toward where the superintendent's office was and said, "I don't care anything about being popular with this crowd. All I care for is to be popular with the man up there."

Likewise our chief concern should be to please God.

235

TODAY

Again, he limiteth a certain day, saying in David, To day, after so long a time; as it is said, To day if ye will hear his voice, harden not your hearts. Heb. 4:7.

A few years ago a visitor was going over the battlefield at Waterloo with an old guide. As they stood by the doorway of the stone château that marked the center of the battle, the guide pointed out the wall that sheltered the old guard of Napoleon and the ditch where Wellington's musketeers were hidden, and the well that was filled with bodies, and from which cries of the wounded were heard on that fateful night.

Upon his asking the direction from which Blucher's troops had come to the relief of the allies, the guide pointed to a road running over the crest of a distant hill and cried, "There's where he came at four o'clock in the afternoon." Then turning to the opposite hill he added, "And there's where Jerome should have planted his great guns at half-past three." Then he wailed, "Too late, too late!"

This is the requiem of lost fame, lost fortunes, lost life, through all the ages, "Too late, too late!" Putting off till tomorrow what can be done today is a common trait of human nature. In things spiritual this may be fatal, for it is the mind of God that determines just when the last approach is to be made. Often we know not the last from the first. It is dangerous to delay doing what God has commanded.

A woman who had not been in church in many years heard an evangelistic sermon, and the Spirit of God gripped her heart. Recognizing her lost condition, she knelt to pray. A Christian nurse in the same seat prayed with her and pointed her to Christ. The penitent woman accepted her Saviour's sacrifice and left the church redeemed. As she was leaving she said to her new-found Christian friend: "Oh, that I had a Bible." The nurse gave her her own, which bore her name. The next day when making the rounds of the hospital she was informed: "We had a sorrowful case today. A young woman was in a traffic accident and died from her injuries. We thought it strange that she had a Bible with your name on it. Before she died she said, 'Thank God this did not happen yesterday.'"

236

NOT DESTROYED

We are troubled on every side, yet not distressed; we are perplexed, but not in despair; persecuted, but not forsaken; cast down, but not destroyed. 2 Cor. 4:8, 9.

The Lord has promised us that although troubled, perplexed, persecuted, or cast down we need not be distressed, in despair, forsaken, or destroyed. Verse 10 assures us that we can always bear in our bodies "the dying of the Lord Jesus," meaning that the consciousness of the fearful price paid by Christ at Calvary for our sins should ever accompany us, witnessing to Him even through severe affliction, so that men, seeing our good works, born of faith in Him, would glorify God.

In Lausanne, Switzerland, a little girl by the name of Adelaide Kamm had a severe heart attack when she was eight years old. For a time physicians thought they could restore her health. After a few years, however, they realized that they could only prolong her life. When the end was near, the invalid heard the truth, but she did not allow herself to give way to gloom. I will smile when I feel ill, she resolved.

Her life became gracious and radiant. For a time she was in the hospital, where she found joy in ministering to other patients. When she was taken to her own home she missed what she had been doing to help others. She wrote a booklet called *Joyful in Tribulation.* It rang with a message of cheer from beginning to end. Life at its worst is bearable, even joyful, when Christ lives in the heart.

A little boy limping down the street on a crutch was whistling a cheerful tune. He was asked, "Sonny, crippled as you are, how can you whistle?"

Replied the little fellow, "I may be crippled in my legs but I am not crippled in my heart. I whistle because I am happy inside."

In a certain hospital isolation ward a Christian woman was in the final stages of a fatal disease. From behind her curtain day and night a cheerful little song could be heard, and then one morning it was still. God, who had given this soul peace in the midst of affliction, had at last given her rest in death.

BROTHERLY LOVE

Let brotherly love continue. Heb. 13:1.

When Frank Higgins, the "sky pilot of the lumberjacks," was in his dying days, he went to fulfill one more engagement, but he was so weakened that it was necessary to call the assistance of a porter. "I'll have to lean on you, brother," Higgins said as the colored man took his grip, "for I am nearly all in." And he placed his arm across the porter's shoulder.

At the train Higgins took out a coin and offered it. "I couldn't take your money, mister," said the porter; "no, sir, I just couldn't."

"Why not?" asked Higgins.

"Mister, you called me brother and you asked about my wife and children and mother. I just couldn't take your money."

It was this kind of love for men—because they were men—that won Higgins' way to the hearts of those among whom he labored.

"Let brotherly love continue," the text says. The scripture presupposes that love has already been born in our hearts. We may try to love people without success. We may associate with them and hate them even more. Divine love must be acquired through prayer and faith in God. It is dispensed by Heaven to the human heart. "And hope maketh not ashamed; because the love of God is shed abroad in our hearts by the Holy Ghost which is given unto us" (Rom. 5:5). Love that comes from God eases tension, destroys prejudice, and prepares a man to live at peace with his fellow man.

A certain Mr. Adams on one of our Western plains had the best stand of grain of all his neighbors. They concluded the difference in their crops must be that he had a better grade of seed, but when they asked him to share it, he refused.

As time went by the inferior crops of these neighbors had a baneful effect on Adams' fields. They began to deteriorate. One day he was seen hauling seed grain to his neighbors with the explanation that no farmer could live to himself.

Brotherly love in action has practical aspects. Lowell's verse applies:

"Who gives himself with his alms feeds three,—
Himself, his hungering neighbor and me."

FORGIVE HIM

And if he trespass against thee seven times in a day, and seven times in a day turn again to thee, saying, I repent; thou shalt forgive him. Luke 17:4.

Following this admonition of the Lord the disciples said, "Increase our faith." They recognized that such forgiveness is a gift of God and that only as they became partakers of the divine nature could they possibly fulfill this injunction.

There is a very beautiful story familiar to many of you of Roy Slaybaugh and his unfortunate accident. The book is before me even as I write this devotional, and even though I have heard it many times, I find it too beautiful to overlook. Two young bandits came hurtling around a highway curve at approximately eighty-five miles an hour and smashed into this Christian gentleman's automobile, leaving the cars a tangled mess on the side of the road. The two boys crawled out unharmed, but Roy Slaybaugh lay still as if already dead. He was taken to the hospital and given the best of medical attention, but those who attended him had little hope of his survival.

When it was thought that death was near, his wife was summoned to his bedside. She remembered the text in the Bible that says to call for the elders of the church and have them anoint the sick with oil and pray for them. This she did, and with amazing results. This man, with an eyeball torn out of its socket, a fractured jaw, a tongue swollen so that breathing was difficult, a broken nose, and the death pallor on his face was made completely well. It was without doubt a divine miracle. When the doctors took the bandage from his eye socket, there was a brand-new eye, and he testified that he could see better out of it than out of the other. His shattered ear too was healed.

When he was discharged from the hospital he and his wife visited the prison where the boys were who had inflicted these injuries upon them. It is here that we see the beautiful principle of forgiveness at work in the hearts of two dedicated Christians. They not only assured the boys of their forgiveness but arranged that gospel literature be delivered to them, and became known as their aunt and uncle.

Forgiveness is a beautiful thing when it is born of love.

IF THEY HEAR NOT

And he said unto him, If they hear not Moses and the prophets, neither will they be persuaded, though one rose from the dead. Luke 16:31.

God will save to the uttermost all who come to Him through Christ, but there is a limit to which the grace of God can go in the salvation of man. From creation He has endowed every man with a free will. He will not override that will in order to save man. Man must cooperate.

In the beginning, before the advent of sin, God communed with man face to face, so solicitous of man's spiritual welfare was He. After sin separated man from his happy estate, God chose prophets, called holy men, through whom He spoke His will to man. He even "bowed the heavens also, and came down" (Ps. 18:9), and at Sinai and Calvary saw to it that man was not without the privileges of divine grace. In the fullness of time He sent Jesus Christ into the world. For thirty-three years He lived among men and at last was lifted up from the earth in ignominious death by crucifixion. All of this was an attempt to communicate with man, to break through to him the story of divine love. And in this contemporary hour there is the Bible—sixty-six books of Holy Writ, a crucible of wisdom of prophets, saints, and seers in all ages wrapped up in a single copy of printed work.

Yes, God has done His best to get the message of love through to the heart of man. No wonder He said, "If they hear not Moses and the prophets, neither will they be persuaded, though one rose from the dead."

Men who reject the messages of the Scriptures do not often hear anything or anyone else. It is true that some men are impressed by visions and dreams, but unless these dreams drive one to a daily dependence upon the Word of God, the conversion is unlikely to be lasting.

We need a day-to-day devotional procedure that cements our relationship with Christ, for belief in and knowledge of the Word of God are essential to growing faith. We need not that one come from the dead to teach us. Sufficient is the light already available to us in His divine revelations.

240

CHEERFUL GIVER

Every man according as he purposeth in his heart, so let him give; not grudgingly, or of necessity: for God loveth a cheerful giver. 2 Cor. 9:7.

Riches are not evidence per se of God's favor to men, nor is poverty a sign of His withholding, for there are some men who don't even go to church and never give a nickel to God, yet who prosper; whereas there are others who give liberally of their means to help those in need, yet who themselves make no profession of religion. It is a law, however, that for the Christian, "he which soweth sparingly shall reap also sparingly; and he which soweth bountifully shall reap also bountifully" (2 Cor. 9:6).

There are some church members who will give only under extreme pressure and even then grudgingly. Such gifts are not honored of God. Perhaps they are better off not giving. Yet others give only when they consider it necessary, otherwise they are busy taking care of themselves. But "God loveth a cheerful giver."

It is said that there are three kinds of givers—the flint, the sponge, and the honeycomb. It takes a blow of steel to get anything out of flint, and then it is often a vicious snap. The sponge must be squeezed, and even then will not yield all it has absorbed. The honeycomb is but the frail cover for a store of sweetness, and at the smallest puncture it yields its sweetness. God loves the "honeycomb" giver.

Bishop Nelson of New Zealand told of two men who met and one asked the other for a donation for his church. The reply was that the church was always wanting money. The other friend said, "When my lad was a boy he was costly. He always wanted shirts, shoes, socks, and clothes, and he wore them out fast. The older and stronger he grew the more money I spent on him. But he died, and does not cost me a shilling now."

"Yes," said the bishop, "a live church always wants money, for it is growing."

Paul charges Timothy to counsel his rich parishioners to be "ready to distribute," that is "open-handed" (Weymouth).

241

FAMINE IN THE LAND

Behold, the days come, saith the Lord God, that I will send a famine in the land, not a famine of bread, nor a thirst for water, but of hearing the words of the Lord. Amos 8:11.

It is difficult to imagine this old world without the words of the Lord. For six thousand years now these words have appealed to human ears, beginning with the conversations that Christ used to have in the Garden of Eden with our first parents. Down through the ages there were prophets, judges, and special messengers, and today we have the Bible printed in hundreds of dialects and spread from one end of the earth to the other. But this will not always be. There will come a famine in the land, not for bread or for water, but for hearing the words of the Lord.

Today the Word of God is treated with contempt, or perhaps worse, ignored. The cinema and night spots and other pleasure dens of the earth enjoy a thriving patronage. Not so with those institutions that feature the Bible, the Word of the living God. Only in crises do men in large numbers show interest in religious services. They seem to say to God when times are normal, "I can get along by myself." Our text indicates that this attitude will not long exist but that there will come a time when men in desperation will seek the words of God and will not find them. "And they shall wander from sea to sea, and from the north even to the east, they shall run to and fro to seek the word of the Lord, and shall not find it" (Amos 8:12).

A farmer boasted of his ample crops year after year, giving God no glory. One year a drought brought him to realize where such simple things as rain come from. In desperation he prayed:

> "God of this planet's dry terrain,
> If I have caused Your great heart pain,
> Forgive me, God, for now 'tis plain
> Except Thou wilt, it cannot rain."

Similarly man will be brought to that situation when he will remember all the moments he has neglected the Word of God.

I SHALL ARISE

Rejoice not against me, O mine enemy: when I fall, I shall arise; when I sit in darkness, the Lord shall be a light unto me. Micah 7:8.

Private Wilson, of the Highland Light Infantry, charged a German gun that was playing on the British position and mowing down his comrades. "Man, I'm angry with the yonder gun, and I'm going to stop it," he said as he charged the gun emplacement. A rifleman followed him but soon fell. Wilson dodged among the haystacks until he got in position, and with a deadly shot, brought down the German gunner. Another took his place at the gun, and Wilson thrust him down. A third, fourth, fifth, and sixth man fell in the same way. When he had silenced the entire crew and rushed forward and bayoneted an officer who had fired at and missed him, he turned the gun around and mowed down a company of enemy reinforcements. He went back unscathed, fell in a faint, only to awaken and ask whether the gun had been brought in. Told that it had not, he staggered back and returned with it on his shoulder.

This is a story of fighting back against impossible odds. It says that a man thrown to the earth need not stay there and that sin, though it may nest temporarily in the heart, should not be given permanent sanctuary. It says what the story of the prodigal son says, that one may arise and return to the Father and renew a relationship with Him that is meaningful and true. Many a backslider would return to the faith were he not fearful that he had sinned too greatly for God to take him back. To all such come these words of welcome: "Ho, every one that thirsteth, come ye to the waters, and he that hath no money; come ye, buy, and eat; yea, come, buy wine and milk without money and without price" (Isa. 55:1).

It was my privilege to baptize a man who had been away from the church for twenty-nine years. During all of this time his heart had been with the church and his faith in its teachings had never wavered. His return to the faith was a relief to him. On the day of his baptism he confessed that he was happy that he had "gotten it done at last."

243

A SMALL MOMENT

For a small moment have I forsaken thee; but with great mercies will I gather thee. Isa. 54:7.

God called Abraham to be the father of a nation of ministers. Out of Egypt He brought His people with a mighty hand, showing signs and wonders in the process. He was with His people in the land of Canaan, protecting Israel from her enemies and building a nation that was the marvel of its age. But with prosperity came transgression, and Israel slighted the hand that had fed her. At last the heavy hand of justice was upon her. She began to lose battles to her enemies. Finally the country was divided, Jerusalem was sacked, and with the stoning of Stephen, Israel ceased to be God's nation of ministers. Then were fulfilled the words of our text, "For a small moment have I forsaken thee."

Ultimately, however, every purpose of Jehovah will and must be fulfilled. A new nation of Israelites has appeared on the scene. "If ye be Christ's, then are ye Abraham's seed, and heirs according to the promise" (Gal. 3:29). Yes, all who accept by faith Jesus Christ as Lord and Master become adopted sons and daughters of Abraham, and hence a new generation of ministers has arisen. What a nation this is of every kindred, tongue, and people of which the kingdom of God is made! With great mercies He is gathering His people in every land.

I am told that in New Guinea there is a young man who cannot read or write but to whom the revelation of God has come by the hand of an angel. He is clear on Bible doctrine and has raised up a church of more than twenty-five believers. Great are the mercies of Jehovah as He extends them to all men to become members of the royal family —citizens of the greatest commonwealth the earth has ever known.

"In a little wrath I hid my face from thee for a moment; but with everlasting kindness will I have mercy on thee, saith the Lord thy Redeemer" (Isa. 54:8). The thought that God ever leaves His children is repugnant to our concepts. "Lo, I am with you alway, even unto the end of the world. Amen," is the blessed assurance He gives to every Christian. The only sense in which He ever "leaves" the Christian is when a believer shuts Him out through disobedience.

PATHS OF RIGHTEOUSNESS

He restoreth my soul: he leadeth me in the paths of righteousness for his name's sake. Ps. 23:3.

On a bitter winter night a minister, Mark Guy Pearce, had taken a cab from a London suburb, and on reaching home, told the driver to come in and get something warm and comfortable but nonintoxicating. He noticed that the cabby had no overcoat, and inquired about it. The man explained his poverty. Mr. Pearce said, "Well, I'm going to give you a coat, but before I give it to you I'm bound to tell you there's something peculiar about it, and it is right that I should explain it to you. That coat has never had a glass of beer inside it from the day that it was made until now. I want you to promise me that as long as you wear that coat you will let the drink alone."

"All right," said the cabby, holding out his right hand. "All right, I won't upset the coat by putting any drink inside of it."

Many months afterward Mr. Pearce met the man and found that he had kept his bargain.

Righteousness has paths. Its ways are clearly defined. It is for His name's sake that He leads us in paths of righteousness. The Christ-loving Christian reflects glory on his Creator. The name of God is exalted when His children live His life. Dr. Bohner has said, "It is easier to follow one's tracks when you follow the person closely, but it is much more difficult when you drop far behind, for time and circumstance may obscure the trail. It is safer to follow closely."

The Ten Commandments are God's standard of righteousness. Righteousness defined here in understandable words makes the will of God plain to the heart of man. It is when we ignore or bypass this clear pinpoint guide that the light dims and right and wrong are not clearly distinguishable. Self-erected standards are self-deluding. Right and wrong are not relative nor may we decide on the basis of general consensus what is right and wrong. The world is in rebellion against standards that are not personally arrived at. But right and wrong are a matter of divine will. The universe must measure itself by this. God's law is an absolute immovable and unchangeable standard, and by it men are judged.

THE POSSIBLE

Jesus said unto him, If thou canst believe, all things are possible to him that believeth. Mark 9:23.

William Pitt, while prime minister of Great Britain, had to go about on crutches. One day the prime minister was approached by a man who complained of having been given an impossible task. The prime minister picked up his crutches, shook them at the man, and shouted, "Impossible, sir? Why, I walk upon impossibilities!"

Jesus definitely encouraged a positive outlook on life. The explosive power of faith is immeasurable. "All things are possible to him that believeth," Christ says. This does not say that all things within human desire are possible. It obviously means all things that are within the will of God. Even seemingly unreasonable things have happened as consequences of faith. Peter walked on water, the dead were raised, the sick were healed, and the Christian church was established and grew. These were all results of faith.

During the French and Indian War, a family of Quakers seemed to have no fear of hostile Indians. They never had any locks or bolts on their doors, but to please their neighbors, they took the precaution, which seemed to them needless, of pulling in at night the string that lifted the latch to the door. One night the Quaker lay awake, thinking. He had always trusted in God, yet he had pulled in the latchstring. This seemed a denial of his faith. He talked the matter over with his wife, and she was of the same opinion. He got up and put the latchstring out. That night the Indians came. They pulled the string and went into the house, talked a little among themselves, and went out, shutting the door softly. The next day the Quakers found that their neighbors' homes had been forcibly entered and the occupants killed. Years later a chief who had been the leader of the attack on the settlement said that when he saw the latchstring out, the sign of confidence made him change his mind, and he said to those with him, "These people are not our enemies. They're not afraid of us; they are protected by the Great Spirit."

Yes, faith is an adequate protector. Should not our prayer be, "Lord, I believe; help thou mine unbelief" (Mark 9:24)?

BY THE GRACE OF GOD

By the grace of God I am what I am: and his grace which was bestowed upon me was not in vain; but I laboured more abundantly than they all: yet not I, but the grace of God which was with me. 1 **Cor.** 15:10.

Paul rightfully ascribes praise to God for his present state of grace and then states that the grace of God was not bestowed upon him in vain. His reasons for saying this are interesting. "I laboured more abundantly than they all," he says. It appears that good works are the language of grace, and that evidence that the grace of God is not bestowed in vain may be seen in the obedient attitude of the Christian, and yet Paul says that his obedience is but the outworking of the grace of God within him.

This marvelous summary of the gospel philosophy should put at rest the theory of some religionists that works are somehow a betrayal of faith and that the two contradict each other. The fact is that one is the outgrowth of the other. Works are the outgrowth of faith and God's grace bestowed.

The thrilling feats of Blondin, the tightrope walker, are well known. Varied stories are extant about his famed crossing of Niagara Falls. Sometimes in one of Blondin's public performances a poor Italian would allow himself to be carried on the acrobat's back across a fearful chasm, to the great terror of the spectators. While visiting a poor district, a city missionary came upon this Italian lying upon his deathbed and was much concerned about the salvation of his soul. "I asked him whether he had ever had any fear that Blondin might fail. 'No,' the man said, 'he was a very able man.'

" 'Then you trusted him with your life because you believed he would not fall.'

" 'Oh, yes. He would not let me fall,' the answer came."

Then the missionary tried to show the dying man that he must trust Jesus for salvation with the same confidence.

Works are an outgrowth of faith. Confidence in this acrobat moved this man to trust him with his life. Confidence in Christ should move us to trust Him with ours, for Jesus never fails.

247

YOUR TREASURE

For where your treasure is, there will your heart be also.
Matt. 6:21.

All about us there is a frantic, almost pathetic, rush for riches. Greed for gold is a passion of both rich and poor. Men steal, lie, cheat, marry, kidnap, and even murder for money. Indeed, we have come to that sorry stage when "men get all they can, can all they get, and sit on the lid." It is not uncommon when inquiring of some young, aspiring person about his life's ambitions to hear him say, "I want to be a rich man." Indeed, it is this underlying motivation that dictates the choice of a life profession in many young college enrollees, both men and women.

Let it be here noted that there is nothing wrong with money in itself, nor is it evil to be rich, but it is the greedy love of money that is the root of all evil (1 Tim. 6:10). And it is exceedingly difficult to have money and not love it. It is equally difficult to be poor without developing an inordinate desire for riches. It is important that we set our affections on eternal and abiding treasures. These are more lasting than silver or gold and shine more brilliantly than diamonds and pearls. These are the inner virtues implanted in the heart of man by the grace of God. To set our hearts upon the acquisition of these God-given traits is to seek treasure in heaven.

John Newton, friend and companion of the poet Cowper, one day called to visit a family that had suffered by fire the loss of all they possessed. He found the pious mistress of the household and saluted her with the words, "I give you joy, Madam." Surprised and deeply sensitive to her loss, she exclaimed, "What, joy that all of my property is consumed?"

"Oh, no," he answered, "but joy that you have so much property that fire cannot touch." This allusion to her spiritual treasures checked her grief and, taking heart, she wiped away her tears, and set her face to rebuilding her life.

"Lay up for yourselves treasures in heaven, where neither moth nor rust doth corrupt, and where thieves do not break through nor steal" (Matt. 6:20).

THE UNEQUAL YOKE

Be ye not unequally yoked together with unbelievers: for what fellowship hath righteousness with unrighteousness? and what communion hath light with darkness? 2 Cor. 6:14.

When a Christian marries a non-Christian, the yoke is unequal. While such a union may succeed, the chances against it are forbidding. Recreational interests are different, so are religious and social; and if children are born, who will decide their spiritual destiny? The unequal yoke also applies to friendship. The influence of two young people upon each other is a fact that cannot be debated. The question of who will affect whom is the question at issue here. Most often the evil overcomes the good. A young person who exposes himself to a wicked environment to show his friendship for another, lays himself open to temptation. He may emerge victorious, but it is unlikely.

The warning against an unequal yoke also applies to Christian fellowship. A Seventh-day Adventist is unique in his beliefs. Whatever faith he may share with other religions and spiritual cultures, he is different. As one man said, "You people don't belong in this world." How true. No Christian is at home in this world. He lives for the world to come. But though we are pilgrims and strangers here, we may make friendship with the lost a redemptive fellowship.

The unequal yoke also relates to one's relationship to religion. Some men find it difficult to live the Christ life. To them religion is a series of do's and don'ts. This, too, is the unequal yoke. "Some Christians carry their religion on their backs. At times it grows heavy, and they would willingly lay it down, but that would mean to break with old traditions, so they shoulder it again. Real Christians do not carry their religion; their religion carries them. It is not weight; it is wings. It lifts them up. It sees them over hard places. It makes the universe seem friendly, life purposeful, hope real, sacrifice worth while. It sets them free from fear, futility, discouragement, and sin— the great enslavers of men's souls. You can always know a real Christian when you see him by his buoyancy."

Yes, it is this yoke that Christ calls "easy." It is this burden that He calls "light."

OF GOD

He that is of God heareth God's words: ye therefore hear them not, because ye are not of God. John 8:47.

A true Christian loves the Word of God. Some people read the Bible from a sense of obligation; others from habit, but a vast majority of Bible owners seldom open the Book. Few approach the Bible with the passion of a thirsty man in search of water or a hungry one in search of food. Perhaps other things claim our attention and sap our spiritual energy. A steady diet of social trauma, jazz, exciting novels, and party-going can easily unfit the mind for spiritual things. If given a chance, the Bible will create an appetite for itself. This is possible only to the spiritual-minded. Those who are of God hear His words.

Often people who profess to love the Word of God handle it carelessly. A typical case of this came to my attention on a street in a southern city. A bearded man, untidy, uncouth, and repugnant to every passer-by held a large open Bible in his hands from which he was haranguing anyone who would listen. The thing that struck me most was that nearly every text he used was misquoted, often to the detriment of its meaning. In such hands the Bible was discredited.

The time will come when none of the novels we have on our bedroom shelf will interest us, and none of the good histories or exquisite essays in which we delight will do us any good. There will be one Book, perhaps its cover worn out and its leaves yellow with age, in whose light we shall see the opening gates of heaven.

Prayer conditions the heart for the reception of the Word of God. We should plead with Him to increase our appetites for spiritual things. To hunger and thirst after righteousness precedes the filling.

The story is told of a young theological student who one day came to Charles Spurgeon telling him that the Bible contains some verses he could not understand, and he was very much worried. To this the great man replied, "Young man, allow me to give you this word of advice: You must expect to let God know some things which you do not understand."

Prayer is the key to understanding the Scriptures, and as we continue to pray and to seek, light will certainly break upon our souls.

YOU FREE

And ye shall know the truth, and the truth shall make you free. John 8:32.

Elder W. J. Hackett, of the North Pacific Union, tells of a visit to a prison in the Philippine Islands while he was a missionary out there, and he preached on John 8:32, our text for today. His listeners apparently had a total misunderstanding of his message for the next day there was a jail break.

But the freedom referred to in the text is not freedom from prison; in fact, if one achieves the freedom here referred to, his testimony may deprive him of his liberty. The Jews of Jesus' day were disappointed in the fact that He did not assume earthly and temporal power and deliver them from the galling yoke of Roman rule. The true practitioner of the faith may find himself a victim of cruelest bondage because of it.

The instigators of the French Revolution characterized their uprising as a war for freedom from economic bondage. However desirable, our text promises no such freedom. It is not in vain that we suffer inconvenience here for the gospel's sake. The fact is, the only true happiness available to man on this earth is through the light of the gospel. The truth allows a man in this world freedom from fear, ignorance, and sinfulness. The truth is indeed the "power of God unto salvation to every one that believeth," but its referent is Christ, the living truth. "I am the way, the truth, and the life," said Jesus. We must know Him for the pardon of our sins. We must know Him as a daily companion and guide. Through repentant faith we may become acquainted with Him. "Acquaint now thyself with him, and be at peace" (Job 22:21).

Yes, Christians stand alone as the truly free, free from the bondage and dominion of sin. "For sin shall not have dominion over you" (Rom. 6:14). We are not slaves to it. Sin's power can be broken, and indeed will be by faith. The provisions of grace are more than adequate.

The "truth" is more than a set of Bible doctrines, more than a statement of belief. It is encompassed only by the total perfection of God as revealed in His Son.

251

I AM GLORIFIED

And all mine are thine, and thine are mine; and I am glorified in them. John 17:10.

Man fulfills his highest destiny when his life glorifies the God of heaven. Paul is specific in his admonition: "For ye are bought with a price: therefore glorify God in your body, and in your spirit, which are God's" (1 Cor. 6:20). Obviously involved here is the problem of health. We are to avoid all habits that would tend to destroy the body and make it unfit to be the dwelling place of the Holy Ghost. This is the very basis of the temperance program of the church. Nicotine, caffeine, and alcohol are destructive agents that are in common use in today's world. Addiction to any or all three constitutes a major physical hazard. Cigarette smoking has now been linked to heart disease in addition to lung cancer and other maladies. Obviously God is not glorified when such health-consuming habits are deliberately practiced.

God may also be glorified in the matter of dress. Men and women are to dress modestly and with sobriety according to the Bible standard. With our current departure from standards of decency in the matter of dress, what an opportunity for the people of God to show the way. Long have we had from the Bible and the Spirit of Prophecy counsel with reference to this important matter. May the day never come when the people of God cannot be distinguished by their personal appearance.

We are also to glorify God in our spirits. This is done through daily devotions. Every home should have a family altar. We also glorify God in our spirits by church attendance. Absenteeism from the house of God has become a chronic spiritual problem. We glorify God in our spirits when we regularly attend the house of worship. The same is true in our service for our fellow man. To visit the sick, the incarcerated, and to minister to the needs of the poor is verily God's work, and we do enrich our own spirits as we seek to help others. Thus may God be glorified in us.

As a good performance by a manufactured product reflects glory on its maker, so well-ordered lives, manifesting the fruits of the Spirit and Christian service, reflect glory on God, our Father and Creator.

THE HOUSE OF PRAYER

It is written, My house is the house of prayer: but ye have made it a den of thieves. **Luke 19:46.**

Seldom have religionists been so deserving of the scathing rebuke of Jesus as when moneychangers were everywhere seen in the Temple, hawking their wares. The dove peddlers and the lamb merchants were undoubtedly the chief offenders. There was a price tag on all spiritual privilege. This was offensive to Christ, whose message was "buy . . . without money and without price" (Isa. 55:1). Violence was done to the spirit of worship by the atmosphere of commerce that pervaded the Temple. Reverting to His authority as the divine Son of God, Jesus purged the Temple of the moneychangers.

Some have looked upon this parable as an excuse for not meeting their monetary commitments to the house of God. Others have even challenged the right of the church to collect offerings on the Sabbath day. While it is true that the collection and counting of monies can be overdone, the legitimate receiving of tithes and offerings on the Sabbath is hardly the subject of rebuke here.

On one occasion a pastor overheard a member complaining of the frequent calls for gifts at church. She considered this offensive to the spirit of worship. A brief check of the church financial records indicated that this sister was a sparing contributor and felt self-conscious whenever money was mentioned. In a subsequent sermon on this subject, the minister stated, "A growing church, like growing children, has many needs that are constant and expanding. As long as my little boy is asking me for something, I am sure that his appetites are healthy and his needs expanding. I get disturbed when he is silent. I ask him what is wrong. So is it with a growing church. The more rapid its growth, the greater its needs."

The taking of the offering must be a part of the spiritual service of the church. It is an act of worship, and when conducted as such is both enjoyable and pleasant. The widow with her mite should find the worship service as pleasant as do the heavy givers. Thus the church of the living God may contribute of its abundance to God and remain a house of prayer for all people.

THEIR UNDERSTANDING

Then opened he their understanding, that they might understand the scriptures. Luke 24:45.

A skeptic was up to his usual pastime of railing on the Scriptures. "There are so many things in it that you don't understand, why read it?" he sneered.

"When you eat fish," answered the Christian, "what do you do when you come to a bone?"

He had to admit that he laid it aside.

It is even so with the Scriptures. Those portions that baffle us, we simply lay aside until we read some text in another passage that will cast light on the text in question. Though many of the writers of the Bible lived great distances from one another and wrote at different periods in earth's history, the writings of one often illumine those of another. This is a proof of the divine origin of the Scriptures. The Bible is not to be approached like any ordinary book. Christ must literally open the eyes of our understanding if we are to understand the Word of God. It is impossible to get its true message and meaning any other way. That is why the infidel can read the Bible and see in it a mass of contradictions. The linguist studies it analytically and avers that a man may reach his own conclusions from what he reads, thus proving the futility of an unaided approach to Scripture.

The story has come down to us that a very wayward young man ran away from home and was not heard of for years. In some way he heard that his father had died, and he returned home and was kindly received by his mother. The day came for the reading of the will. The family were gathered together and the lawyer began to read the document. To the great surprise of all present, the will told in detail of the wayward career of the runaway son. The boy in anger rose, stamped out of the room, left the house, and was not heard of for three years. Eventually he was found. He was informed that the will, after telling of his waywardness, had gone on to bequeath him $15,000. How much sorrow he would have saved if he had only heard the reading through. Thus many people only half read the Bible and turn from it dissatisfied.

ALIVE FOREVERMORE

I am he that liveth, and was dead; and, behold, I am alive for evermore, Amen; and have the keys of hell and of death. Rev. 1:18.

The Author of Christianity was dead and is alive. In this respect the Christian religion is unique. Having tasted death, Christ has the key of the solution to the same, and, thank God, has passed that key to all believing Christians. "One day the grave could contain Him no longer. One day our Lord walked away from death's door, then He arose. Over death He had conquered, and now through my Lord I have life evermore." And because He has the key, death is no longer a mystery. We may literally say, "Though I walk through the valley of the shadow of death, I will fear no evil: for thou art with me."

A little girl had a baby sister who died, and when the little body was put into a tiny coffin, she said, "Mother, baby has a new cradle." That was a pretty name for it. To the Christian death is but being lulled to sleep under the watchful eye of Him in whose hands is the key to hell and the grave.

The Christian may be ministered to daily by the living Lord. As He intercedes for man, He is in a position to substitute His divine merit to man's conscientious insufficiency. As living Lord, He can serve as man's advocate, his go-between, and daily He may confer upon every believer freely of His grace and strength with which to cope with day-to-day problems. We may, therefore, come boldly to the throne of grace, to obtain mercy and grace to help in time of need.

A little boy heard that Queen Victoria was to visit a royal castle, and he stopped by the gate and demanded that he be allowed to see the queen. The soldier laughed and pushed the boy away with the butt end of his rifle. The little boy stood crying when up walked the Prince of Wales, who inquired the reason for his tears. "I want to see the queen," the little boy said, "and the soldier won't let me."

"Won't he?" replied the prince, "then come along with me. I will take you to the queen." Thus a little boy with strong desire in his heart found himself standing before the queen. Even so, through Christ, we may be ushered into the very presence of the living God.

I GAVE HER SPACE

And I gave her space to repent of her fornication; and she repented not. Rev. 2:21.

God was merciful in His dealings with Jezebel, as He is with us. He permitted her long contact with the religion of Israel. In Elijah she had a demonstration of religion that has not been excelled. The years of her prosperity were her days of grace. She repented not though probation lingered. All Israel was filled with evidences of Jezebel worship. The high hills and the groves bore images to her pagan gods. The robed priests of Baal cluttered the streets of Israel, and a once-noble people were led into spiritual bondage. There could be but one solution: the death of Jezebel. She was hurled from a window to the street below, and the dogs ate her. "I gave her space," God said, but she would not repent. God has never hastened to destroy any human being. The privilege of repentance is freely granted to all, but it should be understood that God is no respecter of persons. Those who spite His grace do so at their own peril. "My spirit shall not always strive with man," He told another generation. His mercy is an open door that no man can close. But when the decision is made, it becomes a closed door that no man can open. Justice, though long delayed, must be satisfied.

John Bunyan wrote, "I heard once a story from a soldier, who, with his company, had laid siege against a fort, that so long as the besieged were persuaded their foes would show them no favor, they fought like madmen but when they saw one of their fellows taken and received to favor, they all came tumbling down from their fortress and delivered themselves into their enemies' hands. I am persuaded, did men believe that there is grace and willingness in the heart of Christ to save sinners, as the word imports there is, they would come tumbling into His arms; but Satan has blinded their minds that they cannot see this thing."

Let us repent while there is "space," for the hand of justice, though long delayed, cannot be restrained forever.

One writer has said, "Repentance begins in the humiliation of the heart and ends in the reformation of the life."

THINGS WHICH REMAIN

Be watchful, and strengthen the things which remain, that are ready to die: for I have not found thy works perfect before God. Rev. 3:2.

It seems a universal human trait that men relax their vigilance in moments of greatest danger. We are living in the very shadow of the coming of the Lord. Our primary concern should be readiness to meet Him when He comes, but there is a strange lethargy in Israel. The parable of the Ten Virgins certainly applies here. You may recall that five were wise and five were foolish. Five went to sleep without oil in their lamps. The other five secured the oil, and they too fell asleep. Zion certainly has her share of sleepers. How many can be depended upon to bear the financial burdens of the local church? Only 30 to 40 per cent of the membership. On whom can God count for the individual dissemination of the message to our neighborhoods? Forty per cent of the membership is a liberal estimate.

One Sunday there was a knock at my door, and outside stood a sixteen-year-old girl selling books. She began her canvass, and it wasn't long before I recognized her as a member of another faith. After listening to her, I learned by questioning that she spent at least three hours a week in that same type of enterprise. Knowing what her denomination teaches, I marveled at her zeal, and my mind turned to the people to whom the truth of God has been entrusted. How many hours a week do we spend in personal witnessing? "Be watchful, and strengthen the things which remain," the text warns us. Believers are ready to die, and I suggest that their death is due to lack of activity, lack of communication, lack of transmission. The Dead Sea is dead because it has no outlet. The idle Christian is courting disaster.

As we build our faith in Christ through devotion and service, there occurs a progressive and corresponding perfection of our works. Thus may we be ready when Jesus comes. While imperfection mars all we do, there can at least be a perfect motive. This will in turn ennoble and refine the deed.

YOUR ALMS

Take heed that ye do not your alms before men, to be seen of them: otherwise ye have no reward of your Father which is in heaven. **Matt. 6:1.**

Giving is vital to living. In the divine arrangement all nature is set up on this principle. The clouds sacrifice themselves in showers to the soil. The earth in turn yields her bounties to man and her moisture to the sun. Nature is set up to supply need wherever it exists, and this is a manifestation of the love of God.

This law of sharing holds true in man-to-man relationships. It is ordained of God that man supply the needs of his fellow man wherever they exist. This is the principle behind liberality and almsgiving.

Now, there are some who will give when they are under observation or when their names are trumpeted abroad for their liberality. Our text states that the only reward they will get for their giving is that of men. "Do not sound a trumpet before thee, as the hypocrites do in the synagogues and in the streets, that they may have the glory of men. . . . But when thou doest alms, let not thy left hand know what thy right hand doeth" (Matt. 6:2, 3).

There is nothing made for itself—nothing whose powers and influences are entirely circumscribed to self. Whatever a creature receives it gives out, with the modification and increase of its own force. The clouds borrow water of the ocean but they pour it forth again in refreshing showers upon the thirsty hills, which in their turn send them amongst the valleys. Planets borrow light of their centers, and forthwith fling their rays abroad upon the dark regions of space through which they roll. The tree borrows from every part of the world in order to build itself up; but it gives out, in return, beauty, fragrance, and fruit. Thus, all things give what they appropriate.

Truly, he who appropriates and gives not is an anomaly in the universe. There are those who object to regular financial appeals for funds for the support of the cause of God, but let all such remember that the sacrifice made by Christ at Calvary for us was unlimited, and that He gave without stint or restriction.

THE LIGHT OF THE BODY

The light of the body is the eye: if therefore thine eye be single, thy whole body shall be full of light. Matt. 6:22.

The meaning of our text is clear from its associated passages. It is an injunction against double-mindedness. "No man can serve two masters" (verse 24). "Lay not up for yourselves treasures upon earth . . . : but lay up for yourselves treasures in heaven" (verses 19, 20). The meaning is clear. We cannot have this world and heaven too. A choice has to be made. Each of us must make it. And may our decision be for heavenly treasures.

Earthly treasures do not satisfy. This applies not only to money but to other earthly, fleshly allurements. The carnal heart is appeased but never at rest. Only Christ can bring complete satisfaction to the human soul, but He must be loved, sought after, and believed on to be experienced. "A double minded man is unstable in all his ways" (James 1:8). Unswerving allegiance is Christ's highest demand. "I the Lord thy God am a jealous God" (Ex. 20:5) is no idle expression. It means what it says. Christ will have all of us or none.

According to Charles Spurgeon, when Henry VIII determined to make himself head of the English church he insisted that the convocation should accept his leadership without limiting and modifying clauses. He refused to entertain any compromises. Thus many a sinner would parley with his Saviour on the terms of his salvation. He fain would save some favorite sin. He would amend the humbling terms of grace, but there is no help for it. Jesus must be all in all and the sinner nothing at all. He must without reserve submit to the sovereignty of the Redeemer.

Earthly treasures are temporary in nature. That which is seen will soon pass away. That which is not seen is eternal in the heavens. Because of the permanent nature of heavenly treasure it is only reasonable to expect that we lay up our treasure there. Moses had this in mind when he chose to endure affliction with the people of God rather than enjoy the pleasure of sin for a season. We must, therefore, not be dazzled by the sight of the natural eye but follow the inner eye, discerning between heaven's gold and earth's tinsel.

THE SON OF GOD

Now when the centurion, and they that were with him, watching Jesus, saw the earthquake, and those things that were done, they feared greatly, saying, Truly this was the Son of God. Matt. 27:54.

Nature could not witness the death of the Son of God without protest, and in seeming sympathy with His agony "the earth did quake and the rocks rent." So moving was the scene that the centurion in loud tones confessed his faith. What contrast between his response and the indifference we sometimes show.

The incarnation of Christ testifies that He "was the Son of God." No man was ever born like Him before nor since. As Son of God and Son of man He was both human and divine.

His sinless life stamps Him as the Son of God, for from the cradle to the grave He was without fault in thought, word, or deed.

His ability to raise the dead stamps Him as being the Son of God. All others who performed this miracle did so in His name. He was able to say: "I am the resurrection, and the life" (John 11:25). He did not need help. He could stand before the tomb of Lazarus and call, "Lazarus, come forth" (verse 43), and be obeyed.

At His baptism the Holy Spirit appeared in dovelike form and a voice was heard from heaven saying: "This is my beloved Son, in whom I am well pleased" (Matt. 3:17). God Himself acknowledged Jesus Christ as His Son. Who are we to deny this divine claim?

I offer in evidence His power to transform human life and to bring genuine happiness thereto. Not the trancelike isolation of the Hindu or the Buddhist, but an active, radiating joy that pulsates through our day-to-day activity. As Son of God He is man's only Saviour.

A man attending an evangelistic service was invited to go forward to the altar and seek Christ, but he said, "I do not believe in Him." It was suggested that he test it by prayer. He went to the altar, poured out his test prayer, "O Christ, if Thou be God reveal Thyself." He had not prayed long ere he sprang up with a new conviction, exclaiming, "He is God, He is God!"

THE LORD'S PORTION

For the Lord's portion is his people; Jacob is the lot of his inheritance. Deut. 32:9.

When the Lord divided the nations and gave to each its inheritance He reserved a portion for Himself. The nation Israel was set aside to demonstrate to the world the blessings of divine sonship. They were to be a nation of ministers, a demonstration of the grace of God in human flesh.

Israel is still the Lord's portion though the nature of Israel has changed. She is no longer a nation of Hebrews but a mixture of the honest in heart from every nation under heaven. These are "the Lord's portion," and whatever our circumstances we may claim the promise: "As an eagle stirreth up her nest, fluttereth over her young, spreadeth abroad her wings, taketh them, beareth them on her wings: so the Lord alone did lead him" (Deut. 32:11, 12). God is no less with us than He was with Jacob. "He that keepeth Israel" neither slumbers nor sleeps, and we may be sure that in every emergency Christ stands by our side, for His servants are His portion. By creation the entire human family is akin to God and by right of possession the whole earth is His portion, and in terms of human accountability all men must answer to God for the deeds done in the body.

But because of man's transgression God cannot claim each person as His own. Only those who surrender their lives to Him and accept by faith His righteous character are His. These are called "the Lord's portion." We are His by redemption. We are not our own, for we are bought with a price, and what an awful price that was.

A ship had foundered, and when the lifeboats had been let down it was seen that there was not room in them for all on board. Lots were cast, and among those who had to remain behind was a young and very wicked sailor. He was pale, and those standing near him heard him mutter: "Lost, lost eternally." But he was picked up and thrown into one of the boats. The man who had done that called to him: "You cannot yet die, but I can and am willing to die for you, but mind that I see you in heaven." So Christ has purchased each one of us by His substitutionary sacrifice.

261

LITTLE CHILDREN

But Jesus said, Suffer little children, and forbid them not, to come unto me: for of such is the kingdom of heaven. Matt. 19:14.

Throughout the ages the gospel alone has opened its warm bosom to the young. Christianity alone is the nurse of childhood. Atheism looks on children as on a level with the brutes. Deism or skepticism leaves them to every random influence lest they catch a bias. The Romans exposed their infants. Barbarians and ancient tribes offered them as burnt sacrifices to Moloch. Mohammedanism holds mothers and infants as equally an inferior caste. Hinduism forgets the infant the mother bears and leaves it to perish on the banks of the Ganges. Christianity alone perceives the worth of a child and prescribes its nurture.

Many have criticized ministers for baptizing little children. Such are unacquainted with the fact that between the ages of four and ten a person's destiny is largely fixed, behaviorwise. Statistics also reveal that after the age of thirteen the chance of becoming a Christian grows increasingly remote. No less an authority than Christ Himself said: "Permit little children to come unto Me." Apparently any child beyond infancy can come to Christ.

"Forbid them not." This is a command. How my heart has bled over the years as young people have come to me seeking baptism but their parents forbade it on the grounds that "he is too young, he doesn't know what he is doing." In human life, character is distinctly shown at an early age. Who then with justification can stop a child approaching ten years of age from seeking union with his Lord? Who of us has sufficient wisdom to define the age of accountability?

It is said that the German schoolmaster, John Trebonious, the instructor of Martin Luther, always appeared before his boys with uncovered head. He said, "Who can tell what may yet rise up amid these youths. There may be among them who shall be learned doctors, sage legislators, nay, princes of the empire." Among them there was "a solitary monk that shook the world," the prime founder of Protestantism.

262

THE TEMPERED BODY

For our comely parts have no need: but God hath tempered the body together, having given more abundant honour to that part which lacked. 1 Cor. 12:24.

In this beautiful chapter the church of God and its many parts are compared with the human body. The interdependence of each part upon the other is here stressed, and that each part is important to the success of the whole is the burden of the passage. I am particularly interested in the phrase "having given more abundant honour to that part which lacked." Here Jesus proves Himself to be just the opposite to man. We naturally honor that which is prominent, and what the apostle calls the "comely parts." With reference to the human body we glorify the powers of thought and speech and lavish our praise upon physical beauty, while we take for granted such powers as the ability to walk, hear, feel, and touch. But how important are these powers common and unheralded.

Jesus sought out the unlovely and insignificant and lavished His warmest affection on them. The leper from whom human beings recoiled in His day was required by law to hold up his hand and cry out "Unclean, unclean." One time Christ found Himself in the middle of ten such unfortunate creatures. He healed them and sent them forth normal men. Yes, Christ is able to take "that part which lacked" and make of it a significant thing.

The purpose of this lesson is made clear in verse 25: "That there should be no schism in the body; but that the members should have the same care one for another." Any attitude different from that of the Master is bound to produce schisms based on wealth, race, or social status. This cleavage has threatened the peace of the world.

A Hindu and a Maori who met on a ship were brothers in Christ, but they could not speak to each other because of the language barrier. They pointed to their Bibles, shook hands, and smiled, but that was all. At last a happy thought occurred to the Hindu. In sudden joy he exclaimed, "Hallelujah!" The Maori, in delight, cried out, "Amen!" These two words, not found in their own heathen tongues, brought them together as members of Christ's body.

263

INCREASED IN FAVOR

And Jesus increased in wisdom and stature, and in favour with God and man. Luke 2:52.

In the life of our Lord there was manifested every divine attribute mentioned in verse 2 of Isaiah 11. "And the spirit of the Lord shall rest upon him, the spirit of wisdom and understanding, the spirit of counsel and might, the spirit of knowledge and of the fear of the Lord." Those who associated closely with Him found a wisdom that was beyond human comprehension. Again and again the Pharisees attempted to trap Him in debate only to find Him several steps ahead. When we are faced with perplexities that defy human wisdom, the Bible says, "Ask of God, that giveth to all men liberally."

Jesus exhibited the spirit of understanding. What deep insight He showed when men dragged an ordinary harlot before Him and accused her of being worthy of death. He understood not only her but also her accusers, and after rebuking their hypocrisy, He gave the woman hope and changed her life. As followers of His, should we not pray for divine understanding, and for a heart that beats with other hearts in trouble?

In full stature there was also exhibited in our Lord the spirit of counsel and of might—of counsel to the woman at the well in Samaria, of might when He raised Lazarus from the dead, of counsel when He talked to Nicodemus, of might when He cleansed the Temple of its commercial traffic. The spirit of knowledge in our Lord was demonstrated when at the age of twelve He confuted the doctors and the lawyers in the Temple. Subsequently His congregations marveled that He spake "as one having authority, and not as the scribes" (Matt. 7:29). In favor with God and man—here is the full measure of our stature if we would be like Him. What an ideal to which to aspire!

Jesus taught men the true meaning of "the fear of the Lord." The godly fear enjoined by Paul is not a cringing before the wrath of God but an outgoing devotion arising from love that motivates all life's relationships. This kind of experience Jesus demonstrated to His generation, and it is our privilege to follow His example in claiming God's power for witnessing to His love in this present evil time.

THE HOLY ONE

Cry out and shout, thou inhabitant of Zion: for great is the Holy One of Israel in the midst of thee. Isa. 12:6.

The joy of the Christian is not rooted in any external circumstance. While there is a sense of relief that accompanies financial security, happiness is deeper than a mere sense of relief. It is the presence of the Lord in the heart and in the midst of His people that is the source of true joy. Happiness is based on a relationship between man and his Maker, nothing more or nothing less. "Ye shall find rest for your souls," is spoken to men and women who will put their trust in God and surrender their lives to Him.

In 1917 a large troop ship full of American soldiers on its way to the war zone was zigzagging its way across the Atlantic Ocean. My father was on board. Through a succession of fortunate experiences based on their confidence in my father's religion, the other soldiers looked on him as something of a good-luck charm. As the big ship made its way through the waves, the question went out, "Is preacher on board?" There was genuine suspense until my father was found down in his bunk, reading his Bible. The word went out that he was safely on board and among them. A cheer went up, and the word went about, "Everything will be all right." This attitude followed during many successive battles, leading right up to the Argonne Forest and the cracking of the Hindenburg Line. Before the company would go into battle, my father would have a word of prayer for the men of his unit, and they somehow felt that all would turn out right with "preacher" among them.

With Christ among us we may be sure that all things will work out for our best good, and even our reverses will be turned to our advantage. Often we need the patience of Job to "wait on the Lord." "Behold, he that keepeth Israel shall neither slumber nor sleep" (Ps. 121:4), so the affairs of our lives are never quite out of His reach. When Daniel was plunged into a den of lions, some would think him justified to doubt that God was still with him. But his faith faltered not one instant, and God honored his faith. Great is our peace when our confidence assures us of His presence.

THE STRETCHED-OUT HAND

For the Lord of hosts hath purposed, and who shall disannul it? and his hand is stretched out, and who shall turn it back? Isa. 14:27.

The question of predestination has been a puzzling one throughout the centuries; whether God has already planned the details of men's lives and left them to be mere actors on the stage, being motivated by another's will, or whether they have free will to do as they please. We must first consider that in creating this world God had a plan for every man that is born. It is His purpose that all be saved and contribute to the salvation of their fellow man. It is His purpose that men live lives that will reflect credit on the Creator for having made man to begin with. If man meets the conditions of his creation, then the purpose of God will be fulfilled, and nothing can "disannul it," nor can any power on earth turn back that hand that is stretched out. In short, the Christian who places himself at the center of God's will becomes an invincible force. The powers of hell are helpless to destroy him. How else can you explain the fact that fire could not burn the three Hebrew boys? How else can you explain that a caldron of boiling oil did not consume John the revelator? How else do you explain Daniel's experience in the lions' den? The fact is that when one is at the center of God's purpose for his life, the will of God for that man will be fulfilled. This is the promise of Scripture, and God is not a man that He should lie.

Though God is all powerful, He does not compel the will of man; however, there are consequences of our decisions that we cannot escape. "Be not deceived; God is not mocked: for whatsoever a man soweth, that shall he also reap" (Gal. 6:7).

There are those who reason that if God is all powerful and just, He would stop all the misery and the bloodshed rampant in our world today. All such fail to realize that these things are consequences of our sins and not of God's basic desires and purposes for the human family. In short, He will not withhold from us that which we choose, having stated aforetime that "the wages of sin is death" (Rom. 6:23).

266

UNTO YOU

But unto you that fear my name shall the Sun of righteous-
ness arise with healing in his wings; and ye shall go forth, and
grow up as calves of the stall. Mal. 4:2.

The fate of the wicked is that they will be destroyed. The wages
of sin is death. By contrast the righteous "shall go forth, and grow up
as calves of the stall." "Blessed are the meek: for they shall inherit
the earth" (Matt. 5:5). There will be a full recovery from the wound
that sin has inflicted on the human family, for the "Sun of righteousness" shall "arise with healing in his wings." There will occur in man a
reconstitution of his body. The Bible describes it as a putting on of
incorruption and immortality.

The promises to the overcomer are for our inspiration. They are
not appeals to the selfishness in man nor to the threats of eternal
punishment that inspire service based on fear, for such an attitude
is that of a slave driven to his task. The quality and quantity of
service would be negatively affected in such case. There is no substitute for a labor of love. Love imposes no limitation on its own out-
reach. Its service is measured in terms of human need. Love will give
of itself as long as it is required. This is why the greatest of Christian
virtues is love. As a basic virtue, it is the only creative force in the
universe. Love is the secret of joyful obedience to God. "If ye love me,
keep my commandments," Jesus said (John 14:15). The love relationship between God and man must be fed. This is possible through
worship and service. As love is thus expressed, it is multiplied, and
the capacity to obey is strengthened. Love is that "healing in his
wings" (Mal. 4:2). It is the restorative power of God. By it men's
lives are brought into harmony with the divine purpose. It is thus that
obedience to the law of God becomes the measure of the depth of love
and hence the degree of healing.

Our text concludes, "and ye shall go forth, and grow up as calves
of the stall." There were giants in the land before the Flood, men of
giant stature and intellect. When Paradise is restored, man will once
again grow up to the full stature originally intended for him by his
Creator.

TOO MANY

And the Lord said unto Gideon, The people that are with thee are too many for me to give the Midianites into their hands, lest Israel vaunt themselves against me, saying, Mine own hand hath saved me. Judges 7:2.

It is encouraging to know that God can accomplish much with little and that He can finish a job with few, however large that task. In our text His request to Gideon to reduce his forces is just the opposite to what we would expect, but God wanted to demonstrate a principle to His people then and now; namely, that He can serve His purposes with many or with few. And further, He realized that if man's forces were inadequate, man could not take unto himself credit due alone to God.

We who face the task of world evangelism are often staggered by the population explosion. Some view the disproportion between the bearers of the message of God and the millions to be reached with that message, and grow fainthearted at the prospect. They cannot conceive that so few could ever reach so many, but it shall be. He will finish the work, but He will do it with human beings. God-blessed men are somehow multiplied in their effectiveness. The Spirit-filled man can chase a thousand, and two can put ten thousand to flight. It seems that Heaven's only requirement is that we present ourselves to Him as dedicated vessels.

The Sword of the Spirit, newly edged with power, flashing here and there, will surely gain the day. The phrase, "finishing of the work," is not an idle saying. God will provide providential openings for the proclamation of the message for which we cannot account by natural means. Witness the willingness of the Roman Catholic hierarchy to expose its membership to our literature. There is not even now a satisfactory explanation for this phenomenon. Witness also the sudden and dramatic change of events of Moslem Indonesia. Is not this the deep working of God that the message might go forward? The work of God will be completed and in due time we will reap if we faint not.

God is not limited, but must have clear channels for His work.

GOD THAT PERFORMETH

I will cry unto God most high; unto God that performeth all things for me. **Ps. 57:2.**

A bronze figure of Luther in gown and bands with the Bible in his arms stands upon a pedestal of polished granite under a Gothic canopy at Wittenberg. Upon the base of the monument is the inscription, "If it be God's work it will endure, if man's it will perish." The work of the Reformation was God's work, for it continues and it stands. The long night of medieval oppression was broken by the stalwart performances of the leaders of the Reformation—Luther, Huss, Zwingli, and others. Many of the Reformers paid with their lives for the knowledge they sought, found, and proclaimed, but "the blood of the martyrs is the seed of the Church." Today wherever men walk the earth the light of the gospel has penetrated. "This is the Lord's doing; it is marvellous in our eyes" (Ps. 118:23).

That the work of reformation is the work of God none need doubt. Popular religious bodies have long ago ceased this work. Their lack of emphasis on the fruitage of transformation in the form of obedience to the law of God has produced large numbers of undisciplined Christians. The danger in this is that those so affected imagine themselves in the center of the will of God. Genuine transformation will manifest itself in reformation. The power that converts also reforms, and the work on the lost heart of man is not complete short of reformation. The doctrine that a man may be saved from sin while deliberately continuing to indulge therein is cruel deception. Jesus said, "Ye shall know them by their fruits," but the fruits of righteousness are performed in us by Christ Himself. It is indeed God that performeth all things for me. Says Paul, "I can do all things through Christ which strengtheneth me" (Phil. 4:13). "For it is God which worketh in you both to will and to do of his good pleasure" (chap. 2:13). So, then, the work of grace on the human heart and in the life is the work of Christ first, last, and always. It is ours to make the choice.

With His living presence in our lives the works of righteousness are fulfilled in us, for we then "walk not after the flesh, but after the Spirit" (Rom. 8:4).

A PIT

He that diggeth a pit shall fall into it; and whoso breaketh an hedge, a serpent shall bite him. Eccl. 10:8.

Saul had pursued David for years, trying to take his life. He had little to guide him in this madness but his own jealousy. He trapped David in a cave but did not know it, and lay down to sleep. Under the cover of darkness, with great stealth David made his way to the sleeping Saul, cut off a piece of his garment, and slowly made his escape. Standing on a hill at the break of day, he shouted to Saul and made it clear that as he had cut off a piece of his garment, he might have taken his life. Saul had dug a pit for David. He almost fell into it himself. Arousing from his slumber he shouted, "Behold, I have played the fool" (1 Sam. 26:21).

The causes for pit digging are legion. Malice, avarice, revenge, and jealousy are some of the chief root causes. In the days of the ancient Persian kingdom a statesman by the name of Haman built a gallows for Mordecai, a prominent Jew of his day. Haman was a pompous fellow who liked people to bow down to him and show him honor because of his high position. The Bible says that pride goeth before destruction and a haughty spirit before a fall. This was certainly true in Haman's experience. Having built his gallows, he set about the delicate task of maneuvering his enemy toward the same, but he reckoned without Queen Esther, a cousin of Mordecai. She gave sumptuous banquets until the king was so pleased with her that he would grant her every wish. Then she revealed the evil that was in Haman's heart concerning her uncle and laid bare his plot to hang the innocent Mordecai. In anger the king ordered Haman hanged on his own gallows. He had dug a pit for another, and he fell into it himself.

There is a better way in our world, a happier way, to live. The jealous, the malicious, the envious, are the truly unhappy ones. The better way is the way of love. Love will disadvantage itself for its object. Love "seeketh not her own" and will get out of the way and let pride go hurtling by, but in the end love wins. For the greatest of all virtues is love.

THEY CEASED NOT

And daily in the temple, and in every house, they ceased not to teach and preach Jesus Christ. Acts 5:42.

Our text reveals the key to the power of the New Testament church: "they ceased not." Yes, they were constantly at the task of spreading the good news of the gospel of the kingdom. Every day was a new opportunity to extend the triumphs of the cross. Christians were conscious of each contact being providential with reference to the task of the church.

My wife keeps a good supply of the "Hour With Your Bible" tract series in the automobile and at the house, and anyone chancing to knock on our door who is not a member of the faith will walk away with some aspect of the message in his hand. Stops at service stations and other points along the way are opportunities for disseminating the faith.

This attitude on the part of the New Testament church accomplished three things: (1) It spread the message of the saving grace of the Lord Jesus to the entire known world in the disciples' day, (2) it produced a revival of godliness within church ranks that made its members a spectacle to men and angels, and (3) it brought persecution to the believers, the fires of which are necessary to church purity.

We are also here concerned with the scope of the evangelistic operation. The Bible says, "in the temple, and in every house." The witness of the church was not confined to the precincts of the sanctuary, but in addition to evangelistic meetings in the Temple, there was a meaningful house-to-house visitation program. In the services of the temple the needy soul goes in search of the church. In the house-to-house program the church goes in search of needy souls, and what jewels there are out there, like the woman who prepared the food for a Roman Catholic bishop. She was won to Christ in my recent campaign in Trinidad and is now a colporteur. In her first month she sold more than six hundred dollars' worth of books.

Yes, that which has been predicted by the prophets may be fulfilled in us. There is work for every pair of hands to do and there are places for every pair of feet to go.

EXECUTED RIGHTEOUSNESS

The Lord executeth righteousness and judgment for all that are oppressed. Ps. 103:6.

Since the advent of sin our world has had its fill of oppressor and oppressed. The first example of this is the case of Cain and Abel. Here the issue was a religious one. Because of his faithfulness to God, righteous Abel was murdered by his brother, but God executed judgment upon Cain and made him a miserable wanderer for the rest of his days. This life sentence was harder than instant death. God has always identified Himself with oppressed people and moved for their deliverance. There is the example of Israel in Egyptian bondage. Their cry was heard and God delivered them.

Ellen G. White, in her counsels to the church, refers repeatedly to the intervention of angels in the battles of the Civil War. The government at Washington vacillated for many months about freeing the slaves. The pen of the messenger of the Lord indicates that until the Emancipation Act was signed Heaven would not permit the northern armies to be victorious. God always succors the oppressed.

Witness the life of Christ on earth, how He moved among the lepers and the outcasts of society, relieving their distresses and healing their diseases, giving hope to prostitutes and extreme sinners in His ministry of love. The church of the Lord Jesus Christ can never, like the Pharisee, pass by on the other side, while prostrate humanity cries unheeded for relief. It was an irate Pharisaical crowd that would have stoned Mary of Magdala, but it was Christ who forgave her and sent her forth to "sin no more." It was the hand of God that brought the human family out of the darkness of medieval history into the sunlight of the Reformation. Yes, oppressed humanity could now look and live with a Bible in every home. What a privilege to live in an age of great light and opportunity and pass these blessings along.

In the Detroit riots members of the Seventh-day Adventist church of all racial strains worked together to bring relief to the oppressed, serving the Lord with gladness. It was a Christ-oriented program of organized beneficence. This was righteousness in working clothes. This was judgment for the oppressed.

WITH GLADNESS

Serve the Lord with gladness: come before his presence with singing. Ps. 100:2.

Some people are afraid of anything like joy in religion. They have none themselves, and they do not love to see it in others. Their religion is something like the stars—very high, very clear, but very cold. When they see religion expressed in tears of joy, they cry out against it on the charge of emotionalism. If to sit under His shadow with great delight is emotionalism, let us have more of it. "Now the God of hope fill you with all joy and peace in believing." Here is the norm, so let there be no bounds to our joy. Oh, if God would but open our eyes and give us simple childlike faith to look to Jesus, to sit under His shadow, then would songs of joy arise from all our dwellings. "Rejoice in the Lord alway: and again I say, Rejoice."

In the catacombs where the early Christians were forced to repair for their worship, because of persecution, there is ample evidence of their joy in suffering for and serving their Lord. Dean Farrar says, "Joy and blithe serenity which received death with no alarm or self-abasement were their marked characteristics. St. Luke throws a flood of light on the tone of their society when he says that 'they did take their food with exaltation and singleness of heart.' The words indicate their bounding gladness, their simplicity and smoothness of feeling as of a plain without stones or a field without furrows."

The only genuine joy on earth is the happiness of the Christian. Such a person may indeed "come before his presence with singing," and the joy of his service is based on his love for Him who died for the sinner.

Spurgeon tells of "John Bradford in Newgate who was to be burned the next morning in Smithfield. He swings himself on the bed-post in very glee and delight, for tomorrow is his wedding day. He says to another, 'Fine shining we shall make tomorrow when the flame is kindled.' And he smiles and laughs and enjoys the very thought that he is about to wear the blood-red crown of martyrdom. Is Bradford mad? Ah, no. He has the peace of God that passeth understanding."

273

COMPLETE

And ye are complete in him, which is the head of all principality and power. Col. 2:10.

When Alexander, the crown prince of Russia, was in England, he ordered a watch made. So intricate was its mechanism and peculiar its combinations that when it was broken, not a man in Russia could repair it, and it had to be returned to its maker for repairs. When Adam was called into existence, angels must have beheld him with delighted surprise. By the attacks of sin and Satan, the image of God was lost, and the spirituality of the creature was annihilated. Who can repair the human mechanism? He only who first taught the machine to move in His own image, who is acquainted with all the springs and principles of human action. Pretenders have tried it again and again but to no purpose. When we open the volume of inspiration, we behold the machine once more in the hand of the Maker. He can repair it and not only so, it will be so improved by Him as eventually to comprise many glories to which angels must be strangers forever.

Angels will never know the joy of restoration to divine favor. But in Christ fallen man can be as fully and completely restored as though he had not fallen. Natural birth supplies man with physical and mental capacity. Only when we are born again of the Spirit, is the spiritual nature possible. This is the completion of the job. It is in this sense that we "are complete in him."

The maintenance of our spiritual nature is quite different from the physical and the mental. We can by eating food feed our physical bodies. We may feed our minds through the works of philosophy, history, and science, but the spiritual nature can only be fed through prayer, the study of the Bible, worship, and service to our fellow man. The question of Jesus, "Wilt thou be made whole?" (John 5:6), implies more than physical healing. Christ was offering to this person a fully restored man—physically, mentally, and spiritually balanced. To "him that is able," may we pray today and toward Him direct our faith, for in Him alone is the key to completeness. And He is able to save to the uttermost all who come unto God by Him (Heb. 7:25).

274

LAMB OF GOD

And looking upon Jesus as he walked, he saith, Behold the Lamb of God! John 1:36.

The nature of a lamb makes it a most fitting symbol of Christ on earth as the Saviour of men. Dr. W. R. Nicoll states, "Jesus is described as a lamb led to the slaughter and it is said that as a sheep before his shearers is dumb, so He opened not His mouth. But along with this we must include a reference to the paschal lamb. Few thoughts in John's Gospel are more distinct than that of the relation of Jesus Christ to the paschal sacrifice and feast. The Passover, which was the most conspicuous symbol of the messianic deliverance, was not far off. Flocks of lambs were passing by to Jerusalem to be offered at the coming feast, and the sight may have brought home the thought further, there is no difficulty in believing that the forerunner who had deeply meditated the messianic prophecies and the meaning of the sacrifices, saw with prophetic insight that Christ was to suffer, thus standing for a time on a higher level than any of His disciples."

For four thousand years animal sacrifices had atoned for the sins of men, but their validity rested on the supreme act of atonement at the cross of Calvary by our Lord, Jesus Christ. He was indeed "the Lamb of God." On Him rested the fate of the entire human family. By His mercy thousands would be cleansed while millions who reject Him would suffer the penalty of divine justice, but no one would escape Him.

Now the Bible speaks of the wrath of the Lamb at the end of the age. God's justice, tempered by mercy for six thousand years, will suddenly exact its full price. The unmixed wrath of the Lamb will be visited upon the head of guilty man. How precious then is the "whosoever will" of the gospel invitation.

In Stuart Hamblin we see what looking to Christ can do. Confessing that he had been a great sinner he found his way to the foot of the cross. Then he who had sung the hymns of the world became a great composer of hymns for the church. Touching indeed is the song of his own experience, "It is no secret what God can do. What He's done for others He'll do for you."

275

REMEMBER NOW

Remember now thy Creator in the days of thy youth, while the evil days come not, nor the years draw nigh, when thou shalt say, I have no pleasure in them. Eccl. 12:1.

C. Deyo, who spent thirty years among the Comanche Indians, wrote as follows: "An old Comanche said to a girl that I baptized one day, 'You made me happy today, giving your heart to Jesus while you're in the springtime of life, before you have done much that was wrong. Keep close to Jesus, and your life will be a springtime.' One young man said, 'Today Jesus unlocked my heart and let the Father's Spirit in, now my heart is like a new silver dollar just made, new and bright.' "

Christ saves many a man in his sunset years but He can get more service out of younger people, for they have their lives ahead of them. The flower in the tenderness of full bloom and its early aroma is certainly more serviceable than when wilted and fading and ready to die. The text assures us that one who remembers his Creator in the days of youth will never see a day but what some good must come of it. This is in contrast to his burdened years when he will say, "I have no pleasure in them." The darkest cloud contains a silver lining to the man who has known God through the years. One author writes that he had been passing many enormous billboards, gaudy in hue, striking in design, each claiming superlative merits for its tires. "Buy Live Forever Tires. They last like steel," one ad shrieked. Another: "Use Rockaway Tires. No other rides so smoothly." But the one that impressed most people was the one that said simply, "Smith Tires are good tires." There was a ring of authenticity here; reliability built on years of use and service. I think of this when I think of a Christian who has served the Lord from his youth. His experiences with Christ through the years have built a steadily growing, sound relationship. He simply knows that God is good. With a knowing look in his eye he speaks of the benefits of his lifetime relationship. In his testimony there is none of the bizarre or the sensational, and there are no extravagant claims. God is good. It's as simple as that.

276

SORROW UPON SORROW

For indeed he was sick nigh unto death: but God had mercy on him; and not on him only, but on me also, lest I should have sorrow upon sorrow. Phil. 2:27.

It is a fact that tribulation is not meted out equally to all men, and there are some people whose lives seem to be filled with nothing but "sorrow upon sorrow," while others apparently go through this world on flowery beds of ease. But this is only apparent. Each life receives its measure of sadness, yet none receives more than it can bear. The God of heaven simply refuses to allow the devil to "pour it on." Satan knew whereof he spoke when he argued that God had put a hedge around Job. The fact is, God has put a hedge around all of us. Otherwise the devil, who is by nature a destroyer, would have depopulated the earth.

Harry Lauder had a heart so filled with merriment that for years he had been setting all the world laughing with his songs, but a great darkness fell upon him. As he left the theater one night he received a message that his only son had been killed at the front in France. It was a crushing blow, for the boy was the idol of his father's heart. The grieving father turned to God for comfort. A few weeks later he was canceling lucrative engagements and on his way to France with YMCA forces to sing gospel songs to the soldiers and bear witness for Christ. Commenting on his own experience, Lauder said, "When a great sorrow overtakes any man, there are three things he may do—sour on life, seek oblivion in drink, or turn to God. I have chosen the third path."

This is indeed the object of trial, that it might incline the heart to trust more fully in Christ and in His purposes. There is no joy in the great heart of God when His children suffer. In the case of the death of His own Son at Calvary, His own great heart was torn with sadness. He felt every pain that His Son felt and matched tear with falling tear. If this were understood, there would be fewer clenched fists lifted heavenward and more open hands and suppliant hearts. What an insane and barren world this would be without the spiritual illumination that comes from bearing a cross.

IN NOTHING TERRIFIED

And in nothing terrified by your adversaries: which is to them an evident token of perdition, but to you of salvation, and that of God. Phil. 1:28.

Over the mantel in the ancient Hind's Head Hotel in Bray, England, is a legend all may read: "Fear knocked at the door. Faith answered. No one was there." The force of this message is grasped only when the reader remembers that this was inscribed at the time of Dunkerque, in one of England's darkest hours.

Yes, fear is a coward before onrushing faith. The Bible says, "But perfect love casteth out fear" (1 John 4:18). It was serene confidence inspired by love of God that enabled Christians under direst persecution to face their tormentors serenely and to accept with fortitude whatever punishment they meted out. Dr. John Oliver remarked to one of his patients who was a nervous wreck, "I'll tell you the kind of people who as a general rule I do not see in my office. So far as my experience goes, the people who seem not to be assailed and possessed by fear are those who believe and practice the Christian religion." Christianity even removes from man the fear of death. David in dire trouble said of his experience, "I will fear no evil: for thou art with me" (Ps. 23:4). Addison has said, "What can that man fear who takes care to please a being that is able to crush all his adversaries?" And the secret is that Christ becomes our Protector, Lord, and Master when we surrender our lives to Him. We are in His hands. He will give His angels charge over us to keep us lest we dash our foot against a stone. "God is our refuge and strength, a very present help in trouble" (Ps. 46:1). All of the anxieties of our workaday world sink into insignificance beside the blessed assurance of the eternal presence of the living God.

According to James Russell Lowell:

> "They are slaves who fear to speak
> For the fallen and the weak. . . .
> They are slaves who dare not be
> In the right with two or three."

278

THINK ON THESE

Finally, brethren, whatsoever things are true, whatsoever things are honest, whatsoever things are just, whatsoever things are pure, whatsoever things are lovely, whatsoever things are of good report; if there be any virtue, and if there be any praise, think on these things. Phil. 4:8.

The mind is the seat of all human behavior. It is to this the Bible refers when it says: "Keep thy heart with all diligence; for out of it are the issues of life" (Prov. 4:23). The mind has a tendency to absorb that upon which it dwells, and our thinking assumes the character of that which claims our constant attention. The Bible states that we are changed by beholding (2 Cor. 3:18).

The directional force of all our actions is the will. It controls the thoughts that motivate our actions. The will is comparable to the steering wheel of an automobile. With it we may literally steer our minds in any direction we choose. The problem is that some people make no attempt to control their thoughts. They are submissive to passing emotions. The positive thinking enjoined in our text is foreign to them. It is little wonder that the general pattern of human behavior is erratic and delinquent.

We are in serious need of redirection. The root of our problem is that of unsanctified wills. These must be placed at the disposal of the Almighty. We must literally will to do His will. It is then that He controls the life and guides the footsteps of the faithful aright.

Said Spurgeon, "Good thoughts are blessed guests and should be heartily welcomed, well fed, and much sought after. Like rose leaves they give out a sweet smell that is laid up in the jar of memory." But there are those who claim they are powerless to keep evil thoughts out of the mind.

A certain wise man replied to one who said, "Such and such thoughts have come into my mind," by saying, "Let them go out again." Another wise oracle said, "Thou canst not prevent the birds from flying above thy head, but thou canst prevent them from building their nests in thy hair."

NOT AFTER CHRIST

Beware lest any man spoil you through philosophy and vain deceit, after the tradition of men, after the rudiments of the world, and not after Christ. Col. 2:8.

Human philosophy has all but supplanted the Bible as the standard by which human behavior is measured. It is alleged that right and wrong are relative and that there is no absolute standard by which good and evil can be determined. There is, of course, the human consensus that community of senses is the determining factor, not to mention the philosophy of the streets, that anything is right that you can get away with.

"Beware" we are warned "lest any man spoil you" through these things. These are spoiling philosophies. They corrupt the morals and are often at the root of behavior that is not "after Christ." "Vain deceit"—how many different forms of it there are in the world.

Dr. Bates has said: "Cato and Brutus were both philosophers of the manly sect, and virtue never appeared with a brighter luster among the heathens than when joined with a stoical resolution. And they were not imperfect proficients, but masters in philosophy. Seneca employs all the ornaments of his eloquence to make Cato's eulogy. He represents him as the consummate example of wisdom; as one that realized the sublime idea of virtue described in their writings. And Brutus was esteemed equal to Cato. Yet these, with all the power of their philosophy, were not able to bear the shocks of adversity. Like raw fencers, one thrust put them into such disorders that they forgot all their instructions in the place of trial. For, being unsuccessful in their endeavor to restore Rome to its liberty, overcome with discontent and despair, they laid violent hands upon themselves. Cato, being prevented in his first attempt, afterwards tore open his wounds with fierceness and rage. And Brutus, ready to plunge his sword into his own breast, complained that virtue was but a vain name. . . . As torrents that are dried up in the heat of summer, when there is most need of them; so all comforts fail in the extremity, that are not derived from the fountain of life."

280

YOUR MEMBERS

Mortify therefore your members which are upon the earth; fornication, uncleanness, inordinate affection, evil concupiscence, and covetousness, which is idolatry. Col. 3:5.

The phrase "your members" refers to those organs or faculties that serve evil: (1) "fornication" is a term covering all forms of immorality; (2) "uncleanness" implies a state of impurity; (3) "inordinate affection" is lust; (4) "evil concupiscence" is a lustful conspiring together for that which cannot be lawfully possessed; (5) "covetousness" is secret unlawful desire. All are identified as forms of idolatry. To "mortify" these propensities means to put these things to death, for they are destructive of all that is moral and good. There is no peaceful coexistence between good and evil in the human heart.

But the question arises: How may we mortify or deaden or subdue the unclean, inordinate, concupiscent, covetous desires of the human heart? The fact is that of ourselves we are powerless against these things. Only the sin-bearer—Jesus Christ—can be the sin-remover. "He is able even to subdue all things unto himself" (Phil. 3:21). Thank God there is a solution for sin and a potential mastery of human passion. It is, "Christ in you, the hope of glory" (Col. 1:27).

We must surrender the will to the power of Christ. As a consequence there will be an impartation of the divine nature: "But ye are not in the flesh, but in the Spirit, if so be that the Spirit of God dwell in you. Now if any man have not the Spirit of Christ, he is none of his" (Rom. 8:9). The daily presence of Christ in the life makes possible the fulfillment of Romans 8:21: "Because the creature itself also shall be delivered from the bondage of corruption into the glorious liberty of the children of God."

A little boy saw a bird prancing nervously but helplessly under the gaze of a serpent. The snake moved in slowly but surely, and the bird, charmed by its hypnotic power, seemed powerless to deliver itself. The boy picked up a rock and threw it, hitting the snake on the head. This broke the spell and the bird nervously flew away, never knowing the instrument or person that accomplished its redemption. God is likewise our deliverer in time of peril.

LET US WALK

Let us walk honestly, as in the day; not in rioting and drunkenness, not in chambering and wantonness, not in strife and envying. Rom. 13:13.

The word "honestly" as it occurs in our text means "decently." This text is most appropriate for our time in which the standards of decency are being trampled underfoot.

After listening to a nationally known minister one evening, I would say small wonder that this is so. He said, "Any religion that has rules of dogma is unworkable today. There is no standard by which human behavior may be judged." He discounted the Bible as a rule of faith and practice, declaring it to be valuable as an historical document. He emphasized that each generation has to establish its own code and make its own rules. This is humanism in essence, and under its terms man becomes his own god, and rioting, drunkenness, chambering, and wantonness become the order of the day. Small wonder that men have become lovers of pleasure more than lovers of God, and that the lust for entertainment has become the dominant drive of our age. Man has been cut loose from his moorings and is like a ship without a rudder, adrift at sea, little knowing where he is going. He has been robbed of the security of faith. He exists to serve himself.

The religion of Jesus Christ is just the opposite. It requires that man deny himself and stipulates that the purpose of man is the service of God and his fellow man. Furthermore, it sets up standards by which character is evaluated and deeds are measured. These standards are Heaven born and committed to man as oracles and commandments. As a father gives guidance to his children, so God has given guidance to His people. He has not left them to wander about, to learn by trial and error what is and is not right. He has settled the question of right and wrong forever and has clearly defined it in the Scriptures of truth. Jesus said, "They are they which testify of me" (John 5:39). Herein lies the secret of their power. They reveal Jesus Christ to the human soul. By the Scriptures, Old and New Testaments, Christ is introduced to needy man. These set the standard and guard against the excesses of our times.

WHO IS A GOD?

Who is a God like unto thee, that pardoneth iniquity, and passeth by the transgression of the remnant of his heritage? he retaineth not his anger for ever, because he delighteth in mercy. Micah 7:18.

Gods of metal, stone, and wood were winning their competition with the God of heaven for the hearts of His people, Israel. That this should be so defies all the laws of logic, and yet there is an explanation.

Worship of heathen gods required only outward acts of worship in the form of appeasement. They required no change in the life. The unconverted man's heart liked this, for it relieved him of all responsibility in terms of character reformation. There were no standards of conduct to disturb his conscience or his way of life.

Modern man does not bow down to gods of wood and stone, but men unconsciously set up gods in their own image to whom they need make no sacrifice. The question of Micah then is quite pertinent, "Who is a God like unto thee?" The answer is "None," for only He can pardon iniquity. He only "delighteth in mercy."

An African chief one day ordered a slave to be killed for a very small offense. An Englishman who overheard the order offered the chief many costly objects if only he would spare the poor man's life. But the chief turned to him and said, "I don't want ivory or slaves or gold. I can go against yonder tribe and capture their stores and their villages. I want no favors from you, sir, all I want is blood." Then he ordered one of his men to pull his bowstring and discharge an arrow at the heart of the poor slave. The Englishman instinctively threw himself in front and held up his arms. The next moment the arrow was quivering in his flesh. Then as the Englishman pulled the arrow from his arm he said: "Here is blood, I give my blood for this poor slave and I claim his life." The chief gave the slave to the Englishman, saying: "Yes, you have bought him with your blood and he shall be yours." In a moment the poor slave threw himself at the feet of his deliverer and with tears flowing down his cheeks exclaimed: "You have bought me with your blood, I will be your slave forever."

A MAN NAMED JESUS

He answered and said, A man that is called Jesus made clay, and anointed mine eyes, and said unto me, Go to the pool of Siloam, and wash: and I went and washed, and I received sight. John 9:11.

The testimony meeting is a vital part of worship. I think that next to prayer the devil hates this spiritual exercise most, for in the praise service the believer shares with others a knowledge of the blessings of God to his own soul. Testimonies have a powerful influence for good. The recitation of personal blessings provides clinical evidence that God is alive and active in the spiritual health of human beings.

In my own personal experience I can remember how difficult it was to stand and speak during this vital service. It was almost as hard as getting up to walk down front and signify one's decision to join the church.

The man in our text had been born blind, and lo, in his neighborhood, standing before the neighbors, he is interrogated as to the miracle that gave him sight. Opinion was divided with reference to him. Some said, "Is not this he that sat and begged?" Others said, "He is like him," but he said, "I am he." Then he identified his benefactor as "a man that is called Jesus." There is no boasting here of human merit. The answer is simple and to the point. To God goes all the glory. So prone are human beings to claim credit for their own well-being that few give God the glory that is due His name. Yet "in him we live, and move, and have our being" (Acts 17:28).

After a major world power had accomplished the orbiting of a man and the conducting of certain unusual experiments in space, he was brought back, and in a news conference that I witnessed they were accounting for the miracle that had taken place. I listened in vain for someone to give God the honor that was due His name. Everybody got credit, from the pilot who flew the spacecraft to the technicians on the ground, but there was not a word about God.

"He put clay on my eyes." It was a simple testimony, but this man had discovered the secret of life—to give glory to the God of life. It is still true that "he that humbleth himself shall be exalted," but "whosoever exalteth himself shall be abased" (Luke 14:11).

284

BY GRACE

For by grace are ye saved through faith; and that not of your-selves: it is the gift of God. Eph. 2:8.

In a mood perceptive of universal experience, Fanny Crosby wrote:

"Chords that were broken will vibrate once more."

How true it is that human beings are incapable of judging others, for no man can read the heart. Only God can detect that heart in which "feelings lie buried that grace can restore." The penetrating eye of God sees man not only as he is but as he can become by His grace.

In the Magdalene, a woman of easy virtue, He could see a moral person. In Matthew, the despised tax collector, He could see an honest man. In Peter, the quick-tempered, sharp-tongued sailor, He could see a self-possessed and mighty preacher. In Saul, the zealous persecutor, He could see the world's mightiest evangelist. In James, a son of thunder, He could see an administrator and leader in the church. In John, his brother of violent moods, He could see that meek and mild disciple who would become a favorite.

As we read the words of our text the question comes: Just what does God see in us? The encouraging part is that He sees us, not only as we are, but as we may become by His grace. Ephesians 2:10 says: "For we are his workmanship, created in Christ Jesus unto good works, which God hath before ordained that we should walk in them." When Christ captures the human heart there is a manifestation of new life. The favor of God, unmerited, does for us what nothing else can do.

Carlyle took Emerson through Whitechapel, the terrible slums of London, happily not so terrible today, and then asked him if he had any difficulty in believing in the devil. Had Christ accompanied them through those same slums He might have replied: "There are jewels in those dingy byways for whom I died." The Lord inquired of Ezekiel, "Son of man, can these bones live?" The prophet's reply "O Lord God, thou knowest" expresses our human lack of knowledge of God's way. When will we understand that with God there are no impossibilities, and that miracles are performed in human hearts by His saving grace?

LET US GO

I was glad when they said unto me, Let us go into the house of the Lord. Ps. 122:1.

It is always a source of joy and inspiration to go to the house of a friend. The warmth of love and fellowship justifies any sacrifice that is involved in such a visit. Jesus Christ is a friend that sticketh closer than a brother. The church building is His temple. "And let them make me a sanctuary; that I may dwell among them" (Ex. 25:8), Jesus says. In a real sense, then, when a Christian goes to church he literally meets God there. This accounts in part for the psalmist's joy at being invited into the "house of the Lord." This is significant, because the Bible declares that Christ is a "friend of sinners." This should encourage the weakest child of the King to come humbly into His presence seeking pardon, peace, and power. It is a trait of human nature, however, to want to go in the opposite direction from God when there is guilt in the soul.

This was the case of Adam and Eve in the Garden of Eden. Having transgressed, they hid until God found them. The Bible says that He came walking in the cool of the evening saying, "Adam, . . . Where art thou?" (Gen. 3:9), and having found him crouching in a bush, He asks the next question: "Who told thee that thou wast naked?" (verse 11). No matter how he seeks to avoid the issue, man must eventually confront his Maker.

In my work as a minister I often visit with men and women who have backslidden from their former faith. After I inquire the reason for backsliding, the one most frequently given is that they had a weakness in their life that they could not seem to get rid of, and rather than be a hypocrite they just dropped away. My counsel to such is the reminder of the Master that they who are well need no physician. It is the sick man who goes to the doctor and to the hospital to get his condition corrected. And so the church is God's great center of spiritual healing, and those who go confessing their spiritual needs are blessed and made glad.

When you feel your faith weakening, go to church. It may be just the day God has prepared a message for your own heart.

CHRIST DIED

But God commendeth his love toward us, in that, while we were yet sinners, Christ died for us. Rom. 5:8.

One day early in the eighteenth century a German artist by the name of Stenberg walked through the market place of his home town looking for a model. He was attracted by the face of a gypsy dancing girl and invited her to come to his studio to sit for him, and with her as a model he painted his *Dancing Gypsy Girl.* The little girl was much taken with what she saw in the artist's studio and watched him with great interest as he worked on a painting of the crucifixion. One day she said to the artist, "He must have been a very bad man to have been nailed to the cross like that!"

The artist replied: "No, He was a good man, the best man that ever lived. Indeed, He died for all men."

"Did He die for you?" The innocent question of the girl set the artist thinking, for he had not given his heart to Christ.

One day in a meeting of the Reformers the Scriptures were opened to his understanding and brought him to Christ. He went back to finish his painting of the crucifixion, working this time not only with an artist's skill and technique but with a love that comes out of a believing heart.

Yes, Christ died for our sins—and it was personal. Often the use of the term "our" tends to depersonalize the fact. Perhaps each of us who read this devotional should remember that Christ died for us individually. He was every man's substitute before the bar of justice, but He died for my sin. His atoning blood covers every man's transgression, but the victory over sin must be mine.

J. D. Jones says: "The dweller in Toronto wakes up in the morning and wants a light to dress by. He presses a little switch and his whole room is light as day, and it is Niagara which does it for him. He goes to his bathroom and wants to heat some water for washing or shaving. He presses another switch, and once again Niagara supplies his need. He wants to talk to someone in Montreal or Chicago, he rings a bell, and Niagara carries his message for him." We have a Niagara of that kind of power in Jesus Christ.

PLANTED TOGETHER

For if we have been planted together in the likeness of his death, we shall be also in the likeness of his resurrection. Rom. 6:5.

Baptism is a planting of the Christian by burial in water, similar to the burial of the dead in the earth. It symbolizes in its initial phase the crucifixion and burial of the old man of sin. There are certain similarities between physical death and spiritual death to sin: In death one is unconscious. In a spiritual sense this is also true. We live in the same world we lived in before we died to sin and yet the sinful environment does not get the grip on the inner man that it once did, because within there is a new life, a new nature. In a state of grace Adam and Eve walked by the tree of knowledge of good and evil without temptation, but when tempted to doubt the word of God, Eve yielded, and suddenly that which had formerly had no effect on her became attractive, exercising a pull on her inner life that resulted in transgression. When a man believes the gospel, repents of his sin, and is converted, he receives the spiritual nature that Adam and Eve had at creation. But when the Word of God is doubted and we dally with temptation, the pull is downward in millions of lives. When there is surrender of heart to God's infilling, divine protection is afforded the aspiring saint, and the strength of Jehovah to resist temptation becomes his. How joyful the promise, "We shall be also in the likeness of his resurrection." The new life is then hardly recognizable in terms of the old. In Christ's resurrected body, only the scars remained. And so with us who walk in newness of life, there will be those reminders of our sinful experiences as long as we walk the earth, but never again, having been delivered, need we be impaled on a cross of frustration and spiritual death by the hammer of temptation and the nails of defeat.

During a historic battle, a soldier ran up to the general to salute smartly and report, "Sir, we have captured one gun."

"Fine," replied the general, "take two more."

Living in Christ our spiritually resurrected lives may be one succession of conquests after another. How heartening is the promise, "Five of you shall chase an hundred, and an hundred of you shall put ten thousand to flight" (Lev. 26:8).

NOW IS COME SALVATION

And I heard a loud voice saying in heaven, Now is come salvation, and strength, and the kingdom of our God, and the power of his Christ: for the accuser of our brethren is cast down, which accused them before our God day and night. Rev. 12:10.

This joyful announcement is contained in a chapter that also announces the terrible news that Satan has taken up his abode on the earth. Since this planet is jointly occupied by man and fallen angels, our text is vital to man in terms of his spiritual survival. Satan has come, verse nine announces; salvation has come, verse ten announces, bringing with it strength and the kingdom of our God and the power of His Christ. The sacrifice of Jesus brought from heaven the triumphant shout "the accuser of our brethren is cast down, which accused them before our God day and night." It should cheer our hearts to know that where sin abounds, grace much more abounds (Rom. 5:20), for power against Satan is granted in the hour of need. All God's saints share in the victory, for "they overcame him by the blood of the Lamb, and by the word of their testimony; and they loved not their lives unto the death" (Rev. 12:11).

Thank God, we're not helpless in this world in the face of overwhelming demon strength. "Greater is he that is in you, than he that is in the world" (1 John 4:4). We may, therefore, face each day with the quiet confidence that superior power is on our side. The key to victorious living is full surrender to the will of God.

From my sermon notes I glean this gem: "To play at the edge of God's will is poor business for anyone. 'O Lord,' prayed a consecrated follower of Christ, 'keep us in the center of Thy will.' There, and there only, is concentrated the fullness of the power, and blessing, the love and the glory of God for His children. It is like the center of the current in a swiftly flowing stream. You will catch a little of the flow and momentum if you hug the shore but if you want the whole power of the current back of you, you must get out into midstream. No one ever knows the wealth of life that comes in God's service until he is forever cut loose from the shore and lets the full omnipotence of God drive him."

10   289

ABIDE IN HIM

And now, little children, abide in him; that, when he shall appear, we may have confidence, and not be ashamed before him at his coming. 1 John 2:28.

Christ is coming soon, and we shall all stand before the judgment bar of God to give account of the deeds done in the body. But those who have trusted in Him may face Him in that day with confidence. It is no secret that there will be billions of people who will want to hide from the face of the great Judge of all the earth. These have not made Christ their refuge in the days of their probation. The saddest of all people with whom I have to deal as a gospel minister is an apostate, one who once knew Christ and had a covenant relationship with Him but who has fallen away in sin. Many such persons put up a bristling defense of their apostasy. The errors of some who are still in the church, decisions by church councils with which they do not agree, and shoddy deals, real or imaginary, become the first line of defense for the backslider. Penetrating this smoke screen one often finds a grieving heart saddened by its own failure to keep pace with the long strides of the Master. It often requires patience to reach the real man with whom one is conversing, but this may be done with great blessing to the minister and the one ministered to.

If there is one sin above another of which Christians are guilty, it is that of failure to be concerned with those who have fallen away from the faith. Like the Pharisees of old, many walk by these on the other side. Needed today are more good Samaritans who will lift up the fallen, bind up his wounds, and deliver him to the place of healing and restoration. Thousands who have fallen away from the faith gaze wistfully on the lives they once lived and the associates they once had. But if there is no tender entreaty, no show of interest in the fate of the lost, what hope is there of recovery? These people feel forsaken, shut away, and unwanted. When a member falls away, the church should not rest until every avenue has been exhausted to restore such a one to the foot of the cross.

But how much better that we abide in Him once the covenant relationship is formed between Christ and our souls.

BEFORE ME

This is he of whom I said, After me cometh a man which is preferred before me: for he was before me. John 1:30.

John the Baptist was older than Jesus and yet he declares, "he was before me." In this he recognized the pre-existence of Christ. That our Lord existed before the world was, is a fact clearly taught in Scripture. Isaiah refers to Him in the ninth chapter and the sixth verse as "The mighty God," and he predicts that He would be born unto us. And in John 17:5 Jesus prayed, "And now, O Father, glorify thou me with thine own self with the glory which I had with thee before the world was." Yes, Christ was certainly coexistent with His Father without beginning or ending of days. "In the beginning was the Word, and the Word was with God" (John 1:1). In Him is life unborrowed, underived.

It is Christ who is referred to in Revelation 12:7-9 who fought with Lucifer and his angels before the creation of man. Jesus summarized that battle in these words: "I beheld Satan as lightning fall from heaven" (Luke 10:18). It was Christ who created the world and all that therein is. We read, "All things were made by him; and without him was not any thing made that was made" (John 1:3). But the beauty of this story is that though Christ is the high and Holy One that inhabiteth eternity, He "humbled himself, and became obedient unto death, even the death of the cross" (Phil. 2:8). This is the marvel of the ages, that the Lord of glory, coexistent with God, should identify Himself forever with men, making Himself approachable concerning the minutest affairs of our individual lives.

The story is told of a gentleman who was seen talking to a poor old woman. Friends remonstrated with him, saying, "You ought to consider your rank." To which the gentleman replied, "What if my Lord had considered His rank?" But He did not consider His rank, but took upon Himself the form of a servant that He might be our Saviour. He who was before us made Himself one of us that we might be one with Him, and the cross at Calvary is the symbol of that union.

The greatest place of preference in the world is that area of service to which God has appointed us individually.

A SAFE CONCLUSION

Therefore we conclude that a man is justified by faith without the deeds of the law. Rom. 3:28.

The word "justified" as it is used here means "to render innocent, just, or righteous." Through faith in Christ we are adjudged righteous, innocent, and before God without the works of the law. This priceless revelation is the dearest part of the gospel. If indeed our innocence depended on our works, then all men would now and forever be guilty before God, for it is a gospel principle that guilty man cannot work or buy his way into divine favor. In short, man needs a Saviour, and, thank God, he has one. "Being justified freely by his grace through the redemption that is in Christ Jesus" (Rom. 3:24). It is an act of love on the part of God that accepts man's faith in Him as justification for his transgressions.

Faith in the human heart accepts Christ's merits as its own and on this basis the guilty are declared righteous and innocent and just. Our sins are laid on Jesus, and He in turn credits us with His innocence so that in effect our righteousness is not ours at all, but His. And it is ours "without the deeds of the law." How necessary it is to recognize that neither fast, nor vigil, nor pilgrimage to holy shrines, avails to shrive our souls of evil.

Those who try to appease God by works of merit deceive themselves, and yet obedience does play a part in our salvation. For a loving obedience grows out of living faith. It is the outworking of a personal covenant relationship with Christ, and as faith grows, so obedience becomes more perfect. With growth in grace there is growth in practice. Obedience is a manifestation of an inner change. It is the fruit on the tree, and as our Lord has said, "A good tree bringeth forth good fruit." Thus the law of God is seen to be, not an instrument of salvation, but the standard by which is measured our professed devotion. Transformation of the life comes from following the perfect Pattern, even our Lord Jesus Christ, who was perfect in His obedience.

> "Trust and obey, for there's no other way
> To be happy in Jesus, but to trust and obey."

JOY FOREVER

For the Lamb which is in the midst of the throne shall feed them, and shall lead them unto living fountains of waters: and God shall wipe away all tears from their eyes. **Rev. 7:17.**

There have been great social movements in our world throughout history that have held much promise for the people. In our own time we have seen the Great Society with its utopian promises and idealistic programs. In my father's day he heard proclaimed the peace signed in 1918 as being the beginning of a millennial reign of tranquillity among nations. Just one hundred years ago large religious bodies were proclaiming the kingdom of God upon earth through social legislation and man-concocted schemes and programs. The Christian of good will applauds every humanitarian impulse and gesture to right many of the wrongs that are in our world. Indeed, he participates actively in programs of human betterment in the relief of disease, in education, and in welfare programs for the public good.

This is the program of the Seventh-day Adventist Church in addition to its spiritual emphasis. In lands afar most of our educational institutions are peopled by non-Adventists. This is now, and will increasingly become, a sacred ministry of Adventism. The development of body, mind, and spirit is the philosophy of our service, not only to our membership but to the world beyond. However, our knowledge of the Bible saves us from the error of expecting the eradication of all human problems in this life. For man, in spite of his good intentions, has not solved any of the basic problems that have confronted him for six thousand years. The problems of war and peace are still with us. The problems of disease, of poverty, of human relations, all still plague us today as they always have. The promise of our text is that there will come a day when all these problems will be solved fully and finally. It will be when the kingdoms of this world become the kingdom of our Lord and of His Christ. In that day "they shall hunger no more, neither thirst any more; neither shall the sun light on them, nor any heat. For the Lamb which is in the midst of the throne shall feed them, and shall lead them . . . : and God shall wipe away all tears from their eyes."

WORLD WITHOUT END

But Israel shall be saved in the Lord with an everlasting salvation: ye shall not be ashamed nor confounded world without end. Isa. 45:17.

Life in this world for the true Israel of God is not at all a bed of roses. In every century circumstances have conspired to bring God's people into unutterable hardship. This generation will be no exception. Those who would reign with Christ must suffer with Him, but the promise of God is that there will come an end to the persecution of the righteous and that the apparent prosperity of the wicked will run its course.

There are times when it appears that to do right meets with little reward, whereas evil seems to flourish, and the righteous are often puzzled with this picture. Christians have been burned at the stake, stretched on the rack, and consumed by ravenous beasts—all for doing right. One might conclude that it does not pay to serve the Lord. But the believer has every encouragement to hope.

J. D. Jones has said, "The New Testament gives no assurance that we shall be saved from loss of comfort or material security in this life. It makes no promise that Christians shall be immune from physical danger or death. I remember W. R. Maltby pointing out to an audience of students that in the Sermon on the Mount Jesus promised His disciples three things: That they would be entirely fearless, absurdly happy, and would get into trouble. It came to pass. They did get into trouble and found to their surprise that they were not afraid. Their fears were vanished because they sought only the things of God."

But for the future all Israel, the spiritually faithful, will be saved. The triumphant scene knows no parallel in history. Perhaps the most pompous precession of history occurred in 61 B.C. when Rome gave to Pompey two days of triumph, the magnificence of which has never been duplicated. Tablets were borne by slaves, declaring the details of Pompey's triumphs. Long lines of hostages marched along, symbolizing Roman dominance. It was a heady occasion to say the least, but pale beside the triumphant procession that will usher the Israel of every nation, kindred, tongue, and people into the city of our God.

MY RIGHTEOUSNESS

I bring near my righteousness; it shall not be far off, and my salvation shall not tarry: and I will place salvation in Zion for Israel my glory. Isa. 46:13.

It is true that we need a shining example of what is pure and holy and noble. To fallen man and his descendants, the shining example of a righteous God out there in the heavens is awe inspiring and majestic but of little practical value on this sin-darkened earth. But here is a powerful promise, "I bring near my righteousness; it shall not be far off."

To this end came Christ into the world: (1) to provide an on-the-scene demonstration that the life of God may be lived in the flesh on this sinful planet, and (2) to make possible that demonstration in each believer's heart and life for the salvation of souls and the vindication of God's righteous character. In both instances we see a bringing near of the righteousness of Christ and a fulfillment of the promise that "it shall not be far off." Our text adds yet another element to this promise—"and my salvation shall not tarry." There is evident here a recognition of the immediate need of the human heart for an impartation of the righteousness of Christ if the soul is to survive. It is this part of man's nature that bread alone cannot feed. The character of Christ is Heaven imparted and Heaven sustained. It is the gift of God. Daily prayer and Bible study condition the soul for the reception of Christ in the heart and make each day for the Christian an experience of being hid with Christ in God. And in consequence each Christian becomes a living example of righteousness brought near and an earthly example of the glory of God.

A man once said, "I have no more influence than a farthing rushlight."

"Well," was the reply, "a farthing rushlight can do a good deal. It can set a haystack on fire, it can burn down a house; yea, more, it will enable a poor creature to read a chapter in God's Book. Go your way, friend, and let your farthing rushlight so shine before men that others, seeing your good works, may glorify your Father which is in heaven."

DEBTORS

I am debtor both to the Greeks, and to the Barbarians; both to the wise, and to the unwise. Rom. 1:14.

The apostle Paul considered himself indebted to the whole world, both to the wise and to the unwise. There are some who confine their gospel labors to one class of people on the assumption that those self-sufficient in material things would not be interested. But Christ is the God of the rich and of the poor, the wise and the unwise, the literate and the illiterate, the cultured and the uncultured. To be sure, more of the common people of all countries and races hear Christ gladly, but the rich and the learned are not to be neglected in the gospel approach.

Now we who know the gospel are debtors indeed to the world. We are debtors by reason of our knowledge. We were not chosen to receive the light of the gospel because we were better than others but rather because God had to have ministers through whom He would communicate the righteousness of His character to lost man. In short, it was an act of mercy, an act of love, an act of divine grace that this great honor of possessing truth is conferred upon any human being. But as the possessors of the knowledge of God's grace, like Paul we too must say, "I am debtor."

We are indebted by reason of personal experience. Any man who has experimentally tasted of the good things of God and knows the peace that passeth understanding must share this experience with others. We cannot selfishly clutch it to our bosom and flatter ourselves on our good fortune. We are obligated to "preach the gospel to every creature" (Mark 16:15).

A missionary home on furlough was invited to dinner at a great summer resort where he met many women of wealth and prominence. In his great longing for money to provide the gospel for hungering millions, he could not refrain from estimating the silks, satins, and diamonds of the dinner guests in terms of mission needs. He wrote to his wife: "Dear Wife, I've had dinner at the great hotel. The company was wonderful. I saw strange things today. There were some who wore to my certain knowledge one church, forty cottage organs, and twenty libraries." Our own debt to Christ is of deep personal concern.

IMAGE OF GOD

So God created man in his own image, in the image of God created he him; male and female created he them. **Gen. 1:27.**

It is this likeness to God that distinguishes man above all else in the animal kingdom, and it is significant that wherever Christianity goes it brings a sense of the value of life to all of its adherents. In lands where life is cheap and even the worship of certain false gods is accompanied by human sacrifices, the Christian idea of the sacredness of human life brings about a change. There is instilled within each new adherent a sense of human dignity. This is evident in those large land areas where men formerly lived under primitive circumstances. There is awakened in them a desire for literacy and for communication with the outside world. The strange sleep of heathenism is broken and in its place man becomes an aware, aspiring, progressive, Christlike creature. The marvelous work of the restoration of God's image in man is the continuing miracle of the gospel.

The Christian idea also changes one's environment. In the lands of the aborigine, Christian villages are discernible from the others by their cleanliness and order. The life span is lengthened as man, made in the image of God, assumes his Christlike posture. The image of God is the character of God. When man sinned he lost that image. "To restore in man the image of his Maker" is the end objective of the Christian religion. Man through daily fellowship with Christ assumes more and more of His character and likeness. This is the importance of the daily study of the Word of God and committal of the will to Christ through prayer. Christianity is in essence the restoration of the divine image in man.

The public relations department of most large business organizations concerns itself with the public image of the organization it represents. It has much to do with the impression that organization creates through its policies and services. The success or failure of many a business depends on its public acceptance. However, the gospel does more for the Christian. It not only changes his image, it changes the man. What a difference between him and the man who makes God in his human image.

UNBREAKABLE COVENANT

My covenant will I not break, nor alter the thing that is gone out of my lips. Ps. 89:34.

There have been in human history solemn agreements between men and nations, not a few of which have been ruthlessly broken. Agreements today between nations are hardly worth the paper on which they are signed. They last for a while, as long as it is to the advantage of some new Caesar to use them as a smoke screen for war preparations. Who today can trust the announced intentions of any government? It is indeed refreshing to know that God has made agreements with man that He will not break. As far as His agreements go, a day is as a thousand years, and a thousand years as a day (Ps. 90:4).

Again and again the Bible speaks of God as being "faithful," meaning simply that He honors His word. He promised Adam that He would send a Saviour who would Himself be bruised for the sins of man, thus giving hope to our first parents after their transgression. When the fullness of time had come, God sent His own Son into the world that the world through Him might find life. Later God promised Israel that if they would keep His commandments He would make them a great nation. Their obedience was spasmodic, but God did make them a great nation and bore with them long until the cup of iniquity was full to overflowing.

God promised, "I will put my law in their inward parts, and write it in their hearts; and will be their God, and they shall be my people" (Jer. 31:33). It should be pointed out that this new agreement was not new in the sense that the law was being put into the heart instead of on stone. The law of God has always been written upon the human heart, providing an inner mainspring for obedience.

The newness of the covenant lies in the passing of the "glory of the commandments written and engraven in stone." The old agreement was validated by the blood of goats and bulls and heifers; the new agreement is validated by the precious blood of Jesus Christ.

The old agreement was based on the promises of man to be obedient. This new agreement makes clear that the obedience within man will be performed by Christ. Thanks be to God for this certainty.

LET THEM TURN

But let man and beast be covered with sackcloth, and cry mightily unto God: yea, let them turn every one from his evil way, and from the violence that is in their hands. Jonah 3:8.

Nineveh was at the point of decision when Jonah preached the words of our text. There is a tradition that the people of Nineveh derided Jonah until a black cloud fierce in its ominous rumblings suddenly overspread the city, then they repented with sackcloth and ashes, thus bringing about a stay of judgment. Whether or not this is true, one thing is clear: The day of decision for Nineveh had come. God heard their prayer and turned away His anger.

Here is the cure for lukewarm souls. Here is the cure for the Laodicean spirit. Let us cry mightily unto God for deeper spiritual concern, for sensitivity toward the right, and for will power to fight against inherited and environmental pressures.

Dr. J. Hamilton has said, "You might pound a lump of ice with a pestle into a thousand fragments, but it will still continue ice; but bring it in beside your own bright and blazing fire and soon in the genial glow, the living waters flow. A man may try to make himself contrite, he may search out his sins and dwell on all their enormity and still feel no true repentance, but let him come to Jesus with His words of grace and truth, let his frozen spirit bask in the beams of the Sun of righteousness, then will it melt."

We need more importunate prayers, the kind that never give up. There are examples in the Bible of some remarkable results from this kind of petition, a clinging to the very horns of the altar until the heavens open and mighty things take place. Jesus cites the case of the importunate neighbor who asked bread at midnight. The prayer of Abraham for the city of Sodom is a remarkable instance of God's willingness to go as far as man's faith stretches. Think of Elijah praying for rain. Most of us would have given up after the third or fourth petition. But persistence and the conviction that God would be glorified kept the prophet on his knees until there was "a sound of an abundance of rain."

This is the kind of mighty crying unto God the church needs today.

299

TO SAVE A LIFE

Whosoever shall seek to save his life shall lose it; and whosoever shall lose his life shall preserve it. Luke 17:33.

When the city of Jerusalem should be compassed about by Roman armies, Christ counseled His followers to save nothing, but to flee for their lives. Those who followed this admonition were spared the destruction that came upon the city. Similarly in these last days, the way will become exceedingly strait as we draw nearer to the coming of the Lord. The last price of allegiance will be exacted. Those who plan to leave this world will be stripped of all earthly goods, but there will be those so married to the things of this life that they will not break away. Such will in that day seek to save themselves and those things most dear at the cost of the life to come.

Lot's wife is cited as a prime example. She had followed her husband and Abraham out of Ur in the Chaldees, and later she and her husband settled in Sodom. Because of the wickedness of the twin cities of Sodom and Gomorrah, it was purposed in heaven that they should be destroyed, but God never punishes without first warning. Through Abraham they were warned of judgment to come. An angel escorted Lot, his wife, and two daughters hurriedly out of Sodom. The orders to them were explicit: "Do not look back," but Lot's wife did look back and was turned into a pillar of salt.

In analyzing her behavior, three things stand out: (1) She was married to things of the past. Some of her children were back there in Sodom. It is certain that if we are to enter the joys of the life beyond, we will have to cut loose from even the most precious things of this life. (2) Mrs. Lot was dissatisfied with her refugee status. The discomforts of the way in contrast with the comforts of home made her look back. Many of us fret at our lack of progress. (3) Lot's wife could not find the courage for the unknown terrors before her. The heavy hand of justice was laid upon her shoulder. She sought to save her life and lost it. Ofttimes it is even so with us. "If your heart's in the work hold on, hold on; Tho' the way should be gloomy and sad."

HOW LONG?

And Elijah came unto all the people, and said, How long halt ye between two opinions? if the Lord be God, follow him: but if Baal, then follow him. And the people answered him not a word. 1 Kings 18:21.

Travelers tell us that there is near Jaffa Gate at Jerusalem a small terrace on top of the hill. It is called the Terrace of Indecision. The ground is so level that the rain falling upon it seems at a loss which way to go. Part of it is carried over the west side, where it flows into the Valley of Roses and gives life, fertile beauty, and fragrance to the Sharon lilies and roses. The rest flows down the east side into the Valley of Tophet and onward to the Dead Sea. Every life has its "terrace" of indecision. On the decision of each one hangs his future of helpful life or death.

A poet has said, "On the plains of hesitation bleached the bones of countless millions." The problem of double-mindedness is an old one. The Bible says that a double-minded man is unstable in all his ways. In matters of right and wrong, our eternal interest is at stake. A decision for good is a decision for heaven. An evil choice is a decision for hell. Hesitation can be as fatal as a wrong decision; hence, Elijah's challenge to Israel, "How long halt ye . . . ?"

In the ruins at Pompeii was found evidence of a priest fleeing from the temple when the warning came of the city's approaching doom. He returned to obtain the treasures of the temple, but he had not proceeded far before destruction came and he was lost. Somehow in matters of repentance, tomorrow seems better than today. This is Satan's sophistry. Delay paralyzes the will.

A minister reports that he dreamed one night of a meeting in hell, where demons were challenged to devise some foolproof means to ensnare the souls of men. Various suggestions were made. Suddenly one demon arose and suggested, "I will journey to the world of men and tell them that there is a God, there is a Saviour, there is a heaven; yes, and a hell, but I'll tell them there is no hurry, tomorrow will do." Compromise, delay, dalliance, are all enemies of the soul.

YOUR MODERATION

Let your moderation be known unto all men. The Lord is at hand. Phil. 4:5.

We live in an age of extremes. Few are satisfied with the weather. For some it is either extremely hot or extremely cold. Discontent is the order of the day. Men go from one extreme to the other in politics, religion, and social life. The Christian is an increasingly balanced man. He has a duty to his generation, "Let your moderation be known unto all men." A moderate man is a marked man in this age of excitability and extremism.

The fable is told of Hamet and Raschid, two neighboring shepherds of India, who in a time of great drought made a request of the genius of distribution. Hamet asked for a little brook that would never dry in the summer and in winter never overflow. Immediately the genius caused a fountain to bubble at his feet and scatter its rills over the meadow. The flowers renewed their fragrance, and the trees spread a green of foliage, and the flocks and birds quenched their thirst. Raschid, not satisfied with Hamet's moderate request, desired the genius of distribution to turn the Ganges through his grounds with all its waters and all its inhabitants. As Raschid was looking with contempt upon Hamet and his small request, he heard a sudden roar of torrents and saw a mighty stream come rolling on which was the Ganges broken loose from its bounds. The flood rolled into the lands of Raschid and his plantation was torn up, his flocks overwhelmed, and he was swept away before it, and a crocodile devoured him. The legend bears its own moral.

To be moderate, self-possessed, and always under control is a manifestation of one of the fruits of the Spirit. It is evidence of the keeping power of Christ in the life. When Abraham stood beside his nephew, viewing the rolling plains of Canaan, he manifested the moderation that God produces in the surrendered life. Lot's imagination ran wild, and his covetousness dictated to his reason. Abraham allowed moderation to dictate his decision, and out of his choice God made a people for His name. Excess in any direction is contraindicated in God's work.

AGREE

Agree with thine adversary quickly, whiles thou art in the way with him; lest at any time the adversary deliver thee to the judge, and the judge deliver thee to the officer, and thou be cast into prison. Matt. 5:25.

Christians are called upon by their religion to be as agreeable as is consistent with principle. In his community a Christian should be known as a conscientious cooperator, friendly, pleasant, and helpful. In my neighborhood when I was a little boy, there was a very mean man. As he walked through the streets he didn't greet anyone and always had a dangerous, surly look on his face. Such people were a challenge to me even when I was a child. My job was to bring a smile to that face or at least a greeting from those churlish lips. Day after day I would meet him and speak to him, "How do you do, sir," but with no greeting in reply. This continued for months. One day my boyish brain was preoccupied, and I failed to speak to him. I heard a gruff yet friendly voice say, "Hello, Earl." It was this man. You see, he missed my not speaking to him.

Not only are we to be agreeable with our friends but with our adversaries. This is a good practice at our places of employment.

In Port of Spain, Trinidad, I recently baptized a young woman who worked at the large electro hardware store. She was very pleasant and agreeable as well as a diligent worker at this store. Upon her baptism she explained to her employer that she would not be able to work on the Sabbath. He told her that she could no longer work at that store if this were the case, and fired her. The store manager's father, who owned the place, returned from his vacation meanwhile and missed this young woman. He inquired of his son just where she was. His son explained that he had had to fire her because she wanted to be off on Saturdays to go to church. "You must immediately find and rehire her," exclaimed the father. "And find extra work for her so she will not miss any money from her pay check for not working on Saturdays." Soon the customers were greeted again by the smiling face of this young Christian girl whose agreeable disposition counted so much when she needed it most.

YOUR RIGHTEOUSNESS

For I say unto you, That except your righteousness shall exceed the righteousness of the scribes and Pharisees, ye shall in no case enter into the kingdom of heaven. Matt. 5:20.

The righteousness of the scribes and Pharisees is not difficult to ascertain. It was in essence a rigid adherence to rules without transformed attitudes and regenerated hearts. They would recoil at a man committing overt murder but were guilty themselves of hatred. They were faithful in bringing their alms to the altar but thought little of the attitudes of their brethren concerning them or vice versa. Our righteousness must exceed this. It must involve a transformed spirit from which proceeds the obedient act. The Pharisee could perform a duty while his heart rebelled against it. Righteousness that excels this perfunctory performance must arise out of love for one's duty, and identity with Christ. He would never have submitted Himself to the ignomi022 of Calvary if His heart had not been in it. Christ did not move zombilike through the various phases of His ministry. He was vigorous as a man and vitally interested in human beings and their needs. By contrast the Pharisees interested themselves only in those things that would bring them glory and lead men to bow before them, chanting "Rabbi, Rabbi." Our righteousness must exceed this. We must visit the imprisoned because we love them. We must visit the hospitals because we love the sick. We must distribute literature to the unenlightened because we love them. We must feed the hungry because we love them. We must clothe the naked because we love them, and we must shelter the dispossessed because we love them. Only thus may our righteousness exceed that of the scribes and the Pharisees. From our noblest deeds there may come no publicity, our names may never be trumpeted to the ends of the earth, but of us it will be said, "He loved God supremely and his neighbor as himself."

Also the righteousness of the true Christian is the righteousness of Christ manifested in the life of the believer. It is the goodness of another placed at our account when by faith we accept Christ as Lord and Master, and His perfect obedience as our righteousness.

FALSE WITNESS

Thou shalt not bear false witness against thy neighbour.
Ex. 20:16.

As a young boy I was often told by my parents, "Your word is your bond," and also, "Tell the truth if it kills you, and it seldom will." Whenever I meet a grown person who finds it difficult to tell the truth, I believe his perversity had its roots in childhood. Truthfulness should be one of the first lessons taught a child. Many parents make the mistake of overlooking the tendency of their children to lie with the comment that he or she will outgrow it, but weeds left in the garden on the assumption that the fruit or vegetables will outgrow them will very shortly demonstrate the folly of such practice. They will snuff out the life of the good seed planted and dominate the situation.

The tendency to lie not only will be strengthened if left uncorrected but will manifest itself in other ways. It is commonly believed that a person who will not tell the truth will also steal. Then there is gossiping, twin evil of lying, which is in essence the spreading of a choice rumor about another that may be true or false. The capacity to assassinate with the tongue has long been known. "And the tongue is a fire, a world of iniquity: so is the tongue among our members, that it defileth the whole body, and setteth on fire the course of nature; and it is set on fire of hell" (James 3:6).

I was shocked one time when a young secretary, trying to counsel one of her associates what to do in a certain contingency said, "Of course, you can always garble the facts." Her philosophy was the worldly wise one, "A lie is a very present help in time of trouble."

So important is this matter of tongue control that it is related to the total question of Christian development. "For in many things we offend all. If any man offend not in word, the same is a perfect man, and able also to bridle the whole body" (verse 2). The man who has an unruly tongue is fighting a most persistent demon. "But the tongue can no man tame" (verse 8). Only the power of God can tame the tongue. Let us seek this power of self-discipline through the indwelling Christ.

305

LIKE A TREE

And he shall be like a tree planted by the rivers of water, that bringeth forth his fruit in his season; his leaf also shall not wither; and whatsoever he doeth shall prosper. Ps. 1:3.

A tree or plant sends its roots downward and its stems upward. The roots are the mouths of the tree. Through them they take up from the soil whatever is necessary to their growth. As the trunk and branches of a tree increase, the roots spread out so as to absorb more food. The earth and the air furnish the material with which the tree is built up. The soil contains substances, which loosened by the frost or the plow or by water, are prepared as food for the hungry tree. The leaves are the lungs of trees. With these they inhale the atmosphere and elaborate such gases as the nature of the species requires. The rain, the snow, the frost, the sunshine, and the wind all help to mature the tree until it stands with buttressed roots and giant arms—the king of the forest.

In many ways the growth of a tree and its ultimate stability picture the experience of the Christian. From tiny tendril to spreading oak, its life is one grand story of absorption and committal, of receiving and giving, of collection and dispensation. Every living human being is a beneficiary of the grace of God. We are recipients of blessings, temporal and spiritual, that we neither earn nor deserve. We demonstrate our worthiness to receive these things through service to God and to our fellow man, but it is as important that we be faithful to the principle of absorption as to the principle of dispensation. Intake must match output or there will be destitution of spiritual reserves to meet the issues of day-to-day living, and that is why the study of the Word of God daily is so necessary to our spiritual and moral health, and the Bible principle "Pray without ceasing" is as necessary as breathing, for "prayer is the breath of the soul," and we are not safe one hour without it. Thus may the strength of our souls be as the strength of a tree "planted by the rivers of water, that bringeth forth his fruit in his season; his leaf also shall not wither; and whatsoever he doeth shall prosper."

All a tree needs to do to wither is to be cut off from its nutrients. Our spiritual selves wither when separated from the means of grace.

306

TO BREAK A HABIT

Wash you, make you clean; put away the evil of your doings from before mine eyes; cease to do evil. Isa. 1:16.

S. G. Goodrich has said, "Habit may be illustrated by a beaten path as the traveler is apt to fall into and follow this, so the thoughts and feelings are likely to pursue the track which they have often followed before. As the stream gradually wears the channel deeper in which it runs and thus becomes more surely bound to its accustomed course, so the current of the mind and heart grows more and more restricted to the course in which habit has taught them to flow. These intellectual and moral habits form many peculiarities of character and chiefly distinguish one individual from another. They are, therefore, of the utmost importance."

This anecdote comes out of the War between the States: An officer of a main regiment lay sick with a fever near Savage's Station, Virginia. In his delirium he fought his battles all over again. He would cry to his men, "Deploy to the left," "Keep out of that ambush," "Now go, my braves, double quick. Strike for your flag," "On, on, you'll win the day!" Such were his last words.

Habits developed in life carry until death unless resolutely overcome. Evil habits can and must be broken. The Bible says, "Cease to do evil; learn to do well" (Isa. 1:16, 17). These admonitions complement each other, for the best way to rid oneself of bad habits is to cultivate good habits that take the place of our offensive practices. The habit of criticism will give way to the habit of praise and commendation. Tolerance will supplant evil surmising. Industry will correct a tendency to shiftlessness. Good patterns of conduct can be established by conscious cultivation of desirable traits of character. Such a persistent program will eventually make us abhor the evil and choose the good in every situation.

The power of evil habits can be broken only by the power of God. Indeed, in all the category of evil, there is no bad habit that has not been overcome by someone, somewhere. The strength of Christ is adequate for every emergency, and His grace sufficient. Let us surrender to Him our besetments and evil propensities and He will set us free.

TOSSED WITH THE TEMPEST

O thou afflicted, tossed with tempest, and not comforted, behold, I will lay thy stones with fair colours, and lay thy foundations with sapphires. Isa. 54:11.

The children of God may well expect comfort in affliction in this life. To this end came the third person of the Godhead into the world. The Holy Ghost is called "The Comforter." Many are the afflictions of the righteous. Aside from the everyday problems that plague mankind, the Christian may well find himself enduring the additional affliction of persecution for his beliefs. The early Christian church under the heel of the Roman dictatorship often found itself made the scapegoat for national calamities, and to divert attention from political mistakes, Christians were held up as the offensive agents in said calamities. Persecutions of the most inhuman nature have followed Israel, both ancient and modern, and she has found herself tossed with the tempest and in need of divine comfort.

To be sure, human beings and their deep interest in moments of crisis afford a measure of relief. We cannot discount altogether the power of human sympathy and love, but these can quiet only surface emotion. The healing of our grief can be accomplished only by divine power. "Surely he hath borne our griefs, and carried our sorrows" (Isa. 53:4); therefore He alone through the divine agency of the Holy Spirit can effectively heal the wounds that trial inflicts upon the soul.

"In the exhaustless catalogue of heaven's mercies to mankind, the power we have of finding some gems of comfort in the hardest trials must ever occupy the foremost place; not only because it supports and upholds us when we most require to be sustained, but because in this source of consolation there is something, we have reason to believe, of the divine Spirit; something of that goodness which detects, amidst our own evil doings, a redeeming quality; something which, even in our fallen nature, we possess in common with the angels; which had its being in the old time when they trod the earth and, lingers on yet, in pity."—CHARLES DICKENS.

We know what that redeeming quality is. It is the power of the indwelling Christ through the agency of the Holy Ghost.

ELIJAH THE PROPHET

Behold, I will send you Elijah the prophet before the coming of the great and dreadful day of the Lord. Mal. 4:5.

Christ used this text to refer to John the Baptist, who prepared the way for His first coming to the earth. John, as you know, preached in the wilderness of Judea, crying, "Prepare ye the way of the Lord." His preaching was so powerful that it made a way in men's hearts for the reception of the Master. Of John, Jesus said, "Elias is come already." But John's coming preceded the first coming of the Lord, and the day of His first coming was great, but it was not dreadful; therefore, Malachi 4:5 looks forward to the second coming of Christ, which will be both great and dreadful.

Now the name "Elijah" is a compound word—"Eli" meaning "my god;" "jah" standing for *Yahweh.* The name thus means "Yahweh is my God." The promise, then, is that God will send a people upon the earth whose God is Elijah, who will in the spirit and the power of Elijah prepare the way for the second coming of our Lord.

John's message rang with the authority of truth. He was surrounded by many religions and religious leaders but when men listened to John, his message was different. He spoke with authority. His sincerity and truthfulness gave him power.

So is it today. Men may listen to messages from various ministers proficient in their use of words and flowery in their oratory. But to sit for one hour under the power of the Advent message is a different experience altogether. Hundreds who have done this so testify. There is the ring of authority in this message and the power of truth.

John's message was present truth. "There cometh one . . . after me," he was able to say. He knew what his business was, and his whole ministry was dedicated toward that high and holy purpose. Similarly today the message of Adventism is a special message to this generation. It is aimed at the man who faces the coming of the Lord. It is designed to make strait His way. Like the message of John, it is a message of reformation. It involves primarily the transforming power of God's grace and secondarily the reformation of the life in accordance with the inner experience.

309

MY KINGDOM

Jesus answered, My kingdom is not of this world: if my kingdom were of this world, then would my servants fight, that I should not be delivered to the Jews: but now is my kingdom not from hence. John 18:36.

There will come a day when the kingdom of God will be of this world. Paradise will be restored, and the city of God—the New Jerusalem—will descend from heaven and rest on this earth. Because the throne of God is in that city, it is a symbol of divine authority. Wherever the city goes, that place becomes the capital of the universe. This is significant with reference to the earth, for ours is the only planet in rebellion against God. Sin will be overcome and the rebellion crushed, and on its ashes will be built the new earth wherein dwelleth righteousness.

As the capital of the universe, Christ's kingdom will literally be of this world, but now it is not. While the earth is the Lord's and the fullness thereof, He has nevertheless committed the stewardship of this world to man. In turn the human family has collectively yielded its stewardship to Lucifer. It is he who holds apparent sway in this world checked only by the power of the true owner. And because the way of life on this earth is so alien to the Christian way, Christ would have none of it and uttered this disclaimer, "My kingdom is not of this world." The Master seems to be saying, "Let them have their way now. In this, their day, let them exercise until the cup is full. We must not be guilty of what we condemn in them. They know but one recourse, and that is the sword. I am the Prince of peace. We will confound their power with humility, and we will overcome the world. I could deliver Myself, but, then, what would happen to you and them? If I deliver Myself, who will deliver you? As servants of My kingdom you will fight, but with spiritual weapons."

Thus the kingdom of God is spread in the earth, not with a sword of tempered steel but with a sword of the Spirit, which is the Word of God, and it is the privilege of every Christian to wield this weapon for the extension of the kingdom. When the task seems hopeless, it is ours to work, trusting the Master to fulfill His own purposes.

FOR THEIR SAKES

And for their sakes I sanctify myself, that they also might be sanctified through the truth. John 17:19.

Christ spent whole nights in prayer. The sight of the Son of God agonizing in the Garden strikes awe to the hearts of men and angels. Tempted in all points as we are, He set us an example of daily consecration to God. Here is the secret of sanctification. Thus, day by day He set Himself apart for holy purposes. He did this through prayer. His life seems to have been a constant prayer. Many of His prayers have been recorded for our study. "Lord, teach us to pray," was the appeal of His contemporary disciples. One of the secrets of sanctified living is prayer without ceasing. The mind should be kept in such an attitude that we can pray as naturally as we eat and breathe.

Christ was a student of the Scriptures. His sermons continually reflect His familiarity with Old Testament Scripture, which indeed was "truth" for His time, and in His confrontation with the arch demon, the Word of God was repeatedly his first line of defense. But what if the Scriptures are neglected? How then can they do their perfect work in our hearts?

An African preacher once said in a sermon, "We know that rocks are very hard. Our cutlasses and hoes can do nothing against them, so we leave them alone. But a new thing has come to Calabar, even God's Word, and it has broken up the scattered customs that our fathers thought would remain forever. What must you say concerning the Word? That it is more powerful than the customs of our country. You know how strong our evil hearts are. Hearts as strong as yours have been changed in our town and have been changed by this Word, and what must you therefore say but that this Word is more powerful than a Calabar heart. Bend your heads then before this Word."

Sanctification comes with surrender. Again and again in Scripture we hear Christ surrendering His will to that of His Father. "Nevertheless not my will, but thine, be done" (Luke 22:42). Similar phrases often fell from His lips. It was His ambition while on earth to find Himself ever in the center of His Father's will. It sanctified Him. It will sanctify us.

311

OUR LIGHT AFFLICTION

For our light affliction, which is but for a moment, worketh for us a far more exceeding and eternal weight of glory. 2 Cor. 4:17.

Charles Spurgeon once said, "An old Puritan proverb said, 'God's people are like birds; they sing best in cages.'"

So it is with the child of God; the deeper his troubles, the nearer to heaven he goes if he would live close to his Master. Spurgeon in another place told this story, "In the ancient times, a box on the ear given by a master to a slave meant liberty: little would the freedman care how hard was the blow. By a stroke from the sword the warrior was knighted by his monarch: small matter was it to the new-made knight if the hand was heavy.

"When the Lord intends to lift His servants to a higher stage of spiritual life, He frequently sends them a severe trial; He makes His Jacobs to be prevailing princes, but He confers the honor after a night of wrestling, and accompanies it with a shrunken sinew. Be it so: who among us would wish to be deprived of the trials, if they are the necessary attendants of spiritual advancement?"

In Mexico a method of separating silver from dross is to pulverize the ore, and spread it out on a large platform. Great numbers of mules are driven over it. Quicksilver is poured over the mud, and the trampling is continued. When the metals have thoroughly amalgamated, the mass is cast into the furnace, and the silver runs off clear from the dross. So men are broken and trampled by afflictions. The quicksilver of truth is poured over them, they are cast into the furnace of tribulation, till the precious products of faith and purity are realized.

Faith makes our burdens light. This is true if we compare them with the afflictions visited upon our Lord for our sake. Six thousand years of human transgression was visited upon Him. By comparison, then, our afflictions are light. For the Christian life after the resurrection will more than reward us for the trials of this world. The promised glories reserved for the faithful are hard to visualize. Changes in nature and in human nature, reunion with loved ones, and fellowship with Christ and angels are but a few of the privileges promised.

THEM THAT ARE LOST

But if our gospel be hid, it is hid to them that are lost. 2 Cor.
4:3.

Nothing more effectively shuts out the light of the gospel than
does unbelief. Belief is the primary response of the soul to God's appeal. Unless He is trusted He is not loved or followed. "Them that
are lost" refers to the vast army of unbelievers in our world. "In whom
the god of this world hath blinded the minds of them which believe
not, lest the light of the glorious gospel of Christ, who is the image of
God, should shine unto them" (2 Cor. 4:4).

To the heart of the unbeliever, the gospel is hid. John 3:3 says,
"Jesus answered and said unto him, Verily, verily, I say unto thee,
Except a man be born again, he cannot see the kingdom of God."
Again and again in His parables Christ endeavored to make plain to
His listeners the nature of the kingdom of God. He likened it to a
mustard seed, to a man who took a far journey and left his goods in
the hands of stewards, and to a sower who went forth to sow. His
total teachings were an explanation of the kingdom. He spoke of faith,
of love, of prayer, of obedience to His law, and of service to one's
fellow man; but without the new-birth experience man can see none
of this. From him the gospel is hid.

Augustine relates the story of a certain heathen who showed him
his idol god, saying, "Here is my god. Where is thine?" Then pointing
up at the sun, the heathen continued, "Here is my god. Where is
thine?" And then, pointing to different creatures he said, "Here are my
gods. Where is thine?" But Augustine says, "I showed him not my God;
not because I had not one to show him but because he had not eyes to
see Him." Man, unattended by the Holy Spirit, is incapable of receiving
spiritual things. When we pick up the Bible to read, it must be with
a prayer that God will Himself reveal to our soul the spirit and meaning of the words that greet our eyes. Upon this our spiritual lives depend. It is thus that we drink water and eat bread that will forever
eliminate thirst and hunger.

> "Alas for him who never sees
> The stars shine through his cypress-trees!"

ETERNAL GOD

They shall perish, but thou shalt endure: yea, all of them shall wax old like a garment; as a vesture shalt thou change them, and they shall be changed: but thou art the same, and thy years shall have no end. Ps. 102:26, 27.

"The Bay of Fundy is a romantic, sometimes awesome place. Stories and legends have given to it an atmosphere of mystery. To visit it fresh from the noisy crowds and clanging tumult of the great cities is to experience a new and never-to-be-forgotten sense of greatness that is more than bigness and power and that is more than sound. In the Bay of Fundy the tide runs higher than any known spot in the world, sometimes more than fifty feet. Watching it come pushing, scrambling, pouring in through the bore, over the low flats, over the banks, conquering the rocks, one is left breathless. A young man and lady watching it were silent for a time, overwhelmed by its majestic power. When the tide had spent its force, the girl said quietly, 'Why should the personal affairs of two people like us claim even for a moment the attention of a God of might and mystery like that?' Answered the young man, 'Because He is God.'"—MARGARET SLATTERY.

Human reason cannot contemplate in its limited sphere the awesome fact of an almighty God, exercising the minutest interest even in the falling of the sparrow, but it is true that God always was and always will be equally as unfathomable. It is inconceivable that it would be any other way. All creation had a beginning. God was that beginning, and what is, is sustained by His own perpetual life. God the Father, God the Son, and God the Holy Spirit are unique in the sense that they have life that is unborrowed, unending, and underived. But that we may claim His attention. How overwhelming the thought!

"An aged mother sat in a humble cart, waiting the release of her son from prison. On the vacant seat beside her was a little basket of dainty food and a change of outer garments. Her tearful, eager glances toward the prison gate showed how much love the prisoner who was about to be released would find awaiting him. The mother loved her son though he had been sinful and wrong. So God loved us while we were yet sinners and gave His Son to die for us."

314

WE ARE DUST

For he knoweth our frame; he remembereth that we are dust.
Ps. 103:14.

The story is told that a man once dreamed that God in His eternal council conceived man's creation, and He called to Himself three ministers who wait constantly upon His throne—Justice, Truth, and Mercy—and thus addressed them, "Shall we make man?" Then said Justice, "O God, make him not, for he will trample upon Thy laws." Truth made answer also: "O God, make him not, for he will pollute Thy sanctuaries." But Mercy, dropping upon her knees and looking up through her tears, exclaimed, "O God, make him, and I will watch over him with my care through all the dark paths which he may have to tread." Then God made man and said to him, "O Man, thou art a child of mercy; go and deal with thy brother."

Yes, it is because of God's mercy that we may hope for the more abundant life here and a better world hereafter. "He remembereth that we are dust." This does not allow for or excuse our transgressions, but it does say that we are dealing with an understanding, merciful God who recognizes what He is dealing with. "For he knoweth our frame." He knows what six thousand years of inherited and cultivated sin has done to the human race. But the glorious fact of the gospel is that there is hope for man. As long as mercy pleads his case and shadows his footsteps, man may ever look up with hopeful heart to better days; and like the voice of the bird, his life will become one long symphony of praise to his Maker.

Henry Ward Beecher has said, "Many pray to be made men in Christ Jesus and think that in some miraculous way it will be given them, but God says, 'I will try my child and see if he is sincere.' So He lays a burden upon him and says, 'Now stand up under it, for thus you are made strong.' He sends a provocation to him and says to him, 'Be patient.' He throws him into perplexity and says, 'Where now are thy resources?' If the ambitious ore dreads the furnace, the forge, the anvil, the rasp, the file, it should never desire to become a sword. Man is the iron, and God is the smith, and we are always either in the forge or on the anvil. God is shaping us for higher things."

REDEEMED

And they sung a new song, saying, Thou art worthy to take the book, and to open the seals thereof: for thou wast slain, and hast redeemed us to God by thy blood out of every kindred, and tongue, and people, and nation. Rev. 5:9.

The song of the redeemed can only be sung by those who have had an experience with Christ in the earth, an experience that resulted in their entrance into heaven. It is a song of triumph. The Redeemer Himself will lead it, and appropriately so, for by His blood are the righteous saved.

It is a paradox that wars are often fought to preserve the peace of the world. Elaborate peace movements, of which the Peace Palace at Versailles is a forlorn symbol, have all ultimately failed. The best the United Nations has been able to do has been to achieve an uneasy armistice between belligerent rivals. With nations seething with discontent, global peace seems even to the most optimistic a hopeless ideal. The only peace possible here is that individual joy of heart that comes from a sense of sins forgiven.

The hopelessness of man's case without a Redeemer can only be compared with the condition of a slave without a liberator. Helpless to save himself, he must labor on in servitude, awaiting the day of his redemption. This accounts for the universal admiration in America for Abraham Lincoln, who with his own pen signed the Emancipation Proclamation, setting free millions of enslaved people. Throughout endless ages redeemed sinners will ever love Jesus, the world's liberator. The mention of His name will bring forth shouts of ecstasy, for mankind, forever captive to his sins, was redeemed by the blood of the Lamb. And now liberty, that glorious elixir of spiritual freedom, is ours forever through Jesus Christ our Lord.

If we would be among that great host of the redeemed who will sing the song of the saved, we must begin to learn the score here. Indeed, that is our privilege, for the angels who have not passed through our experience cannot help us then. Although we shall be thrilled to hear the angels sing, they will rejoice to hear the new song that only the saved will bring.

THY CROWN

Behold, I come quickly: hold that fast which thou hast, that no man take thy crown. Rev. 3:11.

The admonition, hold what you have, centers in verse 10 of chapter three of Revelation. There the statement is made, "Because thou hast kept the word of my patience, I also will keep thee from the hour of temptation, which shall come upon all the world, to try them that dwell upon the earth." Pictured here is a relationship between a man and his master. Because that man has accepted Christ as Saviour and believed His Word, he is promised the keeping power of Christ in the hour of temptation.

The love relationship between Christ and His children is a priceless one. Hold it fast. In this regard our determination must match that of Paul, who wrote this testimony, "For I am persuaded, that neither death, nor life, nor angels, nor principalities, nor powers, nor things present, nor things to come, nor height, nor depth, nor any other creature, shall be able to separate us from the love of God, which is in Christ Jesus our Lord" (Rom. 8:38, 39).

The basic ingredient of faithfulness is absolute trust in God. Our crowns depend upon it. The crown in the text is symbolic of our eternal reward. If we fail, another will take our place. God will make up His number. Let "no man take thy crown." It is a lamentable fact that many who have for years sacrificed as members of the church for the cause of the gospel will, because of negligence, turn aside to the mundane things of this world until their love grows cold and will awaken only to find that someone else has persevered and taken their crown. This need not be you.

Somewhere I have read that the crown of England contains 1,700 diamonds, the imperial crown of Russia, 2,500 diamonds, the crown of France, 5,352 diamonds. But the crown of the poorest of God's saints is one solid gem, not to be compared for beauty and value with all the diamonds in the world; for the Lord of hosts is for a crown of glory and for a diadem of beauty to the residue of His people.

317

THEY SLUMBERED

But the wise took oil in their vessels with their lamps. While the bridegroom tarried, they all slumbered and slept. Matt. 25:4, 5.

James White tells of a dream a man once related to him. In this dream he saw the devil sitting fast asleep on a fence post across from the church. Awakening him he said, "Satan, you are not living up to your reputation for being ever busy. I noticed you were fast asleep." To which the devil replied, pointing to the church across the street, "Those people in there are asleep, and as long as they're asleep, I'm safe to nap," and with that he dozed off again, with an occasional snore.

The virgins are the members of the church. In the church there are wise and foolish. The oil represents the Holy Spirit, but even the wise virgins slumbered and slept according to the Scripture. The saints today are asleep to their opportunities for witnessing. Some of our members carry in their bags or pockets small pieces of literature to distribute to strangers they chance to meet. The Lay Activities Department of the church has outlined scores of methods of personal witnessing on the part of laymen. May we be awakened to the high privilege of communicating faith to lost hearts.

Many Christians are asleep to the privilege of Bible study. To victims of this industrial age the twenty-four-hour day seems to be too short. So manifold and complex are the duties of each day that many stagger to their beds not having glanced at the Word of God for strength. There is time to read the paper, to watch television, to listen to the radio, but the Word of God lies neglected on the shelf. The song writer has pictured it thus: "Dust on the Bible, dust on the Holy Word, the words of all the prophets, and the sayings of our Lord." We need to awaken to the joys that accompany the study of the Word of God.

We're asleep to the privilege of prayer. Prayer is indeed the "breath of the soul." We breathe again and again for life. We need the rhythm for spiritual life. The rarefied atmosphere of heaven is life for the soul. Prayer is the principal method of intake.

FLATTERY

Woe unto you, when all men shall speak well of you! for so did their fathers to the false prophets. Luke 6:26.

Flattery is sin. It can only damage the one flattered. The problem is: Which is damaged most, the flatterer or the flattered? One who indulges in this practice cultivates his own insincerity. He may mean well, but the effects of the deed do not match the motive.

There is a psychology that teaches the advantages of flattery, and it may seem to one's temporary advantage to feed the ego of an immediate superior, but the long-range effects of such a program will surely reap its harvest. Flattery has a way of finally catching up with itself and undermining its own influence, and once the word passes that one is an insincere person, his testimony has little weight among thinking people. The tendency to want to be well thought of is a natural one, and the human heart craves praise above reproach and criticism. One would have to be an angel not to plead guilty to this charge. There is something gratifying about receiving a compliment, and to pay one is not necessarily sinful, but it is necessary to mark the difference between flattery and sincere appreciation. Flattery has a false face. It is intended to deceive or to seek advantage for the flatterer. Conversely, a sincere compliment is based on existing fact and is intended to encourage rather than inflate the one complimented.

The flatterer is indiscriminate in his search for a victim. He may find him as a minister at the door of the church, after the sermon, or a soloist whose performance was marginal. He may pick the hat or the dress or the shoes that you wear. On the other hand, there are those who are so afraid that they may flatter that they never pass along a word of praise. It is necessary to our good mental health that we express, with proper reservations, our appreciation to one another for duties well done. Some children have become discouraged because their parents never speak a positive word of good about anything they do. Homes have broken up because husbands and wives have ceased to compliment each other. They take each other for granted. But beware when all men speak well of you.

319

TAUGHT OF THE LORD

And all thy children shall be taught of the Lord; and great shall be the peace of thy children. Isa. 54:13.

The education of our children may determine their spiritual destiny. That is why a Christian education is necessary. While it is true that a parent may not be responsible ultimately for what his child may do, it is equally true that that parent is responsible for the child's getting the best Christian education possible, for this will provide a base on which the child may ultimately make the best decisions in life. No one can deny the good that is being done in the great public school systems of the world. To teach an illiterate man to be conversant in languages is of immeasurable value.

However, there is more to education than the mastery of the humanities. In those early formative years, character is being cultivated, and the best atmosphere for the formation of Christian character is the Christian classroom.

It was my privilege recently to interview the Minister of Finance in an autonomous African country. This man neither smoked nor drank. I learned the reason for his cleanliness of habit. He attended a Seventh-day Adventist school in his elementary years, and the habits of cleanliness he learned in those formative years were still with him. He has a healthy respect for our church school system.

Perhaps one of the greatest benefits of Christian education is that children are taught the Creation story of the beginnings of our world. When a man is convinced of his high origin, there is a corresponding and definite effect upon his behavior. Teach a child that his ancestor was some slimy thing that stood up one day in water, and there is little restraint in terms of behavior that can be expected of him. Christian teachers must also be commended for teaching the moral and ethical standards of the Scripture.

Children are indeed to be "taught of the Lord." It is essential to their peace of mind, "great shall be the peace of thy children." No greater contribution can be made to the stability of the nation, the peace of the world, and the building of the kingdom of God than to provide your child with church-oriented education.

HERE AM I

Then shalt thou call, and the Lord shall answer; thou shalt cry, and he shall say, Here I am. If thou take away from the midst of thee the yoke, the putting forth of the finger, and speaking vanity. Isa. 58:9.

There is nothing more comforting and reassuring than the knowledge that when an emergency arises, Christ is near. And we live in an emergency world.

It is said that the Macedonians had a great general named Eumenes. On one occasion, when he was very sick, they were forced to march against an opposing host without his presence at their head. Seeing the luster of the golden armor and the beauty of the purple vests of their foes, and the immense elephants with towers upon their backs filled with armed men, they halted, declaring that they would not move a step unless their leader could direct their movements. Eumenes, hearing of their indecision, hastened with speed to the front, opened the curtains that hid him from their view, and stretched forth his hands to bid them advance. Catching the inspiration, they saluted him joyously, clanked their weapons, uttered a great shout, and went forward, thinking themselves invincible. They were defeated because he was only a man, but the presence of Christ secures victory.

There are times when men who are not Christians are convicted of their sinful habits and make changes in themselves. They do not know it, but even in this the Spirit of God is at work in the life, reshaping the character in the divine image. All moral reform is Heaven inspired. If an individual convicted of sin never surrenders his life to Christ, of course he is lost, but he is not without the deep movings of the Spirit of God upon his life. In this sense God touches all men. It is His way of taking away the yoke, breaking the power of sin in the life, conditioning man to accept Him as Lord and Saviour. When Christ controls the life there is no pointing of the finger at others, but rather the removal of the beam from one's own eye. There is no idle "speaking vanity," no boasting of one's own righteousness, rather a humble acknowledgment that all goodness is of God and that any changes that occur in the life are due alone to His beneficent grace.

11   321

THE FAST

Is not this the fast that I have chosen? to loose the bands of wickedness, to undo the heavy burdens, and to let the oppressed go free, and that ye break every yoke? Isa. 58:6.

Prayer and fasting are powerful weapons in the arsenal of the Christian. While it is true that many fast as the Pharisees—to be seen of men and applauded for their righteousness—it is equally true that others have seen in this requirement of Christ a means of gaining deeper insights of truth and stronger spiritual experiences.

The disciples had stood helpless in the presence of a demon-possessed child. In disappointment the father witnessed their impotence. Jesus returned to the scene and cast out the devil, to the delight of father and son. The disciples were puzzled. "Why could not we cast him out?" they asked. The Lord replied, "This kind can come forth by nothing, but by prayer and fasting" (Mark 9:28, 29). But it is not the act of fasting that is efficacious, it is the state of mind behind the outward act. "Is not this the fast that I have chosen? to loose the bands of wickedness . . . ?"

We are born in sin and shaped in iniquity. We are held with cords of sin. Sin is a part of our natural selves. We are in this sense slaves to it. Purposeful fasting will be "to loose the bands of wickedness," to break the dominion of sin in the life, to arrest the progress of the sinful habits, to cease from wickedness.

Fasting itself does not win God's favor, but it does clear the mind for a better understanding of His will. It also shows to the heavenly watchers that one is in earnest about what he seeks, for to yield up what one naturally desires in order to receive something of nobler benefit is indeed an indication of earnestness.

Complete victory in the life demands that we "break every yoke." The sin that is not overcome will overcome us. There can be no compromise or peaceful coexistence with our faults. "If Christ is to be Lord at all, He must be Lord of all." This He has promised to be in our experience if we will accept Him as our Saviour. He set the example for us in the wilderness of temptation, and overcame Satan on every point in our behalf.

MANY SHALL COME

And I say unto you, That many shall come from the east and west, and shall sit down with Abraham, and Isaac, and Jacob, in the kingdom of heaven. Matt. 8:11.

The Gentile centurion had just professed great faith in Christ's ability to heal his servant. He had assured Him, "Lord, I am not worthy that thou shouldest come under my roof: but speak the word only, and my servant shall be healed" (Matt. 8:8). In commending this centurion for his faith, Jesus spoke the words of our text. What He said came as a shock to the Israelites, who regarded themselves as the only candidates for the kingdom of God. Jesus assured them that many would come from the east and the west, non-Jews, and sit down with Abraham, Isaac, and Jacob in the kingdom of heaven. To the self-satisfied Hebrews this came as a distinct surprise.

When Jesus sat at the well of Samaria, talking to the Samaritan woman, His own disciples were amazed that He would chat with her. A question is posed here. Just how can the millions of Asia, Africa, and indeed of all the other continents, be exposed to the gospel if we do not carry it? That there should be amazement in the church when a member of one race speaks to a member of another concerning the salvation of his soul, is in itself surprising. Is not witnessing to one and all the church's business? Like Jesus, we should be able to say, "I must be about my Father's business." In His business it is our privilege to share with others the spiritual dividends.

The apostle Paul held his friend, Philemon, responsible for his former slave, Onesimus. He counseled him, "If thou count me therefore a partner, receive him as myself. If he hath wronged thee, or oweth thee ought, put that on mine account" (Philemon 17, 18). That's true Christian involvement, and workable even in modern times.

Yes, many shall come from the east and from the west; from every nation under heaven the saints of God will one day gather, but this will not be unless the church militant bestirs itself in all-out evangelism. We who know the message of God's saving grace must communicate it to lost men wherever they are. This is one of the heavy responsibilities of our privileges as sons of God.

323

THE OLD PATHS

Thus saith the Lord, Stand ye in the ways, and see, and ask for the old paths, where is the good way, and walk therein, and ye shall find rest for your souls. But they said, We will not walk therein. Jer. 6:16.

We live in an age of transition, when it is being contended that right and wrong are relative and that society has a right to set its own standards. It is comforting to know that standards of human behavior have already been set. The moral code—the Ten Commandments—is the unchangeable expression of the will of God with reference to human behavior. God has not left man to decide for himself what is right and what is wrong. It was decided for us before we were born. If indeed God were as changeable as man is, there would be no fixed code of behavior to which we could appeal. Thank God, this is not so. "My covenant will I not break, nor alter the thing that is gone out of my lips" (Ps. 89:34). Right and wrong do not fluctuate from age to age. Men may change, but the law of God is unchangeable. Of His precepts David said, "They stand fast for ever and ever, and are done in truth and uprightness" (Ps. 111:8).

If a man disavows the standard of human behavior set by God, can he indeed be trusted? Look at the fruit of the current permissiveness in conduct, the almost total disregard for standards of decency and morality. The new morality is the old immorality disguised in a robe of sophistication. This is the fruit of the gospel of relativity. This is the consequence of apostasy from God. Let there then be a return to the old paths, a restoration of the good way, and unlike the foolish sons of Jeremiah's day, let us walk therein and find rest for our souls.

Like the giant new ribbons of concrete that constitute our interstate highway system are the new paths and the inventions of men in matters of morals and religion today. These great highway systems have lured traffic away from the old highways that cross our country. The old paths are comparatively forgotten and it is even so with religion. To find these old highways one has to put forth an effort now. Literally he must "look for them." And so is it with the old paths of morality and righteous living. They are becoming extinct in our day.

THE DAY OF THY POWER

Thy people shall be willing in the day of thy power, in the beauties of holiness from the womb of the morning: thou hast the dew of thy youth. Ps. 110:3.

Man's participation in the work of God follows a peculiar pattern. There seem to be periods of refreshing, energetic labor followed by an inexplicable lethargy. There was the unrestrained zeal of the first-century church, which covered the known world with the gospel of the Saviour. Subsequently the relapses from what we call "pentecostal endeavor" left the work of the church to languish. Prophets, however, have predicted a resurgence of Christian witnessing under the power of the Holy Spirit. The Bible refers to this as the latter rain. Our text speaks of the willingness of the people in the day of God's power. Such willingness cannot be artificially stimulated. There must be on the part of the individual a personal surrender to the will of Christ and a willingness to spend and to be spent. He must decide that he can hold back nothing, that all he is and has belongs to his Maker.

It is said that Isaac Newton pored over his problems "til the midnight wind swept over his papers the ashes of his long extinguished fire"; and that Martin Luther in his gigantic labors of preaching, journeying, debating, corresponding, and book writing, had at the time of his death published seven hundred and fifteen works, or more than twenty-five for each year of his public life; and that William Carey preached and prayed for over 300 million non-Christians; and that John Wesley in his preaching traveled on horseback five thousand miles a year, reading history, poetry, and philosophy; and of Clarkson it is said, "He laid aside his vestments of the priesthood and with his fellow workers for twenty years pleaded with the suffering sons of Africa until the cry of the oppressed roused the sensibilities of the nation, until England in her might rose up to say of the traffic in human flesh, 'Thus far shalt thou go and no further.' "

Such is the power of dedicated lives and such will be the witness of God's people in the day of His power. But let us pray and work for it, not fold our hands and merely wait for it. What wonderful opportunities there are for the willing heart.

NOT SAVED

The harvest is past, the summer is ended, and we are not saved. Jer. 8:20.

At the wreck of the *London,* a young woman was urged to take her place in a boat on the point of leaving the side of the ship. She looked at the stormy sea, and the distance to be jumped, although small, appeared very great in her eyes, so she hesitated. While she waited, the danger became imminent. "Jump," cried those in the boat, "we must be off. Jump or you will be too late!" Again she looked, but again she hesitated, and now it was too late, for the boat was moving off. The distance was now really too great. "Stay! Come back!" she cried as the sense of her dreadful situation came to her. "Oh, come back!" This was now impossible, and she was lost.

The greatest neglected opportunity is to put off the decision to accept the provisions of the gospel for personal salvation. For the fearful, the unbelieving, the procrastinator, Jeremiah's lament is in full force. For if we stay in irresolution, the day of probation is already over.

The mother of a Scottish youth about to leave his homeland tried to make him pledge he would begin each day with God. He patted her shoulder and laughed at her fears. "Time enough for God," he said. Taking ship, he sailed abroad, filling his days with profligate living. The months of separation from his home drifted into years. Striking good fortune at last in an Australian gold mine, the young fellow bethought himself of his mother, from whom he had severed all ties. Flush with new-found wealth, he rushed home to make amends for his neglect. But his former townsmen could only take him to the lonely grave of his mother, where they left him crying, "Mother, you knew I loved you." Thus it is that many people trifle with precious privileges they possess until at last they have gone forever.

The danger is very real. For every man there is a line that separates the mercy of God from His wrath. It is possible in this life so to paralyze the will that though the door of opportunity is still open a man is powerless to reach for the life line. Many a man has pursued an evil course beyond the line of no return. Instead of an eternal destiny, his ultimate end is eternal destruction.

PUT IN TRUST

But as we were allowed of God to be put in trust with the gospel, even so we speak; not as pleasing men, but God, which trieth our hearts. 1 Thess. 2:4.

The gospel is the power of God, the good news of His saving grace. That human beings should be trusted with so fearful a responsibility is in itself an act of love, for God would have man a coparticipant in the great work of soulsaving. He would use men through whom to communicate His message of salvation to other men. This necessitates that man be put in trust with the gospel. It is incumbent upon those so honored that they speak the gospel, not as pleasing men, but God, who tries our hearts. We are not at liberty to tone down certain aspects of truth in order to maintain friendship or to curry favor, but the custodian of truth must be a faithful witness.

It is said that a brave old warrior was delayed in reaching the field of battle. He prayed that the battle would not be ended before he arrived. The true soldier of God relishes the arena. He is a part of the warfare between Christ and Satan. He loves combat with the Sword of the Spirit which is the Word of God. The old crusaders used to wear a cross upon their shoulders. This was their badge of service. Peter, the hermit, tore up his gown and distributed the pieces among his enthusiastic volunteers. It was then the fashionable and honorable thing to do. These actions were symbolic of the willingness of the individual to do or die for the cause he loved. It is said that after the battle of Austerlitz, Napoleon Bonaparte struck a medal on which were written the words, "I was there." Veterans of the campaign proudly displayed this badge of honor. It was symbolic of their struggles for the sake of the emperor.

Have we trophies from our struggles with the enemy in God's name? After our Lord gave Himself for us, there were scars in His hands and feet. These emblems of His sacrifice He will bear through all eternity. What scars have we to show for our service of Him, and what trophies mark our toil in the Master's vineyard? Let us speak as dying men to dying men. Can we watch unnumbered millions go to Christless graves without a witness? We are put in trust of the gospel.

REFUGE

That by two immutable things, in which it was impossible for God to lie, we might have a strong consolation, who have fled for refuge to lay hold upon the hope set before us. Heb. 6:18.

The Bible speaks of cities of refuge to which the guilty might flee and find safe haven. They were always situated on high hills so that the person fleeing could easily see them. There were six such cities, and they were always adequate to house another refugee. The roads to these cities were fifty-seven feet wide. All stones and obstructions were removed from them, and at stated intervals priests and elders would go out and inspect them. At every turn or crossroad a finger board indicated the right direction and had written on it in Hebrew characters the word *Miglat;* that is, "refuge," so that he who ran could read. These cities also had ground surrounding them and belonging to them. The moment the manslayer touched that soil he was safe, but he was safe only so long as he remained in the city of refuge.

The Bible says that God is our refuge, and the way to Christ has been plainly marked in the Scriptures so that the runner may read as he runs. Faith in Christ, repentance for sin, baptism, and obedience— all are spelled out very plainly, but we are safe only as long as we abide in Christ our refuge. To wander off these sacred grounds is to court disaster. These cities of refuge were set up for the guilty. God's Word tells us that "all have sinned, and come short of the glory of God" (Rom. 3:23). Christ also is a refuge for guilty man. He is a friend of sinners. He came to seek and to save that which was lost. We may "therefore come boldly unto the throne of grace, that we may obtain mercy, and find grace to help in time of need" (Heb. 4:16).

Some of the names of the cities of refuge are interesting. There is Kedesh. It means "holy place." Shechem means "a shoulder." Hebron means "fellowship." Bezer means "fortress." Ramoth-gilead means "heights." All these are characteristic of our God. It is reassuring to know that as we approach His throne with boldness we may indeed find "grace to help in time of need."

The search for security ends with God, and if we seek Him we will find Him as we search for Him with all our hearts.

IDLE WORDS

But I say unto you, That every idle word that men shall speak, they shall give account thereof in the day of judgment. Matt. 12:36.

In a bitter political campaign of 1884, James C. Blaine was attacked as a corruptionist and Grover Cleveland as an immoral man. In the midst of the campaign the great American preacher Henry Ward Beecher took the stump in behalf of Cleveland. The reason was that, having suffered himself so deeply through slander, Beecher had resolved to defend, if he could, any man who was assailed in like manner. At a great meeting at Brooklyn Rink on October 22 Beecher said: "When in the gloomy night of my own suffering I sounded every depth of sorrow, I vowed that if God would bring the daystar of hope I would never suffer brother, friend, or neighbor to go unfriended should a like serpent seek to crush him. This oath I will regard now because I know the bitterness of venomous lies. I will stand against infamous lies that seek to sting to death an upright man and magistrate." Thus Beecher found honey for others in the carcass of slander.

When even the truth would damage the reputation of another, it should not be spoken. This principle is a requirement of Scripture, and those who follow it obey the dictates of divine love. If indeed an evil must be mentioned, it should be mentioned first to the party involved. All slander comes from a malicious heart. When the grace of Christ has purged the soul, slander is a foreign element. "Either make the tree good, and his fruit good; or else make the tree corrupt, and his fruit corrupt: for the tree is known by his fruit" (Matt. 12:33). What comes out of one's mouth indicates the state of his own heart. In uttering slander we reveal more about ourselves than we do those we talk about.

What shall we say, then, of this tendency to practice cannibalism in verbal form? Hear what Jesus said to His own generation, "For by thy words thou shalt be justified, and by thy words thou shalt be condemned" (verse 37). It is a safe postulate that when we condemn others we condemn ourselves. Then in all our judgments let yea be yea and nay be nay, for in the multiplicity of words there is great peril.

THE BETTER WAY

Better it is to be of an humble spirit with the lowly, than to divide the spoil with the proud. Prov. 16:19.

It is said that on one occasion Abraham Lincoln, while President, visited the home of General McClellan to consult him about a military matter. The general had gone to a reception. Lincoln waited a considerable time, and finally the general returned. Though informed that Lincoln was waiting, he went straight to his bedroom and sent word that he had gone to bed. Lincoln never spoke of the incident, but he did call on McClellan again in the great crisis of September, 1862. He and General Halleck went to McClellan's home to ask him to take charge of the defeated and disorganized army of the Potomac. When Lincoln's friends expostulated with him because of his toleration of McClellan's attitude, Lincoln said, "Why, I would be willing to hold McClellan's horse, if only he would give victory to our army."

Perhaps this is the key to the greatness of this American President. He was a humble man. He would permit personal indignities for the good of the nation. Such humility is rare in our day. The tendency to retaliate and to get even is a universal one, but it is born of pride, and pride goes before destruction and a haughty spirit before a fall. Here is a stanza from Lincoln's favorite poem:

"Oh why should the spirit of mortal be proud?
Like a swift-fleeting meteor, a fast-flying cloud,
A flash of the lightning, a break of the wave,
Man passes from life to his rest in the grave."

In some pathway through a deep glen of the forest, you come upon a jutting rock covered with green moss and through it there trickles a tiny cascade. Nothing on earth is softer than that moss, but when you tear away the moss you come upon the cold naked rock.

Likewise the moss of humility may be ever so soft, clothing the man as does literal moss the rock, but underneath it inevitably lies incorruptible and indomitable courage, for the humble are the steadfast, and the pure are the poor in spirit. Tennyson's Galahad cried:

"My strength is as the strength of ten
Because my heart is pure."

330

WITH SINGING

Serve the Lord with gladness: come before his presence with singing. Ps. 100:2.

Singing and gladness have often been associated. When the problems of life weigh heavy upon us, often a simple song will change our gloom to gladness. Dwight Moody once told of a shipwreck at the mouth of Cleveland harbor. The pilot saw but one warning beam from the lighthouse, the lower light having gone out. The vessel missed the channel and crashed upon the rocks. Many a life was lost. P. P. Bliss subsequently wrote the popular hymn, "Let the lower lights be burning." His career was one of joyful confidence in the Lord. The burning of Chicago inspired him to compose "Billows of Fire." The last melody he wrote was "Hold Fast Till I Come," the words by his wife not long before the fatal journey when both of them were caught up in a billow of fire in the burning train at Ashtabula, Ohio, December 29, 1876. The last words he sang in public before his tragedy were prefaced by "I don't know that I shall ever sing here again, but I want to sing as the language of my heart:

" 'I know not the hour my Lord will come
To take me away to His own dear home,
But I know that His Presence will lighten the gloom,
And that will be glory for me.' "

In the darkness of a December night in the midst of a blinding storm, the train in which he and his wife were riding plunged through a seventy-foot bridge and burned. When last seen before they reached that deathtrap, Mr. Bliss sat with his Bible and pencil in hand composing a hymn. Only God knows the melody of that unsung experience.

Yes, many of the songs that we so unfeelingly sing in our public worship were written from experiences that wrested praise to God out of tragedy. Singing is a part of the joy of religion. The gladness with which we come into His courts is most naturally expressed through songs of praise. How often has the song of the choir in church lifted one's spirits before the message of the hour. The writer was right whose words I quote: "The melody of praise is the atmosphere of heaven. . . . Such song has wonderful power."

331

GIVE TO HIM

Give to him that asketh thee, and from him that would borrow of thee turn not thou away. Matt. 5:42.

A gentleman of wealth was riding horseback when he met an old woman who had not so much of this world's goods as he. He handed her a quarter and rode on. He had ridden only a short distance when he soliloquized thus: "Now, shouldn't I have done better if I had kept my money and bought myself something?" Wheeling his horse, he rode back to the old lady and said, "Give me that money!" She handed it to him. Placing it in his wallet, and at the same time handing her a five-dollar bill, he exclaimed, "There, Self, now I guess you wish you had kept still."

Yes, many of us need to address ourselves sometimes and put ourselves in others' places. That this is a selfish age with life itself contributing to this spirit, I need not say. Richard Whately has said, "It is curious to observe how many people who are always thinking of their own pleasure or interest often, if possessing considerable ability, will make others give way to them, and obtain everything they seek except happiness. For, like a spoiled child, who at length cries for the moon, they are always dissatisfied. And the benevolent who are always thinking of others, and sacrificing their own personal gratification, are usually the happiest of mankind."

Someone has said that the selfish are those that are turned outside in and the unselfish inside out. There is a proverb that says, "Every man for himself and God for us all." Be it understood that God is not for those who are always for themselves. His is an unselfish character. The greatest revelation of this we have in the gift of His Son Jesus. The thirty-three years He spent on this earth were spent in unselfish service for others, and His message to us is, "Go and do thou likewise" (Luke 10:37), the admonition He gave those who commended the deed of the good Samaritan. Liberality is the true road to happiness and peace. Our misery arises out of our constant preoccupation with ourselves. Ultimate satisfaction is the fruit of ultimate service. It is a law of life, and when transgressed it brings upon the life of the hearer all of its attendant miseries.

THOU SHALT REMEMBER

And thou shalt remember all the way which the Lord thy God led thee these forty years in the wilderness, to humble thee, and to prove thee, to know what was in thine heart, whether thou wouldest keep his commandments, or no. Deut. 8:2.

There was good reason for this counsel. Moses knew and so did his Master that we "have nothing to fear for the future, except as we shall forget the way the Lord has led us" (*Life Sketches,* p. 196).

Judges 3:7 records the sad tale: "And the children of Israel did evil in the sight of the Lord, and forgat the Lord their God, and served Baalim and the groves." Yes, they forgot that as a group of slaves, numbering some three million, He had literally plucked them out of the hands of their masters. They forgot His miraculous opening of the Red Sea and His destruction of Pharaoh's pursuing host. They forgot that in the wilderness, where there was no food, He sent them manna from heaven. They forgot that to quench their thirst He gave them water from a rock.

We often speak of people with remarkable memories. Of ancient Israel we must conclude they had remarkable forgetfulness. But is this confined to Israel alone? How often do we in the midst of a perplexing circumstance succumb to the gloom by forgetting how God has led us as individuals in the past. It seems that it is a characteristic of human nature to forget, but it is a characteristic that must be overcome. David admonishes us to "forget not all his benefits."

The prodigal son chose to forget all the blessings of dwelling in his father's house. His was a spirit of restlessness. He longed for the freedom of separation from his father. Not understanding his own impulses he insisted on breaking his family ties, collected his portion of the inheritance, and went to a far country and spent his substance in riotous living. Almost too late he remembered and said, "I will arise and go to my father." His return to the security of his father's house is a message of hope for all who have wandered away. God loves us still and longs for the high privilege of fellowship with His creatures. What a joy it should be for us to remember the Lord and return in humility to the foot of the cross.

HE DID IT NOT

And God saw their works, that they turned from their evil way; and God repented of the evil, that he had said that he would do unto them; and he did it not. Jonah 3:10.

What wonderful mercy is portrayed here. It tells of Nineveh, the great Babylon of its own day, of the repentance of its entire population, and of the mercy of God in sparing the city. We cannot read the story without seeing parallels to our own time. The great cities of the nations are reeking with immorality and vice. They have already earned for themselves the destiny they will receive. These great cities will be overthrown. The anger of God smokes against them, for the transgressions thereof are a reflection on His glory. They demean His character, they defy His justice and despise His mercy. From Moscow to New York and from London to Cape Town the pattern is the same. Man's transgressions reach unto heaven, and the determination has been made there to destroy them. But Nineveh repented. The king "arose from his throne, and he laid his robe from him, and covered him with sackcloth, and sat in ashes" (Jonah 3:6). Of the people it is said that "they turned from their evil way" (verse 10).

God cannot resist repentance. He has listed it as the key to His divine mercy. It was repentance that turned God from the destruction of Nineveh. Repentance will turn Him from the sure retribution that awaits the sinner today.

While it is true that God so loves us that He is not willing that any should perish, it is also true that "whatsoever a man soweth, that shall he also reap" (Gal. 6:7). If we would, therefore, appease the wrath of God, let us repent and turn to Him with all our heart, for He will hear from heaven and forgive our sins.

This world of ours has literally gotten out of hand. Violence with many is a way of life and restraint is flouted. It is as though a demon is loose in our world, and indeed there is, and the tiger within man has been set free. But there is refuge in God. All who put their faith in Him will not be disappointed. All who repent of their sins will experience the warm glow of the divine presence.

BE YE TRANSFORMED

And be not conformed to this world: but be ye transformed by the renewing of your mind, that ye may prove what is that good, and acceptable, and perfect, will of God. Rom. 12:2.

The pressures in our world today toward conformity are many and unrelenting. The whole world has embarked upon a mad dash toward its own destruction, and it would leave none standing on the side lines or going in the opposite direction. The tendency toward drink is a common illustration. It is difficult to find a social function where alcoholic beverages are not served, and from the moment of arrival the pressures to imbibe are there. One has to be a firm personality to resist these pressures.

Then again, it has become fashionable to smoke. The majority of young people feel these pressures to conform. The dangers of smoking are deliberately ignored or made light of. You either do it or you are a "square." Fashion designers the world over also exercise an almost hypnotic influence over the population of the world. If a certain name designer creates a style, it is forced upon the public with almost dictatorial necessity.

God's Book of truth teaches a better way, ". . . be ye transformed by the renewing of your mind." Mind renewal may be accomplished by daily prayer and the reading of the Word of God. This is indeed the only process by which the inner man is refreshed and renewed to meet today's problems. There is need in our world of a demonstration of the character of Christ and of the Godlike life. The daily renewing of our minds enables us to prove what is that "good, and acceptable, and perfect, will of God." Humanity will be moved less by a theory of religion than by a practical illustration of it in everyday life. We preach more effectively by our deeds than by our words. May we demonstrate our inner change, then, by our outward acts and be transformed to doing the will of God.

It is said that when Archimedes discovered the principle of floating bodies he cried out: *"Eureka,"* meaning, "I have found it." So may every soul exclaim in the presence of the King of kings, "I have found Him," and He has brought His peace to my heart.

IN THE MIDST OF TROUBLE

Though I walk in the midst of trouble, thou wilt revive me: thou shalt stretch forth thine hand against the wrath of mine enemies, and thy right hand shall save me. Ps. 138:7.

A Seventh-day Adventist soldier was treating the wounded on the battlefields of Vietnam when he noticed the form of a dead soldier lying there exposed to enemy fire. Though in mortal danger himself he decided to remove the dead man's body lest it be desecrated by the enemy. Cautiously he picked his way to the side of his fallen comrade, lifted him to his shoulder, and began to run with him toward the safety of friendly battle lines. Because of the intensity of fire he had to drop to his knees every few seconds in order to destroy any pattern of fire that might be set up. He had almost reached safety when a sudden burst of machine gun fire tore into the head of the dead man. His head was very close to the head of our missionary-minded medic. As they both fell to the earth, the dead man's body convulsed again as if in final agony, but the shot that would have killed the medic lodged in the dead man's body. He was literally saved by the corpse he carried.

As he crawled to safety he found that his medicine knapsack was bullet riddled and portions of his clothing had been creased with enemy fire. As he reflected, it occurred to him that God had repaid his act of kindness with a miracle.

A good deed is never lost if it is performed with a holy motive. The right hand of God is over the faithful in heart, and one of the joys of the redeemed will be reading the record of how God preserved us in hazards and dangers of which we were unaware.

When we surrender our life to Him and commit our talents, our choicest goods, and our worthy causes to His glory we may be sure that His protecting arm will be over us. The Bible is replete with promises to the moral hero. David gave us an outstanding example when he refrained from taking the life of the sleeping Saul when he himself was fleeing from the king's wrath.

How we need as Christians to develop the habit of disinterested service, good deeds motivated by no thought of reward.

PROTECTED BY ANGELS

For he shall give his angels charge over thee, to keep thee in all thy ways. **Ps. 91:11.**

A stricken Pan American plane headed out over San Francisco Bay with an engine afire and two Seventh-day Adventist ministers aboard. Needless to say, they were praying ministers. Suddenly the engine and one huge section of the wing fell into the water. Ordinarily the plane would have gone out of balance. The pilot himself acknowledges that a higher power kept them in flight. When he sensed that the plane could continue to fly he headed for an emergency landing at a nearby air base.

At this point a passenger rushed to the stewardess saying excitedly, "I must see the pilot! I must see the pilot!"

It is not customary to admit a passenger to the cockpit, but quite against her training the stewardess opened the door and permitted the man to converse with the pilot. "How do you plan to set her down, pilot?" the man asked.

"A belly landing, of course," replied the pilot.

"But you have too much fuel for that," replied the stranger.

"I know," replied the pilot, "but I will just have to take a chance. My hydraulic system is out and we cannot lower the landing gear."

"I am an engineer and I worked at the Boeing Company when they made these planes," replied the stranger. "Give me permission and I will hand crank your landing gear down."

Willing to try anything to save the plane, the pilot took a chance and gave him permission. Sure enough, the man knew exactly where to go. He tore up the floor board in the plane and had somebody hold him by the feet, head down into the undercarriage of the plane as he hand cranked the landing gear into position. Passengers and crew landed safely, but they were indebted not only to invisible angels but to a man who knew the anatomy of the plane.

Even so are we saved from day to day from unseen dangers by unseen angels. But we are especially indebted to Jesus Christ, who made us and who knows just what to do to set us straight and save our souls. Shall we not commit the keeping of our souls to Him today?

THE NECESSITY OF PRIESTHOOD

But Christ being come an high priest of good things to come, by a greater and more perfect tabernacle, not made with hands, that is to say, not of this building. Heb. 9:11.

The sacrifice of Jesus Christ our Lord at Calvary was an all-sufficient offering for our sins. This atoning sacrifice was complete, and as far as the atoning sacrifice for man's sins is concerned, Christ could say: "It is finished." But while the sacrificial offering was a perfect act and complete within itself, the work of reconciling man to God and man to his fellow man did not end at the cross. For the benefits of the atoning sacrifice had to be actively bestowed by a living priest.

This was why the apostle Paul could say of the resurrection: "And if Christ be not raised, your faith is vain; ye are yet in your sins" (1 Cor. 15:17). Please note that he could say this in spite of the fact that Christ had been crucified on the cross for our sins and that this atoning sacrifice was full and complete, yet something else had to be done. "If Christ be not raised, your faith is vain; ye are yet in your sins"! And what was this remaining task? "Wherefore he is able also to save them to the uttermost that come unto God by him, seeing he ever liveth to make intercession for them" (Heb. 7:25).

The significance, then, of the resurrection of our Lord in terms of man's salvation is that He liveth to make intercession. He is alive and therefore is our high priest, bestowing the benefits of His sacrificial atonement upon all who seek His face by faith. In this sense the atonement continues—not of sacrifice but of ministration and application. This also explains why there is an investigative judgment, for there had to occur the validation of four thousand years of animal sacrifices by a living, ministering priest, and a determination for the sake of man and the onlooking universe of the destinies of those who in these symbols of faith had looked forward to the cross, and of all who have named the name of Christ in succeeding ages. Only by this judgment procedure can the creatures of Jehovah understand His workings and declare Him just. And all creation will do just that, and in one final twist of justice Christ will wring from the lips of Lucifer himself an acknowledgment of His righteousness and mercy.

TWO EVILS

For my people have committed two evils; they have forsaken me the fountain of living waters, and hewed them out cisterns, broken cisterns, that can hold no water. Jer. 2:13.

It is tragic enough that men would forsake the Lord, but it is a double tragedy when they seek substitute gods that can only disillusion them at best. Christ is indeed the "fountain of living waters." To the woman of Samaria at the well He offered water which, if she partook, would remove forever the necessity of thirst. He spoke, of course, of His loving words: "The words that I speak unto you, they are spirit, and they are life" (John 6:63). This is literally true, "By the word of the Lord were the heavens made; and all the host of them by the breath of his mouth. . . . For he spake, and it was done; he commanded, and it stood fast" (Ps. 33:6, 9).

Does not wisdom dictate that we go again and again to the fountain for the thirst-quenching streams that flow therefrom? The warning comes, however, of the evil of hewing out "cisterns, broken cisterns, that can hold no water." Herein is pictured the futility of life without Christ. A vain search for an ever-illusive happiness. Having turned one's back on God, it would seem that man has only one vantage ground remaining, and that to confess the hopelessness of his position and plead again for access to the fountain of living waters. But man in his rebellion would add sin to sin. He would build a substitute system of nourishment that is neither workable nor functional. Nevertheless he persists. Such is the deceptiveness of sin.

There are so many today drinking the brackish waters of false philosophies, many of them under the guise of religion. Some have spent their lifetime running from the true Fountain of living waters and digging cisterns of their own devisings. Happy are they who are like that gospel minister who sat on a crowded subway reading *The Great Controversy,* and suddenly decided that here was truth and whatever the cost he would have to make a change. After listening to the message preached in the 1965 New York campaign, he decided to cast his lot with the people of God, and is faithful to this day. And now from Sabbath to Sabbath he happily drinks from the wells of salvation.

THE GATHERING

Fear not: for I am with thee: I will bring thy seed from the east, and gather thee from the west. Isa. 43:5.

There are two great gatherings spoken of in the Bible. One is a gathering of God's people under the instrumentality of the gospel and the other is the great gathering of the saints for the exodus to the world to come at the second coming of our Lord. Both of them are suggested in our text and hence comforting for both here and hereafter.

The first gathering is taking place now. There is a vast mysterious operation of grace going on in human hearts. The gospel of the kingdom is being preached in all the world for a witness unto all nations. Under its influence men and women are being gathered from the ways of transgression to the green fields of Edenic light. What a privilege to have a part in that great gathering. In the providence of God it is the solemn responsibility of every convert to become a convert maker. This is one of the measurements of our fitness to enter the kingdom of God, namely the extent to which we commit our talents to communicating light to others. As a church we are rather amply equipped for this great task. There is a tool for every pair of hands. The harvest is ripe, the laborers are few. Our prayers now should be that the Lord of the harvest will send forth laborers, and rising from our knees, we go.

When this initial gathering is complete, the stage will be set for the final manifestations of God's power. His fury will be felt in the earth unmixed with mercy, and the saints of God will be singled out as the cause for the many mighty manifestations of divine displeasure. And when it seems that they will be destroyed from the earth, the heavens will open as a scroll when it is rolled together and every mountain and island will be moved out of its place. The Lord of glory will return to the earth for the great gathering promised in the Scriptures. From the east, the west, the north, and the south, from every continent under heaven, every nation, and kindred, and tongue, and people—His people will answer the call of the Life-giver. Their mortal, corruptible natures will be immortalized and rendered incorruptible, and we shall all be changed, fitted physically, mentally, and spiritually for heaven.

CALLED UNTO LIBERTY

For, brethren, ye have been called unto liberty; only use not liberty for an occasion to the flesh, but by love serve one another. Gal. 5:13.

Throughout the years of Israel's apostasy Judaism, as a religion, had become increasingly oppressive. On Mount Sinai God gave laws that were intended not merely to regulate human behavior but to explain to man the character of Christ, and in this sense lead man to God. The ceremonial laws were a revelation of the grace of God. They told of the coming of a Saviour who would pay with His life for the sins of the world. These were to meet their complete fulfillment in Him, and all the requirements of this law were to be abolished at His coming.

The civil laws given to Israel were to regulate the conduct of the nation as a government and were binding so long as Israel existed as a nation. These moral, ceremonial, and civil laws if obeyed guaranteed a new freedom. In truth, they were charters of liberty.

Again, the health laws of the Bible were for man's eternal good, for as long as men walk the earth they will need to observe those laws that would perpetuate life. These told of the deep love of a Father-God for His children, that He would take the time to instruct them patiently as to the best way of life on earth—healthwise.

The Ten Commandments are a transcript of the character of God. They tell man just what God loves and what He does not love. They magnify the love of God. This is the only written, concise record of God's nature available to man, and hence an eternally valuable document. In the sense that the law of God, the Ten Commandments, is a description of His will and hence His character, it too, brings men to Christ in the sense that it brings men to a knowledge of His holy will and a revelation of the nature of His love. But in addition to these God-given laws the Jews multiplied restrictive covenants and pledges of their own, thus making religion a burden. Christ came to take these away, for they misrepresented His character of love.

But the Ten Commandments were given a new place of honor in the Christian economy. "I will put my laws into their mind, and write them in their hearts" (Heb. 8:10).

CHILDREN OF PROMISE

Now we, brethren, as Isaac was, are the children of promise.
Gal. 4:28.

The apostle Paul states a parable in this chapter. He compares Abraham's two sons, one by a bondmaid and another by a free woman. In verse 24 of Galatians 4 he compares the Jewish perversion of the purpose of law to their being children of the bondmaid, for to them law became an end rather than a means to an end. Law became master, thus making them slaves. They falsely concluded that by keeping the law they could gain favor with God, and that therefore salvation could be achieved rather than received. This confusion only contributed to their misery, for they were constantly making mistakes, being human, and constantly transgressing the very law they intended to serve and obey. This made them harsh and critical and overbearing. Man became a judge of his fellow man. And the havoc that this spirit wrought should have made the gospel of Christ a welcome message.

The true concept of obedience is that it is the fruitage of faith, and the law of God is joyfully observed only when it is known to be a revelation and manifestation of the grace of God within. Obedience must spring from love. Then it is natural and not forced. This was the Old Testament concept of the true children of God: "I delight to do thy will, O my God: yea, thy law is within my heart" (Ps. 40:8), David could write. "Where there is no vision, the people perish: but he that keepeth the law, happy is he" (Prov. 29:18).

But we are children of promise in another sense. For centuries men of God have predicted the collapse of human civilization and human values. We witness this coming apart of the fabric of human society in our own day. Life on earth is dangerous now, but it will be increasingly so. Many cannot see beyond the catastrophic future. We, however, have placed our hope in the coming of the Lord. We are also in this sense children of promise, for the darker the immediate night, the brighter will be the breaking of the day. The true Christian, then, is an optimist, for he knows that ultimately all things will turn out according to the divine purpose and that his future is a glorious one if in this life he centers his will in the will of Christ.

FOLLOW ME

And as Jesus passed forth from thence, he saw a man, named Matthew, sitting at the receipt of custom: and he saith unto him, Follow me. And he arose, and followed him. Matt. 9:9.

A father and son arrived in a small Western town looking for an uncle whom they had never seen. Suddenly the father pointed across the square to a man who was walking away from them and exclaimed: "There goes my uncle!"

But the son asked, "How do you know? You've never seen him."

The man answered, "Son, I know him because he walks exactly like my father."

Yes, Christians are distinguished by their walk. They are followers of Christ because they imitate Him. For Matthew, following Christ meant to desert the dishonest practices often consequent to customs collections. It was a new way of life altogether. It meant that henceforward he would walk as his Master walked. It also involved breaking with old associates. His daily chats at the customs office were at an end. Henceforth in fellowship with God he would seek only the associations of those who, like him, believed in Christ. Furthermore, this meant for him a deepening spiritual experience. His day-to-day association with the God of heaven in human flesh would work a change in his character. He beheld His miracles, listened to His teachings, and unconsciously began to imitate his Master. Those round about him took note of him that he had been with Jesus.

So may it be with us. To follow Jesus and to walk like Him involves a denial of self. Often the choice must be between what we want and what we know He will allow. Under these circumstances our course is clear. We ought to obey God rather than man, and His precepts rather than our preferences.

Following Christ also involves a cross. We cannot escape its perils if we are to receive its promises. We cannot avoid its trials if we are to reap its benefits, for its trials are in themselves beneficial. The song writer posed a pertinent query when he wrote:

> "Must Jesus bear the cross alone,
> And all the world go free?"

343

A FATHER'S LOVE

For God so loved the world, that he gave his only begotten Son, that whosoever believeth in him should not perish, but have everlasting life. John 3:16.

Satan would have all men believe that God does not love man. He has spent six thousand years trying to prove it. He seizes upon every calamity as evidence of God's lack of care for His children. War, disturbances in nature, sickness and death, which are natural consequences of man's own sins, are turned against God as evidence of His lack of concern and even of hostility toward erring man.

As the revelation of His love God has sent prophets and special messengers to each generation to proclaim the fact of His love, but these men have been misrepresented as working against the interest of the people. Demons have seized upon their words and given wrong impressions of their purposes and incited the anger of the very ones who should have benefited from their ministry.

Then came the Son of God Himself to the earth "that whosoever believeth in him should not perish, but have everlasting life." More than once this miracle-working, selfless Son of the living God was attacked by an angry mob who would have killed Him long before Calvary but for supernatural intervention. The coming of Christ into the world constitutes evidence of a Creator's love that cannot be refuted. But the devil sought to pervert even that. During the thirty-three years of our Lord's ministry on earth He was under constant attack by evil men and demons. His purest motive was misconstrued, and His most benevolent act misrepresented. And finally the anger of the multitude was so kindled against Him that He was delivered to a Gentile to be crucified on Calvary. And though He did this for us, His very hanging there upon the tree was turned against Him as evidence of His helplessness and His lack of divinity. For having saved others, could He not save Himself if He were God? Thus reasoned His revilers. But our Lord knew that if He saved Himself we would all be lost, and so like a sheep led before His shearers, Christ answered not a word. In the language of the spiritual He just "hung His head and died." But His death has meant spiritual rebirth for countless millions.

THE DIVINE PURPOSE

*For God sent not his Son into the world to condemn the world;
but that the world through him might be saved.* John 3:17.

Christ's righteous life stood out in marked contrast to everything
that surrounded Him on earth. But for His love for man, the day-to-
day contact with evil could have been as painful as His suffering at
Calvary. In this sense His very presence on earth was a condemnation
of the apostasy in man. But in all of His contacts with man God was in
Christ reconciling man unto Himself.

Dr. Guthrie says: "How difficult it would be to name a noble
figure, a sweet simile, a tender or attractive relationship in which
Christ is not set forth to woo a reluctant sinner and cheer a desponding
saint. Am I wounded? He is a balm. Am I sick? He is medicine. Am I
naked? He is clothing. Am I poor? He is wealth. Am I hungry? He is
bread. Am I thirsty? He is water. Am I in debt? He is surety. Am I in
darkness? He is the sun. Have I a house to build? He is a rock. Must I
face that black and gathering storm? He is an anchor sure and steadfast. Am I to be tried? He is an advocate. Is sentence passed and am I
to be condemned? He is pardon. To deck Him out and set Him forth
nature calls her finest flowers and brings her choicest ornaments and
lays these treasures at His feet. The skies contribute their stars, the
sea gives up its pearls, from fields and rivers and mountains earth
brings the tribute of her gold and gems and myrrh and frankincense.
The lily of the valley, the clustered vine and the fragrant rose of
Sharon. Yes, there was only one way to save man, the Creator must become the Redeemer. If responsibility is to be assumed, the Maker must
assume it and call upon His own head the wrath of demons and evil
men. But for the joy set before Him, the salvation of souls, He would
tread with steadfast purpose the rugged path to Calvary's brow. There
could be no relief from the pain that would break His heart. A loving
Father would suffer with Him but not deliver Him lest He foil the
purpose for which He sent Him into the world. If I have one thought
left while dying to spend in contemplation it will be of the cross. If
I have one breath left in dying and strength of utterance, one name will
grace my tongue, one word escape my lips—Jesus."

A REASON FOR THE HOPE

But sanctify the Lord God in your hearts: and be ready always to give an answer to every man that asketh you a reason of the hope that is in you with meekness and fear. 1 Peter 3:15.

Elder James White was delivering a message in East Augusta, Maine, concerning the millennium. At the close of the discourse, a Universalist preacher arose and said, "I want five minutes to show that this doctrine has no foundation in the Bible or in common sense."

Elder White suggested that the service be dismissed and that he speak as long as he wanted to in the afternoon.

"No; this is just the place and time for me to speak, and the people want to hear me," the man said.

Brother White said, "We will submit the matter to the congregation, and let them decide it for us." Then he called for a vote. Nearly the entire congregation stood with him.

In the afternoon the Universalist minister spoke.

He said, "I wish to make a few remarks relative to the portion of Scripture commented upon by the speaker this forenoon, which you will find in the sixty-fifth chapter of Daniel." Then he began to ridicule the idea of beasts in heaven.

Elder White interrupted him and told him that it was not Daniel but another prophet who had thus spoken. The Universalist minister rebuked Elder White for interrupting him and continued. Elder White interrupted again and said: "I am not willing that the gentleman proceed any further until he reads Daniel 65, the scripture from which he is speaking." The minister began to search the Scriptures frantically, but of course, could not find it. In fact, he could not even find the book of Daniel. Then he said, "It is torn out of my book," to which Elder White replied, "Here, sir, is mine. Mine has the book of Daniel in it."

After a few more minutes of frustration on the part of the minister, Elder White then quoted the passage the minister sought, and corrected him with the information that it was in the sixty-fifth chapter of the book of Isaiah, and he quoted nine verses from the chapter. This made a great impression upon the congregation. Later this minister stood up and confessed his error and the Spirit of God prevailed.

A GOOD SOLDIER

Thou therefore endure hardness, as a good soldier of Jesus Christ. 2 Tim. 2:3.

Many of us are not too familiar with some of the hardness that the pioneers of the Advent Movement endured to establish what we today enjoy. The following incident is from James White's book, *Life Incidents,* pages 96, 97.

"The second day of April, 1843, I mounted my poor, chest-foundered horse, and started for my native town, much worn by my labors of the winter. The snow was very deep. My horse's feet were much of the time, while passing over the drifts, higher than the tops of fence-posts. My only suit of clothes was much worn, and I had no money. I had not received the value of five dollars for my labors. Yet I was happy in hope. . . . As I was entering the city of Augusta, a farmer was returning home with an empty hay-sled, drawn by six oxen. I chose to ride past this team. The driver sat on the fore part of the sled, and the oxen kept the middle of the road. On being crowded out of the road, my horse became very angry, and as the sled was passing, threw himself over the first set of stakes on to the sled. Seeing strong probabilities that I should be thrown on some one of the second set of sharp stakes and killed, I sprang from the horse, quite over the stakes, into the snow on the other side. The team continued to move along with my horse fairly loaded upon the sled; and by the time I had rescued myself from the snow, was several rods from me. 'Hallow!' cried I. 'Please stop your team and let me have my horse.' The good farmer stopped his oxen, and assisted me in unloading my horse, which, when I had mounted, galloped off as well as before."

There are incidents recorded where Ellen White often traveled while ill in an open sled in freezing weather to meet appointments. These hardy pioneers of the faith were willing to spend and be spent. Perhaps this is why James White could report one thousand converts to the faith within a four-month period. Is it not a rebuke to our Laodicean love of ease? This movement that began in sacrifice must without controversy be finished in sacrifice.

WITHOUT EXCUSE

Therefore thou art inexcusable, O man, whosoever thou art that judgest: for wherein thou judgest another, thou condemnest thyself; for thou that judgest doest the same things. Rom. 2:1.

Human nature is the same, and though one be fully surrendered to God there is in every man the capability of doing evil. This fact precludes anyone's becoming a judge of his fellow man. For we condemn in others that which is characteristic of ourselves. To this fact the Pharisees were evidently blind. At council after council they multiplied rules and established standards by which character could be measured, and thus made themselves judges of the people.

An example of this is the group of men who brought before Jesus a woman caught in adultery. He said to them, "He that is without sin among you, let him first cast a stone at her." Jesus knew these very men had led her into sin, and as He wrote their guilt in the sand they quietly dispersed. But men go on judging other men, assigning motives where they do not exist and imputing meaning to innocent words or gestures. This sensitivity is satanic, and Christ calls this type of judgment "inexcusable."

We cannot read the minds of men. We can only assess words and actions. God alone can read the heart and is qualified to judge.

I have a friend who has a very healthy practice. He refuses to believe that a wrong is intended even when the actions of the other party are obviously perverse. He seeks to excuse the most flagrant act on the ground that perhaps the perpetrator was not thinking or perhaps he was a little ill. This charitable state of mind is the safest to adopt. It is more like the mind of Christ. The philosophy of the three monkeys is apropos here: "See no evil, hear no evil, speak no evil."

One's own peace of mind is also involved, for he who spends his time judging others is a miserable man himself. Doubt and suspicion poison the soul and are destructive of personal peace. The healthy attitude is that which allows for the mistakes of others, recognizing one's own personal weaknesses. It is so easy to misrepresent our true intentions. How can we assess the motives of others?

THE LAW ESTABLISHED

Do we then make void the law through faith? God forbid: yea, we establish the law. Rom. 3:31.

This rebellious generation is reaping what it has sown. We now see an unrestrained society setting its own rules, making its own laws, the results of trial and error and the total rejection of any standard or code of morality. Old-fashioned standards of decency are condemned. Liberty and license are hailed as the new freedom.

Thank God for Adventism, which from the beginning has asserted the binding claims of the law on human behavior and has in addition proclaimed the grace of God, not only as a covering for sin under the terms of justification but as power to break the grip of sin on the soul of the believer. This is the philosophy of salvation taught in the Scriptures. Faith is no substitute for obedience. It is the means. Faith does not make void the law; indeed it is faith that establishes the law as a habit pattern in the life of the saint.

While the law is an external form in terms of its origin and proclamation, under the terms of the gospel that law becomes an internal, integral part of the human make-up. The writing of the law in the inward parts and the putting of it in the heart of man makes obedience to it a joyful outgrowth of the transformed experience. It is not regarded as an external yoke, restraining an otherwise rebellious man, but rather, the converted man finds obedience to the law of God the natural expression of his new state of being. This establishes the law as being "holy, just, and good," and as it becomes a part of the character of man, he reflects the likeness of God.

A woodsman was observed laboriously swinging an ax at the root of a giant tree. Perspiration flowed from his brow, and slowly but surely the giant oak was yielding to the pressure of the rhythmic strokes of the ax. Soon it would come crashing to the earth. Pausing for a bit of rest, the workman heard a voice remark, "That is tough work you are doing there."

"It is not hard for me," he replied, "you see, I am enjoying it. It is what I like to do." When one's heart is not in his work, it becomes drudgery.

INTEGRITY

Therefore, my beloved brethren, be ye stedfast, unmoveable, always abounding in the work of the Lord, forasmuch as ye know that your labour is not in vain in the Lord. 1 Cor. 15:58.

Integrity is a rare quality in this generation. In one section of a Western State alone 250,000 people are employed to watch other people. You see, there is a sin by the name of shoplifting, and seven per cent of the business failures in that area are attributed to shoplifting. It is reported that those apprehended for this form of thievery cut across the entire fabric of the population—ministers, doctors, schoolteachers, movie actors and actresses, juveniles, and even little children are sometimes pressed into service by their parents in this nefarious activity. "Thou shalt not steal" is as necessary an injunction today as ever, but think of the thousands who are never caught, who pride themselves on little contrivances that outwit others to their own financial advantage.

In the matter of telling the truth there is deep need among even the saints for steadfastness. The temptation to spread damaging gossip is ever with us. Character assassination is something to guard against in the church of God. Jealousy and envy are strong contributing factors to that form of thievery that robs a person of his influence and reputation. And then there is integrity with reference to tithe paying. Some who read these words today may have been derelict in their duty as tithepayers. It is the sincere hope of this writer that the lesson will be an encouragement to you to tighten up and square that account with God. Here is an area in which all can abound in the work of the Lord.

A successful businessman once told this experience: "I am particular even about paying my carfare now. When I was a little boy I took a ticket home once and showed it to my father, saying that the conductor had not taken it up and I was that much ahead. My father looked at me and said I had sold my honor for a nickel. That put a new face on it. I always think of what he said when I am tempted to repeat the offense." Sterling honesty and incorruptibility must characterize the child of God.

BE NOT AFRAID

But and if ye suffer for righteousness' sake, happy are ye: and be not afraid of their terror, neither be troubled. 1 Peter 3:14.

During the persecutions of the first century, Christians considered martyrdom the highest honor. In fact, the desire to die for Christ was so strong that men would say and do unwise things to bring it upon themselves. They wanted to demonstrate to the world the power of Christianity over the fear of death.

Freedom from fear of bodily affliction is not a natural thing. In the Christian it is a product of faith. David could say: "Yea, though I walk through the valley of the shadow of death, I will fear no evil" (Ps. 23:4). It is the knowledge that Christ is with us that removes the fear of death. There must also be a clear conscience, which of course is conditional to the Master's presence in the life. One cannot practice deliberate sin habitually without the fear of death embedding itself in the conscience. Such a man is even afraid of life. There is no inward security, no peace of mind. Such a person needs to be warned that there is yet coming upon this world a time of trouble such as never was since there was a nation. And if the trials that await the people of God during this period are fearful, what shall be the end of those who obey not the gospel of God? But to suffer for Christ's sake is the highest of all honors. Did He not give His life for us? The Son of the living God hanging on Calvary, bleeding for the guilt of sinful man, should be enough to strengthen any man for reciprocal sacrifices.

But all suffering for Christ does not involve martyrdom. Many are persecuted for doing God's will in the ordinary affairs of life. Husbands and wives have been known to persecute their believing mates for their faith in God. Men have suffered economic privation, been fired from jobs for their integrity. Social ostracism has plagued yet others. They find themselves deserted by lifelong friends simply because of their profession of faith, and yet others have been physically attacked by mobs for simply being different.

Opposition in this life is the lot of the follower of Christ, for he is literally living a life that is out of harmony with the current.

351

CALVARY

And when they were come to the place, which is called Calvary, there they crucified him, and the malefactors, one on the right hand, and the other on the left. Luke 23:33.

I stood at the base of the large hill of the skull, where it is supposed our Lord was crucified. At the top of that hill is a Moslem graveyard now. It is a place for the dead. Nineteen hundred years ago three crosses adorned its brow, and on the center cross hung the Son of the living God. Yes, this was the scene of earth's most momentous event. Calvary has been called the place of a skull, but it was immeasurably more than this.

It was a place of atonement, for there the sins of all the people were atoned for. The price demanded of God's broken law was paid. The sacrificial atonement of our Lord was full and complete.

It was a place of prophetic fulfillment. For more than four thousand years men had offered animal sacrifices. These in themselves were prophetic of the coming of the Lamb of God that would take away the sins of the world.

Calvary was a place of vindication, and it was this in at least three senses: (*a*) It vindicates the law of God. It says that the law of God is forever binding and that it cannot be changed or done away with. The very death of Christ itself testifies to this, since it was the law that demanded the death of the sinner, the blood of the offending person. (*b*) It is also a vindication of God's original dealing with rebellion. It was He who cast Satan out of heaven. There are those who have not understood this. But at Calvary our understanding cleared, for we saw the evil, malignant nature of Lucifer. (*c*) Calvary vindicates God's love. It says that God loves man, that God is interested in man. So much so that He would give His life for man's salvation. Such is the quality of divine love that it would disadvantage itself for the object of its affection.

Calvary was a place of pardoning mercy. That the Son of the living God would pause in dying to confer pardon upon a repentant thief says something to me. It says that any man who sincerely repents of his sin at whatever stage of his life, can find mercy.

352

ALL THE FULLNESS

For it pleased the Father that in him should all fulness dwell.
Col. 1:19.

When David Livingstone tried to explain the philosophy of God's plan of salvation to the Africans, they, hearing the story for the first time, asked him: "Teacher, how could one man die for the whole human race?"

This is Livingstone's explanation. He dipped his hand into his pocket and brought out two coins, one common British copper penny and the other a little glittering golden sovereign. He explained that in the country from which he came the little golden coin, which was not so large as the penny and did not weigh as much, was actually worth 240 of the copper pennies. The difference in the value was the result of the inherent difference in the metal. So God's holy, perfect, well-beloved Son was worth a whole world of guilty, lost, condemned sinners.

Yes, it is even so with Christ, for "in him should all fulness dwell." "That in all things he might have the preeminence" (Col. 1:18). And Christ alone is worth all creation and more besides. This is why this one life could atone for the sins of the whole world. He could, therefore, make "peace through the blood of his cross, by him to reconcile all things unto himself." Yes, "all fulness" is His—fullness of power, fullness of wisdom, and fullness of love. In all attributes, Christ is equal with His Father and He identifies us as His brethren.

An old Indian chief heard of this glorious provision of the gospel and permitted the missionary to try to persuade him to accept Christ. Finally shaking his head, the old chief said, "The Jesus road is good, but I have followed the Indian road all my life and I will follow it to the end." A year later the old man stood on the borderline of death. As he was seeking a pathway through the darkness he said to the missionary, "Can I turn to the Jesus road now? My road stops here. It has no path through the valley."

The love of God provides the only clear path through the valley of the shadow of death. All other paths stop here. Christ can lead on because He is from everlasting unto everlasting. Eternity past saw no beginning of His life and eternity future will see no end.

BLOTTED OUT

I have blotted out, as a thick cloud, thy transgressions, and, as a cloud, thy sins: return unto me; for I have redeemed thee. Isa. 44:22.

A little boy ran to his mother after he had read the words "I have blotted out, as a thick cloud, thy transgressions." He said, "Mother, what does God mean when He says He will blot out my sins? What is He going to do with them? I can't see how God can really blot them out and put them away. What does it mean 'blot out'?"

The mother said, "Bring me your slate." He brought the slate, and holding it in front of him, his mother asked: "Where is what you wrote on it yesterday?"

He said, "Oh, I rubbed it out."

"Well, where is it?"

"Oh, Mother, I don't know. It was there and now it is all gone."

"Well, that is what God means when He says He will blot out our transgressions," she replied. Our sins are literally gone when they are "blotted out." We may forget them, for God has forgotten them.

No wonder the prophet could exclaim: "Sing, O ye heavens; for the Lord hath done it: shout, ye lower parts of the earth: break forth into singing, ye mountains, O forest, and every tree therein: for the Lord hath redeemed Jacob, and glorified himself in Israel" (Isa. 44:23). You will notice how closely Christ identifies Himself with us. When He blots out our sins He glorifies Himself.

In the game of baseball a team may be one run behind. The losing team comes to bat with a man on first base. There are two men out in the last half of the ninth inning. The batter knocks the ball out of the park. It is a home run! He has changed the score from defeat to victory. His team is delivered, but at the same time he covers himself with glory. By delivering his team he has brought honor to his own name.

This carnal illustration, so easily understandable to those who read this book, illustrates in a measure just how God's marvelous grace exercised toward us brings glory to His own great name.

"Our rainbow arch Thy mercy's sign;
All save the clouds of sin are Thine."

LOOK UP

And when these things begin to come to pass, then look up, and lift up your heads; for your redemption draweth nigh. Luke 21:28.

On a gray morning during World War I the Prime Minister of Britain, David Lloyd George, stood grim visaged before the British Cabinet. The seriousness of the situation was evident upon the faces of all. With grave emphasis the Premier said, "Gentlemen, we are fighting with our backs to the wall. The only way out is up. Our only hope is God."

This statement was less a pessimistic assessment of the immediate situation than an expression of hope of ultimate deliverance. This is the true significance of the doctrine of the second coming of the Lord. Civilization is indeed at the threshold of collapse. Only ostrichlike men with their heads in the sand would deny this. The very fabric of human society is coming unwoven. There is a suspicion now, national and international, that we have tied our stone together with putty and that human solutions are mere stopgap measures at best. "The only way out is up." Our hope is in the coming of the Lord. This is not intended to reflect on the well-meaning efforts of just men, for they are used of God to slow the approach of the gathering storm. Indeed, how dreary life would be without these shining beacons of hope. May the God of heaven lengthen every just man's days and prosper his planning.

But let us not deceive ourselves; the end of all things is at hand. Jesus Christ is coming soon, and He will bring with Him the solution to all of man's pressing problems—problems of war and peace, of hunger, of racial injustice, of unemployment, and of marital disharmony. Yes, all of the problems will find their full and complete solution in the kingdom of our God.

This doctrine, however, is not intended to indulge a state of inertia on the part of us earth-bound creatures. We must not shrug our shoulders in resignation and sit idly waiting for the coming of the Lord. While we know that the only way out is up, we must work as though the only way out is out. Prayerfully sacrificing ourselves for the cause of God, we must live and hope in the coming of the Lord.

SIN

Then when lust hath conceived, it bringeth forth sin: and sin, when it is finished, bringeth forth death. James 1:15.

That lust itself is sin needs no discussion here. Our text simply says that the lustful attitude of the heart is the mother of all lustful acts, and if not overcome, will bring death—spiritual, physical, and eternal. If sin is to be repulsed, the avenues of the mind must be guarded carefully. Sin must be resisted at the point of inception, that is, at the very first point of temptation.

Years ago there was not a single thistle in the whole of Australia. A Scotsman who admired thistles thought it a pity that such a great island should be without that symbol of his great nation. He therefore collected a packet of thistle seed and sent it over to his friends. It was only to be sown in one garden, but now whole districts of the country are covered with it and it has become the farmer's pest and plague. It was only a little seed, but it would have been a blessing if the ship that brought that seed had been wrecked. Take heed of the thistle seed; the little sins are like that.

In Hampton Court garden are several giant oaks that are well-nigh overcome by the huge coils of ivy which, like monstrous snakes, are wound about them. No loosening of the ivy is now possible. There was a time, however, when the ivy was but a tiny aspirant seeking only a little help in its upward climb. Had it been denied, then the oaks would never have become the hopeless and helpless victims of the ivy. So is it with sin. As with Christ in the wilderness, sin must be fought all along the line. There can be no compromise therewith, for the end thereof is death.

Eternal vigilance is the price of freedom. To tamper with evil is to hasten one's own enslavement. "So long as the soul rests with unshaken confidence in the virtue and power of the atonement, it will stand firm as a rock to principle, and all the powers of Satan and his angels cannot sway it from its integrity. The truth as it is in Jesus is a wall of fire around the soul that clings to Him. Temptations will pour in upon us. . . . There is no sin in having temptation, but sin comes in when temptation is yielded to."—*Testimonies,* vol. 4, p. 358.

BLESSED ARE THEY

Blessed are they that do his commandments, that they may have right to the tree of life, and may enter in through the gates into the city. **Rev. 22:14.**

Another translation reads: "Blessed are they that wash their robes." It is a fact that all are born with dirty robes. In sin are we born and in iniquity are we shaped, and only when our robes are washed in the blood of the Lamb do we do His commandments, thus manifesting that we have a right to the tree of life and to enter in through the gates into the city.

There are thousands who walk today in spotted robes. "I think a Christian can go anywhere," said a young woman who was trying to excuse herself for going to some questionable places of amusement.

Replied a friend, "Certainly a Christian can go anywhere, but that reminds me of an incident that happened when I went with a party to explore a coal mine. One of the young women appeared wearing a white dress. Asked she of the old miner, 'Can I wear a white dress down into the mine?' 'Yes'um,' replied the old man. 'There is nothing to keep you from wearing a white frock down there, but there will be considerable to keep you from wearing one back.'"

Yes, to live in this old world is to be exposed to a filthy atmosphere and spotty environments, and once our robes have been washed we cannot carry them just anywhere and expect to keep them spotless. We may walk into certain situations with spotless robes but it is not likely that we will come out unaffected. There must be a rigid adherence to the will of God as is revealed in His commandments. That we are saved by grace through faith does not release us from the claims of obedience demanded in the law. Actually the binding claims of the law are made living reality in the Christian's experience by grace through faith. It is thus that the righteousness of the law is fulfilled in us, and only such have a right to the tree of life.

Finally, there are the gates that lead into the city—twelve of them —with an angel at each gate. What a privilege it will be to enter in. By contrast what bitter disappointment awaits those who will be excluded.

357

AGAINST GOD

There is no wisdom nor understanding nor counsel against the Lord. Prov. 21:30.

Our text first of all calls attention to the Source of all wisdom, understanding, and counsel. God Himself is that only dependable source. Human history is the sad record of nearly six thousand years of human rebellion against this conclusion. God made man upright, but he has sought out many inventions. We could here call the roll of hundreds of so-called wise men who have pitted their wisdom against God, but it has only led man down the long road to defeat and frustration.

After a Week of Prayer on a large college campus, I received a letter from the conference president in which he enclosed a letter from a student to him. The student's letter is dated April 20, 1963. He writes: "There are a few of us here considered to be philosophers because we read the contemporaries from Neitsche, Miller, Sartre, to Hemingway, always paying close attention to those who down God. I have spent most of the year trying to find one proof that God is unjust. I wanted to know about God but I went about it the wrong way. I never prayed or read the Word—funny way to learn about God." And speaking of his roommate he said, "He always bragged that he never prayed in his whole life, but he did pray last night." What that young man did not mention is that in the little philosophical group with which he used to meet they also read Tom Payne's *Age of Reason.*

Thank God for the Week of Prayer plan being followed in all of our schools and churches throughout the world. It enables young and old to explore anew the science of salvation and to discover anew that "there is no wisdom nor understanding nor counsel against the Lord."

Certain so-called wise men have risen in all ages and been used by the evil one to lift their giant intellects in rebellion against God. Plato, Aristotle, Voltaire, Darwin, and others are more widely quoted than the prophets of Scripture, but look at the world that their vaunted wisdom has in part produced. Their postulates are speculative. Their conclusions are sterile. God's truth abides.

THE WAY OF MAN

Every way of a man is right in his own eyes: but the Lord pondereth the hearts. Prov. 21:2.

Deeds are often deceptive, and yet they are the only measure by which man may judge his fellow man. This is probably the basis of the injunction of our Lord: "Judge not, that ye be not judged" (Matt. 7:1).

Even more deceptive is man's own evaluation of his behavior. Unless our hearts are daily attuned to the mind of God through prayer and Bible study, we are likely to look with flattering eye upon our own deeds. This is a part of the deceptiveness of sin. It would lull us into a state of security when there is need of most urgent action and deepest repentance. Laodicean pride is rooted in self-satisfaction when in fact, no deed, however faithfully performed, is beyond criticism, even when viewed with human eyes. Subject that same deed or "way of a man" to the all-searching eye of God and we can understand the reticence of the ancient prophets to even approach the throne of grace without an apology. Read Daniel's prayer in the ninth chapter of his book and Isaiah's prayer in the sixth chapter of his book and you will have little difficulty understanding just what is meant here.

The tendency to flatter oneself can only persist as we neglect prayer and the study of the Word of God. The Bible is God's great mirror to show us just what our true condition is as well as point to the divine remedy. Neglect this and we are sure to be overcome by the stupor of self-satisfaction. Can this be the root cause of the long delay of the promised revival so long looked forward to? Nor may we flatter ourselves if we obey the apostolic injunction: "Pray without ceasing" (1 Thess. 5:17). A man never sees himself better than on his knees. It was the publican who smote his breast and though far more righteous than the Pharisee prayed: "God be merciful to me a sinner" (Luke 18:13). The sensitivity of his conscience was daily cultivated by communion with his Maker, and no man can come repeatedly into the presence of such awesome majesty without being smitten with the vileness of his own nature.

359

OPEN THINE EYES

Love not sleep, lest thou come to poverty; open thine eyes, and thou shalt be satisfied with bread. **Prov. 20:13.**

There is no such thing as a lazy Christian. When the germ of divinity, that is, the heart of the gospel, captures the soul of a man it transforms him into a dynamo of activity. This has been clearly demonstrated in the history of the developing countries of the earth. Now, it is a fact that all countries were at one time or other developing. The continent of Europe was brought out of deep sleep by the approach of Christianity, and it was the revitalized preaching of the Reformation that sparked the Renaissance and the age of enlightenment to which our world has come. On the continent of Africa it was the seed of the gospel sown in hearts that awakened in man a sense of his own dignity. Until the approach of the gospel, Africa also slept a deep sleep.

I have also seen this principle demonstrated in individual human lives again and again. Men whose lives were aimless and worthless and who were a liability to society have upon accepting the terms of the gospel received a new sense of purpose and have become industrious, dependable, honest persons, making their contribution to the betterment of society. In this sense the benefits of the gospel are social as well as spiritual.

As this relates to the family, the Bible says that a man who will not provide for his own household is worse than an infidel.

One of the consequences of man's transgression is that his labor now is not always satisfying. It just may be that a man has to engage in unpleasant tasks to earn his living, but his responsibility as the head of a household requires that he support that household. Many parents allow their children to grow up in idleness. This is a mistake and contributes greatly to the delinquency of our society. Young people should be given tasks to perform at early ages and taught the dignity of labor. Unless the twig is bent in this direction early, recovery from habits of indolence and laziness is unlikely. There is a lot of good religion in the faithful performance of everyday duties with diligence, industry, and faithfulness.

WHERE IS HE?

Now when Jesus was born in Bethlehem of Judaea in the days of Herod the king, behold, there came wise men from the east to Jerusalem, saying, Where is he that is born King of the Jews? for we have seen his star in the east, and are come to worship him. Matt. 2:1, 2.

It has been stated before that the children of this world are wiser than the children of light. The Wise Men of the East were conversant with the prophecies with reference to the birth of the Messiah. The appearance of the mysterious star that had not before been noted in their astronomical observations confirmed in their hearts the fact that indeed the prophecies they studied had been fulfilled. Hence they made their way to the land of light, the country of the Hebrews. These were the possessors of the oracles of God. To their hands had been committed the precious light that was to enlighten the whole world, but what did these Wise Men of the East find? Darkness—gross darkness. On the throne of Israel was a dissipated adulterer and a mere shell of a man who inquired of them as to the whereabouts of the Messiah.

We have here illustrated the supreme peril of hypocrisy. One may live in the very presence of light and yet himself be encased in a world of darkness. We may be participants with others in the ritual of religion while in our innermost souls denying its power.

The cry of the Wise Men, "Where is he?" expresses the basic need of the human family. Humanity was created with one grand basic thirst for righteousness. The sinful cravings of perverted nature are a mutation of righteous desire. The pursuit of worldly pleasure and the use of alcoholic beverages are pathetic expressions of man's deep need of God. It is his feeble cry, "Where is he that is born King?" To all who sincerely seek Him, there is abundant assurance in the Bible that Christ may be found.

As yuletide bells ring out today and the sobering strains of "Silent night, holy night" are heard, may our footsteps turn once again in search for the Redeemer, and let there be no slackening of the pace till He be found.

STRONG TOWER

The name of the Lord is a strong tower: the righteous runneth into it, and is safe. Prov. 18:10.

The words of our text are literally true. Our very approach to God must be in the name of Jesus Christ. It is only thus that we have access to the sympathetic ear of our loving Father. The name of Christ gives protection against demon power. Evil spirits have been exorcised by the mere mention of that name. In the name of Christ the sick have been healed and the dead have been raised. Truly the name of the Lord is a strong tower, and well may the righteous run into it for safety.

But the word "safe" in our text is also translated "set aloft." A bird in his cage may twitter sweet music but there will always be a tinge of sadness, a note of pathos there, for it is the music of the enslaved. In many of the Negro spirituals of our day this plaintive note may be detected. Set the bird aloft and free the man and his spirit soars on wings of hope.

As Sir James McIntosh lay dying whenever a verse of Scripture was read to him he always showed by some sign that he had heard it. "And," says his daughter, "I especially observed that at every mention of the name of Jesus Christ, if his eyes were closed he always opened them and looked at the person who had spoken. Once after a long silence he said, 'I believe.'

"We said in a voice of inquiry, 'In God?'

"He answered, 'In Jesus.'

"He spoke but once after this. Upon our inquiring how he felt he was 'happy.'"

It would seem as if other names on the memory of the saints are like those cut deep into the poet's fabled rock of ice, which, gradually as the sun came around day by day melting the ice, became less and less plain until at length it melted away altogether. But it is not so with the name of Jesus. The psalmist says: "His name shall be continued as long as the sun: and men shall be blessed in him: all nations shall call him blessed" (Ps. 72:17).

THE WISE

The fruit of the righteous is a tree of life; and he that winneth souls is wise. Prov. 11:30.

During one of the great battles of the Civil War a recruit who had lost his company in the tumult of strife approached General Sheridan and timidly asked where he should step in. "Step in!" roared Sheridan, "step in anywhere, there is fighting all along the line." And it is also true that in the great battle for souls there is fighting all along the line. This great controversy for the minds of God's created creatures began away back in the battlements of heaven.

Originally it was a struggle for the minds of angels, but Lucifer was cast out of heaven into the earth and one third of the angels chose to follow him. (Not until the crucifixion of Christ was the true nature of Lucifer fully exposed to the unfallen beings in the universe.)

In the Garden of Eden the struggle entered a new phase. The controversy between Christ and Satan was carried to the mind of newly created man. And as men began to multiply on the earth the two classes became increasingly distinct. Lucifer for his part used men to subvert the faith of other men. Likewise, the God of heaven commissioned His followers to represent His character correctly to those who had lost the way. This in all ages has been the supreme mission of the Christian, and in this grand enterprise we may step in anywhere, for there is "fighting all along the line."

The wise among us become soul winners for several reasons:

1. Unless we work for other souls we will lose our own.

2. Unless men communicate the good news of the gospel to other men many will die without a saving knowledge of the grace of God.

3. Without communicated light this old world would become even more lawless and unfit for human habitation than it now is. It is the glorious light of the gospel communicated by man to his fellow man that literally preserves the earth. Said Jesus "Ye are the salt of the earth" (Matt. 5:13).

IN ORDER

Let all things be done decently and in order. 1 Cor. 14:40.

Of immediate concern to the apostle is the confusion that came from the exercise of spiritual gifts. There were considerable willfulness and a lack of respect for authority existent in the Corinthian church. There was the use of foreign languages in the worship service. To this group Paul explained the need for having an interpreter so that the audience could understand what was being said, and further, no more than three could speak in any one service and they were to do it one at a time. He also had some excellent suggestions with reference to the song service. "Every one of you hath a psalm." We can imagine the confusion resulting from everyone's having his own song and wanting to sing it in a given service!

And then there were those, of course, who had what they called "special revelations." Each one sought time in the worship service to tell his dream or vision or revelation. I have had my share of this in my own personal ministry. Men have stood up in my services saying that the Lord had commanded them to tell a particular dream to the congregation on that day and at that time. I would remind them that it would be best to tell me the dream privately to see if we could find the meaning of it before exposing it to the church, for you must understand that some dreams are traceable to an overloaded stomach, and furthermore, the spirit of dreaming is catching. As all men are dreamers in a sense, a worship service could be totally occupied by examining various visions and dreams. The apostle called all these disorderly procedures to decency and order.

Then there were those who thought they had a new doctrine. For this group the apostle also had some counsel. Would it be wise to stand up before the congregation and expose the "new revelation" before clearing it with other Bible students and checking it for error?

"To the law and to the testimony" is a safe rule by which we may measure new light, and certainly new light should not contradict old light. It is the work of Satan to disrupt the orderly worship of God. Noisy contentions, extravagant claims, a querulous spirit—none of these have the approval of Heaven.

GOD IS ABLE

And God is able to make all grace abound toward you; that ye, always having all sufficiency in all things, may abound to every good work. 2 Cor. 9:8.

When Haydn was composing the oratorio *The Creation* he was seen kneeling by the organ praying for inspiration. Among its grand choruses are "The Heavens Are Telling" and "Let There Be Light." When he heard them for the last time as music is rarely rendered on this earth he exclaimed in tears: "Not mine, not mine, it came from above." Haydn was right. The voice that inspired Haydn to compose *The Creation* and Handel the *Hallelujah Chorus* tuned Perronet's heart to write "All Hail the Power of Jesus' Name."

The world rarely pauses to think of the source of the genius of man. Haydn on his knees by the organ—what a sight, and yet, all men who do creative thinking are recipients of direct revelation. A spark from the throne room of Jehovah ignites the brain and gives direction to the thoughts. God is guiding the mind of man in the search for the secrets of nature, and unlike Haydn, many allow their accomplishments to reflect glory on themselves. But all our sufficiency comes from above. When will we learn this? The applause of men and our own deceitful hearts would tell us otherwise and make of us fools. But the truly great scientists of the earth have acknowledged the source of their inspiration. "Godless science reads nature only as Milton's daughters did Hebrew. Rightly syllabling the sentences but utterly ignorant of the meaning."

The pagan scientist lives a lightless life and man, no matter what his profession, who gathers to himself the honor for his accomplishments is a usurper at heart and will stand at last revealed for what he is. True humility requires that we acknowledge the source of all human goodness, for our God is the giver of every good and perfect gift.

When man assumes to himself credit for any good done he unduly exalts himself. Exalting his own skill or performance or brilliance, he fails to recognize God as the source of all wisdom and judgment and excellence. Our greatest fear should be that we do not faithfully cultivate and use the powers He has given us.

THEN AM I STRONG

Therefore I take pleasure in infirmities, in reproaches, in necessities, in persecutions, in distresses for Christ's sake: for when I am weak, then am I strong. 2 Cor. 12:10.

I submit from the pen of an anonymous author this sportsman's prayer: "Help me to be a good sport and a good loser in this game of life. I don't ask to be the pitcher or have any prominent place in the line-up. Play me anywhere You need me. I only ask that You give me the patience, courage, and stamina to give You the best I've got in every game. If all the hard drives seem to come my way, Lord, I thank You for the compliment. Help me always to remember that You won't ever let anything come my way that I cannot handle, and help me to take the bad bounces as a part of the game. Help me to understand that the game of life is full of hard knocks, bad hops, and foul tips, and make me thankful for them. Help me to get so that the harder they come, the better I will like it, and grant that I shall never sidestep one that is too hot to handle, nor alibi, whimper, nor complain that I have had a raw deal or that the game was a frame-up. Use me wherever You will to play the game in such a way that You will have no regrets for having given me the chance. And finally, when we reach the last inning and the evening shadows are gathering, grant that I may win Your decision and be counted safe at home."

Infirmities, reproaches, necessities, persecutions, and distresses are all negative experiences. No one in his right mind would naturally seek them. The Spirit of Christ in the life enables us to find pleasure in hardness and adversity. This is exactly the promise of Ecclesiastes 12:1. We are assured that if we remember our Creator in the days of our youth, the evil days in which no pleasure is found will not come for the sincere Christian.

Here is the paradox of the gospel: "For when I am weak, then am I strong." Millions have now come to realize that in the battered form of our crucified Lord lay the victory that He came to achieve. His tortured body hanging on a cross reveals more clearly the character of Christ than anything else. And it suggests the source of our strength—that sense of weakness that makes us lean on the everlasting arms.

SURELY I COME

He which testifieth these things saith, Surely I come quickly.
Amen. Even so, come, Lord Jesus. **Rev. 22:20.**

On this the final day of the year, 1969, we look back on 364 days
of precious spiritual opportunity. We are not proud of many things
that we have thought, said, and done. Too often we have been long
on promise and short on performance, and but for the love of a merciful God, between us and Him there would be a great gulf fixed. Thank
God it is not so. We approach the final hours of this year secure in the
knowledge of a Saviour's love, and we are reassured of His love
and deep interest in us by the promise of our text, "Surely I come."

Skeptics will arise to deny this fact. We must, nevertheless, believe
it. We must cling to a belief based on love for our very spiritual lives.
There are those who will give what they call "evidence" that Christ
will not come. "All things continue as they were from the beginning,"
will be the less subtle of all the arguments.

But what does this prove? Sin was allowed to continue for
hundreds of years before the retributive hand of God was seen in the
flood of Noah's day. The fact that the coming of Christ has not taken
place certainly does not say that it will not take place. Yet others argue
that Christ will come but that He "delayeth his coming." But it is not
He who delayeth His coming. We retard the return of our Lord to
this earth by the slowness with which we deliver His message of
mercy. Of necessity must the judgment message be delivered before
the hand of judgment be revealed. A loving, merciful God dare not
destroy the earth without man having opportunity to know of His
saving grace. For be it remembered that He is "not willing that any
should perish, but that all should come to repentance." And that the
Lord has "no pleasure in the death of him that dieth." So, then, let us
day by day reaffirm our faith in the coming of the Lord.

Whenever He comes it will be too soon for many, but the times
and the seasons marking His early return are clearly known to us all.
This is without doubt the end of the age. Let us live our lives with
reference to this fact. "The grace of our Lord Jesus Christ be with you
all. Amen" (Rev. 22:21).